The Therapeutic Relationship

The Therapeutic Relationship Handbook
Theory and Practice

Edited by Divine Charura and Stephen Paul

 Open University Press

Open University Press
McGraw-Hill Education
McGraw-Hill House
Shoppenhangers Road
Maidenhead
Berkshire
England
SL6 2QL

email: enquiries@openup.co.uk
world wide web: www.openup.co.uk

and Two Penn Plaza, New York, NY 10121-2289, USA

First published 2014

A catalogue record of this book is available from the British Library

ISBN-13: 978–0–33–526482–7 (pb)
ISBN-10: 0–33–526482–4 (pb)
eISBN: 978–0–33–526483–4

Library of Congress Cataloging-in-Publication Data
CIP data applied for

Typesetting and e-book compilations by
RefineCatch Limited, Bungay, Suffolk

Fictitious names of companies, products, people, characters and/or data that may be used herein (in case studies or in examples) are not intended to represent any real individual, company, product or event.

Praise for this book

The editors and authors of this book have produced a volume of theory and practice that has tremendous breadth and scope and that is a thorough analysis of the many facets of the therapeutic relationship. Rich in knowledge and practical applications, the authors demonstrate not only an understanding of their field, but also an ability to communicate this with vignettes and examples that are relevant and enable understanding for both students and practitioners alike. The limitations and challenges of each approach are recognised and a detailed list of further references is given for the reader to explore if desired. I highly recommend this book for both students and practitioners and congratulate the editors and authors on their work. I will certainly use it in our Counselling Education Programs for both Bachelor and Master of Counselling students."

Dr Ann Moir-Bussy, Program Leader and Senior Lecturer Counselling, University of Sunshine Coast. Queensland, Australia

To the therapists and practitioners whose hard work, expertise, and sharing helped make this book possible

Contents

Acknowledgements

Thanks to:

Monika Lee, Richard Townrow, and Priyanka Gibbons from McGraw-Hill/Open University Press whose guidance, help, and support helped bring this project to timely fruition.

Colleagues at Leeds Metropolitan University whose advice and support has been much appreciated.

Our family members who have endured alongside us the long hours, countless emails, and numerous versions of chapters that this handbook has necessitated: Kathy Paul, Rosie Paul, and Joan Dexter; Alois and Letisia Charura, Helen Charura and David, Tatenda, Talent, Elizabeth, and Enock Charura.

Sheila Haugh and Colin Lago whose inspiration is present here.

Petruska Clarkson and John Shiers, no longer with us but whose work lives on.

Contributors

Divine Charura is a Senior Lecturer in Counselling and Psychotherapy at Leeds Metropolitan University. He is an adult psychotherapist who works in the NHS, voluntary sector, and in private practice. Divine is also an independent trainer, supervisor, and coach. He has published various papers and contributed to various books, including: *The Transcultural Handbook of Counselling and Psychotherapy* (ed. C. Lago, 2011); *The Handbook of Working with Children and Young People* (ed. S. Pattison et al., 2014) and *Psychotherapy 2.0: Where Psychotherapy and Technology Meet* (Vol. 1) (ed. P. Weitz, 2014).

Stephen Paul retired as Director of the Centre for Psychological Therapies at Leeds Metropolitan University in 2012 after 20 years of service. He is a client-centred psychotherapist. He is co-editor of *The Therapeutic Relationship: Themes and Perspectives* (with S. Haugh, 2008). His published work includes chapters on love, spirituality and therapy, coaching and group therapy. Stephen has worked extensively in both adult and child and adolescent psychiatry. He opened one of the first independent counselling centres in the UK, in Bradford, in 1978. He has been head of a therapeutic school and director of the VSO programme in Bhutan. Stephen now writes, practises therapy, supervision and coaching, and provides training.

In recent years, **Stephen and Divine** have both been supporting therapeutic projects for abandoned and runaway children, slum dwellers suffering from domestic abuse, and people with long-term mental health problems in Bhopal, India. Psychotherapyinleeds@ gmail.com and www.stephen-paul.co.uk

Aida Alayarian BSc, MSc, DocSc, PhD is a chartered clinical psychologist, child and adult psychotherapist. She is a Fellow of the Royal Society of Medicine and an Associate Fellow of the British Psychological Society; MFIP and UKCP-CPJA. Aida has worked with families and children in multidisciplinary and multicultural settings in both the statutory and voluntary sector. She is the co-founder and Clinical Director of the Refugee Therapy Centre. She is the programme leader of the course in Intercultural Psychoanalytic Psychotherapy in collaboration with UEL. Aida has written widely.

Phil Arthington BSc, MSc, DClinPsych is a chartered clinical psychologist and systemic family therapist. Phil has worked as a clinical psychologist in adult mental health services since 2007 and completed his family therapy training in Leeds in 2011. He is a Clinical Lecturer and works part-time at the University of Leeds and part-time in his NHS post. Phil is influenced by social constructionist approaches, particularly collaborative/dialogical therapy.

George Bassett is a UKCP accredited Gestalt psychotherapist, supervisor, trainer, and HCPC Registered drama therapist. He is also a trained narrative therapist and a member of the Royal Company of Storytellers and is currently researching and writing about the use of narrative in Gestalt therapy. He is Co-director of Scarborough Counselling and Psychotherapy Training Institute.

Paula Boston BA, MSW is a UKCP registered family therapist and AFT registered family therapist supervisor. Trained at the Tavistock, Paula has been based at the University of Leeds since 1995 where she is a Senior Clinical Lecturer, Programme Leader for Family Therapy Training, supervisor in family therapy training and research, and course organizer for the MSc in Systemic Family Therapy. Paula is currently involved in a research trial (SHIFT) which is evaluating the effectiveness of systemic family therapy with adolescents who self-harm. She contributed to the original Leeds Family Therapy Research Centre systemic manual and subsequent SHIFT manual.

David Bott is Director of Studies in Psychotherapy at the University of Brighton and a UKCP registered systemic psychotherapist, having originally trained at the Institute of Psychiatry. His publications include a number of papers addressing the relationship between psychotherapeutic theories and models. His book, *The Therapeutic Encounter: A Cross-modality Approach*, co-authored with Pam Howard, was published by Sage in 2012.

Rute Brites (Rute Sofia Ribeiro Brites Lopes Dias) is a Doctor of Psychology, client-centred psychotherapist and trainer, and member of the Psychology Research Center – Universidade Autónoma de Lisboa. Rute is also a board member of APPCPC (Associação Portuguesa de Psicoterapia Centrada na Pessoa e Counselling), and Professor and Researcher at Universidade Autónoma de Lisboa. She is a clinical psychologist.

Anne Burghgraef BA, MA, MSW, PgDip EMDR, UKCP Reg is Clinical Director of Solace Surviving Exile and Persecution, a specialist therapeutic service for refugees and asylum seekers in Leeds and is a Tutor in Family Therapy at the University of Leeds. She has trained and worked in various therapeutic modalities in Canada and the UK, and is interested in the connections between them.

Brian Charlesworth is a Senior Lecturer at the Centre for Psychological Therapies at Leeds Metropolitan University where he is the course leader for the BACP accredited practitioners' course in Relational Therapy. He has some 16 years' experience as a psychotherapist, trainer, and clinical supervisor working from a relational philosophy.

Ken Evans is founder of the European Centre for Psychotherapeutic Studies based in France and the UK and works as a trainer in several training institutes across Europe. He is Visiting Professor of Psychotherapy at the Faculty of Law and Business Studies, USEE. He was elected President of the European Association for Integrative Psychotherapy in 2013, twenty years after being elected its founding President. He has authored numerous articles and books on psychotherapy, supervision, and research. He also runs an eco-friendly farm in Normandy.

Pam Fisher is Director of Dance Voice Centre, Bristol, UK and Course Director for their Dance Movement Psychotherapy MA. Her practice has encompassed work with elderly, youth, children, parent/child, and learning disabilities populations. Her current practice is with groups in recovery from substance misuse, one-to-one and family sessions, and clinical supervision.

Maria C. Gilbert is currently joint head of the Integrative Department at the Metanoia Institute in West London and a Visiting Professor at Middlesex University. She is programme leader of the MSc in Integrative Psychotherapy and of the MA/MSc in Coaching Psychology at Metanoia. Maria has been committed to developing the field of integrative psychotherapy over many years.

João Hipólito (João Evangelista de Jesus Hipólito) MD, PhD, Doctor of Psychology is a client-centred psychotherapist, supervisor, and trainer. He is President of the Psychology Research Center – Universidade Autónoma de Lisboa and Honorary President of APPCPC (Associação Portuguesa de Psicoterapia Centrada na Pessoa e Counselling). He is a professor and researcher.

Pam Howard is Principal Lecturer and Course Leader of the MSc in Psychotherapy at the University of Brighton. She is also a UKCP registered psychoanalytic psychotherapist in private practice. She is past Chief Executive of the UKCP and has chaired the Universities Psychotherapy and Counselling Association. She writes on aspects of the psychoanalytic therapeutic relationship.

Jacob Jacobson is an accredited sex and relationship therapist and clinical supervisor. His doctorate focused on criminal sexual behaviour and he presently specializes in the treatment of illegal online sexual activity. He is an expert witness and provides reports for the Scottish Courts. Jacob currently works in private practice in Glasgow.

Colin Lago has long been inspired by the writings of Carl Rogers, discovered years before he trained as a therapist. He found a deep sensitivity and wisdom in the essential trust that Rogers brought to addressing the nature of humans, relationships, and potentialities. He has worked as a therapist, trainer, and supervisor for over three decades and written extensively on issues of diversity in counselling.

Pete Lavender is a UKCP accredited Gestalt psychotherapist, supervisor, and trainer. Fascinated by the 'relational side' of psychotherapy since his own training, he was able to expound his thoughts when asked to write and run the Diploma in Relational-Centred Psychotherapeutic Counselling in 2003. He is Co-director of Scarborough Counselling and Psychotherapy Training Institute.

Pallab Majumder MBBS, MRCPsych, MIPS, MD works as a consultant child and adolescent psychiatrist for Nottingham City CAMHS Looked After Children's Team. He is also a Senior Fellow at the Institute of Mental Health (IMH), the clinical research establishment of Nottinghamshire Healthcare NHS Trust and affiliated to the University of Nottingham.

Andrew Mirrlees is a relationship counsellor and sex and relationship therapist. After initially training as a psychologist, Andrew completed further training in counselling and psychotherapy at the University of Edinburgh. He then trained as a relationship counsellor, and at present is completing postgraduate work in sex and relationship therapy.

Zenobia Nadirshaw is a consultant clinical psychologist and a senior practitioner with 38 years of NHS experience in the field of learning disabilities and mental health. Through her clinical practice and academic work she has raised the profile of double discrimination for ethnic minorities at national and international levels. She is a recipient of several awards over the years.

Peggy Natiello has worked with the theory and practice of the person-centred approach since 1978 as professor, therapist, consultant, parent, and friend. She considers the embodiment of person-centred values as equivalent to spiritual practice. Her curiosity, these days, wanders towards the field of consciousness, mindful that 'not all those who wander are lost' (J.R.R. Tolkien).

Paul E. Nicholson is a Senior Lecturer in Psychological Therapies and Mental Health at Leeds Metropolitan University. He is a BACP accredited relational therapist who has worked within a range of mental health settings since 1995. He has an enduring interest in relational perspectives in therapy and developing a cohesive language that accurately reflects the processes involved.

Lydia Noor is a UKCP accredited integrative psychotherapist, supervisor, and trainer. From 2009 until 2013 she was Course Leader for the Diploma in Integrative Psychotherapy at SCPTI. In 2013, she launched her own institute with a Diploma in Psychotherapeutic Counselling with Psychotherapeutic Studies in Education. Her current research interest is the impact of a therapeutic voice in the educational context.

Odete Nunes (Maria Odete Neves Fernandes Santos Nunes), Doctor of Psychology, is a client-centred psychotherapist, supervisor, and trainer. She is Scientific Coordinator of the Psychology Research Center – Universidade Autónoma de Lisboa, Director of the Psychology Department of Universidade Autónoma de Lisboa, and President of the Board of APPCPC (Associação Portuguesa de Psicoterapia Centrada na Pessoa e Counselling). She is a professor and researcher.

Geoffrey Pelham is the head of coach training at a leading UK coaching provider. He has also worked for many years as a counsellor, psychotherapist, supervisor, and coach in private practice. Previously he was responsible for the delivery of counselling and psychotherapy courses at Leeds Metropolitan University. His particular area of interest and research is the importance of the relationship in professional settings.

Sally Read is an integrative psychotherapist working in private practice and with people who are homeless or otherwise socially excluded. She was formerly a GP for homeless people and a doctor specializing in the treatment of substance misuse.

Jo Ringrose BSc, MA, DPsych (Prof) is a UKCP registered psychotherapist and director of the Karuna Centre for Psychotherapy and Counselling, Harrogate, UK. She won an award for her research at Leeds University and has published further works including *Understanding and Treating Dissociative Identity Disorder (or Multiple Personality Disorder)* (Karnac Books, 2012).

John Rowan is one of the pioneers of humanistic psychology in the UK, and a leading figure in the transpersonal field. He is a professional member of the Society for Existential Analysis. He is a Fellow of the British Psychological Society, the British Association for Counselling and Psychotherapy, and the United Kingdom Council for Psychotherapy.

Mike Thomas is the Pro Vice-Chancellor (Academic) at the University of Chester and is an experienced clinician and educator, having worked within a variety of settings. Mike has worked as both a mental health clinician and an educationalist for twenty-five years. He is a trustee of three charities. Mike has published and presented papers annually since 1986 and has written chapters in books on patient assessment, sexual health, professional issues, and cognitive behavioural psychotherapy.

Andrea Uphoff is a UKCP registered psychotherapist also licensed to practise in Germany and so divides her work – including training and supervision – across two countries. She is currently engaged in PhD studies at Regent's University, London, where her dissertation research is focused on client experiences of touch in the psychotherapeutic relationship. Andrea is a former convenor of BAPCA (British Association for the Person-Centred Approach) and board member of NEAPCEPC (Network of European Associations for Person-Centred and Experiential Psychotherapy and Counselling).

Val Watson works as a student and staff counsellor at the University of Nottingham. She is also an independent counselling and psychotherapy practitioner, supervisor, and trainer. Val has worked in education settings for over 20 years and has extensive work experience of voluntary and community-based projects.

William West is a Visiting Professor to the Universities of Chester and Central Lancashire. He is a Reader in Counselling Studies at the University of Manchester, where he is most noted for his interest in counselling and spirituality and for his work with doctorate and PhD students. William has written/edited five books and thirty-one academic papers.

Carol Wolter-Gustafson has called the person-centred approach her theoretical and experiential home-base since her first group encounter in 1978. As a therapist, facilitator, and educator, Carol has explored human wholeness and brokenness in personal relationships, and our social arrangements. Her current focus is on cultivating pathways in our body/mind to counteract the 'us-versus-them' rhetoric that fuels pain, suffering, and violence.

Jeannie Wright is Director of Counselling and Psychotherapy programmes at the University of Warwick Centre for Lifelong Learning. She has worked and practiced in Fiji and in 2011 returned to the UK from Aotearoa New Zealand where she was involved in teaching, practice, and research. Her long-held interest is in the therapeutic potential of creative and expressive writing. Jeannie also contributes articles to a range of publications in counselling and psychotherapy.

Introduction

In the modern era there has been an increase in research and associated literature indicating that one of the most important factors within therapy is the therapeutic relationship (Lambert et al. 2004). Although there are an increasing number of different models of practice, practitioners across modalities acknowledge that the therapeutic relationship is central to all therapy and indeed its outcomes (Lambert 2004; Stiles et al. 2006). Others have conducted research and meta-analyses and shown that there is no evidence that any one approach is better than another. Paul and Haugh (2008) have argued that the relationship is the essential component in therapy. We have recently proposed that a successful therapeutic encounter is founded on what may be called love in human life and in therapeutic relationships (Paul and Charura 2012).

The therapeutic relationship as it manifests in the different modes and modalities of therapy thus requires exploration and consideration, as it is the basis of success or failure of any therapeutic interventions.

We concur with Schmid (2001), who points out that ethics has to be the first philosophy when considering the therapeutic encounter. We therefore argue that the therapeutic relationship cannot be reduced to particular words or therapeutic skills but rather is a relationship encounter with a quality of relating, dialogue, contact, and process with each other moment by moment in a way that fully embraces our experiencing.

In this handbook, colleagues across modalities, modes of practice, and settings explore the therapeutic relationship from a range of theoretical positions. They share examples of practice as well as outline the challenges to the therapeutic relationship within different modalities and areas of practice.

Common themes throughout the book include:

- The theoretical and research bases of each modality/model, including a section on theory and practice relating to the client–therapist relationship.
- Examples of therapeutic interventions provided through case vignettes that illuminate the key relational components of the approach and the development and management of the therapeutic relationship within the model.
- The limitations, challenges, and complexities of maintaining a therapeutic relationship within the model: including working cross-culturally; the length, frequency, and duration of therapy; issues of power, difference, and diversity.
- Explorations of new developments within the modality/approach in working with clients capture the work that the authors and other colleagues have been involved in developing in that area.
- Each chapter has a summary and the reader is pointed to key resources.

Who is this book for?

This book is written for all practitioners and trainee practitioners in therapeutic counselling, counselling psychology, psychotherapeutic counselling and psychotherapy, psychiatry, clinical psychology, play therapy, art, dance, drama and music therapies, and related specialisms. Also, practitioners and trainees in mental health nursing, occupational therapy, social work, and specialist education for whom the therapeutic relationship is part of their work. Given the breadth of the subjects covered in this book, it will be of value to students, new and experienced practitioners, academics and trainers across the psychological therapies and helping professions.

To explore different aspects of the therapeutic relationship, the book is divided into five sections:

- Section 1, 'Modalities and the One-to-One Therapeutic Relationship', includes chapters on one-to-one therapy modalities – psychoanalytic, cognitive behavioural, humanistic, and person-centred (Chapters 1–5).
- Section 2, 'The Therapeutic Relationship in Cross-Modality, Relational, Integrative, Creative, and Coaching Therapies', includes chapters on configurations of transtheoretical approaches within a relational paradigm: a cross-modality approach, an integrative approach, and relational therapy. There is also an exploration of the opportunities and complexities of maintaining the relationship in creative therapies, relational dynamics when training therapists, and dimensions of the coaching relationship (Chapters 6–11).
- Section 3, 'Group Therapies, Systemic, Couple/Marital and Family Therapy, and Sex Therapy', includes an exploration of the therapeutic relationship within group therapy, systemic and couple therapy, sex and relationship therapy (Chapters 12–15).
- Section 4, 'The Therapeutic Relationship in the Helping and Mental Health Professions', addresses the therapeutic relationship in the helping professions, and psychiatrists' perspectives on diagnosis, working with adults and young people. It also includes therapists' perspectives on working with dissociative and identity disorder, and an exploration of the relationship when working with learning disabilities (Chapters 16–20).
- Section 5 explores further dimensions of the therapeutic relationship. These include transcultural and diversity perspectives, spirituality, and a consideration of the therapeutic relationship online. The section ends with a critical review of the latest areas of research using neuroscientific perspectives (Chapters 21–24 and the Conclusion).

Although it has not been possible to cover the therapeutic relationship in all the current models of therapy, the place of the relationship is established in our opening chapters when contributors consider the four forces of therapy. In Chapter 1, we look at the research findings considered consistent in relation to outcome across models of practice.

A note on the case vignettes: references to clients are all fictional scenarios based on real life unless detailed in the chapter.

We hope you find this handbook useful and inspiring in considering and developing your practice.

References

Lambert, M.J. (ed.) (2004) *Handbook of Psychotherapy and Behavior Change*, 5th edn. New York: Wiley.

Lambert, M.J., Bergin, A.E. and Garfield, S.J. (2004) Introduction and historical overview, in M.J. Lambert (ed.) *Handbook of Psychotherapy and Behavior Change*, 5th edn. (pp. 509–39). New York: Wiley.

Paul, S. and Charura, D. (2012) Accepting the therapeutic relationship as Love, *The Psychotherapist*, 52: 22–3.

Paul, S. and Charura, D. (2014) *An Introduction to the Therapeutic Relationship in Counselling and Psychotherapy*. London: Sage.

Paul, S. and Haugh, S. (2008) The relationship, not the therapy? What the research tells us, in S. Haugh and S. Paul (eds.) *The Therapeutic Relationship: Perspectives and Themes* (pp. 9–23). Ross-on-Wye: PCCS Books.

Schmid, P.F. (2001) Authenticity: the person as his or her own author. Dialogical and ethical perspectives on therapy as an encounter relationship and beyond, in G. Wyatt (ed.) *Rogers' Therapeutic Conditions: Evolution, Theory and Practice, Vol. 1: Congruence* (pp. 217–32). Ross-on-Wye: PCCS Books.

Stiles, W.B., Barkham, M., Twigg, E., Mellor-Clark, J. and Cooper, M. (2006) Effectiveness of cognitive-behavioural, person-centred and psychodynamic therapies as practised in UK National Health Service settings, *Psychological Medicine*, 36: 555–66.

SECTION 1

Modalities and the One-to-One Therapeutic Relationship

1 The therapeutic relationship in counselling and psychotherapy

Stephen Paul and Divine Charura

Introduction

In this chapter, we contextualize the place of the therapeutic relationship in the talking therapies. The importance of the relationship in therapy has been acknowledged in recent years, mainly as a result of research highlighting the *common factors* across the different modalities of therapy. Most academic researchers now accept that the model or school of practice is not the most important element in effecting therapeutic change.

In the modern era, practice clearly needs to be based on what is effective and grounded in evidence. This evidence shows that the therapeutic relationship is the factor that the therapist has most influence over in therapy – more so than the model or school of practice. Therapeutic practice needs to be refreshed and developed, not remain within what may become a non-evidenced theoretical paradigm (see Haugh and Paul 2008). Furthermore, as Feltham (1999) has indicated, many practitioners develop their own idiosyncratic practice after an initial training that is often grounded in a core model. Other practitioners such as Clarkson (2003) advocate transtheoretical perspectives. Clarkson postulated an integrative, transtheoretical approach to therapy with five dimensions or modes in the therapeutic relationship (Figure 1.1). Recently, we have seen the development of relational approaches that work across the classical models of therapy with the relationship as the focus.

The term 'Eurocentrism' is frequently used in the literature to highlight the influence of European/western people's ideas, concepts, and values (Paul and Charura 2014). Within counselling and psychotherapy, the ideas used to guide theory and practice have traditionally been based on a Eurocentric paradigm that reflects the perspectives of white middle-class males. Until the last twenty years or so, little attention was paid to the impact of adopting a Eurocentric perspective when working with a diverse range of clients whose experiences and cultures are different to those of the therapist (Mckenzie-Mavinga 2005). Eurocentrism permeates assumptions and theoretical frameworks of psychological distress and therapeutic interventions that many therapists ascribe to. An awareness of working with difference in each and every therapeutic relationship will limit the risk of therapists' attitudes and prejudices to 'other' groups being discriminatory within the therapeutic setting.

In Chapter 21, **Colin Lago and Val Watson** explore transcultural theoretical approaches. They consider the limitations, challenges, and complexities of maintaining

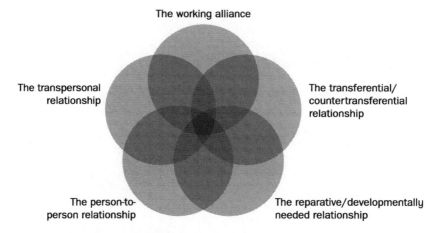

The working alliance

The transpersonal
relationship

The transferential/
countertransferential
relationship

The person-to-
person relationship

The reparative/developmentally
needed relationship

Figure 1.1 Clarkson's model of therapy

a therapeutic relationship within therapy, particularly when working cross-culturally, and the importance of being aware of transcultural issues that may impact on the therapeutic relationship.

Modalities and the one-to-one therapeutic relationship

Four main philosophical forces have developed in the understanding and practice of psychology since the turn of the twentieth century (Figure 1.2).

Psychodynamic/psychoanalytic psychology explores the dynamics between the conscious and unconscious parts of the self and relations with the external world. Classical Freudian therapists analysed their client and held an expert role in interpreting their client's psychic dynamics. Therapists such as Adler, Ferenczi, Abraham, Rank, Jung, Fairbairn, Guntrip, and Klein were influenced by the work of Freud, and were responsible for the development of different analytic approaches to therapy. More recently, there has been an increasing focus on interpersonal relationship in the here-and-now of the therapeutic process.

Behaviourism, which utilizes social learning theory, has been influenced by the work of Skinner, Watson, and others. The focus is on behaviour and its consequences. Practitioners such as Beck, Ellis, and others have developed a range of therapeutic approaches. Recently, there has been an emphasis on cognition and its relationship with behaviour; hence the development of cognitive therapy and cognitive behavioural therapy, in which the therapist acts as an educative trainer.

Existential-humanistic approaches focus on individual responsibility and self-determination. Writers and practitioners such as Fromm, Bugental, Laing, Maslow, Rogers, and Perls have influenced the development of a range of very different models of practice in this area. Bugental and Laing, among others, were instrumental in the development of existential therapy, which differs from humanistic therapies, including client-centred and gestalt therapies. Existential-humanistic therapists typically engage

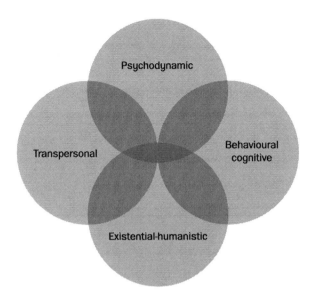

Figure 1.2 The traditional 'forces' of psychology

in helping their client take responsibility for their life situation and act as a catalyst for growth.

Transpersonal therapy takes a holistic view of the individual, including their spiritual development. Writers such as Assagioli, Jung, Grof, and Wilber have contributed to the development of this approach. Transpersonal therapists are mainly concerned with the being of the client and take a guiding role in the client's developmental pathway.

The authors of Chapters 2, 3, and 4 explore the place of the relationship in the four traditional modalities of therapy. **Aida Alayarian** outlines a classical psychoanalytic perspective. She uses case studies based on work with refugees that invite the reader to consider an intercultural perspective. She offers a salient exposition on analytic therapy in the twenty-first century.

Mike Thomas shows that increasingly research and literature in cognitive behavioural therapy (CBT) is focusing on the therapeutic relationship as foreground rather than background. He outlines the shift within the CBT modality of recognizing the importance of the therapeutic relationship over therapeutic cognitive behavioural interventions, which, without a good therapeutic relationship and collaboration of both therapist and client, might be of little benefit.

John Rowan demonstrates the place of relationship, central to these modalities, in the existential, humanistic, and transpersonal traditions. In describing the historical development of European and American schools of practice in the existential-humanistic modality, he notes the quite different philosophical perspectives that underpin this school and their differing emphasis on the relationship from authentic encounter to facilitator to catalyst.

The more recent growth of *postmodern* psychology questions whether there is an ultimate reality that is encompassed within a singular theoretical paradigm. Reality is considered based on multidimensional, subjective realities and practitioners avoid reducing human experiencing within a model based on past social interactive perspectives. In parallel, a range of approaches has developed focusing more on the relationship in therapy. Additionally, there has been the formation of eclectic and integrative approaches. Many therapists train in one core model and later develop their own practice based on what they believe to be effective.

In the modern era, there is consequently a multitude of diverse approaches to the psychological therapies. Corsini and Wedding (2010) number over 400. Many of these may be developments of, or slight nuances in, approaches within established schools.

Further developments have been in the relational approaches, arising out of the traditional modalities, based on the here-and-now of the therapeutic relationship and having a strong body of evidence in the research.

In Chapter 5, **Colin Lago, Peggy Natiello, and Carol Wolter-Gustafson** explore the relationship in person-centred therapy. They remind the reader of the basis of Rogers' research findings as to what works in therapy. They revisit his original theoretical hypotheses and then cite extracts from their three differing counselling practices in support of the central and critical importance, even necessity, of valuing and focusing upon the development of relationship for effective personality change.

In Table 1.1, we summarize the traditional four forces of psychology, the aims of each therapy, and the place of the relationship in therapy.

Table 1.1 The four traditional forces of therapy, the relationship, and traditional position of the therapist

	Methods	Position of therapist	Place of the relationship in therapy	Aim of therapy
Psychoanalysis	Interpretation of transference, countertransference, and resistance	Expert. 'Blank screen' Works with transference and interpretation	Working with the relationship in the here-and-now to resolve past issues	To adjust. To live more fully in the present reality based on the past
Behaviourism And later Cognitive	Deciding goals Action plans New ways of behaving and thinking	Expert Educator Trainer	Focus on practical, goal-based working alliance	To change maladaptive thoughts, feelings, and behaviours
Humanistic-existential	Human encounter In some cases particular techniques may be used	Facilitator Or catalyst	Central Focus on working in the here-and-now	To live a full life Realization of potential To live an authentic life
Transpersonal	Dialogue Imagery Creative visualization	Guide Facilitator Educator	To facilitate holistic change	To achieve spiritual growth To become integrated in mind, body, and spirit

Paul and Haugh identify key themes that have taken place in therapy in recent times:

1   The therapeutic relationship is central to all therapy and the relationship has many different dimensions (or different levels).
2   Evidence points to the relationship, not the theory, as fundamental.
3   Much training, practice, and theorizing is focused on a particular body of theory with little crossover of ideas.
4   Many practitioners view themselves as transtheoretical/integrative as they develop years of practice.
5   The need to focus on the client not the theory.
6   Therapists often marginalize issues of power and culture.
7   The therapeutic relationship is expressed in a myriad of ways, verbally and non-verbally, and takes place in a variety of settings.
8   Increasingly, much current training focuses more extensively on the relationship itself.

(adapted from Paul and Haugh 2008a: 4–6)

Research

The use of meta-analysis of research studies has done much to improve our ability to interpret research studies and factor out inbuilt flaws or discrepancies in methodologies (Lambert and Ogles 2004). Early meta-analyses (Luborsky et al. 1975) discovered the different approaches to therapy were equally effective. The Dodo effect from *Alice's Adventures in Wonderland* was now realized in the talking therapies: 'All shall be winners and all shall have prizes.' It is accepted *de facto* (Luborsky et al. 2002) that therapy is effective and that the major approaches have comparative outcomes. Research has moved on to identify what it is that works in therapy. Findings have indicated that the different schools of practice have the same components, *common factors*, which are now seen to be central to outcome, rather than the idiosyncratic techniques used in a particular model (Imel and Wampold 2008).

Imel and Wampold (2008) note the follow factors affect outcome in therapy:

- General effects – common factors that underlie all psychological therapies: 70%.
- Specific effects – particular aspects linked to a specific model: 8%.
- Unexplained variability – most likely as a result of client differences: 22%.

Effects related to a particular model are therefore limited and much less important than common factors. Lambert (1992) identifies the four common factors as follows:

1   *Extra-therapeutic change*: Those factors that are linked to clients' personal life outside of therapy (such as relationship, family, work, and social factors) that effect wellbeing regardless of participation in therapy.

2 *Hope/expectancy* – also called the placebo effect: gains resulting from the client's belief that they are being treated and that therapy will be effective.
3 *Model/technique*: The factors related to particular therapies (homework, role-play, and so on).
4 *Therapeutic relationship*: All the elements in the encounter, regardless of the therapist's theoretical approach, such as empathy, rapport, and acceptance.

(adapted from Paul and Haugh 2008b)

Asay and Lambert (1999) further identified the importance of the factors shown in Figure 1.3. While the weightings of these factors vary according to the interpretations of different reviewers, the therapeutic relationship is consistently considered the most important in-therapy factor in the therapist's control.

In a meta-analysis of more than 1000 studies, Orlinsky et al. (1994) found that the following key criteria were linked with positive outcomes: empathic understanding, therapist credibility, skill, collaboration, affirmation by therapist of the client, and attention to the client's emotional experiencing (or affect). Furthermore, they identified the most important determinants of outcome to be:

• The quality of clients' participation in therapy – the most important determinant.
• The therapeutic bond – as evaluated primarily by the client.
• The therapist's engagement with the client, especially through 'empathic, affirmative, collaborative and self congruent engagement' (p. 361).
• The skilful use of interventions.

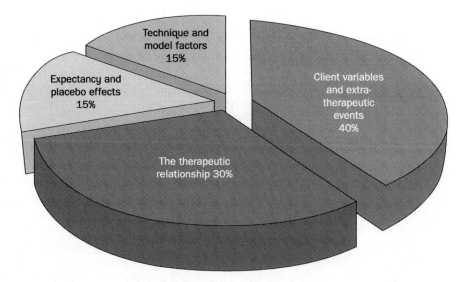

Figure 1.3 Lambert's pie: factors that affect the outcome of therapy
Source: Adapted from Asay and Lambert (1999)

Orlinsky et al. (1994) assert that these variables can 'be considered facts established by 40+ years of research' (pp. 361–2).

Definitions of the therapeutic relationship (Bordin 1979; Gaston 1990; Paul and Charura 2014) highlight the following necessary factors for a successful outcome:

- The collaborative nature of the relationship – therapist and client work together.
- The affective bond between client and therapist – mutual empathic understanding and trust.
- Agreement between client and therapist as to goals and tasks – a shared perspective.

Furthermore, Orlinksy et al. (2004) state that 'the therapeutic bond' has attracted more attention from researchers investigating the link between the process of therapy and its outcome than any other factor. They conclude that the therapeutic relationship is directly related to outcome.

Rogers' research clearly indicated that the 'conditions' of empathy, congruence, and positive regard, when received by the client, led to positive outcomes in therapy (see Chapter 5). Many studies were undertaken of these conditions and a strong correlation has been demonstrated between levels of empathy and positive outcome; and positive regard and congruence correlate with client-reported improvement (Sanders and Cooper 2006). Virtually all the therapeutic modalities accept that these three conditions are instrumental in the practice of therapy.

Research on the relationship in other settings: groups, families, and working with children

Ivey et al. (2012) summarize the research evidence for these modalities.

- Different reviews have concluded that family therapy is effective in a wide range of areas, including marital distress, conduct disorders, substance misuse, eating disorders, depression, and chronic illness (Carr 2000a, 2000b; NICE 2004a, 2004b).
- A recent key study by Girz et al. (2013) evidenced the efficacy of family-based therapy to a day hospital programme for adolescents with eating disorders.
- Schneider et al. (2013) conducted a randomized controlled study on the efficacy of a family-based cognitive behavioural treatment for separation anxiety disorder in children aged 8–13 years: their results showed positive outcomes for this modality.
- Jensen et al. (2012) presented practice-based evidence of group psychotherapy. They argued that apart from the proven efficacy of different forms of group psychotherapy, the designation of its evidence base will continue to hold powerful sway in terms of the teaching, funding, and reimbursement of psychological services.

- Given the present financial climate, the provision of therapeutic relationships that result in positive outcomes is highly regarded by commissioners who fund many services that provide therapy, thereby benefiting clients.

In a summary of current research (further explored in Paul and Charura 2014), we can see that:

- It is now beyond doubt that the therapeutic relationship is the most significant in-therapy factor for positive outcomes.
- There is a strong correlation between levels of empathy, positive regard, congruence, and therapeutic outcomes with clients' reported levels of improvement.
- Special relationship factors such as rapport and positive engagement in therapy, by both parties, are directly linked with outcomes in therapy.
- Client–therapist matching with regards to diversity *may* be linked to outcomes; however, research is limited in this area.
- Neuroscience demonstrates that through the therapeutic relationship, and the provision of empathy and other conditions that foster growth, positive therapy outcomes are achieved.

In Chapter 24, we explore the neuroscience of relationships. Andrea Uphoff reviews the research in neuroscience and its place in understanding the place of relationship in therapy. She questions whether neuroscience may be being presented as the new therapy and whether the relational attitudes of the therapist whatever model of therapy they practise may be more important.

Relational, cross-modality, and integrative approaches

With the changing social and cultural environment, a move towards a postmodernism, and changes in research that have identified effective relational factors in therapy, there has been a movement towards relational approaches to therapy. These approaches may be best considered as located within an overarching paradigm rather than being models in themselves, as relational factors are intrinsic in all schools of therapy. In some approaches they are central to change, in others they are the medium through which therapy happens, and in others they are the basis for the establishment and maintenance of an effective working relationship. As we have seen, all models of therapy utilize the relationship and conceptualize it from different philosophical viewpoints (Figure 1.4).

It is the importance of the relationship as an agent of change that is pivotal. The different forces of psychology have developed schools of practice that work within this principle (see Paul and Charura 2014), such as object relations theory, humanistic views of human development, gestalt and cognitive psychologies.

We are driven to relate and through relationship we change. Our world-view and sense of self are moulded. Our sense of self forms in the context of relationships with others and thus, in relational approaches to therapy, the interaction between client and therapist is considered the forum for change.

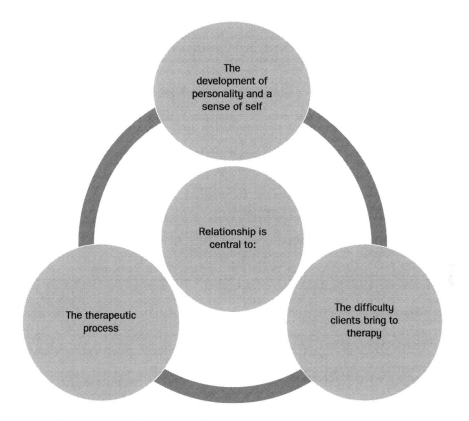

Figure 1.4   The importance of relationship (Paul and Charura 2014)

The key principles of relational approaches are expressed thus:

1   Relations between people are the basis of social and individual life and relational concepts are used to understand human life in all its complexity
2   Relationships are of fundamental importance in:
   • The development of personality and a sense of self
   • The difficulties clients bring to therapy (relations with the self and relations with other people)
   • The therapeutic process (the therapy relationship is the heart of the process)

(Paul and Pelham 2000: 110)

In Chapters 6–9, we look at cross-modality, relational, and integrative approaches to therapy. These particular approaches all outline how therapists can work effectively across different theoretical perspectives or integrate different aspects of theory into practice to facilitate a successful therapeutic relationship.

Every therapist goes through a learning process and this experiential process presents different challenges. In Chapter 10, three psychotherapists outline the challenges and complexities of teaching students to work relationally. In Chapter 11, we also look at dimensions of the relationship in coaching. While it is acknowledged that coaching is different to therapy, it draws from similar psychological theories. It is undoubtedly essential to have a good therapeutic relationship.

In this cross-modality, relational integrative section of the book, the chapters offer the reader a real understanding of the therapeutic relationship from a range of theoretical and experiential perspectives. In Chapter 6, **David Bott and Pam Howard** describe their metaphor of the 'therapeutic dance' between therapist and client. They explore the theoretical base of the cross-modality approach, which draws from humanistic, psychoanalytic, systemic, and integrative approaches.

Maria Gilbert and Ken Evans build on their theory of integrative psychotherapy in Chapter 7, and in particular the relational-developmental approach to theory and practice. They reflect on the depth and essence of their relational-developmental approach to integration. Drawing from integrative theory, they use real-life scenarios to explore how the therapeutic relationship is understood and managed by both client and therapist.

In Chapter 8, **Brian Charlesworth and Paul Nicholson** develop a theoretical rationale for a relational approach to therapy. The relational practice highlighted in this chapter provides a new way of conceptualizing relational psychotherapy practice as a legitimate model. This emerges from a growing paradigm shift towards an accessible, integrated therapy based on the common factors found throughout all therapeutic approaches.

In Chapter 9, **Pam Fisher** presents an overview of the relationship in the theoretical approaches of the creative arts therapies. While she focuses broadly on creative arts therapies, specific examples are drawn from her own practice, which is as a dance movement psychotherapist. There is a strong focus on group therapy perspectives throughout.

In Chapter 10, **George Bassett, Pete Lavender, and Lydia Noor** explore communalities of human relationship and group process in the training of practitioners in Gestalt psychotherapy training, relational-centred psychotherapeutic counselling, and integrative psychotherapy.

In **Geoff Pelham's** chapter on the dimension of the coaching relationship (Chapter 11), he explores coaching psychology, inner game theory, three-way agreements, and different coaching relationships.

Up to this point, we have introduced chapters in which the therapeutic relationship is mostly between two people (therapist and client). There is also a complex dynamic in the therapeutic relationship in modes of practice in which therapists work with more than one client at a time. These include group therapy, systemic and family therapies. The relationship is a central common feature throughout.

Group therapies, systemic therapies, couples/marital and family therapy, and sex therapy

Therapists engaging with couples, families or groups find themselves conceptualizing the therapeutic relationship in a different way to a therapist working with a single client. Couples, families, and groups often come for therapy because of complexities and different tensions in their relationships. Rober (2008) stated that what the therapist meets at first encounter is a group of distressed people apprehensive about what the future has in store for them, and some may have been less willing to attend for therapy. These dynamics present a challenge for the therapist. Chapters 12–16 address the therapeutic relationship when working with couples, families and groups.

The place of the relationship in group therapy is established in Chapter 12. **Stephen Paul and Divine Charura** review research that shows that cohesiveness is the agent for therapeutic change in groups. They identify the therapeutic components for establishing a cohesive and effective group.

In Chapter 13, **Phil Arthington and Paula Boston** introduce the relationship in systemic therapy and explore the different theories that argue that families as systems function to maintain stability, while also adjusting to internal and external pressures to change. They review systemic engagement and alliance building, the self of the therapist, systemic therapy in context, and supporting the therapeutic relationship via supervision.

In Chapter 14, **Anne Burghgraef** and **Divine Charura** consider the relationship in couples/marital and family therapy. The focus here is on working with couples and families and the complexities that arise in the therapeutic relationship. How does the therapist manage the therapeutic relationship when couples/families have problems? The authors discuss some of the challenges and ways of managing complex dynamics in the therapeutic relationship when working with couples and families.

Jacob Jacobson and Andrew Mirrlees review the place of the relationship in sex therapy in Chapter 15. They illustrate the multi-faced role of the therapist as medical expert, therapist, and role model and the place of the therapeutic relationship in this.

The relationship in the helping and mental health professions

In Section 4, the reader is introduced to the therapeutic relationship in the helping professions such as in medical general practice and nursing, in which the primary role of the professional is not as psychological therapist. The chapters in this section focus on the challenges and complexities of working with clients within the psychiatric/ mental health system as well as those who have a diagnosis or learning disability. Although the models of practice that are discussed in this section are very different, they offer the practitioner insight into the opportunities, challenges, and complexities of working with clients in these settings.

In Chapter 16, **Sally Read** examines the therapeutic relationship for therapists and health and social care professionals when working in multidisciplinary teams, particularly those where at least some colleagues are working to a 'medical model'. She discusses the challenges of working in such teams: balancing the needs of clients, managers and service, while striving to maintain effective therapeutic relationships.

João Hipólito, Odete Nunes and Rute Brites consider the importance of the therapeutic relationship in psychiatric services in Chapter 17. Often within these settings, individuals/clients have diagnoses and multidisciplinary teams work closely in supporting and helping to maintain a therapeutic relationship. The challenge is primarily on maintaining a therapeutic relationship with clients, who may be within a service against their will, or who may have a diagnosis of a mental disorder for which particular medications may be prescribed. They propose how the two paradigms of psychiatry/diagnosis and psychotherapy can co-exist, and propose therapeutic ways of working with clients who may be diagnosed or have experienced psychiatric diagnosis.

Children may also use psychiatric services. In a psychiatrist's perspective on working with young people (Chapter 18), **Pallab Majumder** argues that a special therapeutic relationship has to be established when working with young people in order to foster the best therapeutic alliance. Furthermore he proposes that when working with young people from other cultures, it is important to note that the traditional western model of psychiatric care and therapeutic engagement may not be effective, particularly given that their understanding of mental health, mental illness, and mental health care services can be very different from established mainstream therapeutic practice. Thus the development of a positive working relationship is essential.

In Chapter 19, Jo Ringrose outlines and explores the therapeutic relationship with clients with disorganized attachment, dissociative identity disorder. She argues that the therapist will need to become one of the client's main attachment figures through a containing therapeutic relationship.

In 'Making the invisible visible: the relationship when working with learning disabilities' (Chapter 20), **Zenobia Nadirshaw** considers the equities and inequities of therapeutic work with people from this often ignored group. She proposes proactive ways of working that are truly client-centred.

Further dimensions of the therapeutic relationship

The final section of this book focuses on further dimensions of the therapeutic relationship. In Chapters 21 and 22, the authors consider the importance of transcultural and diversity perspectives, as well as spirituality in therapeutic relationships. In moving forward with further developments within theory and practice, focus shifts to the therapeutic relationship in working online and through video-linked relationships. Paul and Haugh (2008b: 19) stated that regardless of the paradigm, the relationship is the most significant factor for a positive outcome. Our last chapter confirms this through neuroscientific evidence and exploration of how the therapeutic relationship contributes to neurological changes in the brain.

Colin Lago and Val Watson explore transcultural theoretical approaches in Chapter 21. They consider the limitations, challenges, and complexities of maintaining a therapeutic relationship within therapy, particularly when working cross-culturally, and the importance of being aware of transcultural issues that may impact on the therapeutic relationship.

In Chapter 22, **Stephen Paul and William West** consider the place of spirituality in therapy. They look at dimensions of the therapeutic encounter, exploring explicit and implicit spirituality, and religiosity. They highlight the centrality of spirituality to clients and how it is important for therapists to be open, fearless, and non-defensive in working with psycho-spiritual issues in the therapeutic relationship.

In Chapter 23, **Jeannie Wright** extends the therapeutic relationship to working online and suggests ways in which therapists can build therapeutic relationships both online as well as when working with video platforms. She explores the place of metaphor and the power of figurative language.

In Chapter 24, **Andrea Uphoff** reviews the research in neuroscience and its place in understanding the importance of the relationship in therapy. She questions whether neuroscience may be being presented as the new therapy and whether the relational attitudes of the therapist, whatever model of therapy they use, may be more important.

Summary

In this chapter, we considered the following:

- The main philosophical forces of psychology, namely psychodynamic/ psychoanalytic, behaviourism, existential-humanistic, and transpersonal psychology. The method, position of the therapist and place of the relationship in therapy, and aim of therapy for each of these forces was outlined.
- Research to show the centrality of the therapeutic relationship and common factors as central to outcome was presented and discussed.
- The relationship in cross-modality, relational approaches.
- The place and application of the relationship in a range of professional settings in health and social care.

Further reading

Haugh, S. and Paul, S. (eds.) (2008) *The Therapeutic Relationship: Perspectives and Themes*. Ross-on-Wye: PCCS Books. Summarizes the research, modalities, and issues.

Lambert, M.J. (ed.) (2013) *Handbook of Psychotherapy and Behavior Change*, 6th edn. New York: Wiley. The 'gold standard' summary of research in the talking therapies.

Paul, S. and Charura, D. (2014) *An Introduction to the Therapeutic Relationship in Counselling and Psychotherapy*. London: Sage. A practitioner's textbook.

References

Asay, T.P. and Lambert, M.J. (1999) The empirical case for the common factors in therapy: quantitative findings, in M.A. Hubble, B.L. Duncan and S.D. Miller (eds.) *The Heart and Soul of Change: What Works in Therapy* (pp. 33–56). Washington, DC: American Psychological Association.

Bordin, E.S. (1979) The generalizability of the psychoanalytic concept of the working alliance, *Psychotherapy*, 16: 252–60.

Carr, A. (2000a) Evidence-based practice in family therapy and systemic consultation I: child-focused problems, *Journal of Family Therapy*, 22 (1): 29–61.

Carr, A. (2000b) Evidence-based practice in family therapy and systemic consultation II: adult-focused problems, *Journal of Family Therapy*, 22 (3): 273–95.

Clarkson, P. (2003) *The Therapeutic Relationship*, 2nd edn. London: Whurr.

Corsini, R.J. and Wedding, D. (eds.) (2010) *Current Psychotherapies*, 9th edn. Pacific Grove, CA: Brooks/Cole.

Feltham, C. (1999) Contextualising the therapeutic relationship, in C. Feltham (ed.) *Understanding the Counselling Relationship* (pp. 4–32). London: Sage.

Gaston, L. (1990) The concept of the alliance and its role in psychotherapy: theoretical and empirical considerations, *Psychotherapy*, 27: 143–53.

Girz, L., Lafrance Robinson, A., Foroughe, M., Jasper, K. and Boachie, A. (2013) Adapting family-based therapy to a day hospital programme for adolescents with eating disorders: preliminary outcomes and trajectories of change, *Journal of Family Therapy*, 35: 102–20.

Haugh, S. and Paul, S. (2008) Conclusion: is the relationship the therapy?, in S. Haugh and S. Paul (eds.) *The Therapeutic Relationship: Perspectives and Themes* (pp. 247–54). Ross-on-Wye: PCCS Books.

Imel, Z. and Wampold, B. (2008) The importance of treatment and the science of common factors in psychotherapy, in S.D. Brown and R.W. Lent (eds.) *Handbook of Counseling Psychology*, 4th edn. (pp. 249–62). Hoboken, NJ: Wiley.

Ivey, E.A., D'Andrea, J.M. and Ivey, B.M. (2012) *Theories of Counselling and Psychotherapy: A Multicultural Perspective*, 7th edn. London: Sage.

Jensen, D.R., Abbott, M., Beecher, M.E., Griner, D., Golightly, T.R. and Cannon, J.N. (2012) Taking the pulse of the group: the utilization of practice-based evidence in group psychotherapy, *Professional Psychology: Research and Practice*, 43 (4): 388–94.

Lambert, M.J. (1992) Implications of outcome research for psychotherapy integration, in C. Norcross and M.R. Goldfried (eds.) *Handbook of Psychotherapy Integration* (pp. 94–129). New York: Basic Books.

Lambert, M.J. and Ogles, B.M. (2004) The efficacy and effectiveness of psychotherapy, in M.J. Lambert (ed.) *Handbook of Psychotherapy*, 5th edn. (pp. 139–93). New York: Wiley.

Luborsky, L., Rosenthal, R., Diguer, L., Andrusyna, T.P., Berman, J.S., Levitt, J.T. et al. (2002) The Dodo bird verdict is alive and well – mostly, *Clinical Psychology: Science and Practice*, 9 (1): 2–12.

Luborsky, L., Singer, B. and Luborsky, E. (1975) Comparative studies of psychotherapies: is it true that 'Everybody has won and all must have prizes'?, *Archives of General Psychiatry*, 32: 995–1008.

Mckenzie-Mavinga, I. (2005) Understanding black issues in postgraduate counsellor training, *Counselling and Psychotherapy Research*, 5 (4): 295–300.

National Institute of Clinical Excellence (NICE) (2004a) *Eating Disorders: Core Interventions in the Treatment and Management of Anorexia Nervosa, Bulimia Nervosa and Related Eating Disorders*. London: NICE.

National Institute of Clinical Excellence (NICE) (2004b) *Depression: Management of Depression in Primary and Secondary Care*. London: NICE.

Orlinsky, D.E., Grawe, K. and Parks, B.K. (1994) Process and outcome in psychotherapy: Nocheinmal, in A.E. Bergin and S.L. Garfield (eds.) *Handbook of Psychotherapy and Behavior Change*, 4th edn. (pp. 270–376). New York: Wiley.

Orlinksy, D.E., Rønnestad, M.H. and Willutzki, U. (2004) Fifty years of psychotherapy process-outcome research: continuity and change, in M.J. Lambert (ed.) *Bergin and*

Garfield's Handbook of Psychotherapy and Behavior Change, 5th edn. (pp 307–90). New York: Wiley.

Paul, S. and Charura, C. (2014) *An Introduction to the Therapeutic Relationship in Counselling and Psychotherapy*. London: Sage.

Paul, S. and Haugh, S. (2008a) The therapeutic relationship: background and context, in S. Haugh and S. Paul (eds.) *The Therapeutic Relationship: Perspectives and Themes* (pp. 1–8). Ross-on-Wye: PCCS Books.

Paul, S. and Haugh, S. (2008b) The relationship, not the therapy? What the research tells us, in S. Haugh and S. Paul (eds.) *The Therapeutic Relationship: Perspectives and Themes* (pp. 9–23). Ross-on-Wye: PCCS Books.

Paul, S. and Pelham, G. (2000) A relational approach to therapy, in S. Palmer and R. Woolfe (eds.) *Integrative and Eclectic Counselling and Psychotherapy* (pp. 110–26). London: Sage.

Sanders, P. and Cooper, M. (2006) Research into person-centred counselling, in P. Sanders, *The Person-Centred Counselling Primer*. Ross-on-Wye: PCCS Books.

Schneider, S., Blatter-Meunier, J., Herren, C., In-Albon, T., Adornetto, C., Meyer, A. et al. (2013) The efficacy of a family-based cognitive-behavioral treatment for separation anxiety disorder in children aged 8–13: a randomized comparison with a general anxiety program, *Journal of Consulting and Clinical Psychology*, 81 (5): 932–40.

2 Psychoanalysis and conceptualization of the therapeutic relationship

Aida Alayarian

Introduction

In this chapter, I look at psychoanalysis, its method of treatment and identity as a theory of human nature, development, and experience. Specific focus will be on the unconscious and transference-countertransference within the therapeutic relationship. Psychoanalysis is enriched by the social sciences and the intercultural aspects of the therapeutic relationship. I present two case vignettes and discuss the validity of psychoanalytic psychotherapy in developing the therapeutic relationship from an intercultural perspective.

Foundations of psychoanalytic theory and practice

The foundations of the therapeutic relationship within psychoanalysis are based on collaboration between a therapist and a client to overcome resistance that blocks change and the healing process. Sandler et al. (1973) emphasized the need for a therapeutic alliance sustained by interpretation. It is the power of this relationship for patient self-understanding that allows psychoanalytic interventions to be effective. Freud's (1915) view on transference was on unconscious aspects of the patient's suffering which are not yet reachable. As manifestations of the patient's unconscious mind, they can lead to relational conflicts during early developmental processes as well as in adulthood, indeed be acted out in transference within the therapeutic relationship with the therapist – that is, feelings of love, desire for closeness and intimacy, as well as feelings of anger, rejection, hatred, and hostility. Transference within the therapeutic relationship is resistance to remembering. The therapist needs to work on this resistance by opening a space to explore the symbolic meaning of what is being acted out in transference. With such space and exploration, patients gain insight of developmental failure.

Different theorists have contributed to the foundations of psychoanalytic theory and practice. For example, Klein's (1946) work with infants raised theoretical arguments that the 'pre-oedipal' phase is relational, indicating that babies have conflicting feelings of love and hate towards the mother or other (the primary care giver). Her concepts of the 'good breast' and 'bad breast' in the baby's phantasy refer to the frustrations of dependency through mechanisms of projective identification, projection, and introjection that focused on earlier developmental processes (Klein 1957). Other contemporary psychoanalysts also focus on earlier developmental processes. Examples include (1962a, 1970) notion of containing and Winnicott's (1965) facilitating environment. Indeed, Joseph (1987), Heimann (1950), Searles (1959), Anna Freud (1989), Fairbairn (1952), Bowlby (1969, 1973, 1980, 1988), Guntrip (1992), Langs (1992), and Hinshelwood (1997) referred to conceptualizations of the m/other's function as container; they all strengthened the object-relations theories and intercultural aspects of psychoanalytic theory and techniques.

Freud's (1915, 1917, 1920) reference to repression in the analysis of dreams, literature, jokes, and slips of the tongue illustrates the route through which our desires continue to find an outlet. Freud (1920) argued that affects owe their aetiological importance to the fact that they are accompanied by the production of large numbers of excitations, and that these excitations, in turn, call for discharge in accordance with the principle of constancy. In his view, traumatic experiences and pathogenic forces produce levels of excitation that are too great to be dealt with. The treatment of traumatic memories by abreaction is thus based upon this more fundamental principle of constancy (i.e. the level of excitations). He suggested that powerful affects restrict association, and that active affects level out the increased excitations via motor discharge. However, anxiety is unable to bring about this reactive discharge and may paralyse the power of movement and association, creating abreaction through facilitation of verbal expression alongside emotional discharge via motor activities (Breuer and Freud 1895). Freud (1920) formulated two principles of mental function: (1) produce and represent to the psyche experiences that have produced pleasure in the past or are likely to produce pleasure in the present; (2) avoid or eliminate experiences resulting in *unpleasures*.

One principle of pleasure seeking is to avoid pain, and the reality principle defers gratification when necessary. In a good enough environment, one learns to endure pain and defer gratification with a tolerable and functioning ego. Such an ego is not only governed by the pleasure principle, but also obeys the reality principle – it seeks pleasure through taking account of reality, even though pleasure is postponed. This is termed 'principle selection' and is exercised through hallucinatory wish-fulfilment for pleasurable experiences, or through repression of unpleasures.

Psychoanalysis aims to develop an affective, therapeutic relationship by creating a safe and responsive environment that allows for accessing, reworking, and integrating the client's traumatic material. As psychoanalysis has continued to evolve and respond to different populations, an intercultural psychoanalytic approach has developed. This intercultural approach provides a medium to facilitate both the patient's reintegration of self and the re-establishment of trustworthy relationships with others within a relational context.

The therapeutic relationship

It is important to note the unique subjectivity of the therapist–patient dynamic inherent in the therapeutic relationship. Despite this fact, psychoanalysis is refuted to be influenced by subjective views of reality at a particular moment, within the therapeutic relationship, through the transference/countertransference interpretation. Transference/ countertransference[1] should be constantly evaluated in the therapeutic relationship. It is important to acknowledge that transference/countertransference is idiosyncratic to psychoanalytical societies. Its significance in the therapeutic relationship has yet to be widely explored in a systematic dialogue with therapeutic disciplines not closely allied with psychoanalysis. It is the responsibility of the psychoanalytic community to help its critics learn the strength of psychoanalytic intervention as an effective therapeutic model that prepares and enhances patients' psychic space, the sense of self and resilience – a heuristic approach for positive integration.

One of the paradoxes of the therapeutic relationship is that of the therapist who can combine the use of heuristics and personal learning to implement the theory and knowledge they gain in appropriate and genuine practice. It is important to recognize that psychoanalysis can cause uncertainty in the face of complex, ambiguous, and unique material, and as a rule must be addressed by psychoanalysts. Psychoanalysis presents as an enquiry that is continuously developing through multidimensional evidence within the context of daily life. Thus, pragmatic 'facts' emerge through the patient–therapist dyad within transference/countertransference, never become concrete, and are unfixed; thus objectivity of the inner world occurs just as objectivity of the outer world.[2] In over three decades of clinical practice, I have learned that: (a) individual characteristics are prompted spontaneously; (b) idiosyncratic fit mediates the effect of effort on patient response within the therapeutic alliance; and (c) psychoanalytic theory is for me the best approach for the development of a genuine intercultural therapeutic relationship, focus on personal development, and a perceived relative advantage to fit with the individual's needs and preferences.

I offer two vignettes[3] of my experience of working with real clients in the hope of illuminating the key relational components of the approach and the development and management of the therapeutic relationship within the intercultural psychoanalytical model; and how a case can be contextualized. This is increasingly important since we live in a multicultural world and our theoretical framework has to be applicable to working with clients from different cultures.

Case vignette

Eram was just 16 years old when she was tortured by the authorities owing to her parents' involvement in a peaceful protest. In our first meeting she told me, 'They come to our home and take me and my sister two years older than me. She was 18. They covered our head and brought me to an interrogation room separate from my sister. This was the second time they arrested my sister but was first time for me – I was scared. They beat me with . . . It was painful and scary. I didn't say a word. The angry policeman pulled out a gun and pressed it against my forehead and said, "If you don't tell me who your parents meet and how to organize people for demonstration, I will kill you and your sister immediately." I was really scared. I didn't know what to do. I went silent. He shouted something. I could not hear him more. Some man brings my sister. I looked at her and she looked at me in silence for few seconds. He put his gun on my sister head and shot her and he sat in his chair . . . I was screaming and I faint . . . don't remember what happened next.'

Eram's mind clearly had been over-exposed to disturbing and intrusive violent experiences. In exploring this case, it is striking that at the start I, as Eram's 'listening other' (Alayarian 2011), bear witness to her experience of being paralysed with uncertainty regarding what might be found behind a closed door if we were to develop a therapeutic relationship.

In the sessions following on from this disclosure, Eram's counter-reaction to having shared this information with me was acted out by arriving late and cancelling some sessions. This left me wondering whether I had responded in a way that had made it harder for her. I spoke to her about this and it became clear that her anger was not only linked to her choosing to share her feelings with me, but was also a reaction to a conflicting part of her for surviving her sister and now wanting to trust and embrace her therapy. I also spoke of any worries she might have about the impact on me of sharing these troubling experiences. This helped her develop the ability to engage more fully with exploration. She attended regularly, but still appeared to have a problem with focusing on her problems. If I tried to make some connection with part of her need for processing her experience (not just the trauma she had endured), I immediately felt I was forcing her into uncomfortable and distressing territory and contributing to an assault on her mind – whereas my experience of time passing without further exploration of these thoughts left me feeling as though I was a neglectful parent, colluding with her avoidance.

In a session following disclosure of her abandonment as a child by her parents, Eram again became guarded and said little. She left me with little sense of what happened to my attempts to sustain contact with her. I felt that for the time being she had closed the door on thinking about her painful experience.

Having had little expectation of making contact and of being heard, I felt Eram had not the psychic space to think further about the trauma she had endured. I put this to her and indicated that we could focus on her experiences in the here-and-now and could deal with her unbearable feelings when she was ready. She happily agreed with this.

The challenges within psychoanalysis, the value of working interculturally, and issues of power and diversity

One challenge in all therapeutic approaches is unique subjectivity; but in psychoanalysis, subjective experience is openly accepted. As Kareem and Littlewood (1992) suggest, intercultural therapy is beyond the fact of our shared humanity. Positivism, for example, argues that the only true knowledge is scientific knowledge, and that only positively established proof is scientific knowledge. Ernst Mach (1897), an influential logical positivist, indicated that all knowledge is derived from sensation, thus phenomena under scientific investigation can be understood only in terms of experiences, present in the observation of the phenomena.

If we accept that each individual is unique, then within each interaction there are always interpersonal dynamics; thus within therapeutic relationships, there are always intercultural aspects. It is important to be aware of the influence of our own culture, both from a personal and professional perspective, on the on-going process of our learning within therapeutic relationships, and of the importance of understanding that: (a) each individual is unique; (b) there are factors outside of a person's awareness – unconscious thoughts, feelings, and experiences – that influence the thoughts and actions of both patient and therapist; (c) our past shapes who we are at present; (d) human beings are engaged in the process of development throughout their lives.

The intercultural approach becomes a framework for an explicit edification of perceptual thinking of the mind as a form of creative clinical practice without prejudice, thus focusing on the person's psyche for a deeper understanding of self and relating to others. In therapy, patients typically see what they expect, and therapists are seen as experts, but there are always unconscious elements influencing transference/countertransference feelings and interactions within the therapeutic dyad.

An intercultural approach offers a way for therapists to support patients to build resilience (Alayarian 2008) that can potentially be sustained throughout their lives rather than merely addressing one emergent problem. Determining the extent to which psychoanalysis has the capacity to foster more enduring resiliency and recovery (Alayarian 2011) in patients, requires disciplined implementation of clinical monitoring and evaluation to provide evidence of effectiveness.

Here I present another vignette to illustrate a difficult aspect of the therapeutic relationship based on an intercultural consultation I was engaged in.

Case vignette

Bernadette, a young woman in her late twenties who had been sexually abused by her father from the age of four and her brother, eleven years her senior, from the age of six, contacted me in a state of panic asking for therapy. She had been in therapy for the last two years, but felt her therapist did not understand her. After calming her down on the phone, we arranged to meet for a consultation, on the condition that I might conclude that I couldn't help her and recommend that she continue seeing her therapist. When we met she reported that she had begun to vividly remember the sexual abuse, and began to recount how these invasive memories were influencing her relationship, leading her to display emotional reactions that involved distinct parts of her body; mainly trembling in her legs, which became violent shaking when her partner touched her. She felt uncared for, embarrassed, and humiliated by asking for help from her therapist – indeed angry and frustrated at her request being ignored by the therapist's silence.

I said I would be interested to hear her view and her thinking about her shaking and its effects on her relationship with her partner, and her partner's view on the situation when she was in that state. She replied, 'My partner freezes and leaves me, not daring to ask anything: surely she would look down on me with contempt, seeing me as a damaged mess beyond help . . . it must be something seriously wrong with me as my therapist never responded and she thinks I am not really lesbian and I have chosen my sexuality because I hated my father and brother and therefore fear of having a relationship with men in general, but my relationship is not working either, because I am so damaged. Can you please help me? I want to get better and I would do anything you might say.'

In our brief encounter, instead of shaking, she talked about her terror of annihilating intrusion. I asked her to tell me about her mother and how she approached her about the sexual abuse. She said, 'it is difficult to talk about my mother as she shamed me severely, repeatedly telling me I was a wicked little girl for making up such lies about my father and my brother . . . humiliated further, I decided not to tell anyone until my partner told me I should seek therapeutic help.'

In just one meeting, I observed that Bernadette underwent a process of transformation from being in exclusively bodily states into ones in which the bodily sensations came to be united with words. This left me wondering what was preventing her from doing the same with her therapist whom she had been seeing three times a week for nineteen months.

I explained that I wondered whether her experience of horror and trepidation regarding her therapist's lack of response to her narratives were the same feelings that she experienced of her mother shaming and humiliating her. She burst into tears with agreement. With further exploration, Bernadette's perception of her therapist as humiliating her changed to an acceptance and understanding that her therapist's lack of response might be to give her space without intrusion, or being overwhelmed by narratives of the trauma she endured. I encouraged her to talk to her therapist about her feelings, especially her feeling of being humiliated. I also offered to talk to her therapist, something that Bernadette welcomed, and we parted by agreeing that we both talk to her therapist.

In communicating with Bernadette's therapist, she confirmed that she was struggling, but had no one to turn to. She indicated that she needed to work with Bernadette because she was her trainee patient for twenty-four months, but she could not continue beyond that as the material she was presenting was too unbearable for her (as a trainee therapist) and she felt that her supervisor was not giving her sufficient support. She asked to see me and I offered to see her for one or two sessions, if her supervisor agreed, to help her with the intercultural aspect of the case. We discussed how helpful it would be if she could communicate her countertransference feelings and thoughts with Bernadette in a professional manner. The therapist agreed to openly communicate both their needs and limitations. I informed Bernadette that I had spoken to her therapist, who would be informing her of the content of our discussions.

Bernadette contacted me and said that she had spoken with her therapist and they had agreed to work together for another five months and that she would like to come and see me after. I suggested it would be good for her not to see me or another professional straight afterwards and take time to reflect on the work she had done with her therapist, which she found acceptable. She said that her states of mind shifted from an exclusively bodily form to an experience that could be felt and named.

As a result of being heard, patient and therapist were able to build a better relationship that allowed them to focus on transference/countertransference, where the patient came to recognize that her perception of the therapist reflected the feelings she had experienced of her mother, and the therapist was able to accept her limitations and work with her patient more effectively – although not the best, a genuine therapeutic relationship was built between them.

My intention for this brief encounter as a piece of consultative intercultural work is to highlight how a good enough therapeutic relationship can help form such somatic-linguistic unities of emotional experience into an expressive language to a genuine human relation, in which a sense of being can be born, restored, and consolidated, without a need for dissociating from reality. Bernadette's situation was complex and there may be a great many things that I was incapable of immediately recognizing; the provision of a safe space to be heard and felt understood was what she was searching for to make her life manageable. She was yearning for a 'listening other' who she could relate to. Her bodily manifestation of her somatic forms of shame and humiliation that she had felt in transference by remembering, associating, recounting and, in her mind, exposing herself to her therapist with the hope of being helped was the cause of her great anxiety. Her therapist's lack of experience, the fear of losing Bernadette, and not feeling supported by her supervisor were the cause of the therapist's anxiety, which was preventing them from building an effective therapeutic relationship. One of the most fundamental aspects of a therapeutic relationship is that there are two people in the room at the conscious level with many unconscious elements that can influence the process by projections, introjections, and projective identifications.

Therapists' power and power imbalance within the therapeutic dyad is a reflection of the culture and forms of diversity by which power can manifest. In Bernadette's case, it can be observed that both therapist and patient were vulnerable and with different needs, but the therapist was in a powerful position. The therapist's need to keep Bernadette in therapy created a strong transference in Bernadette that the therapist, like her mother, was not listening and not caring for her. So, power in the therapeutic relationship and the differences in power that exist influence the patterns of communication. Incorporating an intercultural psychoanalytic approach will prevent inner projections between people from diverse cultures and subcultures. Intercultural psychoanalytic psychotherapy places the relationship between client and therapist at the centre with a focus on the deficits resulting from the individual's early development, external trauma, and/or culture-bound symptoms that may be presented within the therapeutic context. The intercultural approach uses the psychoanalytic clinical structure allowing space for some flexibility, so that consideration may be given to issues of race, culture, and the genuine concerns of the client that may otherwise fall outside the experience of professionals trained and working only within the western framework. Bernadette's expectations were based on her social and cultural context – identifying herself as vulnerable and disadvantaged compared with her therapist. The therapist's expectation of Bernadette was based on her need to be her patient – listening other and her container in the consulting room.

Therapeutic interventions will be successful if the therapist gives value to their own internal world, reflecting, exploring, and monitoring their unconscious as an important part of the therapeutic relationship with the intersubjective unconscious sphere where the transference/countertransference is constantly discussed and examined. Heimann (1950) noted the importance of the use of countertransferential feelings to gain insight into the transferential material and prevent the construction of inadequate and feeble interventions that do not address the unconscious communications within the patient–therapist therapeutic dyad.

An understanding of psychic space and function is central to intercultural psychoanalysis and brings unconscious processes to the preconscious/conscious domain in transference/countertransference interpretations within the therapeutic dyad; the therapist explains the patient's unconscious patterns in the pre-conscious/conscious. Therefore, the patient attains an apparent and perceived insight into facts, helped by the descriptive mappings conveyed by the interpretations.

If the client suffered during their early development, and has unsuccessful relationships similar to the relationship they had with their parents or primary carer during that early development, the patterns of relating will become more apparent in therapy. Those facts are rational for interpretation, which can provide insight into the repetitive patterns of behaviour in relating to others. The therapist may use the presence of a causal factor in transference to establish whether a patient is fearful of commitment, and whether in transference the pattern of the patient's behaviour is similar to their relationships of the past.

It is fair to say that in any therapeutic relationship there is no possibility of testing all ideas at the same time. Thus, any new measure provides more knowledge or enquiry for further understanding, and the potential for falsification, which lends credibility to the theory.

New developments

Psychoanalysis has seen many new developments. These include an intercultural psychoanalytic relational approach with a focus on resilience. Clinical illustrations and research are needed to investigate how effective the approach is for those with long-term mental health issues as a result of the trauma they have endured or of being a marginalized member of society, owing to race, colour, culture, gender, class, sexuality, disability, language, or marital status, for example. One of the difficult tasks for people who are affected by trauma is the feeling of loss, including the loss of the self – or at least a part of the self; and the lack of mourning of the self that is lost or at least partly lost.

Laplanche and Pontalis (1973: 277–8) indicate 'the object-relationships of a specific subject, but also types of object-relationship by reference either to points in development (e.g. an oral object-relationship) or else to psychopathology (e.g. a melancholic object relationship)'. From an object-relations perspective, what a person internalizes from early childhood sets the foundation for establishing and maintaining relationships. Object-relations theory is primarily concerned with love, especially the need for parental love, which developed from drive theory that removed from the discharge mechanics of the libido. Psychopathology is an expression of traumatic self-object internalizations from childhood acted out in our lifelong relationships. Objects refer to people, parts of people, or physical objects that symbolically represent either a person or part of a person.

Revisiting object-relations theory (Alayarian 2011; Paul and Charura 2014), new developments within the intercultural psychoanalytic approach provide a better therapeutic relationship within the constantly changing society we live in. From this perspective, the relational model accounts for the distortion of objects by pointing to the inherent difficulty of the search for relatedness. An important facet of object-relations theory is that it looks not only at what others have been for us, but also what we wanted them to be, indeed what we are to others. Although cognitive development is not independent of affective factors and psychodynamic struggles, early primitive forms of cognition are universally unavoidable. Early forms of perception and cognition lacking a sense of time, space, and object constancy, contribute to the painful intensity of the struggles within early object relations.

From an intercultural perspective, the role of subliminal messages from the environment shapes object-relations dispositions. With psychic space and a secure sense of self, insecure situations will be distinguishable from secure ones. There is a tendency to bounce back from setbacks with a developmental advance as a result of a positive interaction between the self and the environment; psychic space, sense of self, and an ability to dissociate healthily from unbearable thoughts and memory are key ingredients that provide the ability to be reflective, and the ability to relate.

An intercultural psychoanalytic approach is a form of therapeutic relationship that enhances resilience by providing space for exploring vulnerabilities; helping to maintain a focus on the healthy/functional parts of the patient, while working on the disturbed parts in order to achieve resilience.

Summary

If we accept that personal development is on-going throughout life, and psychoanalytic therapy is an opportunity to pick up where we left off to re-address our developmental deficits, we can hypothesize: resilience is an important component of analysability in treatment; so is the ability to dissociate with memory that we are at times not able to process and to deal with.

How can we distinguish between resilience and vulnerability? For a vulnerable person, memories may pose as thoughts, feelings, or images that do not reveal themselves as memories. They may come to mind, but seem relatively meaningless; at other times they overwhelm consciousness and go into a vividly remembered past. For a resilient person, these memories emerge into consciousness clearly when there is enough psychic space to give pause for thought and process (Alayarian 2011).

The effects of external trauma in one's psyche can be so powerful that it enforces rejection of desire, and can take the form of projections and introjections; there is no 'psychic space' or coherent 'sense of self' and power for the self to achieve the pleasure (Alayarian 2011). Therefore, there is no sense of self, no psychic space to be relied on and used within the therapeutic relationship, and the therapist will not be perceived as the 'listening other' – thus, the patient feels unheard and uncared for (see vignette on Bernadette).

Thus a therapeutic relationship is simply the relationship between therapist, in a helping role, and the patient, being helped, working together to build the capacity in a way that supports the healing and ensures positive outcomes. It also enables supportive supervisor–supervisee relationships, and enhances the capacity of therapists as a whole, by understanding the role of empathy, genuineness, and positive regard in interpersonal communication.

Considering psychoanalysis as a scientific practice offers a critical position from which the field has the ability to increase its effectiveness and relevance in working with people who suffer from complex psychological problems that are too often failed by other therapeutic methods that are conventionally accepted and practised within mental health services. As with all scientific methods, continued scrutiny is essential to maintaining the validity of psychoanalytic findings. Thus, intercultural psychoanalytic interventions remain open to finding new ways to provide evidence that has the potential to falsify as well as adhere to methods of collecting and collating data for the purpose of increasing patient resilience and sustainable psychological recovery and growth. Establishing the relevance of scientific research in improving the effectiveness of the intercultural psychoanalytic approach is fundamental to developing best practice for therapeutic relationship.

Notes

1   Transference and countertransference are normal phenomena that may arise during the course of the therapeutic relationship. Understanding these phenomena is important for any therapeutic relationship. Transference involves the redirection of the client's feelings, conflicts, and thoughts regarding unresolved or unsatisfactory childhood experiences in relationships with parents and other important figures onto the therapist. Countertransference involves the same principles, except the direction of the transference is reversed. Countertransference involves redirection of the therapists' feelings, thoughts, and reactions towards the client.

2   I argue that if the inner world can be conceived of as a source of objective data, then it has to be testable. In order to test observations, therapists inevitably impact the results acquired; however, this occurs in every approach and data gathering.

3   Some information in both vignettes has been changed to ensure anonymity and confidentiality, including names and some facts, by altering elements of the case history.

Further reading

Alayarian, A. (2011) *Trauma, Torture and Dissociation: A Psychoanalytic View*. London: Karnac Books. This book helps the reader to understand trauma from a psychoanalytic perspective.

Kareem, J. and Littlewood, R. (1992) *Intercultural Therapy: Themes, Interpretation and Practice*. Oxford: Blackwell Scientific. This book responds to the need for an awareness of various ethical, theoretical, and practical issues. It is suggested that in the UK people from ethnic minorities are less likely to receive psychotherapy.

Winnicott, D.W. (1965) *The Maturational Processes and the Facilitating Environment*. London: Hogarth Press. This collection of Winnicott's papers applies Freud's theories to infancy and the failures of development in infancy.

References

Ahumada, J.L. (1994) What is a clinical fact? Clinical psychoanalysis as inductive method, *International Journal of Psychoanalysis*, 75: 949–62.

Alayarian, A. (2008) *Consequences of Denial: The Armenian Genocide*. London: Karnac Books.

Alayarian, A. (2011) *Trauma, Torture and Dissociation: A Psychoanalytic View*. London: Karnac Books.

Bion, W.R. (1962) *Learning from Experience*. London: Heinemann.

Bion, W.R. (1970) *Attention and Interpretation*. London: Tavistock.

Bowlby, J. (1969) *Attachment and Loss, Vol. 1: Attachment*. New York: Basic Books.

Bowlby, J. (1973) *Attachment and Loss, Vol. 2: Separation, Anxiety and Anger*. New York: Basic Books.

Bowlby, J. (1980) *Attachment and Loss, Vol. 3: Loss, Separation and Depression*. New York: Basic Books.

Bowlby, J. (1988) *A Secure Base: Clinical Applications of Attachment Theory*. London: Routledge & Kegan Paul.

Breuer, J. and Freud, S. (1895) *Studies of Hysteria*. Standard Edition, 2: 19–305. London: Hogarth Press.

Fairbairn, W.R.D. (1952) *Psychoanalytic Studies of the Personality*. London: Tavistock.

Freud, A. (1989) *Normality and Pathology in Childhood: Assessments of Development*. London: Karnac Books.

Freud, S. (1915) *The Unconscious*. Standard Edition, 14: 159–205. London: Hogarth Press.

Freud, S. (1917) *Mourning and Melancholia*, Standard Edition, 14: 243–58. London: Hogarth.

Freud, S. (1920) *Beyond the Pleasure Principle*. Standard Edition, 18: 7–64. London: Hogarth Press.

Guntrip, H. (1992) *Schizoid Phenomena, Object Relations and the Self*. London: Karnac Books.

Heimann, P. (1950) On countertransference, *International Journal of Psychoanalysis*, 31: 81–4.

Hinshelwood, R. (1997) Catastrophe, objects and representation: three levels of interpretation, *British Journal of Psychotherapy*, 13: 307–17.

Joseph, B. (1987) Projective identification: clinical aspects, in J. Sandler (ed.) *Projection, Identification, and Projective Identification*. London: Karnac Books.

Kareem, J. and Littlewood, R. (1992) *Intercultural Therapy: Themes, Interpretation and Practice*. Oxford: Blackwell Scientific.

Klein, M. (1946) Notes on some schizoid mechanisms, *International Journal of Psychoanalysis*, 16: 145–74.

Klein, M. (1957) *Envy and Gratitude: A Study of Unconscious Forces*. New York: Basic Books.

Langs, R. (1992) *A Clinical Workbook for Psychotherapists*. London: Karnac Books.

Laplanche, J. and Pontalis, J.B. (1973) *The Language of Psycho-Analysis* (trans. D. Nicholson Smith). London: Hogarth Press.

Mach, E. (1897) *Popular Scientific Lectures* (trans. T.J. McCormack). LaSalle, IL: Open Court.

Paul, S. and Charura, D. (2014) *An Introduction to the Therapeutic Relationship in Counselling and Psychotherapy*. London: Sage.

Sandler, J., Dare, C. and Holder, A. (1973) *The Patient and the Analyst: The Basis of the Psychoanalytic Process*. New York: International Universities Press.

Searles, H.F. (1959) The effort to drive the other person crazy, in *Collected Papers on Schizophrenia and Related Subjects* (pp. 521–55). New York: International Universities Press.

Winnicott, D.W. (1965) *The Maturational Processes and the Facilitating Environment*. London: Hogarth Press.

3   Cognitive behavioural therapy and the therapeutic relationship

Mike Thomas

Introduction

Cognitive behavioural therapy (CBT) is one of the most enduring forms of talking therapies, having been around for more than 150 years. Drake et al. (2013) provide an overview of its inception, pointing out its early proponents such as Charles Darwin (1872) and William James (1884). From the mid twentieth century onwards, CBT was influenced by psychoanalytical approaches alongside cognitive and behavioural techniques. Aaron Beck (1976), who was a trained analyst, attempted to apply psychoanalytical techniques in his behavioural treatment practice, which focused his work towards cognitive behavioural therapy (Thomas 2008). Cognitive behavioural therapy has developed from this early foundation to its modern approach where the client and therapist work together in a therapeutic partnership to identify and comprehend problems and instigate an awareness of thoughts, feelings, and behaviours. Over the years there has been further emphasis on the impact of the physical and the environment. Cognitive behavioural therapy views the interconnectedness of thoughts, moods, and physical sensations as influencing both negative and positive behaviours. The therapy helps clients to alter unhelpful and distressing negative thoughts and behaviours using evidence-based interventions.

The outcome of therapy, therefore, is for the client to understand the dynamics that support the interrelations between thinking, feeling, and behaviour and to have learnt different and more effective methods of managing their problems and have more resilient coping skills. Cognitive behavioural therapy does not provide a curative therapeutic approach but one that supports the client to develop new techniques to deal with their presenting problems. For example, if the condition is severe or enduring or they experience a life situation that cannot be changed, then CBT will adopt a variety of different interventions to support the client, including third-wave CBT techniques such as mindfulness, dialectical therapy or compassionate CBT. If the condition is more short term, then brief therapy interventions can be adopted.

Foundations of theory and practice

Beck's (1976) cognitive triad puts forward the theory that the individual may be influenced by negative thoughts about the self, the world, and the future. For some individuals, certain life events can be perceived as negative, which lowers mood and develops unhelpful thinking. A dysfunctional circle is then established where low mood increases negative thinking, which in turn increases low mood until there is a generalized distortion of thinking. Cognitive behavioural therapy refers to the process of moving from a negative to a more positive view of the self, the world, and the future as cognitive reframing or restructuring.

Beckian approaches see reframing or restructuring as occurring on three different levels of thinking, mood, and behaviour, each of which influences the other two. The three levels are often termed core beliefs, intermediate assumptions, and negative automatic thoughts (NATs) respectively. Core beliefs are the deepest level of thinking, which supports a structure (schema) that clusters thinking, past events, and current experiences into existing beliefs.

Core beliefs act as the foundation for a second level of thinking called under- lying (intermediate) assumptions, which refer to individual attitudes. Attitudes can be both negative and positive for the individual and are called dysfunctional or functional underlying assumptions. Assumptions in turn support the more reachable level of thinking called automatic thoughts, which occur immediately and some- times below conscious awareness in response to daily life events. Beck took the view that dysfunctional underlying assumptions supported negative automatic thoughts.

The most accessible and fastest therapeutic response occurs at the level of automatic thought, and so it is no surprise to find that most CBT therapists practise at this level with six to twelve sessions. Inevitably in a period of financial constraints there is less work seen at the intermediate and core levels, although reframing thinking at core level has more long-term benefits because these impact on underlying assumptions and automatic thoughts. Beck's cognitive triad and the three levels of cognition have been developed over subsequent years and several different CBT models are now established. Some of the most common are Ellis's (1977) rational- emotive model, Padesky and Mooney's (1990) five aspects of life experience model, and Lazarus's (1997) model of brief CBT therapy.

There are six sequential steps to applied CBT: socialization, assessment, case formulation, treatment interventions, evaluation, and end or termination of therapy. *Socialization* involves informing the potential client, in words that are understandable, about the principles of CBT, the methods of assessment and the potential levels of interventions available to the client.

Assessments sometimes span several sessions and direct the treatment intervention at immediate, intermediate or core level. Assessments help the client to gain understanding of the most dominant mode of negative thinking and how the interactions between thoughts, feelings, moods, behaviours, and environment maintain each other in a dysfunctional way.

Assessment tools can be categorized into two groups: comparative and exploratory (Thomas and Drake 2012). Comparative tools are generally validated instruments that provide scores for specific results, such as those for measuring anxiety levels, low mood states or general wellbeing. Others use criteria for diagnostic purposes, as in the Diagnostic and Statistical Manual of Mental Disorders V (DSM-V; APA 2013) or the International Statistical Classification of Diseases 10th Revision (ICD-10) (WHO 2007).

Exploratory tools are individualized and relate to the client's history, life experiences, relationships, employment, general health, and any important issues such as alcohol intake, drug use or prescribed medication. Exploratory assessment can also take into account visual evaluation (skin condition, gait, speech, and general presentation) that may provide information related to the client's mental state, while question-and-answer assessment can take into account issues such as cognitive functioning or physical problems. Exploratory assessments include measurements of sleep, diet, mood, behaviour or thinking.

Assessment leads to *formulation*, which is the process whereby the client's problems are linked to CBT approaches to demonstrate the level of thinking (immediate, intermediate or core) and their association with mood, behaviour, and environment, which negatively influences the general life of the client. The formulation is the basis for the agreed treatment plan.

There are three types of formulation: protocol-driven, generic, and idiosyncratic (individualized) case formulation. Protocol formulations have been tested in practice, are normally problem-specific, and provide treatment guidelines for common mental health issues such as anxiety or depression. Generic formulations tend to follow a specific model such as Padesky and Mooney's (1990) five aspects model or Lazarus's (1997) brief therapy model, which emphasize particular aspects of thinking, feeling, physical sensations, behaviour, and the environment. Individual or idiosyncratic case formulations combine generic and problem-specific approaches with information related to the client's particular and unique presentation, complexity, and lifestyle.

Two other types of formulation are maintenance and longitudinal. Maintenance formulations focus on immediate problems and the issues that maintain the problems via the interrelations between thoughts, feelings, physical sensations, and the environment. Because the aim of therapy is to manage the immediate problems, maintenance formulation works at the NATs and intermediate level, is useful in short- to medium-term therapy, and protocol-driven and generic formulations are most useful. Longitudinal formulations work on early childhood influences and at the core or schematic level, where therapy inevitably takes longer and so individualized formulations are better.

Treatment interventions follow on from discussion of the case formulation and normally focus on issues at NATs, intermediate or core level. For protocol-driven treatments there are pre-packaged interventions, whereas for idiosyncratic/ individualized or generic treatments the client and the therapist discuss potential treatment options before agreeing on those that provide the most realistic outcomes.

Within treatment are continuous on-going measurements of progress, so various methods of collecting relevant data are used, including diaries, sleep charts, mood and behaviour records, negative-thought records, panic diaries alongside measurements of specific diagnostic conditions such as anxiety, obsessive-compulsive disorder or depression. Results of such records are analysed and discussed at set sessions throughout therapy to demonstrate progress or highlight issues that require a different approach. A constant in CBT treatment is the exploration of the interrelations between thoughts, feelings, physical sensations, behaviour, and the environment so the client can initially see how they maintain difficult issues. As therapy progresses, the client tries different ways of changing the pattern into a more positive interrelationship and improving coping skills. Sometimes this is by identifying triggers for negative responses such as memories, negative automatic thoughts or specific situations, and altering the impact of the triggers through improved recognition, responses or avoiding the triggers. At other times, the problems may be perceived as recent but the roots for the emotional responses may be due to childhood events or trauma, and treatment explores the impact of early memories on emotions and dysfunctional underlying assumptions which support negative automatic thoughts.

Treatment may include problem-solving exercises, rehearsals for real events, talking through speculative and potential responses from others, exploring anxieties and fears, and learning new skills such as mindfulness, distraction techniques, relaxation exercises or developing raised awareness of the effects of NATs and dysfunctional underlying assumptions. Objectives tend to be realistic and less sophisticated at the start of therapy but contemporary CBT practice can go on to include complex multi-method interventions that may integrate family therapy, systemic work, dialectical techniques, narrative therapy, person-centred principles, e-CBT, text and mobile-apps support, self-help and educational resources, and existential approaches. Treatment involves improving self-concept, self-esteem, and self-image, so it is important to ensure goals are both realistically achievable and within a suitable time frame.

Evaluation of the treatment intervention occurs properly during the final two sessions of therapy but can occur throughout treatment whenever analysis of the client's homework, charts or scores is undertaken. End-of-treatment evaluation begins by looking at the original treatment objectives which followed the compiling of the case formulation and deciding if the objectives have been achieved. Evaluation is more effective if there are demonstrably improved scores on the measuring instruments used in treatment; for example, a reduction in anxiety, improved mood scores, better relations with others, improved sleep patterns. Discussing measurement scores can be a good platform to go on to talk about future management techniques and self-help interventions after therapy has ceased.

There are two reasons for carrying out the evaluation phase at least one session before cessation of therapy: to allow time to make plans if required for further referrals, perhaps to a support group, local charity, general practitioner or more specialized services; and to support the client if they have difficulties with the thought of dealing with their problems without therapeutic support. It is not easy to take on therapy and it takes courage to open up to a stranger but equally it can be difficult to say goodbye to the therapist who has shared difficult and traumatic thoughts and feelings. Evaluation provides time for the client and the therapist to review the therapeutic journey, to provide suggestions for self-help techniques once therapy is over, and to support the client's increased independence.

This element of evaluation thus takes the therapy into the end, or termination, phase. As in the socialization phase, this aspect of therapy requires a high level of interpersonal skills and involves both the client and therapist planning post-therapy work, such as referring on to other agencies, joining support groups or taking on new objectives outside of therapy. It involves recognition of the trust and depth of the therapeutic relationship and the impact a cooperative partnership approach has had on the client's initial problems. It also involves saying goodbye with a positive and reflective approach.

The therapeutic relationship

The client should at all times retain the understanding that they have choices and can control where they want therapy to focus in the context of their problems. As such, socialization is an essential skill for the CBT therapist and assimilates elements of person-centred and humanistic approaches with an emphasis on establishing a trusting relationship and demonstrating genuine interest in the client's problem. Thomas and Drake (2012) stress that this stage of establishing the therapeutic relationship should be viewed as a similar ethical stance to gaining informed consent for therapy to continue. A working relationship involves coming to a joint agreement on therapeutic issues such as confidentiality, boundaries, the client's input into 'homework' and out-of-session activities, the importance of assessments, how feedback should be provided, when evaluations will be carried out, explanations of concepts and assessment of results, a full explanation of their diagnosis, and so on. This therapeutic alliance is sometimes referred as the therapeutic contract and its importance in the context of relational skills cannot be overestimated, since within CBT it is generally held that a solid therapeutic relationship increases the beneficial outcome of the therapy (Roos and Weardon 2009; Daniels and Weardon 2011).

Like other talking therapies, CBT relational skills involve listening, asking the right questions, acknowledging the other, reinforcing positive elements of change, being genuine, demonstrating support, being kind and compassionate, and being honest with responses and answers, as these are key to positive CBT outcomes.

Challenges

Cognitive behavioural therapy retains a reputation for its instrumental approach to clinical conditions and the individual that is hard to shake off; for instance, Salkovskis (1996) argued against the application of a mechanical approach in CBT. Thomas and Drake (2012) suggest that this reputation is due to a number of different issues: that psychotherapists and psychologists have carried out more clinical research studies on CBT than they have on other psychotherapeutic approaches; that the application of objective research methods using validated measuring instruments and the requirements of peer-reviewed publications restrict emotional involvement or natural observations; and that the introduction of the Improving Access to Psychological Therapies (IAPT) programme with its utilization of pre-prepared protocols has increasingly restricted, and in some cases prevented, the application of individually based case formulations and treatment plans. Thomas and Drake go on to argue that IAPT may, over time, dilute the skills of CBT therapists to carry out individualized case formulations.

In response to such criticism, CBT therapists are increasingly adopting developments in mindfulness and compassionate-based approaches to stress that trust and empathy remain core competences and objectives of CBT interventions. Yet this is not new. For example, Gelder (1989) observed that the thoughts and feelings of clients were an essential part of CBT approaches. Judith Beck (1995) consistently argued for CBT practitioners to demonstrate empathetic skills and the requirements for authenticity and genuineness in the therapeutic relationship, while Padesky (1996) emphasized that skilled application of psychotherapeutic principles would prevent the development of a mechanistic and prescriptive CBT approach. More recently, Westbrook et al. (2011) argued that CBT is actually a therapy of understanding, and Leahy (2008) suggested that a more positive therapeutic outcome is achieved by a therapist who demonstrates a deep understanding of the client's suffering.

Before the IAPT programme (which has gained widespread application across many parts of England due to the support of central governmental funding), the assessment stage of CBT led to conceptualization of the problem and presentation to the client in various forms prior to case formulation. The rise in protocol-driven or problem-specific protocols was mentioned above, but it is worth noting that its initial development and acceptance by CBT practitioners was due to a growing concern that CBT was losing its theoretical integrity as practitioners expanded into new clinical conditions and started to adopt different approaches. Dominant figures in the field, led by Clark (1986), provided research findings supporting specific CBT interventions for certain conditions (Warwick and Salkovskis 1990; Clark and Wells 1995; Ehlers and Clark 2000), and it has been argued that the utilization of protocol-driven techniques was an attempt to bring CBT back into a more structured, theoretical, and research-supported arena (Drake et al. 2013). The fact that this drive for a return to a more traditional CBT paradigm occurred at the same time as a huge rise in demand for therapy probably helped in the development of the IAPT model, which is more about service re-design and delivery than CBT.

Layard et al. (2006) argued that mental health issues prevented employment and negatively affected the UK economy, which, alongside NICE (2004) guidelines and its emphasis on research studies, provided the right environment for the government to jump at the chance to provide low-cost and effective interventions and led to the dominance of CBT within the IAPT programme. This may explain why IAPT continues to be referred to as a development in CBT despite the fact that IAPT is concerned with service delivery and not therapeutic principles.

Other challenges within CBT have occurred with more stealth. Drake et al. (2013) argue that IAPT has now reached the point of theoretical exhaustion and can provide no further enhanced CBT-based understanding without recourse to new forms of CBT practice. The work of Clark and others to hold back the tide of entrepreneurship and creativity within CBT is failing, as individual clients present with increasing levels of complexities and a rising consumerist-driven desire to be seen and accepted as individuals rather than as part of a mass demand on therapeutic services.

For example, despite the dominance of protocol-driven formulations there is continuing debate about the formulation approach to be used in response to clients' problems. Protocol-driven formulations are recognized as pre-packaged treatment models that often have received research scrutiny and provide standardized sets of interventions for mental health problems; often those most commonly encountered in clinical practice such as anxiety and depression. Supporters such as Grant et al. (2010) state that the therapist has a professional duty to carry out protocol-driven formulations as they are based on research findings, whereas others such as Kinsella and Garland (2008), Thomas and Drake (2012), and Drake et al. (2013) argue that protocol-driven formulations are restrictive in their inability to deal with real-life situations. Clients present with complex, enduring or severe conditions and it is unlikely that experienced therapists will only encounter individuals with only one mild type of condition. Generic or idiosyncratic (individualized) formulations are better able to support more in-depth personalized interventions. And there is a growing view that protocol-driven (IAPT) formulations are good at developing the skills of early therapists and are useful for short-term mild conditions, but as more experience is gained the therapist adopts more individualized and generic formulations because they provide more flexibility to meet clients' needs.

Another challenge to CBT is the ending phase of therapy. For some practitioners, the demand of high-volume turnover makes the ending phase an administrative formality with the last session comparing pre-treatment scores with the final results, a short discussion on further referrals, and the completion of the requisite paperwork. This is not how CBT should be completed and is more a reflection of the therapist, the care system or a management objective if that is the case. Clients deserve better and have a right to be treated as equal partners in therapy, including the ending stage and afterwards.

New developments within CBT

Despite its drawbacks and the growing dominance of CBT as the public services therapy of choice over the last two decades (Moorey 2012; Trower 2012), IAPT has provided a reason for successive governments to fund a new type of therapeutic worker – the psychological wellbeing practitioner (PWP). A PWP need have little, if any, background therapeutic experience or be CBT trained but can still deliver low-intensity CBT programmes with a high level of throughput and minimum facilitation. More complex cases can be referred to the high-intensity IAPT worker who will work in the more structured CBT tradition covered above.

There is, however, a movement away from the reductionist and economically driven IAPT delivery. Within the research environment there are more studies on CBT outcomes that adopt qualitative rather than quantitative approaches; for instance, more studies using phenomenological and grounded theory methods (Coldwell et al. 2011; Moore et al. 2012). There are also further developments regarding the benefits of multi-modal therapies with CBT delivered within a model that encompasses family and psychosocial therapies with analytical, systemic, and narrative techniques (Bertrando 2011). Third-wave CBT and multi-modal approaches involving CBT techniques will continue to be more effective as research increases our understanding of approaches involving digital-based CBT, mindfulness, motivational interviewing, metacognition and dialectical-behaviour therapy, as well as cognitive-interpersonal and psychoanalytical techniques.

Cognitive behavioural therapy will also be further practised outside the traditionally trained therapist approach as the work of the PWP has indicated that different health workers can be effective. Health visitors, midwives, general practitioners, and other healthcare workers will increasingly practise low-intensity interventions, while a more multidisciplinary approach will be taken between health and social care workers. The work of Collins et al. (2013) indicates that future psychotherapists will also be more skilled in intervening in physical disorders and providing increased insights into the relationship between thoughts, feelings, and physiological symptoms.

Cognitive behavioural therapy is developing away from a treatment-focused approach to one that can be used by the client as a therapy that provides support at different periods of their lives rather than one which seeks an end to specific problems *per se*. In addition, although brief interventions will continue to be a mainstay, there will be more interest in long-term solutions and less access to state-funded CBT. This will provide an expansion into more longitudinal therapies with more focus on intermediate and schema-centred work, as working at this deeper level prevents further relapses and simultaneously deals with NATs and immediate problems in the early stages of therapy.

Summary

Cognitive behavioural therapy has a long history and has demonstrated an ability to develop and evolve to suit the prevalent societal needs of the day. It has an admirable research record to show its effectiveness in dealing with individual problems and provides efficiencies in an environment of central government ideological and economic objectives to cut central state funding.

This form of therapy provides a logical set of underlying principles and sequencing in its application. It also provides practitioners with freedom to explore immediate presenting problems or deeper schematic issues as well as a huge range of validated measuring tools to evaluate progress. Cognitive behavioural therapy continues to develop different formulation approaches and new treatment techniques with the growth of third-wave therapies and new ways of delivering therapy (particularly via digital media). It further lends itself to multi-modal approaches and increasingly multidisciplinary teams with different individuals and professions adopting CBT techniques in their everyday work.

Finally, CBT continues to explore new ways of making the interpersonal aspects of therapy more equal and is increasingly incorporating existential, person-centred, and psychoanalytical techniques into the CBT repertoire while retaining the principles of supporting the client's understanding of the relationship between their thoughts, feelings, physical sensations, behaviour, and environment.

Further reading

Collins, E., Drake, M. and Deacon, M. (2013) *The Physical Care of People with Mental Health Problems: A Guide for Best Practice*. London: Sage. One of a very small number of texts available that explores the physical disorder dimension experienced by individuals with negative thinking and feeling symptoms.

Drake, M., Ross, I. and Thomas, M. (2013) Cognitive behavioural therapy: past, present and future, *Journal of Psychological Therapies in Primary Care*, 2 (1): 51–70. Provides an overview of the historical development of CBT and potential diversification of CBT into multi-modal practice.

Dryden, W. and Branch, R. (eds.) (2012) *The CBT Handbook*. London: Sage. Contributions from different practitioners and theorists provide a good practical guide for those seeking to know more about CBT delivery.

References

American Psychiatric Association (APA) (2013) *Diagnostic and Statistical Manual of Mental Disorders*, 5th edn. Washington, DC: APA.

Beck, A.T. (1976) *Cognitive Therapy and the Emotional Disorders*. New York: International Universities Press.

Beck, J.S. (1995) *Cognitive Therapy: Basics and Beyond*. New York: Guilford Press.

Bertrando, P. (2011) A theory of clinical practice: the cognitive and the narrative, *Journal of Family Therapy*, 33: 153–67.

Clark, D.M. (1986) A cognitive model of panic, *Behavioural Research and Therapy*, 24: 461–70.

Clark, D.M. and Wells, A. (1995) A cognitive model of social phobia, in R. Heimberg, M. Liebowitz, D.A. Hope and F.R. Schneier (eds.) *Social Phobia: Diagnosis, Assessment and Treatment* (pp. 69–93). New York: Guilford Press.

Coldwell, J., Meddings, S. and Camic, P.M. (2011) How people with psychosis positively contribute to their family: a grounded theory analysis, *Journal of Family Therapy*, 33: 353–71.

Collins, E., Drake, M. and Deacon, M. (2013) *The Physical Care of People with Mental Health Problems; A Guide for Best Practice*. London: Sage.

Daniels, J. and Weardon, A.J. (2011) Socialisation to the model: the active component in the therapeutic alliance? A preliminary study, *Behavioural and Cognitive Psychotherapy*, 39: 221–7.

Darwin, C. (1872) *The Expressions of Emotions in Man and Animals*. London: John Murray.

Drake, M., Ross, I. and Thomas, M. (2013) Cognitive behavioural therapy: past, present and future, *Journal of Psychological Therapies in Primary Care*, 2 (1): 51–70.

Ehlers, A. and Clark, D.M. (2000) A cognitive model of post traumatic stress disorder from different sources of trauma, *Behavioural Research and Therapy*, 38 (4): 319–45.

Ellis, A. (1977) The basic clinical theory of rational-emotive therapy, in A. Ellis and R. Grieger (eds.) *Handbook of Rational-Emotive Therapy*. New York: Springer.

Gelder, M.G. (1989) Foreword, in K. Hawton, P.M. Salkvoskis, J. Kirk and D.M. Clark (eds.) *Cognitive Therapy for Psychiatric Problems: A Practical Guide*. Oxford: Oxford University Press.

Grant, A., Townend, M., Mulhern, R. and Short, N. (2010) *Cognitive Behavioural Therapy in Mental Health Care*. London: Sage.

James, W. (1884) What is an emotion?, *Mind*, 9 (34): 188–205.

Kinsella, P. and Garland, A. (2008) *Cognitive Behavioural Therapy for Mental Health Workers*. London: Routledge.

Layard, R., Bell, S., Clark, D.M., Knapp, M., Meacher, M. and Priebe, S. (2006) *The Depression Report: A New Deal for Anxiety and Depression Disorders*. London: London School of Economics.

Lazarus, A.A. (1997) *Brief but Comprehensive Psychotherapy*. New York: Springer.

Leahy, R.L. (2008) The therapeutic relationship in cognitive-behavioural therapy, *Behavioural and Cognitive Psychotherapy*, 36: 769–77.

Moore, G.F., Moore, L. and Murphy, S. (2012) Integration of motivational interviewing into practice in the National Exercise referral scheme in Wales: a mixed methods study, *Behavioural and Cognitive Psychotherapy*, 40: 313–30.

Moorey, S. (2012) CBT: past, present and future, in W. Dryden and R. Branch (eds.) *The CBT Handbook* (pp. 45–65). London: Sage.

National Institute for Health and Clinical Excellence (NICE) (2004) *Management of Depression in Primary Care*. Guideline CG23 [www.nice.org.uk/CG23].

Padesky, C.A. (1996) Developing cognitive therapist competence: teaching and supervision models, in P.M. Salkovskis (ed.) *Frontiers of Cognitive Therapy*. New York: Guilford Press.

Padesky, C.A. and Mooney, K.A. (1990) Clinical tip: presenting the cognitive model to clients, *International Cognitive Therapy Newsletter*, 6: 13–14 [http://padesky.com/clinicalcorner].

Roos, J. and Weardon, A. (2009) What do you mean by 'socialisation to the model'? A Delphi study, *Behavioural and Cognitive Psychotherapy*, 37 (3): 341–5.

Salkovskis, P.M. (ed.) (1996) *Frontiers of Cognitive Therapy*. New York: Guilford Press.

Thomas, M. (2008) Cognitive behavioural dimensions of the therapeutic relationship, in S. Haugh and S. Paul (eds.) *The Therapeutic Relationship: Perspectives and Themes*. Ross-on-Wye: PCCS Books.

Thomas, M. and Drake, M. (2012) *Cognitive Behaviour Therapy Case Studies*. London: Sage.

Trower, P. (2012) CBT theory, in W. Dryden and R. Branch (eds.) *The CBT Handbook* (pp. 25–44). London: Sage.

Warwick, H.M.C. and Salkovskis, P.M. (1990) Hypochondriasis, *Behavioural Research and Therapy*, 28: 105–17.

Westbrook, D., Kennerley, H. and Kirk, J. (2011) *An Introduction to Cognitive Behavioural Therapy: Skills and Application*. London: Sage.

World Health Organization (WHO) (2007) *Multi-Axial Presentation of the ICD-10 (International Statistical Classification of Diseases and Related Health Problems, 10th Revision), for use in Adult Psychiatry*. Cambridge: WHO/Cambridge University Press.

4 Existential, humanistic, and transpersonal therapies and the relational approach

John Rowan

Introduction

Existential, humanistic, and transpersonal traditions have many similarities but some important differences. This chapter does justice to both, but it is quite hard to get the balance right, and there may well be some disagreements about the judgements made. However, I have a good deal of involvement in all three specialities, and have been fascinated to see how each new development has affected the ins and outs of this. The relational approach has affected every therapy over the past twenty or thirty years, and today almost everyone pays at least lip service to it. And in a way this is particularly challenging to the three approaches outlined here, because authenticity is so basic to them, and at first sight so incompatible with the relational approach.

Foundations of theory and practice

Existentialism is a philosophy that goes back a long way. Indeed, in the magisterial collection *The Worlds of Existentialism*, Friedman (1964) takes us back to Heraclitus and the Old Testament. However, it seems to be generally agreed that Soren Kierkegaard is the spiritual founder of existentialism, and that Ludwig Binswanger and Medard Boss are the first existential therapists, together with Viktor Weizsacker and Hans Trub. One of the ideas of existentialism is that there are four dimensions to an individual's world-view: the Umwelt, the Mitwelt, the Eigenwelt, and the Uberwelt. The Umwelt is the natural world with its physical, biological development; the Mitwelt is about the social world and the relations people have with one another; the Eigenwelt is the private world of our own experience and identity; and the Uberwelt is about the ideal world with its spiritual dimension where we are in touch with beliefs, aspirations, and values that go beyond ourselves. Emmy van Deurzen (2002) has addressed this in the many books she has written, edited or co-edited. Existentialists were the first to insist that the person coming for therapy and the person conducting the therapy were in the same world and on the same level, and that the relationship between them was crucial. It should be open and accepting, not role-bound and formal. 'It cannot suffice that I have an insight *for myself*: it is important that the insight arise *between* us, the participation in this insight by me and by you is important. One cannot convey truth to another, one finds it with another' (Trub 1952: 103, quoted in Friedman 1964: 504).

This quote is clearly in line with the latest thinking on the relational approach, but it was written long before the present ferment. However, the existential approach did not make much impact on the world of psychotherapy until the advent of a remarkable book, which made such a big impression: *Existence: A New Dimension in Psychiatry and Psychology*, edited in 1958 by Rollo May, Ernest Angel and Henri Ellenberger. *Existence* presented the American public for the first time with the translation of the writings of leading European phenomenological and existential psychologists such as Ludwig Binswanger, Eugene Minkowski, Erwin Strauss, Viktor Emil von Gebsattel, and Roland Kuhn. May wrote two introductory chapters that were no less influential than the rest of the volume. May's chapters were epoch-making. They were re-published many times and became classic writings in the field. Thereafter, May was commonly viewed as the spokesman for the existential approach to psychology. Many years later, Bugental confessed that the reading of May's essays in *Existence* had had a kind of conversion effect on him. Alvin Mahrer, president of the humanistic psychology division of the APA in the 1980s, wrote that *Existence* had been his Bible in the 1960s (De Carvalho 1991: 63).

Existential psychotherapy divided into European, British, and American versions, which became progressively differentiated as the years went by, and are now strikingly different. The British version became identified with the Society of Existential Analysis, founded by Emmy van Deurzen. The American version followed Rollo May, in the manner suggested above, although Irvin Yalom was also considered a leader. But one of the most influential existentialists has been Martin Buber, who contributed the idea that there was an important contrast between the I-It (the way we treat things) and the I-Thou (the way we relate to people). The mistake we can make is to treat people in an I-It manner. This is to treat people like things, which is inauthentic. 'Buber also argues that such an I-Thou attitude requires the I to take the risk of entering itself fully in to the encounter: to leap into the unpredictability of a genuine dialogue with all of its being – including its vulnerabilities – and to be open to the possibility of being fundamentally transformed by the other' (Cooper 2003: 20). Mick Cooper describes all of this very well, and his short book has already become a classic.

Closely allied to the existential approach is phenomenology. The best known of the phenomenologists is Husserl (1931/1960), who contributed all the basic ideas. Spinelli (1967) has pointed out that phenomenology and humanistic psychology actually meet in the work of Carl Rogers. And later writers like Merleau-Ponty (1962) have been hugely influential, not only to the existentialists, but also to the humanistic writers.

Turning now to the humanistic therapies, we can go back to 1963, when the Association for Humanistic Psychology was born. Of course, humanistic therapies had existed before 1963, but that was the first time the term 'humanistic' had been used to describe them. One of the first was psychodrama (Karp et al. 1998), which comes from Jacob Moreno in the 1920s. Moreno is the true father of group work, and his approach is still flourishing today. Carl Rogers started his work in the 1940s, and the person-centred approach has continued to flourish after his death. Recently, there has emerged a new aspect to this approach, with a group describing 'working at relational depth'

(Knox et al. 2013), which is a very clear move into a more relational version. The classic book on Gestalt therapy, *Gestalt Therapy: Excitement and Growth in the Human Personality* (Perls et al.), was published in 1951, and this approach flourishes in a number of countries today, although much changed. Perls did not have a relational approach, and of course we are all relational now. This means that current gestaltists such as Rich Hycner (1991) and Philip Lichtenberg (2008) have moved far away from the Perls manner and technique. One of the great theorists of humanistic psychology is Alvin Mahrer (1996), whose classic book *Experiencing* first appeared in 1989, and was later reprinted. And one of the most important names is that of James Bugental (1981), whose account of authenticity is the humanistic classic on the subject.

The transpersonal emerged from the humanistic tradition, based on the work of Abraham Maslow, who with Anthony Sutich founded the Association for Transpersonal Psychology. Maslow's (1973) book *The Farther Reaches of Human Nature* only appeared after his death. The work spread rather rapidly after that, and today about thirty countries in Europe alone have active transpersonal psychology associations, with many more worldwide. One of the specialized versions of the transpersonal approach was developed by Roberto Assagioli in Italy, and today there are institutes of psychosynthesis in many countries [two.not2.org/psychosynthesis]. The recent handbook of transpersonal psychology gives an up-to-date account of all this (Friedman and Hartelius 2013).

The therapeutic relationship

The following is a key quotation: 'By authenticity I mean a central genuineness and awareness of being. Authenticity is that presence of an individual in his living in which he is fully aware in the present moment, in the present situation. Authenticity is difficult to convey in words, but experientially it is readily perceived in ourselves or in others' (Bugental 1981: 102). In other words, what Bugental is saying is that authenticity is an experience.

Case vignette

To illustrate this, take the example of a young man in therapy who became very angry with the therapist, saying: 'I don't think we are getting anywhere. When I say something, you just repeat it back to me, and never really give me what I want.' The therapist says: 'It really irritates you that I simply give your statement back to you, without offering any cure or correction.' Back comes the young man: 'There you are, doing it again! If it don't get anything better than that, I am just going to leave!' The therapist says, 'You are so angry with me not giving you anything more, that you really feel like leaving.' The young man gets up out of his seat and goes to the door. The therapist says: 'Just before you go, I want to say that I really respect what you have just been saying. It is more alive and more direct than anything you have said before, and it must have taken real courage to say all that.' The young man leaves. But he comes back the following week, much more involved and much more self revealing.

In developments from classic existentialism, many modern writers consider that the real self, the self that is to be actualized in self-actualization, is not a concept but an experience. It is not something to be argued at a philosophical level, but is something to be encountered at an experiential level. If we say that authenticity is merely 'an openness to existence, an acceptance of what is given as well as our freedom to respond to it' (Cohn 1997: 127), then there is no way of perceiving authenticity. It becomes an abstract and useless concept. Other existentialists have gone much further. For example:

> Authenticity consists in having a true and lucid consciousness of the situation, in assuming the responsibilities and risks that it involves, in accepting it in pride or humiliation, sometimes in horror and hate. There is no doubt that authenticity demands much courage and more than courage. Thus it is not surprising that one finds it so rarely.
>
> (Sartre 1948: 90)

For me, authenticity is a direct experience of the real self. It is unmistakable, self-authenticating. It is a true experience of freedom, of liberation, and as such it can be considered a mystical experience. We have already heard what Bugental says about it. And that is not all.

There is an important link between authenticity and genuineness, or congruence, as described by Carl Rogers. 'It is my feeling that congruence is a part of existential authenticity, that the person who is genuinely authentic in his being-in-the-world is congruent within himself; and to the extent that one attains authentic being in his life, to that extent is he congruent' (Bugental 1981: 108). Again it takes Bugental to draw our attention to the heartland of the humanistic approach, which is also the heartland of the existential approach. Both Bugental and Rogers are clear that congruence is difficult and demanding, and recent writers like Dave Mearns (1994, 1996, 1997) have made it clear that it cannot be taught as a skill.

So, if we want to go beyond the most basic levels of consciousness, we have to do it for ourselves, on our own account. We have to step off the escalator of social approval. We have to take responsibility for our own lives. And what do we get then? Primarily, and most obviously, it is authenticity. More recently, Jenny Wade (1996: 160) wrote:

> Authentic consciousness differs dramatically from earlier stages because it is free from commonly recognised forms of ego-distorted cognitive and affective perception. Traditional theorists view this stage as markedly free of the ego defenses seen prior to this level, so that persons at this level are able to experience and express themselves fully (Maslow 1987; Belenky et al. 1986; Graves 1981). Their increased capacities have led Maslow and the Gravesians to designate this stage the first level of another developmental order.

What we are saying, then, is that the real self which we are aiming at in humanistic psychotherapy is not something very abstract and hard to pin down – it is situated both in the empirical realm of psychological research and in the conceptual realm of philosophy. It is closest to the self as described in existential psychotherapy, as described by Friedenberg (1973: 94):

> The purpose of therapeutic intervention is to support and re-establish a sense of self and personal authenticity. Not mastery of the objective environment; not effective functioning within social institutions; not freedom from the suffering caused by anxiety – though any or all of these may be concomitant outcomes of successful therapy – but personal awareness, depth of real feeling, and, above all, the conviction that one can use one's full powers, that one has the courage to be and use all one's essence in the praxis of being.

This seems to me a ringing and crystal clear assertion, which is echoed many times in existential writings (Spinelli 1994; van Deurzen 1997; Cooper 2003; Schneider and Krug 2010). To sum up, then, we can say that all three of these approaches have in common a real devotion to the real self on the one hand, and to the real relationship on the other. But they do not slip into the mistake of assuming that the field is everything and the person nothing – that is wrong for all three approaches.

The challenges and complexities of maintaining a therapeutic relationship within an existential perspective

Let us now turn to another source of wisdom. Clare Graves was the researcher who developed the theory that was later taken up and further elaborated by Beck and Cowan (1996), and named by them as spiral dynamics. This theory states that the early stages of development are actually tribal in their thought patterns, and still very common in the less developed parts of the world. Obviously this terminology is not familiar to everyone, but it is so useful that we sometimes have to introduce it. The middle stages exhibit first-tier thinking, which is most people's idea of rationality in the more developed areas of the world – what is usually called formal logic, and is the kind of logic built into computers, where everything is either/or, one or zero. This is tremendously useful when dealing with things – the inanimate world. The stages after that use second-tier thinking, which is more like dialectical logic, or vision-logic, which starts from the premise that A is not simply A. Graves calls this a 'momentous leap'. If a client comes into the room and I as the therapist say to myself, 'Arthur is Arthur', that gives me no hint of what might happen later. But if a client comes into the room and I say to myself, 'Agnes is not simply Agnes', that immediately opens up vistas of future change in unspecified directions. This is the logic we need when dealing with people – the human world. We are now in the realm of self-actualization.

Of course, there is far more to self-actualization than authenticity or dialectical thinking. Maslow (1987) laid down seventeen characteristics, and I added to these (Rowan 2001) to give a total of thirty.

Case vignette

Consider the following example. A young man writes to his therapist months after finishing therapy, and relates the episode that moved him most. He was walking along the beach near his home, and saying to himself, 'I am such a failure: I have disappointed my parents, I have disappointed my teachers, I have disappointed my boss, there is just no hope for me.' But then, all at once, as he walked along, he saw the sun setting across the water, and suddenly went into a quite different mood. He said to himself, 'My parents had the wrong expectations for me, my teachers had the wrong expectations for me, my boss has the wrong expectations for me – I am not the picture they painted. I am me!' – and his heart leaped up, and he opened his eyes, and he kept repeating 'I am me!', louder and louder. And when he got home, he covered a big sheet of paper with the words 'I am me!', 'I am me!', 'I am me', over and over again. And it was as if he opened his heart, and saw the world through his own eyes, for the first time. He wrote that he had not thought too much about his therapy before that time, but all at once he got it.

It is important to make the point that authenticity is profoundly relational. When I am in the therapy room with a client, I can almost see the web of connections between us, alive in the common space. We are able to communicate at the deepest level, as if we were members of the same race and background. Because of the extreme adherence to presence and co-presence, we can communicate directly and without our roles getting in the way.

For example, one man was talking about his relationship with his wife, and describing the way in which some of the things she said triggered strong reactions in him. Instead of empathizing with him and exploring this, I confronted him with the idea that it was his 'big fat ego' that was the problem, demanding to be undisturbed and flattered. I challenged him to move into his authentic self (he was a long experienced therapist) and to meet her criticisms directly and sincerely. He was mature enough (aged 52) to be able to accept this and work with it, and in fact our relationship grew through this.

Philip Lichtenberg put it like this:

> She wasn't looking at me; she was just talking in front of me. So after a period of time I said. 'Do you know that I'm here? Would you tell that to me, and would you ask something of me in respect to what you've told me? How do you think I feel when you tell me that story?' I did a series of things like this; she was stunned. And it changed, dramatically, the whole relationship between us. Now she had to say, 'This happened to me. What do you think of that? Or how do you feel when I tell you that?' And I could say, 'Well, I really feel very sad when I hear you tell me that. And, is there something I could do when you tell me that that would be OK for you?' And she said, 'But you've already done it. You've heard me. You acknowledged . . . my loneliness.'
>
> (Lichtenberg 2008: 82)

I could say, 'Tell me about yourself, but also, ask me for something, and ask me how I react when you tell me about yourself'. That's what I do now. 'When you tell me this, what do you want? When you tell me this, what do you imagine I feel? When you tell me this, are you defining who you are? And how does that feel?' There are varieties of ways in which I would now incorporate all of the elements, rather than, 'I'm listening.'

(Lichtenberg 2008: 85)

One of the strengths of the existential approach is this ability to cut through the surface presentations and call on the authentic self lying behind. There is, of course, a danger that this can turn into a demonstration of the rightness of the therapist and the wrongness of the client, but once we are aware of this possibility we can watch out for it.

To summarize, then, we can say that all three of our approaches believe in risk-taking, and in breaking down any formalized forms of interaction between client and therapist – or, as we prefer to say, between person and person.

New developments

Moving on more into the transpersonal, it would appear that there are two levels within the transpersonal that need to be considered. The first of these is called the Subtle, and it is characterized by being the home of many concrete representations of the divine. This makes it very approachable, because all of us can relate to symbols, images, dreams, imaginary beings, archetypes, and all the rich panoply of material explored so brilliantly by Jung (2009), Hillman (1979), von Franz (1964), Assagioli (1975), Houston (1982), and others. It has been pointed out that we are all familiar with this level of consciousness, because it is the realm of dreams, and we all have dreams. As far as therapy is concerned, it is the home of the deepest form of empathy, which has sometimes been called transcendental empathy (Hart 2000). This level has also been called the process of Bhakti yoga, which also takes very seriously the presence and importance of spiritual beings who can be prayed to. This has been called the region of third-tier thinking (Rowan 2012). This is terribly important, because it pushes at the limits of therapy as usually understood, and speaks to the possibility of pushing even further into the realm of spirituality.

At this level, in addition to being with the client, I can be the client, in the sense of entering into the same mental space. This is particularly obvious in the case of dreams, where the therapist can come into the dream with the client. I remember a time when a client said, 'And then my mother came into the room', and I replied, 'Yes, and she is wearing a yellow dress, isn't she?', which the client confirmed. This kind of closeness is starting to be recognized more widely today, with the publication of such books as *Relational Depth: New Perspectives and Developments* (Knox et al. 2013). Not everyone recognizes this as transpersonal work, but my own chapter (Rowan 2013a) spells out this argument in some detail.

The other level of the transpersonal, less travelled and less used, is called the Causal, and it represents the deep water of mysticism, where there are no signposts, no landmarks, and no resting places. This is the level of Jnana yoga. It is the realm where we say that 'All is One', that there are no distinctions and no differences, just the vast ocean of spirituality. This is much less used in transpersonal therapy, although important contributions have been made by Epstein (1996), Rosenbaum (1999), Eigen (2011), Brazier (1995), and others, and therefore there is no point in dwelling on it at length, but is has to be recognized as a separate realm. Paradoxically, at this level there is no empathy, because there are no problems. For this reason, in my opinion, clients have to be asked for their permission before working at this level with them. But when doing so, some very deep work may be done in a very short space of time.

Coming back, then, to the Subtle, it is here that we find that imagery very largely takes the place of words, and that instead of asking questions like 'And what happened then?', the therapist may say, 'If that situation were illustrated by a fanciful picture, what would the picture be like?' We would then explore the picture. Not only is this a very effective way of doing therapy, it can be good fun as well, and at this level we tend to find a good deal of shared laughter.

But since this is a spiritual level, it may call for direct communication with a person's soul, or guardian angel, or higher self, or daimon, or inner shaman, as is quite obvious in the work of James Hillman (1989). And this can conveniently be done using the theory and methods of the dialogical self (Rowan 2010), which can again be very vivid and compelling. Clients are thus enabled to get in touch with what is deepest inside them, according to their own spiritual map. The fact that this is now possible makes it more likely that the transpersonal will at last be recognized and appreciated more widely.

In transpersonal therapy, the process of therapy has been likened to the alchemical process (Rowan 2005: Ch. 6) and this seems very useful, pointing out for example that therapy can go through negative moments and periods, which are indeed important components of the whole process.

The transpersonal approach is particularly well suited to multicultural work (Fukuyama and Sevig 1999) because it is open to spirituality, a key element for some cultures, and in any case a valuable bridge between cultures. Fukuyama and Sevig's (1999) book has many examples of how this works out in practice. It is also clear that although religion often claims the whole region of spirituality, it is in fact a vast mixture of higher and lower levels of consciousness, and most of it is prejudiced against women. We therefore have to be careful in distinguishing between religion and spirituality (see Chapter 22 in this volume).

The most recent writings on the transpersonal (Friedman and Hartelius 2013) cover many areas, including altered states of consciousness, somatic therapies, dreaming and other relevant areas, and it is good to see the expansions of the work which now seem to be coming along, including my own chapter (Rowan 2013b) in Dryden and Reeves.

The transpersonal realm is therefore a very rich and fruitful space in which to be working, and it opens up possibilities that are often denied by other and earlier forms of therapy. In the past, it was difficult for this kind of work to be recognized and respected for what it is; in some countries, for example, the work of that great pioneer of the transpersonal, Carl Jung, is not recognized as a therapy at all. Let us hope that the new work, rich as it is, will bring about the change that we all want to see.

Summary

It can be seen from the above that there is a huge paradox at the bottom of these approaches – the existential, with its philosophical basis, the humanistic, with its experiential emphasis, and the transpersonal, with its aspirations to go beyond all the others. We are dealing here with a real relationship that is at the same time totally freeing. It is a relationship designed to end the need for a relationship. Instead, we can appreciate our relationships and make the most of our relationships, but we are not needy for any relationship. We are authentic beings, well able to reach out to others, but not dependent on them for our goodies. We each create our own world, and take full responsibility for that. We are whole persons.

Further reading

Fukuyama, M.A. and Sevig, T.D. (1999) *Integrating Spirituality into Multicultural Counselling*. London: Sage. This book helps to show how the transpersonal approach makes it easier to approach multicultural clients and help them to make sense of counselling and/ or psychotherapy.

Knox, R., Murphy, D., Wiggins, S. and Cooper, M. (eds.) (2013) *Relational Depth: New Perspectives and Developments*. Basingstoke: Palgrave Macmillan. This is an important contribution to the whole intersubjective realm, showing how it is relevant to even the most basic forms of counselling.

Schneider, K.J. and Krug, O.T. (2010) *Existential-Humanistic Therapy*. Washington, DC: APA. A spirited account of the importance of connecting the existential and the humanistic, to the benefit of both.

References

Assagioli, R. (1975) *Psychosynthesis: A Manual of Principles and Techniques*. London: Turnstone Press.

Beck, D.E. and Cowan, C.C. (1996) *Spiral Dynamics: Mastering Values, Leadership and Change*. Oxford: Blackwell.

Belenky, M.F., Clinchy, B.M., Goldberger, N.R. and Tarule, J.M. (1986) *Women's Ways of Knowing: The Development of Self*. New York: Basic Books.

Brazier, D. (1995) *Zen Therapy*. London: Constable.

Bugental, J.F.T. (1981) *The Search for Authenticity* (enlarged edition). New York: Irvington.

Cohn, H.W. (1997) *Existential Thought and Therapeutic Practice*. London: Sage.

Cooper, M. (2003) *Existential Therapies*. London: Sage.

De Carvalho, R.J. (1991) *The Founders of Humanistic Psychology*. New York: Praeger.

Eigen, M. (2011) *Contact with the Depths*. London: Karnac Books.

Epstein, M. (1996) *Thoughts without a Thinker*. London: Duckworth.

Friedenberg, E.Z. (1973) *Laing*. London: Fontana/Collins.

Friedman, H.L. and Hartelius, G. (eds.) (2013) *The Wiley-Blackwell Handbook of Transpersonal Psychology*. London: Sage.

Friedman, M. (1964) *The Worlds of Existentialism: A Critical Reader*. Chicago, IL: University of Chicago Press.

Fukuyama, M.A. and Sevig, T.D. (1999) *Integrating Spirituality into Multicultural Counselling*. London: Sage.

Graves, C. (1981) *Summary statement: the emergent, cyclical, double-helix model of the adult human biopsychosocial systems*. Handout for presentation to World Future Society, Boston, MA, 20 May.

Hart, T. (2000) Deep empathy, in T. Hart, P. Nelson and K. Puhakka (eds.) *Transpersonal Knowing*. Albany, NY: SUNY Press.

Hillman, J. (1979) *The Dream and the Underworld*. San Francisco, CA: Harper & Row.

Hillman, J. (1989) *The Essential James Hillman: A Blue Fire*. London: Routledge.

Houston, J. (1982) *The Possible Human*. Los Angeles, CA: Tarcher.

Husserl, E. (1931/1960) *Cartesian Meditations: An Introduction to Phenomenology*. The Hague: Nijhoff.

Hycner, R. (1991) *Between Person and Person: Toward a Dialogical Psychotherapy*. Highland, NY: Gestalt Psychology Press.

Jung, C.G. (2009) *The Red Book*. Hove: Routledge.

Karp, M., Holmes, P. and Tauvon, K.B. (eds.) (1998) *The Handbook of Psychodrama*. London: Routledge.

Knox, R., Murphy, D., Wiggins, S. and Cooper, M. (eds.) (2013) *Relational Depth: New Perspectives and Developments*. Basingstoke: Palgrave Macmillan.

Lichtenberg, P. (2008) The four corners at the intersection of contacting, *International Gestalt Journal*, 31 (1).

Mahrer, A.R. (1996) *The Complete Guide to Experiential Psychotherapy*. Chichester: Wiley.

Mahrer, A.R. (1989) *Experiencing: A Humanistic Theory of Psychology and Psychiatry*. Ottawa, ONT: University of Ottawa Press.

Maslow, A.H. (1973) *The Farther Reaches of Human Nature*. Harmondsworth: Penguin.

Maslow, A.H. (1987) *Motivation and Personality*, 3rd edn. New York: Harper & Row.

May, R., Angel, E. and Ellenberger, H. (eds.) (1958) *Existence: A New Dimension in Psychiatry and Psychology*. New York: Basic Books.

Mearns, D. (1994) *Developing Person-centred Counselling*. London: Sage.

Mearns, D. (1996) Working at relational depth with clients in person-centred therapy, *Counselling*, 7: 306–11.

Mearns, D. (1997) Achieving the personal development dimension in professional counselling training, *Counselling*, 8: 113–20.

Merleau-Ponty, M. (1962) *The Phenomenology of Perception*. London: Routledge.

Perls, F.S., Hefferline, R.F. and Goodman, P. (1951) *Gestalt Therapy: Excitement and Growth in the Human Personality*. London: Souvenir Press.

Rosenbaum, R. (1999) *Zen and the Heart of Psychotherapy*. Philadelphia, PA: Brunner/Mazel.

Rowan, J. (2001) *Ordinary Ecstasy: The Dialectics of Humanistic Psychology*. Hove: Routledge.

Rowan, J. (2005) *The Transpersonal: Spirituality in Psychotherapy and Counselling*, 2nd edn. Hove: Routledge.

Rowan, J. (2010) *Personification: Using the Dialogical Self in Psychotherapy and Counselling.* Hove: Routledge.

Rowan, J. (2012) Third tier thinking and subtle consciousness, *Journal for the Study of Spirituality*, 2 (1): 91–7.

Rowan, J. (2013a) The transpersonal and relational depth, in R. Knox, D. Murphy, S. Wiggins and M. Cooper (eds.) *Relational Depth: New Perspectives and Developments.* Basingstoke: Palgrave Macmillan.

Rowan, J. (2013b) The transpersonal in individual therapy, in W. Dryden and A. Reeves (eds.) *The Handbook of Individual Therapy*, 6th edn. (pp. 497–518). London: Sage.

Sartre, J.-P. (1948) *Existentialism and Humanism.* London: Methuen.

Schneider, K.J. and Krug, O.T. (2010) *Existential-Humanistic Therapy.* Washington, DC: APA.

Spinelli, E. (1967) The phenomenological method and client-centred therapy, *Journal of the Society for Existential Analysis*, 1: 15–21.

Spinelli, E. (1994) *Demystifying Therapy.* London: Constable.

Trub, B. (1952) Healing through meeting, in M. Friedman (ed.) *The Worlds of Existentialism: A Critical Reader.* Chicago, IL: University of Chicago Press.

van Deurzen, E. (1997) *Everyday Mysteries: Existential Dimensions of Psychotherapy.* London: Routledge.

van Deurzen, E. (2002) *Existential Counselling and Therapy in Practice*, 2nd edn. London: Sage.

von Franz, M.-L. (1964) The process of individuation, in C.G. Jung (ed.) *Man and His Symbols.* London: Aldus Books.

Wade, J. (1996) *Changes of Mind.* Albany, NY: SUNY Press.

5 The person-centred approach: courage, presence, and complexity – a template for relationship in a postmodern/ post-structuralist world

Colin Lago, Peggy Natiello and
Carol Wolter-Gustafson

Person-centred therapy is the original relationship therapy.

(Tudor 2010: 52)

Introduction

This chapter briefly introduces some of the essential components of the person-centred approach, and illustrates that this approach is both a theory of relationship as well as of therapy. We argue that the approach requires courage to practise and illustrate this through several case reflections recording significant and dramatic moments in therapy. Newer developments in the theory and practice are briefly discussed and some key resources to further reading are included at the end of the chapter.

The foundations of the client-centred/person-centred approach

The theory of the person-centred approach is open, clear, and elegantly accessible. The principles of the approach, however, are complex, challenging, and unwavering. Rather than reifying theoretical abstractions, Rogers created space for the uniqueness and personality distinctions of its many practitioners. These radical paradigm changes he offered continue to challenge all of us to think again about our own theory and practice of psychotherapy.

Our extensive deliberations to construct this chapter, conducted between the USA and the UK on joint Skype phone calls, led us one evening to the subject of courage in therapy – the courage to be and the courage to be in relationship. We had been discussing the nature of the therapeutic relationship, as formerly conceptualized by Carl Rogers (1951, 1959),[1] and agreed that courage is inherent in person-centred practice. The reader will find the theme woven into each section of this chapter.

Rogers is perhaps best known in the wider therapeutic world and beyond for his elaboration of what he termed as the 'necessary and sufficient conditions' for the psychotherapeutic process. Briefly stated, Rogers asserted that for therapy to occur, it is necessary that the following conditions exist (Rogers 1959: 213):

1 That two persons are in *contact*.
2 That the first person, whom we shall term the client, is in a state of *incongruence*, being *vulnerable*, or *anxious*.
3 That the second person, whom we shall term the therapist, is *congruent* in the *relationship*.
4 That the therapist is *experiencing unconditional positive regard* toward the client.
5 That the therapist is *experiencing* an *empathic* understanding of the client's *internal frame of reference*.
6 That the client *perceives*, at least to a minimal degree, conditions 4 and 5, the *unconditional positive regard* of the therapist for him, and the *empathic* understanding of the therapist.

The overall theory, developed through extensive clinical research, fundamentally recognized and respected the unique subjective experiencing of both persons in the relationship (client and therapist) and specified both the client's relational aspects (conditions 1, 2, and 6) and the therapist's relational tasks within this process (conditions 3, 4, and 5).

The therapeutic relationship

The person-centred approach is thus a theory of relationship as well as one of therapy. It is based upon a disciplined attempt to 'wrest from the phenomena of experience the inherent order which they contain' (Rogers 1959: 189). Unlike therapists of other approaches who work with theories of personality or prescribed sets of intervention strategies, person-centred therapists strive to enter into each relationship with a client with an acceptance, openness, and respect to what the client will bring and to how the client may process this material. Thus person-centred therapists only have their own self and experiences to call on while conducting therapy. Rogers (1959: 215) writes, 'For therapy to occur, the wholeness of the therapist in the relationship is primary, but a part of the congruence of the therapist must be the experience of unconditional positive regard and the experience of empathic understanding.' Succinctly expressed by Rogers, he said: 'If I can be all that I am, then that is good enough.' The therapist is thus 'naked' or, more accurately, devoid of psychological protection, when entering a counselling relationship. Thus the need for courage!

Colin recalls a moment he experienced in a seminar in which he had been invited to give an exposition of the person-centred approach to third-year postgraduates studying the psychodynamic approach. Only too conscious of how theoretically simple the person-centred approach might look from this other framework, Colin was understandably anxious about the student criticisms he might have to deal with. However, in the subsequent dialogue with the student group, Colin was moved that one student volunteered that she now more fully understood the nature of the relational stance advocated by the person-centred approach in contrast to many other forms of therapeutic engagement, as it truly required a depth of trust and courage in the self of the therapist by the therapist. 'I now understand what my person-centred colleagues have been trying to explain to me', she said. As postulated on one website, 'ordinary courage is about putting your *vulnerability* on the line. In today's world, that's pretty extraordinary' (www.brenebrown/ordinary-courage).

Rogers wrote extensively that this complete theoretical perspective is based solely upon the postulate of the 'actualizing tendency'. He explains:

> This is the inherent tendency of the organism to develop all its capacities in ways which serve to maintain or enhance the organism. It involves not only the tendency to meet what Maslow [1954] terms 'deficiency needs' for air, food, water, and the like, but also more generalized activities. It involves development toward the differentiation of organs and of functions, expansion in terms of growth, expansion of effectiveness through the use of tools, expansion and enhancement through reproduction. It is development toward autonomy and away from heteronomy, or control by external forces. Angyal's [1941] statement . . . could be used as a synonym for this term: 'Life is an autonomous event which takes place between the organism and the environment. Life processes do not merely tend to preserve life but transcend the momentary status quo of the organism, expanding itself continually and imposing its autonomous determination upon an ever increasing realm of events.
>
> (Rogers 1959: 196)

Rogers later referred to the wider 'formative tendency' of the universe (Rogers 1980). Although we have little space here to develop these concepts, we are of the view that, at its best, when the quality of therapeutic relationship is working well, when the client fully experiences, perceives, and values the relationship, when the therapist is authentically able to come close to deeply accepting and understanding the client's experiencing of the world, then a process is released that proves not only healing for the client but touches the deepest conjoint flowing of experiencing between them – something which Rogers, later in his life, came to suggest as touching the transcendental core of life itself (Rogers 1980). This deep level of connection between client and therapist was noted by a participant who commented, after a particular demonstration interview Rogers gave at an expressive arts therapy workshop late in his life, 'you were her soul-mate' (Natiello 2001: 47).

Other writers within the person-centred approach have noted such profound moments and described them variously as: 'the quality of tenderness' (Thorne 1985), 'passionate presence' (Natiello 2001), and 'relational depth' (Mearns and Cooper 2005; Knox et al. 2013). Monteiro dos Santos (2013) has described it thus: 'we move gracefully with the moment toward whatever or wherever the moment takes us. This graceful movement is what I call magical moments. This sometimes takes us to laughter, crying, or simply to a moment of silence with the client.' Yamashita (2013) notes that this is about meeting a 'person as a whole in the deepest meaning'.

While already having travelled in this chapter from Rogers' early conceptualizations based upon relational factors to these somewhat 'heady heights' of peak moments described immediately above, we do not wish to ignore the middle ground of this spectrum – that is, the industrious, committed, everyday strivings that occur between clients and person-centred therapists. Rogers' belief in the wisdom of the human organism led to his deep commitment to being 'client-directed', most popularly known as 'non-directive' – a description that has historically led to much critique, but a term that strove to capture the essence of therapists' eschewing of their own power and expertise. Such a radical stance, we believe, facilitates the client's inherent internal explorations, and has the potential to release their own organismic wisdom. In addition, this relational conceptualization joins partners – client and therapist – in a human interaction that facilitates deep connections intra-psychically (within each of them), inter-psychically (between the two of them), and existentially (connecting with the wider ramifications of human life). We return to this principle in the next section.

Challenges

Below, we attempt to reveal the depth and challenge of Roger's theory through stories from our own practices. As we consider the three therapist conditions for growth – congruence, empathy, and unconditional positive regard – and the principle of non-directiveness in person-centred practice, we remind you that they are intricately connected. One condition rarely exists in isolation from the others. When we are able to bring all the conditions forward, our full presence releases the healing process to which Rogers refers above. No strategies or techniques or directions are needed. The actualizing tendency of the client and our presence are enough! Although we highlight one or two of the conditions for growth in each of the following anecdotes, reflection will reveal that all conditions are present in each story.

Non-directiveness and the actualizing tendency

Person-centred therapy relies heavily on the presence of the therapist and trust in the client's actualizing tendency. The practice of the approach resists articulation. Tudor and Worrall (2006: 220–1) remind us that Rogers' task was 'to describe in words that are public, linear and discrete a process that is continuous, normally private, often unspoken, always subtle and invariably subjective'. Perhaps Rogers himself issued the greatest challenge to person-centred practitioners:

> But is the therapist willing to give the client full freedom as to outcomes? Is he genuinely willing for the client to organize and direct his life? Is he willing for him to choose goals that are social or antisocial, moral or immoral? If not, it seems doubtful that therapy will be a profound experience for the client. Even more difficult, is he willing for the client to choose regression rather than mental health? to choose neuroticism rather than growth? to choose to reject

health rather than accept it? to choose death rather than life? To me it appears that only as the therapist is completely willing that *any* outcome, *any* direction may be chosen – only then does he realize the vital strength of the capacity and potentiality of the individual for constructive action.

(Rogers 1951: 48)

This statement reveals the profound courage required of practitioners to be always committed to the client's authority to choose whatever future he or she decides is right, without interference! Non-directiveness requires therapists to let go of control, expertise, and authority over the client. It demands deep trust in the actualizing tendency of clients, conviction that the organismic wisdom of the client is superior to any guidance the therapist can offer – a genuine desire to support client empowerment rather than therapist success. Holding true to this principle can keep a sense of surprise and wonderment alive, as documented in the example below.

Case vignette

Rebecca spoke quietly, monotonously, about parts of her life . . . high school in a convent boarding school, a marriage to a wealthy man 17 years her senior – a marriage in which she did not feel like much of a person, and finally dissolved.

She droned on. I began to lose my focus. Her disclosure about a lover who moved into her home months ago and recently killed himself snapped me back. Her tone was unchanged, and I almost missed the tragic disclosure.

I shifted to the edge of my chair. She said, 'I haven't had a visitation.' A 'visitation?', I inquire. She responded, 'Like an appearance of him standing beside my bed.'

As Rebecca droned on, I saw a bird resting outside the window behind her. I rarely interrupt a session, and surprised myself by saying, 'Oh, there's a bird outside. It must be a quail.' She did not respond, nor look behind her. I bit my tongue (to no avail) when I realized that the feathers, veiled by the opaque shade, seemed black. 'Oh, that's NOT a quail,' I muttered, astonished at my second intrusion. The feathered creature disappeared from behind her and jumped to the patio floor in front of the unshaded middle window. 'Oh my God,' I exclaimed, "That's a Road Runner! I have never seen one here before.'

The bird stood in the patio, right outside the window . . . tall, with long elegant neck and spikey tail that stood out stiffly behind. This bird fixed his eyes on the client for a long moment, then turned and walked slowly across the patio.

The client gasped, and said softly, 'John was a Marine, and had a huge tattoo on his arm – from shoulder to elbow. That tattoo was a Road Runner.'

My intuition knew there was value in this coincidence. 'Rebecca,' I said reverently, 'I think you are having a "visitation".'

Her head dropped; she was silent; finally the sobs came. She allowed herself a few minutes of unaccustomed grief and said, 'That's enough.' Her face and her body softened, and she said quietly, 'I feel much lighter,' tapping her heart gently. The bird hopped back to the window, gave her a final look, and disappeared.

'This session was completely idiosyncratic,' explained the therapist. 'Neither of us could have planned it, and I came close to spoiling it in my need to do something. The lesson: Be fully present. Have no agenda. Dwell in the uncertainty and the experience of the client. Everything you both need for the work to unfold is always there, and will eventually reveal itself. This principle can only be met when therapists bring themselves fully into the therapeutic relationship, holding the three conditions for growth.'

The three conditions

Congruence asks of therapists a consistent effort to become more self-aware, a commitment to presenting oneself with integrity and self-knowledge. High value is placed on the ability to be present with clients without façade or pretence. When the therapist is authentically able to come close to deeply accepting and understanding the client's experiencing of the world, then a process is released that proves not only healing for the client but also for the therapist. A session with a very sad client reveals the practice of congruence and empathy.

Case vignette

Fifteen minutes into the first session with Nathan, I was completely enamoured of this small, frail, physically challenged, irreverent man. His stories were incredible. Nathan, whose parents fled Poland during the Second World War with their two small sons, revealed a former life as a powerful Broadway producer. Recently divorced by a wife he still loves, he has lost most of his money, his home, one of his four sons, and his serious heart disease has already disabled him to an alarming degree.

He arrived late for a morning session announcing, 'I've just come from my cardiologist. He says I could drop dead at any second.'

As we passed the dining room, he said, 'You had a dinner party last night. Did you have wine?' I told him we did. 'Oh, how I'd love a taste of wine,' he said longingly. 'When we lived in Puerto Rico we had wine for dinner every night, and I miss it.'

I knew he was asking me for wine. The therapy rules came crashing in on me, and I reminded him that his doctor said he could drop dead at any second. 'Really Nathan, I cannot give you wine. Your health is in serious jeopardy.'

'I just meant a little taste,' he said wistfully. My response was firm.

We proceeded with the session. Suddenly, the losses of Nathan's life washed through me. His profound grief became my own and I realized how professional rules were preventing me from offering him genuineness, empathy, and caring. Without thinking, I excused myself. In the kitchen, I asked Bob to reach into a high cupboard for a Stuart wine glass. I poured a small portion of white wine into the glass, walked back to the office, and placed it in front of Nathan. Startled he mumbled, 'Thank you, Peggy,' put the glass to his lips and wet them. We continued the session; later he savoured one more sip of wine. Then he slid the glass toward me, and said, 'You will never know how much this means to me – and in such a beautiful glass.'

We both knew Nathan was not talking about the wine, but rather about the congruent, deep relationship that was offered – the breaking of the therapy rules and my willingness to dwell in his profound experience of loss and grief. He was seen, felt, understood – no longer alone.

Empathy occurs when the therapist 'senses accurately the feelings and personal meanings that the client is experiencing and communicates this understanding to the client' (Rogers 1980: 116). Empathy, often taught as parroting, is not a technique! If the therapist cannot really grasp what it feels like to stand in a client's shoes, it is best left unsaid. Insincere empathy is manipulative. A story from John Shlien reveals the true, gut-wrenching depth of empathic connection.

> He began to cry softly, saying, 'They talk about love and affection. I know what that means. The only good thing I ever had [his engagement to a girl] was taken away from me, broken up.' He blew his nose, dropped his handkerchief, and as he picked it up, glanced at me . . . He saw tears in my eyes. He offered me the handkerchief, then drew it back because he knew he had just wiped his nose on it and could feel the wetness on his hand. We both knew this, and each knew the other knew it; we understood the feel and the meaning of the handkerchief, the stickiness and texture, the sympathy of the offering and the embarrassment of the withdrawal . . . It is not the tears, but the exquisite awareness of dual experience that restores consciousness of self and not a word was spoken during this episode.
>
> (Shlien 1961: 316)

Unconditional positive regard is grounded in the belief that all individuals deserve non-manipulative, non-possessive caring simply because they exist. We leave to your imagination the challenge of offering such caring to persons of questionable character who often become our clients – criminals, addicts, rapists, or simply those with whom therapists cannot feel deeply connected. Bozarth (1998: 83) believes it is the 'curative factor'. Carol describes an experience of positive regard and empathy with a difficult client.

Case vignette

Samantha told me that for more than fifty years she had never fit in anywhere. Her family had nicknamed her after a variety of cactus. I experienced her sharp edges often.
She explained, flat-voiced, that she had been dead on the inside for so long, that she needed several hours of stillness and silence from me, in order for any sensation, any hint of feeling, to arrive. I received her request without the need to label her 'too needy' or as trying to 'manipulate me'. Instead, I found a stretch of time during which I met her once a week for four hours. Steeped in Carl Rogers' deep understanding of the empathic relationship, I was able to be with her 'as if' I were experiencing her same need to control me, and to make sure I did nothing at all to intrude on her silence. However,

there was a difference. I knew I was not controlled by her. Without the need to pathologize her deeply experienced sensitivity, I was free to receive her fierce need to manage my responses to her.

With closed eyes, she awaited any sensation she could identify as hers. I sensed her whole being straining to exist, despite my presence in that room. She would not let herself be intruded upon, to be vaporized and sent into oblivion. The sound of me shifting in my chair, or my coffee cup gently placed on the table would cause her to jump. She would open her eyes, fix them on me, and angrily describe the way I had scared her and made her lose everything she had been working on up to that point in the session. Without the need to pathologize her, or defend myself from her anger – although she was good at delivering it – I would acknowledge how disrupted, angry, and defeated she felt as I moved when she didn't want me to. Early in our sessions together she would squint her eyes, and implore me to answer, 'Then why do you do it to me?!'

After a quiet moment I simply replied I had been uncomfortable and needed to move a bit, and that I had seen it had really frustrated her. Essentially, my dangerous assertion was that I was a separate person in the room with her, but I was with her extreme sense of danger and betrayal.

After one such 'interruption' there was an hour of extreme silence between us. She opened her eyes and asserted, 'You are not my dead mother in the tomb. She wanted me to be there with her. I am not.' We sat, perhaps for the first time, together in the room. That moment lasted just nanoseconds, but it was the ground upon which our relationship took root.

I believe that her reality contained more layers of complexity than any diagnosis, label or treatment plan could encompass. I also believe that had I used a proscribed technique to encounter her, I would have become one more person trying to control her. Had I relied on my professional expertise instead of my human attempts at understanding her construction of reality, nothing in her experience would have changed very much. My willingness to fully receive her complexity allowed her journey to be slightly less complex. No less painful, to be sure, but at least she didn't have to fight my fighting for authority over her.

We hope these anecdotes reveal some challenges and complexities of person-centred practice. It is astonishing that a system that calls on the most primal courage and holistic commitment of the practitioner is often described as naïve and simplistic.

New developments

In recent years, several strands of emerging person-centred theory and practice have been recognized as offering new and valuable contributions to the approach. Among these we include 'relational depth' (Knox et al. 2013), 'the quality of tenderness' (Thorne 2004), 'configurations of self' (Mearns and Thorne 2000), 'plurality of selves' (Cooper and Rowan 1999), 'idiosyncratic empathy' (Keys 2003), 'love' (Keys 2010), clients as 'self-righting' (Bohart 2013), and 'difficult, fragile and dissociative process' (Warner 2013).

In addition, in recent decades, some theorists and practitioners, while acknowledging the person-centred approach as their grounded philosophic origins, have branched out into advocating differing aspects of practice to the point that, in some cases, these are now recognized as quite distinct bodies of work and have been collectively named as the 'Tribes of the PCA' (Warner 2000; Sanders 2004). We have chosen the following examples precisely because they relate directly to the subject of this chapter, that of the therapeutic relationship. For example, Garry Prouty developed pre-therapy to work with clients traditionally called 'psychotic' and 'schizophrenic' (Prouty et al. 2002). These people are the ones relegated to institutions, considered to be 'beyond psychotherapeutic reach', who are treated pharmacologically instead of personally.

A student of Carl Rogers and Eugene Gendlin, Prouty remained radically committed to be with a client, empathically following every breath, every movement, every nascent point of contact he could in concrete micro-steps. He lived these steps, and wrote, lectured tirelessly, and trained others internationally, until his death in 2009. His work continues to be developed in the USA and throughout the world, being implemented in a variety of mental health situations where clients are enabled to be contacted, to be invited into relationship.

Margaret Warner (2013) has worked with Luke, a client who among other things has been hearing voices for many years. Working without diagnostic language, she sought a way to communicate with others in the field. She has developed a descriptive language, empathically tuned to the real issues facing 'difficult' clients in a 'fragile process' or 'dissociative process' in a way that bridges the linguistic and conceptual gap. Through her research, writing, and international facilitation, Warner develops her empathic theoretical framework of her work with clients like Luke, and opens dialogues across differing theoretical perspectives. Additionally, Joseph and Worsley (2005) edited a book addressing 'person-centred psychopathology', offering a radical reconceptualization of this arena.

Dave Mearns, who first introduced the concept of 'relational depth' writes, in the foreword to the recently edited text by Knox et al.,

> relational depth is not merely about establishing enough contact and trust such that the client allows the therapist to do their work – it is about establishing such a powerful contact at a range of depths that the client feels joined by the therapist. This joining will make it possible for them to go to places within themselves that they have previously had to avoid.
>
> (Mearns 2013: vii)

We appreciate that this section on new developments is desperately truncated and we are only too aware that we have not been able to acknowledge, in any depth, the various contributions created by a wide range of colleagues, all seeking to enhance the effectiveness of this overall approach. Just before closing this section, however, we do want to acknowledge the sterling work carried out by various colleagues in the research field. Contemporary society, in its many forms, has re-enforced the need for all approaches to psychotherapy to ascertain their efficacy and effectiveness. Colleagues from within the person-centred-humanistic tradition have been particularly industrious in this arena, and internationally eminent figures such as Mick Cooper, Robert Elliot, Beth Freire, Art Bohart, Jerold Bozarth, Leslie Greenberg, and many more, have created a research base that profoundly validates the person-centred approach as a medium for relational therapy.

Summary

In this chapter, we have sketched out a vision of the person-centred approach to therapy that grounds the whole theory and practice within the context of an interpersonal relationship, which, in turn, facilitates the client's intrapersonal relationship with themselves and ultimately impacts their own existential field in life. Key theoretical propositions have been described and challenges to practice have been illuminated through the presentation of case material. The person-centred approach continues to influence new developments that are currently somewhat expanded from the original hypotheses, as befits a theory that strives for openness in relationship and openness to contemporary contextual demands. One such example of this is demonstrated in the new British NHS programme 'counselling for depression', which is directly implementing key person-centred principles and for which a new ten-item processing scale assessing the impact of therapy has been developed by Elliot and Westwell (2012).

Note

1   Carol Sutton, a former academic colleague of Colin's at De Montfort University, Leicester, always believed that Rogers' greatest theoretical contribution had been his 'naming of the constituent aspects of the therapeutic relationship'.

Further reading

An extraordinary explosion in person-centred literature has occurred within the UK during the last two decades. The following key texts therefore represent just the tip of the iceberg:

Barrett-Lennard, G.T. (2013) *The Relationship Paradigm: Human Being Beyond Individualism*. Basingstoke: Palgrave Macmillan. This is the latest book to emerge from Goff in a long line of texts inspired by the person-centred tradition and which has continually focused upon the relational elements of therapy.

Tudor, K. and Worrall, M. (2006) *Person-Centred Therapy: A Clinical Philosophy*. Hove: Routledge. The authors critically examine the theory and generate radical new implications for practice.

Wood, J.K. (2008) *Carl Rogers' Person-Centred Approach: Towards an Understanding of its Implications*. Ross-on-Wye: PCCS Books. This book provides a series of thoughtful and wide-ranging radical critiques of the person-centred approach that refuse to be seduced by any simple ideological view of the theory and practice.

An expansive consideration of 'Rogers' therapeutic conditions' is provided by a series of four books published by PCCS Books in Ross-on-Wye, edited by G. Wyatt, S. Haugh, T. Merry, P. Sanders, J. Bozarth and P. Wilkins. These texts are most useful in deepening understanding of the sheer depth and significance of Rogers' original hypotheses.

Sanders, P. (2004) *The Tribes of the Person-Centred Approach: An Introduction to the Schools of Therapy Relating to the Person-Centred Approach*. Ross-on-Wye: PCCS Books.

References

Angyal, A. (1941) *Foundations for a Science of Personality*. New York: Commonwealth Fund.

Bohart, A. (2013) The actualising person, in M. Coopers, M. O'Hara, P. Schmid and A. Bohart (eds.) *The Handbook of Person-Centred Psychotherapy and Counselling*, 2nd edn. Basingstoke: Palgrave Macmillan.

Bozarth, J. (1998) *Person-Centered Therapy: A Revolutionary Paradigm*. Ross-on-Wye: PCCS Books.

Cooper, M. and Rowan, J. (1999) *The Plural Self: Multiplicity in Everyday Life*. London: Sage.

Elliot, R and Westwell, G. (2012) *Person-Centred and Experiential Psychotherapy Scale*. (Contact Robert Elliot directly at the University of Strathclyde for further details.)

Joseph, S. and Worsley, R. (eds.) (2005) *Person-Centred Psychopathology: A Positive Psychology of Mental Health*. Ross-on-Wye: PCCS Books.

Keys, S. (ed.) (2003) *Idiosyncratic Person-Centred Therapy: From the Personal to the Universal*. Ross-on-Wye: PCCS Books.

Keys, S. (2010) *Love in therapy: risks, costs and challenges*. Lecture presentation to the Belgian PCA Association. June.

Knox, R., Murphy, D., Wiggins, S. and Cooper, M. (eds.) (2013) *Relational Depth: New Perspectives and Developments*. Basingstoke: Palgrave Macmillan.

Maslow, A.H. (1954) *Motivation and Personality*. New York: Harper.

Mearns, D. (2013) Foreword, in R. Knox, D. Murphy, S. Wiggins and M. Cooper (eds.) *Relational Depth: New Perspectives and Developments*. Basingstoke: Palgrave Macmillan.

Mearns, D. and Cooper, M. (2005) *Working at Relational Depth in Counselling and Psychotherapy*. London: Sage.

Mearns, D. and Thorne, B. (2000) *Person-Centred Therapy Today: New Frontiers in Theory and Practice*. London: Sage.

Monteiro dos Santos, A. amdsantos54@hotmail.com. *When the heart speaks: The essence of Person Centred Psychotherapy*. 10 June 2013.

Natiello, P. (2001) *The Person-Centred Approach: A Passionate Presence*. Ross-on-Wye: PCCS Books.

Prouty, G., Van Werde, D. and Portner, M. (2002) *Pre-therapy: Reaching Contact-impaired Clients*. Ross-on-Wye: PCCS Books.

Rogers, C.R. (1951) *Client-Centered Therapy: Its Current practice, Implications and Theory*. Boston, MA: Houghton Mifflin.

Rogers, C.R. (1959) Client-centered framework, in S. Koch (ed.) *Psychology: A Study of a Science*. Study 1, Vol. 3: *Formulations of the Person and the Social Context* (pp. 184–256). New York: McGraw-Hill.

Rogers, C.R. (1980) The foundations of the person-centered approach, in *A Way of Being* (pp. 113–36). Boston, MA: Houghton Mifflin.

Sanders, P. (2004) *The Tribes of the Person-Centred Nation: An Introduction to the Schools of Therapy Related to the Person-Centred Approach*. Ross-on-Wye: PCCS Books.

Shlien, J. (1961) A client-centered approach to schizophrenia: first approximation, in A. Burton (ed.) *The Psychotherapy of the Psychoses* (pp. 285–317). New York: Basic Books.

Thorne, B. (2004) *The Quality of Tenderness* (revised edition). Norwich: Norwich Centre Publications.

Tudor, K. (2010) Person-centered relational therapy: an organismic perspective, *Person-Centered and Experiential Psychotherapies*, 9 (1): 52–68.

Tudor, K. and Worrall, M. (2006) *Person-Centred Therapy: A Clinical Philosophy*. London: Routledge.

Warner, M. (2000) Person-centred psychotherapy: one nation, many tribes, *Person Centred Journal*, 7 (1): 28–39.

Warner, M. (2013) Difficult client process, in M. Coopers, M. O'Hara, P. Schmid and A. Bohart (eds.) *The Handbook of Person-Centred Psychotherapy and Counselling*, 2nd edn. Basingstoke: Palgrave Macmillan.

Yamashita, K. (2013) *How Dharma-based Person-centred Approach/Shin-shu Counselling is Living Within Myself* [http://amidatrust.ning.com/group/buddistcounselling andpsychotherapy/forum/topics/shinshu-counsellingdharmabased; accessed 20 May 2013].

SECTION 2

The Therapeutic Relationship in Cross-Modality, Relational, Integrative, Creative, and Coaching Therapies

6 The drama of the therapeutic encounter: a cross-modality approach

David Bott and Pam Howard

Introduction

Strictly speaking, the 'cross-modality approach' proposed here is not an 'approach' *per se* and might be more accurately described as 'an approach to approaches'. There are a number of elements to this. The first takes the position that there is no basis upon which to privilege one relational approach or modality over another but that it is necessary to have a coherent therapeutic account (Wampold 2001). At the same time, it is recognized that there are underpinning commonalities found in all relational modalities in the attempt to deal with unresolved developmental dilemmas in contemporary life (Lapworth Sills and Fish 2001; Stern 2004; Evans and Gilbert 2005). With this, the therapeutic relationship is framed as a dramatic encounter, challenging therapeutic passivity. Informed by theories and principles that invite active intervention, the therapist is enjoined to be human, spontaneous, and creative, engaging directly in the performance of the client's narrative of distress.

Foundations of theory and practice

The foundations for this are to be found in what has come to be termed 'the postmodern turn', referring to the European cultural and social movement whereby the aspirations of modernism in providing social progress on the basis of rationality and objective scientific evidence have been brought into question. Postmodernism rejects the possibility of universal truths in the form of 'grand narratives' like Marxism and psychoanalysis in favour of local knowledge constructed out of particular interests and perspectives. In its impact on the field of counselling and psychotherapy, postmodernism has been informed by a conflation of American social constructionism and French post-structuralism. The former has had direct implications for therapeutic activity, while post-structuralism has provided a critique of the philosophical and theoretical context within which therapy takes place (Bott and Howard 2012).

The origins of post-structuralism can be located in France with a post 1968 challenge to enlightenment principles in general, and the work of Hegel and Marx in particular. The post-structuralists, in effect, turned their back on the grand but flawed enlightenment programme of humanity, progress, and freedom in favour of a number of themes, many of which find their origins within the writing of Nietzsche. These are: the rejection of a programme of cumulative and progressive historical change; the celebration of difference over conformity; the privileging of local and irrational knowledge over the universal and objective; moral relativism; and a fascination with the surfaces of things. Significantly, Nietzsche's notion of perspectivism – that every thought is also an interpretation – would have it that there are no such things as facts but that knowledge is a function of competing sets of interests.

Thus Lyotard (1979) declares 'an incredulity towards meta-narratives', bringing into question the bid by any particular approach to claim supremacy. Derrida's (1974) proposition, 'Il n'y a pas d'hors texte', questions the adequacy of language in accounting for an objective world, since it can only ever refer to other language. Much of the impetus for the 'postmodern turn' in therapy has come from what is seen as oppressive 'modernist' practice, and Foucault (1979) provided an analysis of the subtle forms of domination implicit in the client–therapist relationship.

The other strand of postmodern thought, social constructionism, has had a profound and direct impact upon therapeutic practice, most significantly in the field of systemic/family therapy. Social constructionism reflects a North American cultural world-view characterized by optimism, openness, and pragmatism. Its underpinning principles date back to the work of G.H. Mead (1934), subsequently developed in the 1960s and 1970s by social theorists like Becker, Goffman and, notably, Berger and Luckmann (1967). There has been a resurgence of interest in these ideas by contemporary thinkers, pre-eminent among these the academic psychologist Kenneth Gergen (1999, 2008). Social constructionism would have it that theories construct the world in their own terms (Warhus 2001). Significantly, this requires that we give up on competition between schools of therapy and regard them as socially constructed communities of meaning. The challenge is to recognize the value of therapeutic approaches in that they provide accounts which make human distress intelligible, while knowing them to be reifications of ideas arising out of the concerns of particular social, historical, and cultural contexts (Bott and Howard 2012).

The implications of the postmodern critique are that no theoretical or methodological approach can claim pre-eminence. At the same time, breaking down the boundaries between theories and models risks losing a coherent position from which therapy can be conducted. Brown and Stenner (2009) question the tendency to drag a phenomenon out of the rightful place in which it has meaning. Psychotherapeutic concepts and interventions can only be understood within the linguistic, theoretical, and ideological framework in which they are embedded (Safran and Messer 1997).

Furthermore, Thomas Kuhn's (1962) notion of paradigm requires that we respect the fundamental epistemological distinctions between approaches. As this volume will have demonstrated, there are a wide number of well-established therapeutic accounts that have shown themselves to be effective in responding to human distress. This raises issues of difference and integration. One response has been to take a position of exclusive adherence to a particular approach (*monism*). At the other extreme, *eclecticism* puts epistemological distinctions on one side in favour of a pragmatic combination of techniques. While *eclecticism* in essentially atheoretical, selecting out on the basis of utility, *integration* seeks to bring principles and practices together from a range of approaches into a consistent whole (Hollanders 2000; Wachtel 2011). Cooper and McLeod (2011) propose a pragmatic *pluralism* on the basis of what is meaningful to the client. By contrast, the cross-modality approach proposed here sets out to respect the differences between theories of counselling and psychotherapy while seeking to promote a relationship between them that is respectful and actively engaged. This is encapsulated in the notion of 'respectful co-existence' (Bott 2005).

As the title suggests, the cross-modality approach takes a meta-position in proceeding from the principle that there are enduring themes that are a feature of human relatedness. These are a function of human growth and development, family context, and social/cultural arrangements. The narratives emerging from common human experience have relevance beyond theoretical distinctions. Arguably, 'narrative' and 'enactment' feature in all relational therapeutic approaches. The client will bring to therapy a 'problem-saturated story'. At the same time, therapy can be viewed as a dramatic event since the story is not only told it is also performed. Cross-modality intervention places particular emphasis on the latter. The therapeutic encounter is viewed as a dramatic event within which the therapist takes an active part as *Deus ex machina*, finding creative and imaginative ways to subvert potential 'tragic outcomes'. In this regard, depending on their core modality, they are invited to draw on principles that underpin working with process.

Psychoanalytic practitioners, for example, will be mindful of the 'transferential invitation' (Bott and Howard 2012) being unconsciously communicated by the client. The management of the transference/countertransference relationship is at the heart of successful therapeutic outcome. The therapist who is provoked into enacting the part in the drama that they have been unconsciously given by their client will ensure a repetition takes place as opposed to a working through of early relational trauma (Freud 1914). We repeat, argued Freud, in order not to remember, and in this way the drama of the therapeutic encounter can be seen as a paradoxical attempt to communicate our distress but not have to risk the anxiety of new relational possibilities.

In taking the view that therapeutic encounter is shared dramatic event (Bott and Howard 2012), there are a number of ideas and principles in systems theory that have utility. Significantly, it challenges the taken-for-granted view of the world as a linear matter of cause and effect, in favour of circularity, where each cause is at the same time an effect. Salvador Minuchin (1976) coined the term 'family dance' to capture the intricate way in which family members maintain their positions in relation to one another. In the drama of the therapeutic encounter this becomes the 'therapeutic dance', where the client brings to therapy the steps of existing 'dances' with an invitation for the therapist to join in. A relational model of resistance requires the therapist to engage in the dance graciously respecting the lifetime of investment that the client has put in to learning the routine. This in itself is not enough and much of what might be considered effective therapy risks being no more than a replay of old moves as the therapist becomes, in systems parlence, 'inducted into the system'. For productive therapy to take place, the therapist is required to introduce new possibilities. This is achieved by introducing some new steps while ensuring that both partners remain on their feet.

As suggested above, there has been a resurgence of interest in social constructionism. Berger and Luckmann's *The Social Construction of Reality* (1967) takes forward Mead's original proposal that what we take for reality is based upon taken-for-granted assumptions. Social arrangements arise from repeated actions that are passed on to the next generation as social facts. From this perspective, the therapeutic encounter becomes a social setting where taken-for-granted assumptions on the part of the client are challenged by a 'significant other' in the form of the therapist. The work of Erving Goffman has particular relevance here given his emphasis upon the place of 'performance' in social life. Here, the social world consists of a series of dramatic acts where, through turn-taking, we alternate between the role of actor and audience. Identity is constructed and maintained through a series of dramatic acts (Goffman 1956). Goffman identifies social situations where this process becomes problematic. In *Asylums* (1961), he attaches the term 'total institution' to organizations like prisons and psychiatric hospitals where 'inmates' sleep, play, and work in the same place with the absence of possibilities to construct a satisfactory identity. *Stigma* (1963) is concerned with the dilemma of the individual who is socially disqualified by virtue of a discrediting attribute or negative label. Taking this forward, the therapeutic hour becomes a context where identities are confirmed and constructed. The 'client' or worst 'patient' is presented with the challenge of managing a potentially stimatizing context. From this perspective, notions like 'resistance' and 'identification' can be seen as a function of the therapeutic relationship and the setting within which it takes place.

Earlier, mention was made to the therapist as *Deus ex machina*. This refers to a device originally encountered in Greek Tragedy whereby a dilemma is resolved by the unexpected intervention of an outside character or event. Central to the tragedic experience is the notion of *harmatia*. An incident in the plot leads the protagonist on a path of tragic error. In therapy, the client is both author and protagonist of his or her own tragedy. As therapists, our appreciation of the client's courage in adversity is not enough in itself. We are required to join the client on stage and take an active part in the drama. Typically, in Greek Tragedy, a god would appear, intervening on behalf of the protagonist. In the therapeutic encounter, the therapist is craned on to the stage in order to interfere with the tragic outcome of the client's drama. Human experience is far too conflicted and complicated for simplistic intervention and even good endings are seldom happy. At the same time, predicted outcomes can be confounded and the way opened for a richer narrative to replace a thin and predictable plot.

The therapeutic relationship

The philosophical and theoretical position we have argued leads us to challenge the status of theory and therapeutic 'modality' as a particular kind of truth. That said, there is a convincing body of research to suggest that having a sound theoretical orientation is a key factor in successful therapeutic outcome. All therapeutic narratives constitute an attempt to understand the complexities of human experience and have a tendency to construct the world in their own terms (Warhus 2001). Quoting Korbzyski, Gregory Bateson (1972) reminds us that 'the map is not the territory'.

At the same time, all relational therapeutic narratives have, at their heart, the notion that we are born into the world incomplete and utterly vulnerable. This lends the early years of a human's experience a disproportionate impact on a life span.

Central to this understanding is an acceptance of the primacy of human relationships in the development of self and identity. We are so profoundly shaped by the others we encounter in our infancy to the extent that this not only shapes our mind but, notably, our brains (Cozolino 2006; Schore 2012). We bring coherence to bear on our experience through the construction of a narrative: a story in which we define who we are, what other people are like, and how we might understand our place in the world.

When the client enters the consulting room, they tell his or her story to the therapeutic Other. This will typically be an account of the troubles that have brought them to seek help. As has been suggested, this story is not just told but enacted. Therapy therefore takes the form of a dramatic encounter in which the client 'invites' the therapist to play their part in their familiar script. Theory thus provides a lens through which to challenge this world-taken-for-granted. A therapist without a theoretical 'map' will most often find themselves unwittingly accepting the part in the play that is unconsciously handed to them and the predictable tragic ending, which has brought the client here in the first place, will be recreated.

Case vignette

Holly entered therapy in her mid-thirties as she struggled with anxiety and loneliness after feeling rejected time after time by 'unfeeling' partners. She described her relationships as 'turbulent' and 'intense'. Her early life had been characterized by hostile, disorganized, and intrusive parenting. The therapist was moved by Holly's story and the level of anxiety she was experiencing both within and outside of relationships. As the therapy progressed, however, the therapist found himself working terribly hard to keep the 'therapeutic frame'. Holly constantly sought to rearrange session times, would take phone calls within sessions, and often arrived late, finding it hard to leave. She became increasingly 'interested' in her therapist's private life and would enquire as to his whereabouts on weekends and a whole host of other inappropriate questions. The therapist found himself quite rigidly holding boundaries and fell more and more silent during sessions in an attempt to 'guard' against what he experienced as her intrusive requests and demands.

We could think of Holly's behaviour as an attempt to recreate her chaotic, disorganized early life within the consulting room. Through her inquisitions of her therapist's private life she was persisting in recreating the intrusive relational pattern she herself had experienced at the hands of her mother. As the therapist retreated from her, she experienced him as abandoning her in the same way in which she felt her partners did and, ultimately, echoing the lack of attuned parenting from her past.

A range of theoretical accounts exists for why we 'persist' in recreating the relational encounters that prevented us from having our needs met in infancy. Freud's (1920) notion of 'repetition compulsion' conceptualized this phenomenon, and has been taken up in 'game-theory' and attachment theory among others. These are all equally valid theoretical accounts of 'persistence', as coined by Lynne Hoffman (1993). Drawing on extensive child observational research, Daniel Stern introduced the concept of 'implicit relational knowing' (Stern et al. 1998). This helpful term refers to the infant's – and subsequent adult's – implicit expectations of others that they will feel, respond, and behave in particular ways. What underpins this concept is the notion that infants operate largely on the basis of prediction. Stern argues that infants become upset and unsettled when their mothers respond in surprising ways, even if the predictable outcome has negative connotations for the infant.

As clients we will actively, if unconsciously, work to preserve our unique perspective on the world. On the one hand, we will seek help in the form of therapy; on the other, we will seldom be willing to bring our version of events, and our ways of being and relating, into question. As therapists our role, irrespective of modality, is to politely, yet actively, decline the invitation to play out the client's familiar drama. The key here, however, is to do so without inviting resistance in the client. It is our position that 'resistance' is not a property of the client but a function of a failing therapeutic relationship. If a client is 'resisting', then the therapist is failing to engage with the client's story and enactment is a creative and safe way. The therapist's own 'implicit relational knowing' will of course play a part in the dramatic encounter. Blaming a failed therapeutic relationship on the client's 'resistance' is a common manifestation of a therapist's inability to confront their own blind-spots.

Drawing on their therapeutic model of choice, the therapist's task is to engage actively in the dramatic presentation of the client's story while drawing attention to the limitations of their account. We should not forget that our patterns of relating and their accompanying narrative accounts were devised under desperate circumstances while we were utterly dependent and cognitively immature. These relational strategies were designed to protect us from feelings of loss, shame, anxiety, and rejection. Poignantly, though, now as adults these defensive strategies are often at the route of our distress. As the therapist actively subverts the client's attempts at persistence, these difficult feelings come to the fore and the client experiences the necessary emotional crisis. As anxiety about the unpredictable is experienced, this provides the opportunity for the therapist to offer him or herself in the role of what Stern (1985) would call a 'self-regulating other' – an other who is available to help the client to contain, process, and bring previously unintegrated and disregulating affective experiences into the self. This is not about any kind of 'cure' or about making difficult feelings disappear but, as Freud suggested, about helping the client to learn to bear the pain of being human.

We could see Holly's behaviour towards her therapist as an unconscious request for containment and for a safe and boundaried environment. If he became too rigid, the therapist risked recreating the very rejection Holly experienced from others but to indulge her requests would of course be destructive to therapy. The challenge for this therapist was to hold the boundaries enough while remaining non-defensive and, when this gave rise to her inevitable anxiety, not abandoning her and giving voice to her need of containment.

Fritz Perl's notion of the 'safe emergency' is of central relevance here (Perls et al. 1951). The framing that the therapist plays the role of the 'polite but unpredictable guest' should not be confused with an inability to provide consistent safety. It is the safety that the therapist fosters that determines whether the client is able to negotiate an expansion of the client's 'implicit relational knowing'. In the place of 'self-regulating other' the therapist must be open to spontaneous emotional experience, in order to provide the necessary attunement and mirroring that will allow the client the opportunity to familiarize him or herself with aspects of their hitherto unfamiliar internal world.

The proposal that the therapist should engage directly in interrupting and challenging the dramatic presentation of the client's dilemma stands in stark contrast to the tendency towards therapeutic passivity. One variant of this emerges when the therapist becomes more engaged with their approach than with the client; lost in obscure papers and elegant conceptual accounts of the 'material'. At the other extreme is to be found a quasi-religious commitment to the 'relationship' that shows itself in a mindless warm relating without any meaningful engagement with the client's phenomenal world. Arguably, therapy takes its most passive form when the process of the relationship is reduced to procedure and the uncertainties of the encounter are avoided by engaging in activities and following manuals (Bott and Howard 2012).

Challenges to the therapeutic relationship

The client who struggles with a sense of imperfection may be all too ready to find fault with the world in general and the therapist in particular, leaving the latter feeling criticized and with a sense of failure. Successful intervention requires the therapist to take a position of having nothing to prove or protect while being cautious in their invitations for the client to express emotion. Developmental models help in making sense of this dilemma. In intervention, the therapist will be well served by psychoanalytic principles with particular reference to transference and the Oedipal.

Case vignette

John comes to therapy bringing with him a theme of loss and abandonment in early life. His pain and longing for connection are hidden behind an angry exterior. In the therapeutic encounter, the request for help is experienced by the therapist as a kind of attack, and attempts to establish a warm connection are met with some hostility. Treating fear as information, the therapist seeks to form a productive engagement by recognizing and respecting John's protective strategy.

Here, we may turn to systems thinking and strategic intervention in the form of a therapeutic bind. The therapist might be inclined to suggest to John that, since she does not know him, he should not trust her too soon. Some readers may be uncomfortable with this kind of paradoxical intervention but, arguably, it speaks directly to John's dilemma, while opening the way to the potential for a trusting relationship.

Again, where expressions of need have been met by emotional unavailability, the client may well have learnt to 'cut-off', negating relationships as threatening and unsatisfying. Here, the therapist needs to look beyond the absence of obvious signs of distress seeking connection with the client's internal world. Attachment theory and the work of D.W. Winnicott provide a way of understanding and working with this dynamic.

Equally, while the subject of love, a particular child in the family may be 'allocated' the task of keeping others happy. This can show itself in therapy by a process whereby the therapist finds himself looking forward to her next session with Jane, who was so appreciative of the skilful interventions in the previous session. Reflection upon this opens the way to a concern that Jane is acting out an old story. Here, unlike with John in the previous case vignette, the therapist is faced with the challenge of engaging with warmth while remaining wary of seduction. The therapeutic task is to challenge actively self-disqualification while endorsing the client's right to be 'important'. This kind of positioning is informed by script theory and game theory.

Faced with the oppositionality that can be a feature of a childhood characterized by restrictive or punitive controls, the therapist will do well to sidestep the transferential invitation to be controlling in favour of humour and playfulness. Analysis of the transactions with reference to ego-states can provide a useful framework for this kind of intervention.

Where the need for intimacy has been experienced as a threat, either in terms of intrusion or abandonment, the therapist may find him or herself allocated the role of applauding audience to the client's achievements. Productive intervention will require that this passive position is graciously declined and connection is made with the frightened, lonely toddler hiding behind the desperate performance. Here, accounts of narcissism underpin therapist engagement.

New developments and research findings

Common factors theory (Imel and Wampold 2008) suggests that all evidenced-based therapies lead to similar outcomes. The idea is that therapeutic narratives that have stood the test of time have commonalities that underpin their effectiveness. This is often amusingly described as the 'Dodo bird effect', which suggests that 'everyone has won, so all must have prizes'. That said, this is not the same as arguing that coherence and intellectual rigour with regard to modality is not of equivalent importance. Indeed, such common factors as advocated by Wampold (2001) in *The Great Psychotherapy Debate*, suggest very clearly that 'adherence to a treatment model' is absolutely essential for positive outcome. While most of us would not speak of 'treatments', the point is firmly made. Eclecticism, we argue, leads to confusion with regard to the orientation and objective of the work. In articulating a 'cross-modality approach', we are inviting the practitioner into an important, albeit seemingly paradoxical position. We must embed ourselves within our modality and employ it coherently while remembering the self-referential nature of all 'conventions of intelligibility' (Warhus 2001).

The 'therapeutic alliance' of course is quoted as the most important common factor underpinning all effective psychotherapy. In this chapter, we are arguing that therapy takes place within the relationship in the form of a dramatic enactment. Drawing on their chosen modality, the therapist intervenes in this drama in surprising and creative ways. This then is consistent with the accepted notion that the person delivering the therapy is deemed within contemporary research literature as being more important than the approach being employed. This leads us to consider the types of traits, or characteristics, associated with individuals who are effective in helping their clients. Verbal fluency, interpersonal perception, affective modulation and expressiveness, warmth and acceptance, and being action-orientated are all therapist variables that are now associated with positive outcome (Wampold 2001). Additionally, the ability to make alliances with individuals with a broad range of relational patterns is essential, as is a tendency to be 'other-focused' (Anderson et al. 2009). Having the ability to reach, connect, and sustain a relationship with individuals with a history of broken or traumatic attachments is the bedrock on which therapy rests. Action-orientated psychotherapies, in which practitioners can provide cogent explanations, are those that have the greatest chance of bringing about change and creating the type of 'safe emergency' we describe above.

Summary

- The contemporary philosophical position which underpins the field of counselling and psychotherapy challenges the view that it is possible to privilege one approach over another and this is supported by outcome research findings.
- The vehicle for therapeutic intervention is the relationship but this needs to be located within a coherent paradigm.
- Effective therapy is a function of the extent to which the practitioner exhibits certain qualities and actions.
- A cross-modality approach respects the distinction between therapeutic paradigms while valuing exchanges between practitioners in the form of a dialogic pluralism.
- Therapy is taken to be a dramatic process where the therapist engages actively with the enactment of the client's dilemma, and resistance is taken to be a function of the therapeutic relationship, not a property of the client.

Further reading

Bott, D. and Howard, P. (2012) *The Drama of the Therapeutic Encounter: A Cross-Modality Approach*. London: Sage.

Stern, D. (2004) *The Present Moment in Psychotherapy and Everyday Life*. New York: Norton.

Wampold, B.E. (2001) *The Great Psychotherapy Debate: Models, Methods and Findings*. Mahwah, NJ: Erlbaum.

References

Anderson, T., Ogles, B.M., Patterson, C.L., Lambert, M.J. and Vermeersch, D.A. (2009) Therapist effects: facilitative interpersonal skills as a predictor of therapist success, *Journal of Clinical Psychology*, 65: 755–68.

Bateson, G. (1972) *Steps Towards an Ecology of Mind*. Chicago, IL: Chicago University Press.

Berger, P. and Luckmann, T. (1967) *The Social Construction of Reality: A Treatise in the Sociology of Knowledge*. Harmondsworth: Penguin.

Bott, D. (2005) Person-centred counselling and systemic intervention: respectful co-existence, *Counselling and Psychotherapy Journal*, 16 (6): 19–21.

Bott, D. and Howard, P. (2012) *The Drama of the Therapeutic Encounter: A Cross-Modality Approach*. London: Sage.

Brown, S. and Stenner, P. (2009) *Psychology without Foundations: History, Philosophy and Psychosocial Theory*. London: Sage.

Cooper, M. and McLeod, J. (2011) *Pluralistic Counselling and Psychotherapy*. London: Sage.

Cozolino, L. (2006) *The Neuroscience of Human Relationships: Attachment and the Developing Social Brain*. New York: Norton.

Derrida, J. (1974) *Of Grammatology*. Baltimore, MD: Johns Hopkins University Press.

Evans, K. and Gilbert, M. (2005) *An Introduction to Integrative Psychotherapy*. Basingstoke: Palgrave Macmillan.

Foucault, M. (1979) *Discipline and Punish: The Birth of the Prison*. New York: Vintage Books.

Freud, S. (1914) Remembering, repeating and working-through (further recommendations on the technique of psycho-analysis II), in *The Standard Edition of the Complete Psychological Works of Sigmund Freud, Vol. XII (1911–1913): The Case of Schreber, Papers on Technique and Other Works* (pp. 145–56). London: Hogarth Press.

Freud, S. (1920) Beyond the pleasure principle, in *The Standard Edition of the Complete Psychological Works of Sigmund Freud, Vol. XVIII (1920–1922): Beyong the Pleasure Principle, Group Psychology and Other Works* (pp. 1–64). London: Vintage Classics.

Gergen, K. (1999) *An Invitation to Social Constructionism*. London: Sage.

Gergen, K. (2008) Therapeutic challenges of multi-being, *Journal of Family Therapy*, 30 (4): 335–49.

Goffman, E. (1956) *The Presentation of Self in Everyday Life*. New York: Anchor.

Goffman, E. (1961) *Asylums: Essays on the Social Situation of Mental Patients and Other Inmates*. New York: Doubleday.

Goffman, E. (1963) *Stigma: Notes on the Management of Spoiled Identity*. Englewood Cliffs, NJ: Prentice-Hall.

Hoffman, L. (1993) *Exchange Voices: A Collaborative Approach to Family Therapy*. London: Karnac Books.

Hollanders, H. (2000) Eclecticism/integration – historical developments, in S. Palmer and R. Woolfe (eds.) *Integrative and Eclectic Counselling and Psychotherapy*. London: Sage.

Imel, Z. and Wampold, B. (2008) The importance of treatment and the science of common factors in psychotherapy, in S. Brown and R. Lent (eds.) *Handbook of Counseling Psychology*, 4th edn. (pp. 249–62). Hoboken, NJ: Wiley.

Kuhn, T. (1962) *The Structure of Scientific Revolutions*. Chicago, IL: University of Chicago Press.

Lapworth, P., Sills, C. and Fish, S. (2001) *Integration in Counselling and Psychotherapy*. London: Sage.

Lyotard, J. (1979) *The Postmodern Condition: A Report on Knowledge*. Manchester: Manchester University Press.

Mead, G.H. (1934) *Mind, Self, and Society*. Chicago, IL: University of Chicago Press.

Minuchin, S. (1976) *Families and Family Therapy*. Cambridge, MA: Harvard University Press.

Perls, F., Hefferline, R. and Goodman, P. (1951) *Gestalt Therapy: Excitement and Growth in the Human Personality*. New York: Julian Press.

Safran, J.D. and Messer, S.B. (1997) Psychotherapy integration: a postmodern critique, *Clinical Psychology: Science and Practice*, 4: 140–52.

Schore, A. (2012) *Affect Regulation and the Origin of the Self: The Neurobiology of Emotional Development*. Hillsdale, NJ: Psychology Press.

Stern, D. (1985) *The Interpersonal World of the Infant: A View from Psychoanalysis and Developmental Psychology*. New York: Basic Books.

Stern, D. (2004) *The Present Moment in Psychotherapy and Everyday Life*. New York: Norton.

Stern, D.N., Sander, L.W., Nahum, J.P., Harrison, A.M., Lyons-Ruth, K., Morgan, A. et al. (1998) Non-interpretative mechanisms in psychoanalytic psychotherapy: the 'something more' than interpretation, *International Journal of Psychoanalysis*, 79: 903–21.

Wachtel, P. (2011) *Therapeutic Communication*, 2nd edn. New York: Guilford Press.

Wampold, B.E. (2001) *The Great Psychotherapy Debate: Models, Methods and Findings*. Mahwah, NJ: Erlbaum.

Warhus, L. (2001) Therapy: a social construction, in K.J. Gergen (ed.) *Social Construction in Context*. London: Sage.

7 An integrative approach to the psychotherapeutic relationship: therapeutic challenges and successes

Maria Gilbert and Ken Evans

Introduction

We have chosen to introduce our approach to integrative psychotherapy by providing a critical reflection on a brief case vignette of a significant event in a long-term psychotherapeutic relationship involving Ken Evans. We begin with an outline of the epistemological foundations underpinning our theory and values, followed by our integrative perspective on the psychotherapeutic relationship, including some key theoretical concepts that inform our reflections on our clinical practice. We then provide a brief introduction to the case vignette, the case vignette itself, and offer a commentary on the process.

Professional context and background

Maria Gilbert is Joint Head of the Integrative Department at the Metanoia Institute in West London, while Ken Evans is co-director of the European Centre for Psychotherapeutic Studies based in France and the Channel islands. Both institutes are accredited members of the European Association for Integrative Psychotherapy (hereafter EAIP), which was founded in 1996.

The EAIP believes there can be no single approach to integrative psychotherapy. The EAIP defines as integrative,

> any methodology and integrative orientation in psychotherapy which exemplifies, or is developing towards, a conceptually coherent, principled, theoretical combination of two or more specific approaches, and/or represents a model of integration in its own right. In this regard there is a particular ethical obligation on integrative psychotherapists to dialogue with colleagues of diverse orientations and to remain informed of developments in the field.

> (www.euroaip.eu/about-eaip/)

While EAIP is home to, and positively encourages a wide variety of approaches to integration, each accredited institute within EAIP must adhere to the EAIP generic training standards, which are set at Masters level or equivalent. Member institutes of EAIP are currently represented across 14 European nations. The EAIP was the first Europe-wide school of psychotherapy to become accredited as a European Wide Accrediting Organization by the European Association for Psychotherapy in Berlin in 1996.

Epistemological bases of our approach to integrative psychotherapy

'In our opinion the epistemology, theory and clinical practice of any approach to psychotherapy should be consistent and explicit and thus accessible to critique' (Evans and Gilbert 2005: 15). The basis of our approach to integrative psychotherapy supports the non-linear and multi-causality of field theory, which, according to Lewin (1952), is a way of looking at the total situation whereby human phenomena are recognized as interconnected, interdependent, and interactive. What this means is that human experience is intimately connected with current contextual conditions and cannot be understood in isolation. This underpins the importance of sensitivity to the context of the client's life, inside and outside the clinical room. Indeed, in a very real sense the client brings his or her world into therapy.

Secondly, the illumination of subjective personal experience of phenomenology honours the importance of the client's subjective bodily experience as a valid source of knowledge. 'There is no "me" apart from my history just as there is no "me" apart from the world' (Kennedy 2013: 79). We maintain that the client's phenomenological experience should not be contradicted by the therapist's theoretical dogma. Prior 'knowing' on the part of the therapist can undermine the client's view of reality. In this sense, we subscribe to Bion's (1967/1992) well-known statement that we approach each session 'without memory or desire' in the sense of not being attached to any desires, results or presuppositions about outcomes.

Holism supports the simultaneous exploration of both inner and outer engagement with the client. From a holistic perspective, nothing is deliberately ignored. Holistic observation is not simply 'looking' but looking reflexively and in depth, not only mindfully but with the whole of one's being, mind, body, and emotion. The integrative psychotherapist attempts to bring the whole of him or herself to what is figural in the engagement with the client and to attend to the full complexity of the client's experience.

Thirdly, we draw on the dialogical perspective of the existential philosopher Martin Buber (1923/1958), and the contemporary unfolding of his ideas in dialogical psychotherapy (Friedman 1985) and dialogical gestalt therapy (Yontef 1993; Hycner and Jacobs 1995; Kennedy 2013) to bring a further crucial dimension to our approach – the inter-human dimension. Buber criticized the overemphasis on individual experience at the expense of inter-human experience. Buber's emphasis on the I-Thou of relationship underpins our belief in the co-creation of all relationships. Indeed, central to our concept of integrative psychotherapy is the focus on the co-creation of the therapeutic relationship, which leads us to our theoretical foundations.

Finally, our approach is further underpinned by a constructivist view with an emphasis on the co-constructed psychotherapeutic relationship within a two-person psychological perspective. From this perspective, the therapist and client make up an interactional field where the focus is on 'subject to subject relating'. This relational emphasis is at the heart of current intersubjectivity theory and relational psychoanalysis

(Stolorow and Atwood 1992; Benjamin 2012). This perspective is further supported by neurobiological research, which also highlights the implicit level of relating – that is, the non-verbal, somatic basis, which has been described as 'embodied simulation' by Gallese (2009: 519).

Foundations of theory and practice

Integrative perspective on the psychotherapeutic relationship

Congruent with our above philosophical assumptions and at the core of our thinking we view the psychotherapeutic relationship as a co-created process to which both the psychotherapist and the client contribute. Drawing from the intersubjective perspective (Stolorow and Atwood 1992), we are interested in the creation of the therapeutic dialogue, the conversation in the therapy room, and how this facilitates change, or at times hinders growth. From the intersubjective perspective, we are interested in the co-creation of the dialogue of therapy and the 'subject' to 'subject' relating that is central to a mature interaction. We agree with Lewis Aron's perspective that this relationship is mutual but not equal: 'The relational approach that I am advocating views the patient–analyst relationship as continually established and re-established through ongoing mutual influence in which both patient and the analyst systematically affect, and are affected by, each other' (Aron 1999: 248). It is this dialogue between the two participants that is at the heart of the psychotherapeutic process. However, ultimately we go beyond the subject to subject dialogue and surrender not to the client but rather to the 'between' (Yontef 1993; Hycner and Jacobs 1995) or the 'relational unconscious' of relational psychoanalysis, as exemplified by Mitchell and Aron (1999) and Gerson (2004). In focusing on the relational ground 'between' the participants, we would emphasize the importance of respecting the 'otherness' of the client, the essential 'differences' in our experience of life, and also the shared existential realities with which we all live. True contact requires the appreciation of difference (Evans 1996).

The therapeutic relationship

All relationships are simultaneously alive at explicit verbal levels of engagement, and at implicit non-verbal levels of communication (BCPSG 2010). These two levels interact and inform one another, so we are not describing an isolated process but an interactive one (except where there is dissociation from split-off parts of the person). Since the time of Freud, therapy has been viewed as the 'talking cure', but it is only recently as the result of child development research, neurobiological research, and work on 'implicit relational knowing' by the BCPSG (2010) that the implicit levels of therapeutic communication have received due attention. This process, described by the BCPSG as 'implicit relational knowing', has also been described as 'unformulated experience' by Donnel B. Stern (2010) in recent relational literature. The implications of these findings for an integrative relational psychotherapy approach, is the focus on the non-verbal, somatic levels of communication being honoured as much as the conversation in the room. Change is facilitated by the implicit level of understanding communicated by the therapist's tone of voice, accepting body language, the rhythms of his or her voice, and generally the 'sense' of his or her presence that is conveyed non-verbally to the client by the therapist's vitality affects (D.N. Stern 2010).

We experience a particular affinity with the 'three principles of salience' described by Lachmann and Beebe (1996), which have evolved from their child developmental research. They consider these applicable to the psychotherapeutic process.

- *Self and interactive regulation*: a focus on the regulation of affect, both internally and in relation to the other, highlights how affect dysregulation is often at the heart of a client's problems. That is, the client's difficulties in accessing their emotional experience and understanding its meaning and purpose surface in their relation with the therapist such that the therapy becomes a microcosm of the client's 'way of being in the world'.
- *Rupture and repair*: they see that ruptures are expectable in therapy, akin to the 'mistakes' written about by Casement (2002), or 'therapeutic alliance ruptures' emerging from Safran and Muran's (2000) work where a misunderstanding occurs between therapist and client. The repair of such a rupture can have profound healing power for the client.
- *Heightened affective moments*: these are emotional moments of contact, called 'moments of meeting' by Buber (1923/1958) and referred to by Stern (2004) as 'now moments'. Such moments of being 'seen' and 'fully acknowledged' by the other of the therapist mark change moments in therapy.

Ruptures in the relationship are often evident in 'enactments' between therapist and client, in which unconscious material for both parties seems to get enmeshed in a process that may lead to hurt, miscommunication, and subsequently to a rupture in the relationship, unless the enactment is recognized and discussed (Chused 1991). We may be unaware at the time of our own contribution to the enactment either as therapist or client beyond a sense of confusion about what 'has gone wrong' in the communication. Such an enactment when counterproductive will lead to discomfort in the relationship, which will be experienced by both parties. In our experience, being open and ready to acknowledge one's own part in this process can foster a reparative experience for the client, as is evident in the following case vignette.

Case vignette

James Is 38 years old and a project manager with a UK national building company. He is based in the Midlands where he lives with his partner Louisa, an occupational therapist, and their two-year-old daughter Lily. James and Louisa own their own home and James has a small portfolio of property that provides rental income. James is highly intelligent and successfully completed a three-year counselling diploma course in 2002. Prior to this key episode he was just a month or two away from finishing a four-year psychotherapy training programme and subsequently went on to achieve a distinction for his clinical case study and is registered as an accredited psychotherapist. Alongside his busy working life James manages a small psychotherapy practice.

This brief introduction to James portrays a picture of family stability, prosperity, and contentment and while this is the case today, it was not always so. James has truly taken 'the road less travelled', a long and very hard road characterized by physical brutality, emotional deprivation, crime, and incarceration.

James is the middle of three children with a sister two years older than him who is a school teacher and a brother two years younger who is a mechanic. James's father had been estranged from James and his siblings for several years prior to his death in 2009. He died of a heart attack after a lifetime of alcohol misuse. Neither James not his siblings have any desire for contact with their mother, who James describes as manipulative, deceitful, and unstable.

James's parents went to live in Ireland twenty-five years ago, apparently so that his father might escape his mother's family who had a notorious reputation for fighting, gambling, and drinking. His parents' relationship was volatile and frequently at breaking point and after a few years his mother left her husband and children and returned to the UK. The children remained with their father in Ireland for several years where the two boys suffered physical violence at the hands of their father, who also goaded them to fight each other and frequently tested their loyalty to him rather than their mother. Paradoxically, James's father conveyed a depth of love, albeit brutal at times, for all his children, regrettably contaminated with a style of parenting that he in turn transferred from his own impoverished and brutalized upbringing.

James's salvation was school. He was a bright pupil who enjoyed sport and related well with other children and his teachers. This came to an abrupt end when his father packed his bag and 'persuaded' him he should go and live with his mother in the Midlands. Years later he was able to acknowledge it was like being 'sold out'. Bewildered, cut adrift, James travelled alone to the UK – he was fourteen years old.

Initially, his mother greeted him enthusiastically but he soon realized his mother wanted him to live with her simply to secure extra points on the council housing list. Once achieved, she dropped all pretence of wanting her son and distanced herself from him with relentless verbal abuse. She brought men into the house and was thoroughly careless about her dress and sexual activity such that James was constantly humiliated.

In Ireland, James had taken refuge in school and among school friends. Now he found himself in an educationally failing school in a deprived area of a major inner city where his Irish accent singled him out as different. He learned very quickly that in order to survive it was necessary to fight. He discovered he was good at it, very good. Here was his survival strategy and his downfall.

James took karate training and excelled at full contact karate. He was taken on as a doorman, club bouncer, and built a significant reputation. After years of devastating humiliation from both parents, he now found he had respect, for being a 'hard man'. Drug-related crime was inevitable and by his late teens he was commanding significant sums of money. He was generous to his friends and dangerous to their enemies. James experienced the 'under belly' of society and witnessed things most people never see below the veneer of so-called civilized society. In a subculture of crime, street justice was brutal and profoundly antisocial but nevertheless elicited a kind of ruthless honesty. In such an environment, a form of dignity and credibility was bestowed upon those who successfully challenged societal norms and values. In this counter-cultural greenhouse James found meaning, respect, and a degree of self-worth.

Eventually, he ended up in prison and locked away in solitary confinement because of his aggressive behaviour. James describes how, paradoxically, the isolation provided an opportunity for reflection. The futility of his chosen path in life finally dawned on him when he received a challenge from a fellow prisoner. Even in solitary confinement the need to maintain status and face emerged as a prisoner in an adjoining solitary cell tapped out a coded challenge along a water pipe to James. The message affirmed that they would have to engage in a brutal fight at some point to ascertain who was going to be the man. James said he began to laugh at the futility of it all and continued with a gallows kind of humour long into the night. James recognized the need to change his life.

The subsequent story of James's struggle to be a member of lawful society is neither smooth nor easy but is characterized by sheer determination and courage. Some people have seen him and believed in him, while others have seen no further than his former reputation and record. He has justified the faith of those who had looked below the surface and proved the others profoundly mistaken.

His first counselling experience offered him clear boundaries and acceptance. His counsellor clearly liked him. Three years of counselling training helped him believe he could go further. The senior staff at his interview for psychotherapy training saw beyond his criminal record and took him at face value. Subsequently, he proved to be a conscientious and committed trainee who consistently achieved high marks for his coursework despite a dearth of educational background prior to his counselling education. The distinction for his case study, confirmed by the external examiner, was a remarkable achievement.

Critical reflection of the therapy session

James and I had worked together for three years up to this point and he acknowledged he saw me as a mentor and positive role model. Together we had built an effective therapeutic alliance, which had been tried and tested on a number of occasions. I liked James and respected his steadfast commitment to his personal and professional development. He impressed me with his capacity for vulnerability and courage in working through the consequences of his abusive childhood and the impact of his troubled history upon his life and relationships.

Towards the end of the therapy session, James said he wanted to attend a professional conference but a former colleague was one of the speakers and he had decided not to attend. She had abruptly ruptured a professional relationship with James some years earlier. James believed she had been unprofessional and caught in a process she was not willing to explore. I recall him bringing this to therapy much earlier in our work. He had been hurt and angry but for his part recognized the process and, though wounded, eventually moved on with dignity.

To my subsequent astonishment and dismay, I jokingly suggested he go to the conference and shrug off his concerns. I even made a mild excuse for her and remarked something to the effect that she was 'only human'. My overall stance was to 'let it be, everything will be fine'. James's body language appeared heavy and subdued. He began to frown and appeared to be struggling to find the words with which to reply to my comment. Time ran out and the session ended somewhat abruptly.

After the close of the session, I was preoccupied with James's experience of hurt in relation to the colleague. I realized he was now likely more immediately hurt by my 'throw away' remarks. About an hour after the end of the session he texted me with a message protesting his belief that he had been rejected by the colleague who he believed had behaved unprofessionally. The message was direct and his anger and hurt contained. I intuited James was defending his position, while working hard not to dismiss me and discount the mutual regard we had co-created. I was impressed with James and disappointed with myself and curious!

Here was a critical episode that required serious reflection on the dynamics of the process between therapist and client. What might I have repeated from James's history and why now?

My dismissal of James's issue was a significant therapeutic error reminiscent of his father's declaration that 'everything will be okay', when James was sent back to the UK at age fourteen. His father had let him down at best and betrayed him at worse. I realized I had repeated this process in this enactment. Why?

Invariably, effective therapeutic relationships need to be tested to show that they are truly trustworthy. Apparent therapeutic mistakes may unconsciously be co-created in order to repeat history and confirm life script (Berne 1961), although we believe with a deeper desire to generate healing (Stolorow and Atwood 1992). The strong and effective therapeutic alliance forged between us was putting James's early survival decisions at risk. James was experiencing with me the sort of relationship he would have wanted from his father. However, our relationship threatened the core of his belief system. If I let him down he would relive again some of the humiliation and hurt he experienced as a child and adolescent, but his script would be intact and life would be predictable.

I also considered a recent challenging encounter with an important person in my life to be significant in acting as a magnet and feeding the unconscious process. The interaction leading to the rupture was not a 'one-way street', with James's unconscious process setting it up and the therapist being drawn into the projective identification (Searles 1978–79). The therapist's unconscious was also at play (Gerson 2004). Indeed, we would go so far as to maintain that projective identification can only operate when both parties are contributing to the process at some level on a co-created unconscious level. We are also increasingly convinced that so-called therapeutic errors are in fact therapeutic necessities calling forth the possibility of repetition but also calling forth the possibility of reparation and with a profound potential for healing. But who is healed? The client certainly, but what of the therapist? We agree with the notion that in the interactive matrix of the therapeutic relationship, the client heals something in the therapist so that the therapist may heal something in them (Casement 1985).

At the beginning of the next therapy session, I sensed James's ambivalence. I intuited from his body language he was feeling anxious and wanting to be present but struggling with an opposite need to keep his distance. I was aware of experiencing something similar and I imagined James was reading my body language also.

Self-disclosure is a controversial intervention in psychotherapy, though increasingly acknowledged across the range of relational oriented approaches as having considerable potential to move therapy forward when used with discrimination (Zahm 1998).

I began with an apology. 'James, near the end of our last session I was left concerned about my manner of being with you. I realize I was dismissive of you and I want to apologize, I am sorry I did not take your concern seriously.' James visibly relaxed, breathed out, and expressed a tearful smile. He acknowledged he came feeling some anger and justified self-righteousness but said he had been able to hold onto his regard for me and the work we had done together over the years. He added with a wry smile that 'he was left wondering what was going on for me.' I was touched by his reception of my apology and I felt myself breathing out. My lived body experience was one of relief and I sensed a renewal of contact between us, a mutuality of I-Thou. I was impressed with the maturity of James's self-support. The interpersonal bridge (Kaufman 1992) between us that had experienced a rupture was re-established and I believe even deepened.

Challenges: theoretical reflection

In writing about the interactive matrix of therapeutic relationship, Greenberg (1995) suggests that precise techniques are impossible when seeking to re-establish contact after a rupture in the relationship. Instead, he believes an apology is a necessary precondition for the re-establishment of relationship. He goes further, maintaining the view that the meaning of an act, like an apology, cannot be determined by theory but rather the meaning of such an act arises out of the interaction itself. It is as if in such moments we are on an unknown path and what carries us through is our vulnerability, honesty, and not knowing – our authentic presence. Martin Buber would understand this as the I-Thou attitude, which can never be employed as a mere technique but can only arise in a moment of transparency, openness, and courage. In such a 'now moment', we model to the other the I-Thou attitude, which may in turn call forth reciprocity in the other.

The paradigm shift towards a two-person psychotherapy gives less emphasis to techniques and 'rules' of practice and more significance to spontaneity in the exploration of the process emerging between therapist and client. How might the client and therapist repeat history? How might the client and therapist repair history? (Lachmann and Beebe 1996). There is no rule book on relationality; no prescriptions on how to engage in a relational oriented psychotherapy as two people meet each other, influencing each other, challenging each other consciously and unconsciously, sometimes at a deep and profound level.

Without needing to go into detail and switch the focus of therapy towards myself, I nevertheless shared with James that our last session had likely touched on a recent experience in my personal life and that I was 'primed' like a magnet to fall into a process. James appreciated my acknowledgement of my part in the rupture.

Grounded in the significant degree of horizontality in our lived experience in the moment, and supported by James's psychotherapy training, we embarked on a collaborative theoretical exploration of what may have happened. This 'theoretical dialogue' was also an acknowledgement that James was now an accredited psychotherapist in his own right. So together we unpacked the co-created nature of the transaction between us, the projective identification, the conflict between the repetition, compulsion, and the reparation of the relationship. This was made possible by and dependent upon how we both dealt with the aftermath or 'fall out' from the rupture.

It was through mutual transparency, openness, and honesty, rather than technique – a rulebook – that we began to understand the historical dynamic at work in the present and moved beyond its psychic grip.

James had been waiting for an apology from his father for over twenty years!

Summary

Among the most significant developments in contemporary psychotherapy has been the move towards the centrality of the therapeutic relationship, which has challenged the classical notion of drive theory, therapist neutrality, and the notion of 'objectivity'. The primary need of human beings is for contact with the other.

Considered therapist self-disclosure, the inevitability of enactments, and the recognition of the influence of the therapist in the co-creation of the therapeutic relationship are current areas of exploration among a range of relational oriented approaches. The occurrence of enactments and ruptures in the therapeutic alliance, if recognized and reflected upon, are now widely recognized by diverse authors as opportunities for learning and change.

Although reliance on theory, techniques, and a rulebook is counterproductive in such clinical encounters, it is also true that techniques and dialogue need not be mutually exclusive. Sometimes a well-timed technique can add substantially to the therapeutic endeavour. Similarly, sound theory can support good practice. However, theory needs always to be held lightly, to gently inform our critical reflection in order to help understand a process rather than direct clinical practice when it can often be little more than a box into which we neatly place the client. The latter gives but transitory respite in situations of not knowing, while the former gives hope for the continued development of the profession of psychotherapy.

Further reading

Evans, K.R. and Gilbert, M.C. (2005) *An Introduction to Integrative Psychotherapy.* London: Palgrave Macmillan. This is one of the key texts on the theory and practice of integrative psychotherapy.

References

Aron, L. (1999) The patient's experience of the analyst's subjectivity, in S.A. Mitchell and L. Aron (eds.) *Relational Psychoanalysis: The Emergence of a Tradition.* Hillsdale, NJ: Analytic Press.

Benjamin, J. (2012) Beyond doer and done to: an intersubjective view of thirdness, in L. aron and A. Harris (eds.) *Relational Psychoanalysis, Vol. 4: Expansion of Theory* (pp. 91–129). New York: Routledge.

Berne, E. (1961) *Transactional Analysis in Psychotherapy*. New York: Grove Press.

Bion, W. (1992) Notes on memory and desire, in *Cogitations* (new extended edition). London: Karnac Books [original work published 1967].

Boston Change Process Study Group (BCPSG) (2010) *Change in Psychotherapy: A Unifying Paradigm*. New York: W.W. Norton.

Buber, M. (1958) *I and Thou*, 2nd edn. (trans. R.G. Smith). New York: Scribner [original work published 1923].

Casement, P. (1985) *On Learning from The Patient*. London: Routledge.

Casement, P. (2002) *Learning from our Mistakes*. Hove: Brunner-Routledge.

Chused, J.F. (1991) The evocative power of enactments, *Journal of the American Psychoanalytic Association*, 39: 615–39.

Evans, K.R. (1996) True dialogue requires the appreciation of difference, *International Journal of Psychotherapy*, 1 (1): 91–3.

Evans, K.R. and Gilbert, M.C. (2005) *An Introduction to Integrative Psychotherapy*. London: Palgrave Macmillan.

Friedman, M.S. (1985) *The Healing Relationship in Psychotherapy*. New York: Jason Aronson.

Gallese, V. (2009) Mirror neurons, embodied simulation and the neural basis of social identification, *Psychoanalytic Dialogues*, 19: 519–36.

Gerson, S. (2004) The relational unconscious: a core element of intersubjectivity, thirdness and clinical process, *Psychoanalytic Quarterly*, 73: 63–98.

Greenberg, J. (1995) Psychoanalytic technique and the interactive matrix, *Psychoanalytic Quarterly*, 64: 1–22.

Hycner, R. and Jacobs, L. (1995) *The Healing relationship in Gestalt Therapy*. Highland, NJ: Gestalt Journal Publications.

Kaufman, G. (1992) *Shame: The Power of Caring*. Rochester, VT: Schenkman Books.

Kennedy, D.J. (2013) *Healing Perception: An Application of the Philosophy of Merleau-Ponty to the Theoretical Structures of Dialogic Psychotherapy*. Peregian Beach, QLD: Ravenswood Press.

Lachmann, F.M. and Beebe, A.B. (1996) Three principles of salience in the organization of the patient–analyst interaction, *Psychoanalytic Psychology*, 13: 1–22.

Lewin, K. (1952) *Field Theory in Social Science: Selected Theoretical Papers*. London: Tavistock.

Mitchell, S.A. and Aron, L. (eds.) (1999) *Relational Psychoanalysis: The Emergence of a Tradition*. Hillsdale, NJ: Analytic Press.

Safran, J.D. and Muran, J.C. (2000) *Negotiating the Therapeutic Alliance*. New York: Guilford Press.

Searles, H. (1978–79) Concerning transference and countertransference, *Journal of Psychoanalytic Psychotherapy*, 7: 65–88.

Stern, D.B. (2010) *Partners in Thought: Working with Unformulated Experience, Disassociation, and Enactment*. New York: Routledge.

Stern, D.N. (2004) *The Present Moment in Psychotherapy and Everyday Life*. New York: W.W. Norton.

Stern, D.N. (2010) *Forms of Vitality*. Oxford: Oxford University Press.

Stolorow, R.D. and Atwood, G.E. (1992) *Contexts of Being*. Hillsdale NJ: Analytic Press.

Yontef, G.M. (1993) *Awareness, Dialogue and Process: Essays on Gestalt Therapy*. Highland, NJ: Gestalt Journal Publications.

Zahm, S. (1998) Therapist self-disclosure in the practice of Gestalt therapy, *Gestalt Journal*, 23 (2): 21–52.

8 Relational therapy: defining the therapeutic relationship

Brian Charlesworth and Paul Nicholson

Introduction

The relational approach to psychotherapy and counselling describes contemporary perspectives that emphasize the role of *relationship* in both how we practise with a client and consider the development of human personality. Relational philosophy offers a language through which to frame traditional theoretical conceptualizations, and a rationale for integrative practice that acknowledges the relational nature of the practitioner in the process.

Foundations of theory and practice

Viewing personality development and the therapeutic encounter in relational terms has been a recurring theme throughout the development of psychotherapy, yet one that somehow eluded being placed at the centre of mainstream interest (Baker Miller and Stiver 1991). Prompted by the wider attention given to this evolving paradigm by authors within the field during the 1980s and continuing up to the present (Paul and Pelham 2000; Kahn 2001; DeYoung 2003; Mearns and Cooper 2005) there has been a gradual increase in awareness of relational perspectives, currently represented as a set of assumptions and principles rather than a unified theory of development (Pelham 2008).

The central premise of relational philosophy is that our initial sense of self is developed through relationship and that we maintain and perpetuate this sense of self through relationship also. We are not separate, we do not exist in a vacuum, and our sense of reality and identity is formed *in relation to* our experience and the meaning we divine from it (Mitchell 2000). So from our first breath, we embark on the journey of becoming an individual in a reality where we are perpetually in relationship with others and objects around us, with the sense of ourselves we construct based upon the conclusions we draw from those relationships (Mitchell 2000).

This mode of perception is described as the 'self with other' relationship (DeYoung 2003). It represents a way of considering human perception which forms the key basis of understanding the full extent of the term *relational* utilized within the approach.

The concept of the individual as a constantly shifting, reflexive entity, who's own perception of self and reality is based upon interpersonal and environmental contact is a growing position that stands as an alternative to the traditional concept of the individual, disconnected self, existing in isolation (DeYoung 2003; Mearns and Cooper 2005).

The relational perspective offers an alternative view, with human personality being seen as something which exists within a complex matrix of self-with-other relationships building up an ever forming and malleable self-structure. This distinction is not a new concept. Despite tracing its genesis to the early days of psychoanalysis, relationalism has only become more widely articulated within the world of psychological theory since the latter decades of the twentieth century (Pelham 2008).

The therapeutic relationship

The concept of identity through relationship has influenced the nature of the role of the therapist in practice (Reynolds 2007), from the promoting of insight into unconscious conflicts, to the client experiencing a new sense of self through the therapeutic relationship. Humanistic approaches developed practice traditions that mirrored relational perspectives for change. Radical at their inception, the idea of positioning the client's view and the therapeutic relationship as being of prime importance to successful outcomes, placed huge emphasis upon the whole therapeutic enterprise being a relational process. The inclusion of *congruence* into Carl Rogers' core conditions introduced a definitive relational dimension into practice (Schmid 2002) and reinforced the belief that through the therapeutic relationship, a therapy had been devised that *actually* worked (Paul and Haugh 2008).

Not only is there no significant evidence to indicate that any one model of practice is more effective than another (Lambert 2004; Stiles et al. 2006) but the supposition that a relationship of some description is necessary within therapy is reflected in over a thousand studies (Wampold 2001; Orlinsky et al. 2004). The therapeutic relationship is now considered a significant determinant in therapeutic change (Paul and Haugh 2008).

Again this notion of viewing personality construction through relationship is not new. Infants are innately disposed to be attracted to human features and display capacity to relate to others before they develop cognitive skills (Gerhardt 2004). The psychiatrist R.D. Laing, believed the desire for relational contact with others is linked to our own sense of *ontology*; of how we perceive and manage our sense of existence (Laing 1969).

Gerhardt (2004) argues that relationship is key to our development and maintains that we are arriving at a period in time where unrelated disciplines are converging to produce new understandings of emotional life, with biochemistry and neuroscience identifying relational contact as a necessary ingredient for the individual to self-regulate their affectual world. The therapeutic value of relationship is in its capacity to establish *confirmation* of the self; a mutual affirming of existence and opportunity to offer acceptance of how we relate to the world (Friedman 1988). This is seen as the key transformative factor in therapy (Schmid 2002).

We use the term *relational ontology* to describe a central theme found across many developmental models within psychotherapeutic theory – a sense of enduring ontological stability and identity through relationship (Howard 2008; Lapworth and Sills 2010).

Within cognitive behavioural therapy research, an emphasis has emerged over the last thirty years on similar ideas (Paul and Haugh 2008), and in an attempt to point out broader parallels, Lapworth and Sills (2010) outline a spectrum of comparable concepts adopted across schools, with many traditions voicing similar themes of relational forces forging personality from infancy. Despite these commonalities, there is still little acknowledged crossover of ideas or language between theoretical models (Paul and Haugh 2008). Ultimately, versions of the *truth*, as defined model to model, remain separated by the language they use to describe comparable phenomena.

Language is a relevant factor in how we relate to our own experience of existence, construct our relational worlds (Mitchell 2000), and subsequently work with these relationships in therapy. Self is linked to language, and borne from a 'sociolinguistic context' that manifestly unites our conception of ourselves to the existence of others (Mearns and Cooper 2005: 5). Language allows us to process emotions in a conscious fashion, articulate meanings from our perceptions, and provide the opportunity to reconfigure them through relationship (Gerhardt 2004).

Developmental theories, once accepted as true, objective reflections of reality, are now being increasingly considered as subjective interpretations of observed phenomena and therefore not generalizable (Hansen 2006). A wide variety of effective theoretical approaches to healing emotional suffering have been recorded (Croteau et al. 2002) that question the necessity of *truth* in therapeutic change and suggest alternative explanations may be appropriate. Rather than squeeze the client into a model that is unavoidably subjective, the counsellor's theory is considered no more than a 'narrative structure that helps to "re-story" the client's experience, create new meanings and causes the client's experience to be considered from other perspectives' (Hansen 2006: 293). This allows the client to create new symbolic connections for comprehending living, and invites the formation of new relationships to experiences that were previously problematic.

With each theoretical approach viewed as a valid narrative, but not an unequivocal and objective truth, the opportunity for an accessible and mutual language that reflects the client's and counsellor's experiencing, can be created in relationship to allow for new relating to be formed in the client's world. Relational philosophy offers a reasonable narrative to accommodate and rationalize the linguistic differences between models and as such offers a coherent and ethical platform to incorporate them within a framework (Paul et al. 1996; DeYoung 2003).

The importance of personal narrative to therapeutic identity is reflected in the growing trend for more personalized approaches to practice. In 1996, 21 per cent of BAC(P) practitioners classed themselves as integrative and in a study across random regions within the UK in 2008, that figure rose to between 30 and 50 per cent (Lapworth and Sills 2010).

Personal inclinations directly influence the choices involved in developing practice philosophy (Watkins and Scaturo 2013) with theoretical preferences heavily influenced by the personal attributes and experience of the individual. This occurs within a self-defined and consistent framework (Lapworth and Sills 2010), with each individual applying their own relational sense of self and reality onto how they conceptualize and choose the way they practise (Charlesworth 2010).

Key propositions in the development of integrative relational practice include:

- That the therapist's sense of self is central to their development.
- That theoretical freedom of choice is central to integrative development.

- The impact of personal experience is far greater in the practice of therapy than theoretical allegiance.
- That the developing practitioner is by nature dynamic and process bound, not static.

(Charlesworth 2010)

We believe that integration is particularly possible through a relational framework, as it offers a range of broad assumptions that act as the foundation for practice. Without being overly fixated on the specifics of any one vocabulary, a relational position allows the practitioner to draw upon compatible specifics across models, and develop their own practice philosophy in accordance with the following assumptions:

- Personality is formed and maintained through a complex and perpetually updating matrix of relationships to our experience of existence.
- How we relate to our experience of being forms the basis of our beliefs and subsequent behaviour.
- There are patterns and a rationale to these beliefs and behaviour, even if they are not easily apparent or self-defeating.
- The relationships we form with our existence can be safely reviewed and reorganized within an authentic and empathic therapeutic relationship.
- Both parties involved bring into the therapeutic process their own unique perspectives and contributions.
- The client's narrative is respected and is central to the process, with the use of theory being offered as informative, not definitive, in assisting the client to create a more meaningful personal narrative/self-structure.

Working relationally we aim to:

- Work within a therapeutic relationship built on trust, empathy, acceptance, and therapeutic presence.
- Identify distressing patterns of relating for the client, name them and work with them in the here and now.
- Develop a practice philosophy rooted in relational assumptions, holding the quality of the therapeutic relationship and its symbolic importance central to the process.
- Work in awareness, respond in the best interests of the client, and contribute productively to the therapeutic relationship.

We see two primary levels of relating in the therapeutic encounter: first, the *here and now* between the therapist and the client (Rowan 1983); and second, between the client and their own experience of existence. The more the therapist is able to enter into the therapeutic relationship, the more able they are to contribute productively to the therapeutic process, with responsibility for providing a useful presence resting with the practitioner and their ability to employ a *therapeutic use of self* (Clarkson 2006; Paul and Charura 2014).

Training containing diverse learning experiences plays its part in the process of developing the practitioner's ability to do this (Lapworth and Sills 2010). Through reflective practice, theoretical knowledge, and self-awareness, a process of individuation occurs, matures throughout the therapist's career, and results in a uniquely individual practice philosophy (Rowan and Jacobs 2003; Charlesworth 2010; Lapworth and Sills 2010).

Relational practice requires the therapist to track the client's (and their own) way of being in the session moment by moment, in order to respond reflexively and contribute meaningfully to the therapeutic process.

Case vignette

A woman in her early thirties came to counselling to address problems she acknowledged she had with feeling obsessive about the safety of her four-year-old son. This was expressed as a narrative embracing a number of historical factors, including more recent events regarding allowing her son to be cared for by others. She disclosed that she was aware of what she was doing, but felt unable to change. This was causing her some distress, yet simultaneously she felt this behaviour was justified.

The therapist's internal response was to recognize the immediate need of the client to be heard, and acknowledged the conflict she encountered between the competing emotions within her.

The client's initial disclosures were tentatively conceptualized into theoretical terms (DeYoung 2003) – in this case, a possibility of attachment issues immediately coming to mind.

Emotionally, the therapist also empathized with the client's feeling of being stuck and unable to reconcile her opposing feelings. This was subsequently conveyed by the therapist reflecting on his here-and-now experience of the embryonic relationship, affirming the client's reality and difficulties.

Over a period of time, historical aspects of the client's narrative presented clues to patterns of relating which emerged from childhood experiences into the present, but did so without any concrete acknowledgement of their emotional impact.

Up to this point, the relationship felt somewhat tentative, with the client guarded and uncomfortable in exploring the meanings attributed to her life experiences. The therapist explored the nature of their relationship together, reflecting on levels of trust between them and the vulnerability she felt when in relationship with others. In experiencing a consistent, trusting relationship, her reluctance to address issues of trust reduced and a willingness to accept her patterns became more prevalent.

The client now felt able to acknowledge the patterns emerging from her past and realized that her childhood living alone with her mother from the age of four mirrored her current situation as a mother herself. This led to the realization that her over-protection was in fact an attempt to avoid repeating her early experiences.

In the client experiencing a depth of trust within the therapeutic relationship, she felt able to modify her relationship to trusting others and subsequently allow herself to release her sense of anxiety when out of contact with her son.

Challenges

Working relationally places specific responsibility on the individual therapist. The therapist needs to be willing to engage in relational philosophy and participate fully in the therapeutic process. It is also imperative that the therapist has sufficient training, theoretical awareness, and personal development in order to be able to adequately develop their own individuated model of practice that is consistent and competent.

Regarding established theory as something that can be useful as a means of framing understanding but not as objective truth is a challenge, and risks being perceived as eclectic rather than a disciplined and coherent approach to practice.

Like the client, the therapist is required to reflect on their place in the therapeutic encounter, their own relational patterns and how they may impact upon it. This means that the ability to engage in reflective practice is an essential quality required of the relational practitioner, as is being able to create an authentic and genuine relationship with the client.

In developing relational practice, we consider the following three components of training crucial:

- Theory encompassing a range of approaches from which the therapist develops a pool of knowledge in line with their philosophy. We see little value in teaching single-model approaches but rather offer a range of models that reinforce principles of change (Fitzpatrick et al. 2010), which support integrative growth. The therapist will decide on their style of relational practice and develop a cohesive rationale based on reflective practice. This is individualistic integration as opposed to eclecticism.
- The relational therapist is required to self-assess, meaning that some effort is given to developing their awareness of how they relate to their world. We believe that the more the therapist knows about their own patterns of relating, the more able they will be to develop a productive therapeutic relationship with the client.
- Relational competencies: Paul and Charura (2014; after Roth and Pilling 2007) present the competencies needed for working in this model, and cover three main areas: the practical, personal, and professional.

Effectively, the *practical* area covers development and maintenance of the therapeutic relationship, including agreeing the therapeutic aim, assessment, and ability to work collaboratively. The *personal* aspect covers qualities including authenticity, empathy, and the ability to work competently in the here and now to help clients reflect on, develop, and articulate their emotions, experiences, and personal meanings. *Professionally*, ethics, knowledge, use of supervision, and commitment to ongoing personal and professional development are all qualities deemed necessary for relational practice to operate successfully.

New developments: distillation and point of contact

In the above example, relational practice involved the meeting of two unique relational perspectives interacting within a safe, therapeutic relationship. Attention was paid to personal meanings each brought into the relationship and through the therapist's use of self, the client was confirmed in their own sense of existence. For this to occur, the therapist must be willing to draw upon resources originating from their own relational framework that may be considered useful to the therapy process.

This inherently personal process may include the following:

- Awareness of personal patterns of relating, to self, others and the world
- Training, theory and skills development
- Development of the inner self-supervisor
- Use of clinical supervision
- Spirituality
- Cultural heritage
- Awareness of difference
- A range of rich life experiences

This process takes place continuously, influencing the reasoning behind individual contributions, and reflects the level of engagement necessary from the therapist within the therapeutic relationship (DeYoung 2003). We term the presentation of the factors involved in any one single exchange within the therapeutic relationship as *distillation* (Figure 8.1).

The distillation model outlines a snapshot view of the moment-by-moment interactions between client and therapist at the point where they are in contact, where contributions from both are visible, and choice of contribution and response can be processed. The intended result of which is a heightened awareness of the flow and meaning of reciprocal contributions made across the lifespan of the relationship in support of therapeutic change within the client.

The client undertakes a process of distillation themselves, prioritizing what to present in the moment in accord with their relational patterns with the therapist in the session. The challenge for the therapist here is in locating these patterns and working with this knowledge within the therapeutic relationship.

The *point of contact* process (Table 8.1) seeks to outline the role of the therapist within each dialogical interaction, illustrating a sequence of stages in each exchange, from disclosure to intervention. This reflects how each person's contribution is a result of individual distillation of their own relational phenomenology and how they impact upon each other within each moment of the therapeutic relationship.

Example: a common boundary issue

The client is continually late to sessions and apologizes profoundly to the therapist each time. This behaviour seems familiar to how the client encounters distress out of session and is expressed regularly.

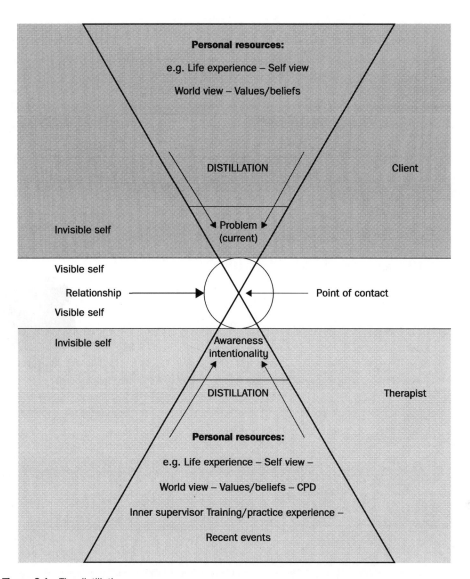

Figure 8.1 The distillation process

The therapist considers the nature of the existing therapeutic relationship, and will have distilled this here-and-now awareness into a considered response to the client. Working relationally, the therapist first considers his own reaction and immediate response to the client's presentation, before considering how to process this more functionally, based on experience, training, and therapeutic considerations distilled into awareness (Table 8.2).

Table 8.1 Point of Contact: exploration of relational process

1	2	3	4	5
Disclosure	Therapist's automatic response (reaction)	Internal therapist process (awareness)	Therapeutic consideration	Intervention
Contribution from the client	*Stimulus from client triggered in the therapist, e.g.*	*Is this useful to the therapeutic process?*	*Choice of what to contribute to the process*	*Actual contribution from the therapist at the point of contact*
Client's own personal experience Personal narrative Personal communication – own language and physicality	Emotions Theory Historical Behaviours	Intentionality? Relationship, timing, disclosure Is it happening/ repeating here and now? Between us? Anticipating the client's response	For example, reflection of feelings, use of theory, silence, Socratic questioning What next? Do I share my perception? Does awareness at this stage add to the therapeutic process?	The intervention

Table 8.2 Example of relational dynamic

1	2	3	4	5
Disclosure	Therapist's automatic response (reaction)	Internal therapist process (awareness)	Therapeutic consideration	Intervention
Client's distress – verbal and non-verbal – at being late	Irritated, aware of theoretical links to patterns from previous sessions	What sense do I make of this awareness?	What do I do from this awareness? What can I add to the therapeutic process?	Being late seems to upset you

In this example, there are several theoretical choices possible at the point of contact, all of which will live to a greater or lesser extent within the therapist's theoretical framework and be brought into play. This process will repeat itself throughout the lifespan of the therapeutic relationship and directly reflects the relational dynamic between two individual personalities meeting in order to re-evaluate and reorganize current working models of self in the client.

Summary

The concept of idiosyncratic practice has been a growing phenomenon over recent years, with increasing numbers of therapists regarding themselves as integrative (Lapworth and Sills 2010). This shift in emphasis from therapeutic technique to the personal dimension of therapy (Halgin 2006) will be reflected in the development of future training provision and founded on a growing belief that single-model approaches are limited in their suitability for treating a wide variety of client issues encountered in contemporary practice (Lampropoulos and Dixon 2007).

We believe that relational philosophy offers a working language more compatible within the mainstream mental health services, which adopt evidence-based philosophy (Larner 2011), and provides an opportunity for integrating more qualitative approaches into health care in the future.

In outlining our perception of the relational approach to psychotherapy, we have provided a comprehensive representation of the interpersonal and developmental factors involved in the activity of therapy. From common themes found across traditional approaches, relationalism has emerged as a contemporary paradigm within an increasingly integrative landscape, presenting a platform to effectively reframe established theoretical structures and develop integrative practice in a consistent and principled manner (DeYoung 2003; Lapworth and Sills 2010).

The personal qualities and characteristics of the individual practitioner involved are considered essential to the formation of individuated practice. Through the process of distillation we have accounted for how each practitioner draws upon their own unique relational resources to navigate their way through the therapeutic encounter.

In presenting this approach, we hope to empower the therapists of the future to be creative, courageous, and willing to access their own resources in entering into productive therapeutic relationships.

Further reading

DeYoung, P. (2003) *Relational Psychotherapy*. London: Routledge. This book provides a detailed exploration of relationalism in psychotherapy, building upon the fundamental concept of the self-with-other relationship and its relevance to practice.

Lapworth, P. and Sills, C. (2010) *Integration in Counselling and Psychotherapy*. London: Sage. This book offers a comprehensive examination of the issues related to integration in its many forms and their impact on practice considerations for the contemporary counsellor/psychotherapist.

Paul, S. and Charura, D. (2014) *An Introduction to the Therapeutic Relationship in Counselling and Psychotherapy*. London: Sage. This book offers an in-depth exploration of the therapeutic relationship by proposing a relational approach in psychotherapy and counselling practice.

Paul, S. and Pelham, G. (2000) A relational approach to therapy, in S. Palmer and R. Woolfe (eds.) *Integrative and Eclectic Counselling and Psychotherapy*. London: Sage. This book chapter provides a thorough analysis of the conceptual and historical components of the relational paradigm and its relationship to therapeutic practice.

References

Baker Miller, J. and Stiver, I.P. (1991) *A relational reframing of therapy*. Presented as part of the Stone Centre Colloquium Series, 5.6.91 [http://www.relationaltheory.org/pdf/previews/preview_52sc.pdf; accessed 19 August 2013].

Charlesworth, B. (2010) *Counselling/Psychotherapy and Integration – 'I did it my way': An Enquiry into the Influential Factors in Creating the Integrative Practitioner*. Leeds: Leeds Metropolitan University.

Clarkson, P. (2006) *The Therapeutic Relationship*, 2nd edn. London: Whurr.

Croteau, J.M., Talbot, D.M., Lance, T.S. and Evans, N.J. (2002) A qualitative study of the interplay between privilege and oppression, *Journal of Multicultural Counselling and Development*, 30 (4): 239–58.

DeYoung, P. (2003) *Relational Psychotherapy*. London: Routledge.

Fitzpatrick, M.R., Kovalak, A.L. and Weaver, A. (2010) How trainees develop an initial theory of practice: a process model of tentative identifications, *Counselling and Psychotherapy Research*, 10 (2): 93–102.

Friedman, M. (1988) The healing dialogue in psychotherapy, *Journal of Humanistic Psychology*, 28 (4): 19–41.

Gerhardt, S. (2004) *Why Love Matters*. Hove: Routledge.

Halgin, R.P. (2006) Thoughts about journeys to integrative psychotherapy, *Journal of Psychotherapy Integration*, 16 (1): 73–83.

Hansen, J.T. (2006) Counseling theories within a postmodernist epistemology: new roles for theories in counseling practice, *Journal of Counseling and Development*, 84 (3): 291–7.

Howard, P. (2008) Psychoanalytic psychotherapy, in S. Haugh and S. Paul (eds.) *The Therapeutic Relationship: Perspectives and Themes*. Ross-on-Wye. PCCS Books.

Kahn, M. (2001) *Between the Therapist and the Cient: The New Relationship*, revised edition. New York: Holt.

Laing, R.D. (1969) *Self and Others*. Harmondsworth: Penguin.

Lambert, M.J. (ed.) (2004) *Bergin and Garfield's Handbook of Psychotherapy and Behaviour Change*, 5th edn. New York: Wiley.

Lampropoulos, G.K. and Dixon, D.N. (2007) Psychotherapy integration in internships and counselling psychology doctoral programs, *Journal of Psychotherapy Integration*, 17: 185–208.

Lapworth, P. and Sills, C. (2010) *Integration in Counselling and Psychotherapy*. London: Sage.

Larner, G. (2011) Deconstructing theory: towards an ethical therapy, *Theory and Psychology*, 21 (6): 821–39.

Mearns, D. and Cooper, M. (2005) *Working at Relational Depth in Counselling and Psychotherapy*. London: Sage.

Mitchell, S.A. (2000) *Relationality: From Attachment to Intersubjectivity*. Hove: Routledge.

Orlinsky, D.E., Ronnestad, M.H. and Willutski, U. (2004) Fifty years of psychotherapy process-outcome research: continuity and change, in M.J. Lambert (ed.) *Bergin and*

Garfield's Handbook of Psychotherapy and Behaviour Change, 5th edn. New York: Wiley.

Paul, S. and Charura, D. (2014) *An Introduction to The Therapeutic Relationship in Counselling and Psychotherapy*. London: Sage.

Paul, S. and Haugh, S. (2008) The therapeutic relationship: background and context, in S. Haugh and S. Paul (eds.) *The Therapeutic Relationship: Perspectives and Themes*. Ross-on-Wye: PCCS Books.

Paul, S. and Pelham, G. (2000) A relational approach to therapy, in S. Palmer and R. Woolfe (eds.) *Integrative and Eclectic Counselling and Psychotherapy*. London: Sage.

Paul, S., Pelham, G. and Holmes, P. (1996) A relational model of counselling, *Counselling: Journal of the British Association of Counselling*, 7 (3): 229–31.

Pelham, G. (2008) The relational approach, in S. Haugh and S. Paul (eds.) *The Therapeutic Relationship: Perspectives and Themes*. Ross-on-Wye: PCCS Books.

Reynolds, R. (2007) How does therapy cure? The relational turn in psychotherapy, *Counselling, Psychotherapy and Health*, 3 (2): 127–50.

Roth, A.D. and Pilling, S. (2007) *The Competences Required to Deliver Effective Cognitive and Behavioural Therapy for People with Depression and with Anxiety Disorders*. London: Department of Health.

Rowan, J. (1983) *The Reality Game: A Guide to Humanistic Counselling and Therapy*. New York: Routledge.

Rowan, J. and Jacobs, M. (2003) *The Therapist's Use of Self*. Maidenhead: Open University Press.

Schmid, P.F. (2002) *Contact and Perception*. Ross-on-Wye: PCCS Books.

Stiles, W.B., Barkham, M., Twigg, E., Mellor-Clark, J. and Cooper, M. (2006) Effectiveness of cognitive-behavioural, person centred and psychodynamic therapies as practiced in the UK National Health Service settings, *Psychological Medicine*, 36: 55–66.

Wampold, B.E. (2001) *The Great Psychotherapy Debate*. Mahwah, NJ: Erlbaum.

Watkins, C.E., Jr. and Scaturo, D.J. (2013) Toward an integrative, learning-based model of psychotherapy supervision: supervisory alliance, educational interventions, and supervisee learning/relearning, *Journal of Psychotherapy Integration*, 23 (1): 75–95.

9 The opportunities, challenges, and complexities of maintaining a therapeutic relationship within the creative therapies

Pam Fisher

Introduction

This chapter presents an overview of the theoretical bases and research approaches of the creative arts therapies. Two case studies drawn from practice illustrate some of the challenges and complexities of the therapeutic relationship. A third case study introduces social/cultural perspectives. Significant emergent themes discussed are bias, risk, and inter-subjectivity. While the chapter focuses broadly on creative arts therapies, all specific examples are drawn from the author's own practice, which is as a dance movement psychotherapist. As the author's work in practice is primarily in group rather than individual therapy, there is a stronger focus on group therapy perspectives throughout.

Foundations of theory and practice

The theoretical and research bases of different modalities of creative psychotherapies

Creative arts therapies/psychotherapies present a diversity of approaches to the therapeutic relationship. Modalities within the creative arts therapies/psychotherapies are art, dance/movement, drama, music, and play. Across the creative arts therapies the underlying psychotherapeutic theoretical foundations are diverse, from modality to modality. Also, they may vary within each of them. Examples of the theoretical bases from different trainings are psychodynamic, systemic, and person-centred. In some models, these theories will be more explicitly used, whereas within the model in which I practise they are more implicit in a relational approach. However, irrespective of the model, the therapist works reflexively to integrate her understanding of any dynamic shifts that arise.

All modalities have the potential to foster the therapeutic alliance using a wide range of mediums, skills, and processes (Levine and Levine 2000; Jones 2005; Chaiklin and Wengrower 2009). This can enable a therapeutic relationship to emerge in practice in a process that may be more non-verbally that verbally based. Thus the relationship may be subtle, unspoken, and located across the sensory range.

Arguably, the one crucial underpinning theory across all creative arts therapies is that creative arts processes have the potential to foster growth and change, and/or to support a client to be at their best. Therefore, within creative arts therapies the process may be in place to support a person – to *maximize wellness* in an individual – rather than to be a *change agent*. For example, clients with a lifelong learning disability or autistic spectrum disorder would be referred to dance movement psychotherapy sessions to support them to be at their best. Thus communication, social interaction, and the ability to express emotions would be fostered within a non-verbal, creative framework. This differs from the perhaps more traditional perceived view of the purpose of talking therapies.

Across the creative arts therapies there may be more directive or non-directive approaches in practice together with eclectic or integrative theoretical perspectives. A creative arts therapist may support the emergence of playfulness so that a person can re-access earlier life stages, or in the case of a child can express non-verbally what is needed to be expressed through the medium of play (Winnicott 2001).

Research in the creative arts therapies presents challenges, in that it is located more naturally within a qualitative paradigm (Payne 1993, 2006; Grainger 1999; Higgs and Titchen 2001; Hollway and Jefferson 2002; Denzin and Lincoln 2003; McNiff 2005). Thus it may not translate into or offer the kind of measurable data that will readily support the growth of our work within health and social care settings. From a wider field, the recent work in neuroscience (Goleman 1996; LeDoux 1999; Bloom 2006; Cozolino 2006; Gerhardt 2010) has begun to unravel some of the big questions as to how and why the creative arts therapies are effective. Specifically, the identification and role of mirror neurons presents possibilities to give credence to our work. Mapping mirror neurons shows that they fire in response to stimuli; 'feel good' or empathic emotional responses can be monitored and so it may be possible to demonstrate the effects of creative arts therapies from a neuroscientific evidence base.

The validity of research that relies on qualitative data is not always accepted within health and social care contexts. There is sometimes a struggle to translate our research into forms that will be accepted and/or understood. Examples drawn from my role as a research supervisor are of dance movement psychotherapy students researching across a range that often comprises non-verbal, differently abled groups or individuals. Research may be focused on the value of a creative psychotherapeutic process in dementia care, with clients on the autistic spectrum, or those with profound and multiple learning disabilities. In each of these examples, written or verbal communication would be unlikely or impossible to contribute to research data. Research in creative arts therapies grapples with issues of bias and validity and values the depth of data that emerges from individual experiences. Our research seeks answers to deeply personal questions and examples of methodologies chosen may be narrative, case study, ethnographic – but predominantly within a qualitatively based frame.

The therapeutic relationship

The therapeutic relationship is fundamental in psychotherapy, stemming from Carl Rogers' work that developed the thinking that without such a relationship there was no possibility for change or growth to occur (Rogers 1967/1995; Kahn 1999; Haugh and Paul 2008). Thus the prime focus on development of the therapeutic relationship is as central in creative arts therapies as in other forms.

All creative arts therapies use a creative process to initiate and develop the therapeutic relationship. The process is non-directive – there are no right or wrong ways of doing things and the sounds, movements or images that may be produced are not judged. The focus is on attunement to self and other, to promote mutuality within the therapeutic relationship.

The key components to build therapeutic relationship within the model of dance movement psychotherapy that I practise are based on the core conditions of person-centred practice (Rogers 1990; Mearns and Thorne 2007). Empathy, congruence, and unconditional positive regard will be strongly present. (In creative arts therapies, empathy may be used in a non-verbal, kinaesthetic way to support the development of therapeutic relationship.) Non-directiveness, together with the Rogerian sense of prizing the individual, is strongly present in the author's practice and she witnesses this as enabling a therapeutic relationship to develop. She is saying both verbally and non-verbally to the client, 'You are fine, I see and appreciate who you are.' Empathic connection with the client is important; the feeling is of body, mind, and spirit creating a bridge between the client and self. Thus it is safe enough for her/him to find parts of self that may have been long defended or hidden to self and others.

Two case study examples now follow; one is focused on a one-to-one and the other on a group dynamic perspective. The first two examples are drawn from a dance movement psychotherapy group in the second stage of rehabilitation from alcohol/substance misuse. The clients attended a weekly dance movement psychotherapy group for up to twelve weeks as part of a structured rehabilitation programme. The group was mixed gender but the male/female ratio usually was skewed towards there being significantly more men than women.

A range of complex needs underlies the presenting 'addict' label (a term which they themselves use even though we 'professionals' might not): thus in any group anxiety, depression, eating disorders, obsessive compulsive disorder, and more may be represented (Ortman 1997). Add to this the emotional mix of anger, shame, confusion, and 'lost-ness', together with issues of broken families, perhaps probation or a custodial sentence, and a complex therapeutic environment will have been created. Issues about personal space, touch, emotional engagement, body image, and being seen or judged by their peers are familiar themes. This client group was always comprised of a wide cross-cultural mix of attendees. A discussion of the creative process/person-centred approach in practice, interventions, development, and/or management of the therapeutic relationship follows each of the case studies.

Case vignette: One-to-one therapist/client engagement within a group process

Jon was a male client, at the mid-way point of the twelve-week rehabilitation programme and was a regular attender of the dance movement psychotherapy group. He presented as an articulate, confident member of the group, using the sessions to maximum potential to explore creativity in a non-verbal frame. The majority of interactions were playful and upbeat, with requests from him for therapeutic props to support creative engagement.

Someone suggested group sculpts, a process in which individuals move into the centre of the studio to create a sculptural group shape. On this occasion music was used and clients moved seamlessly in and out of the central space so that a constantly shifting 'sculpture' was unfolding. Jon was positioned opposite the therapist and came into the centre, knelt and extended his hand, giving her direct eye contact. She went into the centre, also kneeling, and connecting her hand with his, palm to palm, holding his gaze. Her felt sense was of Jon presenting a challenge and need to be met and held. Client and therapist stayed in this connection for at least one minute; the therapist was conscious of synchrony of breath and a sense of intimacy in the shared gaze. She experienced no sense of confrontation or discomfort coming from Jon but was conscious of being very visible to the group; she felt a degree of uncertainty about this 'witnessed intimacy'.

Following the session, Jon and the therapist had a brief conversation; her uncertainty about the connection they had made led her to check with him that it had not been an unwanted or intrusive intervention. He affirmed that he had felt met and held; that he trusted the situation and recognized that he was being 'unconditionally held'. Jon then disclosed parts of his life story that illustrated and emphasized the value of this meeting and holding. Several weeks later he initiated the same connection and there was a strong, powerful sense of him owning and guiding the process.

Reflection

Approach

The approach was strongly creative, person-centred, and process based. The therapist's non-directiveness supported the group's choice to create sculpts. The approach also enabled Jon to connect with his own spontaneous response to this. He had chosen to put himself at the centre of the sculpt, and had used non-verbal signals of eye contact and openness in his posture. He was able to make the choice to do this and felt safe in doing so. There was a perceived element of challenge to the therapist, which she accepted.

Intervention

The therapist's intervention, which she recognized had an element of risk, offered spatial proximity, appropriate touch connection, and an opportunity for a mutual sense of intimacy. The risk was that she had misread the situation, that this could or would be not what Jon wanted, that he would reject the connection. If that had happened, she might have moved back gently and changed her body shaping to be less directly focused on him. The other risk was that others could perceive the intervention negatively in the group process. I suggest that this risk is always present in creative arts therapies/psychotherapy groups and other group therapy. In any creative process there is an element of risk and one has to take this risk in order for anything to happen (Yalom 1995) – but risk has to be managed and this will be revisited later in the section on *challenges*.

Development and/or management of the therapeutic relationship

The therapeutic relationship within this relatively brief time frame had been constructed using principles of dance movement psychotherapy: Chacian circle form (Levy 1995) at the start of each session, non-directiveness together with the core conditions of person-centred practice (Rogers 1990; Mearns and Thorne 2007). At this mid-way point in therapy, therapist and client had co-created mutuality and Jon was feeling 'safely held'. Congruence was a key component of the interaction and the therapist's responses were tested out by the brief conversation, which she initiated with Jon after the session. This was her way of checking and managing the outcome; had Jon given a more circumspect response, it would have been different.

Case vignette: Working with the dynamics of a group

There was only one female client in the group (in the preceding weeks there had been three women and four men) and she was quite combative towards one of the male clients. Her body shaping was predominantly low, heavy with symmetry; in contrast, the male client had a mix of light and heavy weight, expressing height and asymmetry in his movements.

The female client took control of a game with hoops, choosing to umpire it, disqualifying him straight away for 'rule violation' but did not do the same with any other group members. Later in the session when the male client asked for a creative dance wearing 'dressing up' costume, no-one supported him in this; the rest of his (male) peer group sat out so that in effect he was marginalized. But then, later in the session his peers expressed concern for him when he left the room briefly (for a trip to the WC, it transpired). Finally, in a guided relaxation at the end of the session, for the first time since this particular activity has been requested, the group created a circle rather than being scattered randomly around the room. The therapist perceived this to be an unconscious coming together into cohesion.

Reflection

Approach

It seemed that this was about allowing the group to settle and find it's own way of being (Yalom 1995). Interventions by the therapist were minimal and the focus was on safe holding with no bias towards one or another participant. Trust was needed on the part of the therapist to allow the creative process to unfold. However, the therapist's feelings within this process were not always so clear. She noticed herself wanting to defend the male client, challenge the female one, and to direct the group to 'join in' with the creative dance. Had she done so she wondered whether the outcomes would have been different?

Intervention

This case study illustrates the value of minimal or no intervention by the therapist – in other words, there *was no intervention*. The therapist was a container to hold the therapy space safely so that issues could emerge and be worked through by the clients (Chodorow 1994; Yalom 1995). However, as stated in the previous paragraph, this was, to coin a phrase, easier said than done and provided a rich seam for personal reflections.

Development and/or management of the therapeutic relationship

Having focused so strongly on the non-directive, person-centred creative process, this case study illustrates the challenges of developing and managing the therapeutic relationship in any group psychotherapy process. The harmonious, ending circle form was of the group's own doing and very different from the scattered form of previous weeks. The following week there was a sense of group camaraderie; the specific female and male client were more relaxed in each other's company. Each person within the group had been able to explore her/his position.

Wider questions that emerge from this case study (to be explored in the next section) are: How does (un)conditionality play out with a number of different energies in place? Is it possible to be truly person-centred, congruent to a diverse range of needs in a group context?

Challenges

Unconditionality

Challenges have already been identified in this chapter and the complexities of the therapeutic relationship are now discussed in more depth. Returning to the question of unconditionality, transference and countertransference certainly were being played out in each of the case study practice scenarios described and this needs to be held in awareness (Whitehouse, in Pallaro 1999; Fischman, in Chaiklin and Wengrower 2009). Creative arts therapies/psychotherapies hold the potential for a rich and daunting number of ways in which a transference (or countertransference) might arise. Ways of moving, art images being made, music or play interactions – in all of these the challenge is to integrate understanding of underlying transference and/or countertransference and to work creatively with this. The challenge and perhaps limitation to therapeutic relationship building might be to do this within what may be a predominantly non-verbal process.

Bias of perception and understanding of the inter-subjective framework within which CAPT (and arguably all forms of psychotherapy) operate is a constant challenge.

As with transference and countertransference, which closely aligns with the concept of inter-subjectivity, this may be exacerbated by the multi-faceted, multi-sensory opportunities that CAPT can offer. Thus, using the example of a play therapist, the challenge when working with a child who plays out symbolic nurturing of a doll in her therapy sessions would be not to assume obvious meanings from such graphic symbolism. In practice, a practitioner might reflect on this in the context of her clinical supervision to explore all the potential layers of meaning that might be presenting.

Congruence/person-centredness within a group context

In the modality within which I work, there is a predominance of group rather than one-to-one psychotherapy. This challenges every aspect of forging therapeutic relationships with individuals. For clients, in practice a group brings both positives and negatives: clients can and do set up peer support structures within a group but also may struggle with inter- and intra-personal dynamics. For therapists, in practice it is the same principles of openness, unconditionality, and creative process that support therapeutic relationship whether it is with one person or a group. Arguably this presents even a greater challenge than when working in therapeutic relationship with one person. However, group therapy also presents a wealth of opportunities for rich, deep therapeutic encounter, relationship, and connection.

A final point of relevance in this section is that of risk-taking. Both the above cases involved risk for client(s) and practitioner. Creative arts have the potential – for example, in art to depict feelings on paper; in dance/movement to be seen in a dance that expresses one's own emotional expression. This requires courage on the part of the client and certainty that their creative outcomes will not be judged or assessed as not good enough. Risk of judgement is heightened in a group therapy context. Thus the practitioner must create a container that feels safe (Chodorow 1994). Risk may be essential to effect change but can only occur if a safe enough environment has been created (Yalom 1995; Ringer 2002; Mearns and Thorne 2007).

Working with difference/cross-culturally

Moving now to working with cross-cultural difference, there are opportunities for CAPT to draw from an eclectic range of resources to support processes. Challenges might be to avoid the social, cultural, and ethnic stereotypes and to stay rooted in creative practice, which assumes nothing as a given for each client. Difference is not always on the surface – it may be hidden. Keen observation, awareness, and attunement are required. Empowerment of clients is critical; my offer to attempt an African style dance, which he had requested, resulted in a client shaking with laughter at my ineptitude. He was then empowered by being able to teach me how to do it better.

A brief case example now follows that demonstrates how some issues of cultural difference emerged within a group process.

Case vignette: Cultural dynamics

Every time the music played and the group were invited to improvise, to 'find their own dance', Meena turned to face the wall or the window and moved in her seamless flow of graceful, undulating movement. She appeared confident and able – she was a professional person, training as a counsellor to support her work – apparently very much western in dress, language, and custom. It was the fourth day of a five-day intensive introduction to dance movement psychotherapy. The group was standing in a circle, holding hands when Meena began to speak. She shared two things – one was that she had been brought up to believe it unseemly, shameful to be seen by anyone while dancing. This was part of her cultural heritage. The group realized that she had managed this by turning away from the group as she danced and they found this deeply moving. There was a sense that she had found her own way to transcend the cultural boundaries. The second thing Meena shared was that it was hard to stand in a circle and hold hands – as a child she had been teased about her skin colour and told that she was dirty and therefore untouchable to her peers. The acceptance of the group and her strength enabled her to break through to a place she had not been able to find before. At this point, most of the group were weeping as they realized how much harder her week had been than she had been able to say until this point.

Reflection

Approach

How could any one else in the group, peers or myself, possibly have known what Meena's internal process was? Building on all that has already been identified in this chapter, this vignette reinforces the value of a process in which nothing is assumed, where the therapeutic relationship is safe enough for an individual to explore, to take risks, and finally to articulate parts of her story.

Intervention

As in the previous case, the guiding principle here was that of there *being no intervention*. That was my 'on the surface' or, in my own language, 'front brain' thinking during each creative exploration that Meena participated in. To explain this in more general terms, as a creative arts therapist I am presenting with open-ness, empathy, and effectively giving each client the 'space' to explore, access as deeply as they need, and if necessary to take risks. That is my 'front brain' thinking mode, but on a deeper, farther back level I am assessing possibilities, noticing, and if necessary planning creative interventions that could be useful to support a client's process. It is important to have a range of therapeutic props, a range of music choices but also not to hold any assumptions about cultural and/or ethnic preferences for any client.

Arguably, when working within a creative therapy modality there is potential to maximize exploration. However, there is also the risk of pre-empting or assuming what choices a client will naturally make. For example, a colour choice or rhythm preference needs to rest with the client, not the therapist; when working with colour, using black or white may not hold the same symbolism for people of different cultural heritage.

Coming from an English sociocultural perspective (where, for example, we now have chalkboards rather than blackboards), I was aware of potential risk in the use of black, but an assumption I made early in practice about the 'non-threatening' quality of a piece of white voile fabric was swiftly dispelled by a client who said it 'reminded her of weddings', which had a very negative connotation for her, while another told me that in her culture white was the colour of mourning.

Thus every creative stimulus or intervention used within a creative process therapy model needs to be offered with awareness of its potential impact on the process, but also with the understanding that risk is integral. If the client has power and feels safe enough, they will be our guide.

Summary

The creative arts therapies/psychotherapies offer a framework and potential for practitioner and client to develop and work at the deepest level of relationship. Managing risks and maximizing potential calls for a strongly reflective approach to practice. The author's way of managing is through reflections that encompass writing, music, art, movement, role-play, playfulness, embodiment, and non-verbal peer group interaction. Using and developing these creative, reflective tools in personal practice and supervision has supported my practice. They are recommended to practitioners to provide a holding frame and ongoing deepened awareness of self and others.

Further reading

The following books will help the reader to gain a deeper understanding of the relationship in different aspects of creative and art therapies:

Jennings, S. (2011) *Healthy Attachments and Neuro-dramatic Play*. London: Jessica Kingsley.

Jones, P. (2007) *Drama as Therapy*. Hove: Routledge.

Kirklin, D. and Richardson, R. (2003) *The Healing Environment, Within and Without*. London: RCP.

Liebmann, M. (1996) *Arts Approaches to Conflict*. London: Jessica Kingsley.

Malchiodi, C.A. (2007) *Expressive Therapies*. New York: Guilford Press.

Warren, B. (2004) *Using the Creative Arts in Therapy and Healthcare*. Hove: Brunner-Routledge.

References

Bion, W.R. (2011) *Experiences in Groups and Other Papers*. Hove: Routledge.
Bloom, K. (2006) *The Embodied Self*. London: Karnac Books.

Chaiklin, S. and Wengrower, H. (2009) *The Art and Science of Dance/Movement Therapy.* Hove: Routledge.

Chodorow, J. (1994) *Dance Therapy and Depth Psychology: The Moving Imagination.* London: Routledge.

Cozolino, L. (2006) *The Neuroscience of Psychotherapy.* London: Norton.

Denzin, N.K. and Lincoln, Y.S. (2003) *Strategies of Qualitative Inquiry.* London: Sage.

Gerhardt, S. (2010) *Why Love Matters: How Affection Shapes a Baby's Brain.* Hove: Routledge.

Goleman, D. (1996) *Emotional Intelligence.* London: Bloomsbury.

Grainger, R. (1999) *Researching the Arts Therapies: A Drama Therapist's Perspective.* London: Jessica Kingsley.

Haugh, S. and Paul, S. (eds.) (2008) *The Therapeutic Relationship: Perspectives and Themes.* Ross-on-Wye: PCCS Books.

Higgs, J. and Titchen, A. (2001) *Professional Practice in Health, Education and the Creative Arts.* Oxford: Blackwell.

Hollway, W. and Jefferson, T. (2002) *Doing Qualitative Research Differently.* London: Sage.

Jones, P. (2005) *The Arts Therapies: A Revolution in Healthcare.* Hove: Routledge.

Kahn, M. (1999) *Between Therapist and Client: The New Relationship.* New York: Freeman.

LeDoux, J. (1999) *The Emotional Brain.* New York: Orion.

Levine, K. and Levine, G. (2000) *Foundations of Expressive Arts Therapy.* London: Jessica Kingsley.

Levy, F.J. (1995) *Dance and Other Expressive Art Therapies: When Words are Not Enough.* New York: Routledge.

McNiff, S. (2005) *Art-based Research.* London: Jessica Kingsley.

Mearns, D. and Thorne, B. (2007) *Person-Centred Therapy Today.* London: Sage.

Ortman, D. (1997) *The Dually Diagnosed: A Therapist's Guide to Helping the Substance Abusing, Psychologically Disturbed Patient.* Northvale, NJ: Jason Aronson.

Pallaro, P. (1999) *Authentic Movement.* London: Jessica Kingsley.

Payne, H. (1993) *Handbook of Inquiry in the Arts Therapies.* London: Jessica Kingsley.

Payne, H. (2006) *Dance Movement Therapy: Theory, Research and Practice.* Hove: Routledge.

Ringer, T.M. (2002) *Group Action.* London: Jessica Kingsley.

Rogers, C. (1990) *Client-Centred Therapy.* London: Constable.

Rogers, C. (1967/1995) *On Becoming a Person: A Therapist's View of Psychotherapy.* New York: Mariner.

Winnicott, D.W. (2001) *Playing and Reality.* Hove: Brunner-Routledge.

Yalom, I.D. (1995) *The Theory and Practice of Group Psychotherapy.* New York: Basic Books.

10 Process-based relational-centred training: preparing psychotherapy students to work at relational depth

George Bassett, Pete Lavender and Lydia Noor

Introduction

This chapter emerged out of several process meetings between the three authors in which we explored the essential common elements in our process-based relationally centred philosophy for training. At the time of writing, we were each responsible for training students at the Scarborough Counselling and Psychotherapy Training Institute (SCPTI), which is accredited by UKCP as a training and accrediting member organization. George is the course leader for the Gestalt psychotherapy training, Pete leads the relational-centred psychotherapeutic counselling course, and Lydia leads the integrative psychotherapy course; all three courses sit in the humanistic integrative tradition. In this jointly authored chapter, we aim to share how we work relationally with our students, a process which, in turn, we argue, transfers positively to their therapeutic relationships in the future.

We are united by our passionate belief in, and commitment to, relational-centred work. Relationships (be it with trainees, between trainees, between ourselves or with the outside world) are our continuing focus and concern, and these relationships can easily get tangled. Our goal is to train the students to be relationally centred practitioners equipped to engage therapeutically at depth in sensitive, attuned, and aware ways. Through our encounters in 'group process' in particular, students learn more and more about who they are in relationship, and thus prepare themselves to be with, and alongside, future clients.

How do relational-centred therapists learn and hone the skills of therapeutic presence (Clarkson 2003) and relational availability? How might students be prepared to embrace the complexities of the therapeutic relationship and of each client's uniqueness, as conveyed relationally? Group process has much to offer both the developing and qualified therapist. This process-based containing encounter gives witness, challenge, and deeper understanding of what we imagine about each other. Group process is an opportunity for what is hidden and shaming to emerge – a potentially rich opportunity to find a sense of dwelling comfortably within ourselves and a sense of belonging with others.

Although we are joined in our relational project, we each have our own unique ways of enacting and teaching our relational approach. Our differences stem both from our personal values and ways of being, and from the special concerns of our respective professional fields. In the sections that follow, we each describe our particular 'take' towards preparing students to engage effectively in therapeutic relationships. At the end of this chapter, we offer several references and suggestions of further reading for you to pursue. First, however, we outline our basic stance, which is a shared vision.

Foundations of theory and practice

Process-based relational-centred training

The SCPTI approach is both process based and relationally centred. It also embraces an implicitly relational-developmental model (Evans and Gilbert 2005). In our view of therapy, not only does the therapist pay close attention to what is conveyed in the here-and-now of the relationship, we are also curious about the potential of each expanding moment to reveal something about the there-and-then of the client's history (Yontef 1988).

From a relational-developmental perspective, the therapist steps into the therapeutic relationship with a curiosity; a willingness to be impacted and a preparedness to learn about the uniqueness of this client's relational expectations and experiences. The therapist might wonder who the client needs me to be at this moment – a holder of clear boundaries, a safe container of overwhelming sensations, a new secure base (Wallin 2007) – so that the client's previous inadequately met developmental needs can emerge. In this it is important to remember that 'stepping-in' relationally may lead potentially to a repeat of the client's history rather than provide a reparative experience (Evans and Gilbert 2005).

The therapeutic relationship: learning through training

Relational-centred counselling

In writing this course, I (Pete) drew from Rogers' humanistic person-centred model and Gestalt theory alongside transactional analysis, to form a coherent relationally centred model. This is the theoretical stance of the model with each day of our counselling training, starting with group process – the most important part of the training day in my view – followed by skills practice with some direct teaching interspersed. Group process is a time where I facilitate and encourage the students to encounter each other, share, and risk meeting at increasing relational depth (Mearns and Cooper 2005). This requires constant attention on my part to the content of what the students are saying and, more importantly, who they are saying it to. For example, I have been in many group situations over the years where participants speak out to the centre of the room focusing on the ceiling, carpet, heater or other object. As my colleague Lydia once observed to someone apparently talking to the rug, 'try looking at me instead of the rug; you won't get any empathy from the carpet!' Often group members will try to deflect by talking superficially (about something or someone outside of the room). I will draw their attention to this, and ask them to 'own' what they are saying, bringing their content into the immediacy of a relational here-and-now encounter (Wilkinson 2008).

Inevitably, this way of directing their words to an-other increases the chances of their being able to locate avoided feelings that usually go alongside this more emotionally laden way of being and relating together. To work successfully this relies on the individuals feeling safe and being willing to risk exposing their vulnerable selves, the threat of shame being an ever-present (though often unspoken) fear. My part in this process is to guide the trainees, in essence 'holding their hand' as they undo years of cultural and familial conditioning allowing them to show each other (and me) who they really are.

As course leader, I am in relationship with all of my students, one which the test of time has demonstrated can endure over many years; not just the duration of the course. I am also the recipient of many powerful projections (Clarkson 2004) from the group members, both powerfully positive and powerfully negative. I see my job as being to allow these projections to manifest, and to encourage their development, enabling both myself and the trainees to gain an understanding of how they have learnt to be in relationship, and also (often) what their relational-developmental needs are. For example, projecting a kindly father (or grandfather) figure onto me may be showing that the student needs to repair a relational deficit with their own father/grandfather. (Projection is no respecter of gender; I have been someone's mother/grandmother on many occasions.) Equally, there may be a subconscious need to view me negatively, as an authoritarian or adversarial figure, again to work through an archaic, unfinished relationship.

Once the students have been together for a number of months, and their ability to 'trust the process' has been affirmed, they are able to relate to each other in a very immediate, intimate 'present-centred' way, without archaic learned ways of being getting in the way (Delisle 2011). They are then increasingly able to take this ability of relating in, to, and with the present, rather than their history, into their client work, enabling them to be 'relationally centred' in their approach.

It is vital to hold in mind that group process is about here-and-now experience (Yontef 1988) not simply superficial inquiry. Asking of another student 'how are you today?' will result in a challenge from the tutor (or, even better, from another student), with the suggestion that they ask what it is they really want to know. During group process, the students' relational-past often gets triggered as they recreate their history in their present relationships. This provides 'fuel' for the skills practice part of the day.

Skills practice takes place over two sessions, first in small groups of between three and five students, where (from the first day of training) they take turns to be therapist and client with the other(s) acting as supportive witness/observer(s). The therapeutic relationship is thus foregrounded from the beginning. Some trainees have previously had training in counselling skills elsewhere and are used to role-playing counsellor and client on 'invented' issues. However, on arriving at SCPTI they are often shocked to find that they are expected to work 'live' on their own baggage and deal with current issues triggered by group process. Once again, the potential for shame to manifest in the client/student is enormous because they are being observed not only by tutors, but also their peers. Following this exercise (and a sorely needed tea-break), the skills practice continues in the full group with the students again working as client and therapist – this time volunteering themselves to take the 'hot seat'. This now takes place with the whole group watching and giving feedback, magnifying the anxiety of the new recruits (and some not-so-new), and increasing the potential for shame and exposure.

Having experienced (too often) teaching 'by humiliation' during my schooling in the 1970s and 1980s, I hold in my awareness that for many adults returning to learning brings with it a fear that they might be revisiting their first experience of public shaming; usually at the hands of thoughtless teachers. I emphasize with any prospective trainees that my teaching style is based upon my intent to communicate in a non-shaming manner (Klein 2010). It is also crucial that group members respect each other's confidentiality, and treat other's personal material with the same respect they would like to see accorded their own. It has to be acknowledged, however, that it is impossible to eliminate shame altogether (and neither would I want to, 'healthy shame' has a useful place in our emotional palette).

Over the years, I have been teaching this course I have noticed that what emerges in group process often reflects the taught theoretical content of the module – even when the students don't know in advance what that might be. It's as if the planned content is already 'in the air' and somehow becomes figural.

Beyond the specific teaching/learning content, the focus is always on the relational process. In our profession, I hear the word 'process' used frequently ('trust the process', 'it's your process', 'parallel process', and 'we need to process' being just a few examples). However, when I decided (for this chapter) to research its meaning, I could find very little written. I noticed some time ago that in nearly every instance the word 'process' could be replaced with 'relate' or 'relationship'; when we talk about process are we in reality talking about (being in) relationship? Thus the examples above become 'trust the relationship', 'it's how you relate', 'parallel relationship', and 'we need to relate'.

My dream is to see this psychotherapeutic, relational-centred counselling course become completely 'process based'. I envisage our day being spent processing [relating], with the tutor pausing the process at intervals to expound the theory of what is occurring in the student's relationships in the room right now – what better way to grasp the link between theory and practice using the immediacy of the here-and-now process? It would be easy to build the skills practice component into this revised model, again by pausing and inviting individuals to work as client and therapist to gain deeper insight into their emotional baggage. I suspect this will remain a dream for some time yet, but I live in hope; hope that more research and writing specifically on 'process' will back up my belief.

Integrative perspective

As I (Lydia) begin to write my section of this chapter, I am momentarily back in the training room with vivid memories of myself as a trainee. The many challenging, demanding, and rewarding moments of group process are at the forefront of my thoughts and feelings. During my own training, there were times when I wanted to run away, where I felt indignant about other people's projections onto me, when my own shame was activated almost, but not quite, beyond a tolerable level. It is through the group process aspect of my training that I learnt most about myself in relationship to others. This was the deepest learning for me and it is this awareness that I bring to my work with clients and to my role as leader of the integrative psychotherapy course. And my personal journey continues, as my co-trainer and I hold the space for our trainees to spend one and a half hours each training day engaged in group process.

Group process is demanding, as we explore what we co-create in the 'between' of our relationships, when we respond in the here-and-now (Yontef 1988) of our meeting. When a group of people invest in 'being' together, with the sole purpose of relating, histories can collide. But group process offers the opportunity to increase our awareness of what we bring of ourselves and our own process to this relational space. We engage the discomfort of hearing about ourselves which we might prefer to shy away from – knowing our impact on others when we dominate, stay hidden, appear critical, lack empathy or are too overwhelming. Equally, it may come as an uncomfortable surprise to hear that in our difference we are welcome, interesting, exciting or worthy of someone's attention. This increased awareness, whether uncomfortable or joyous, is fuel for our individual therapy, as we explore and integrate our own history.

To be relationally present for our clients, we need to know the difficulties and gifts we bring to this singular task of relating. What might emerge in group process could be our desire to escape, our need to deflect, our boredom, jealousy or resistance to someone's narrative. We might also learn what is appreciated, loveable or delightful about ourselves and those around us. We learn what we can and cannot tolerate. Here we can test our sense of safety, reshape our boundaries, and find out what is needed from the environment in order to allow the shamed, previously unwelcome parts of ourselves, to emerge.

Learning about the therapeutic relationship through experiential group process

The relational-developmental model (Evans and Gilbert 2005) I embrace requires that the therapist commits to the uncertainty of the co-created relationship between therapist and client and, in doing so, is open to the client's potential transferences (Clarkson 2003) and projections. Although our intention is to provide a developmentally needed reparative relationship (Clarkson 2003), the client may feel that what we offer is a repeat of an unhealthy dimension of their history. Unwittingly, we may become the parent who does not allow enough autonomy, is too over-nurturing or does not welcome anger. We might become relationally tangled with the client who presents with the all too familiar personality style, similar caustic tongue or parallel fragility of our own parent. The therapists who know the pitfalls of these relational inductions are better equipped for their work.

This response to relational process that repeats and repairs is the very stuff of group process. As we sit with each other in the training group, with our attention engaged in the process 'between', we encounter the transferences that we induce (Clarkson 2003) and the projections that come our way. We learn what we might similarly search for in others and what we also project. The request towards us, or from us, may come from an adversarial stance or from a desire to merge or idealize (Clarkson 2003). One person may find us nourishing and responsively attuned (Stern 1998), whereas another experiences us as toxic. We learn about the wide assortment of responses to parts of ourselves with which we are familiar, and are challenged to expand our awareness to other less immediate aspects. How can we sit with clients and create a field in which they can, for example, voice their fears, move towards greater autonomy or tolerate difference, if we do not know this for ourselves?

A frequent pattern of relating, triggered in group process, and certainly played out in the therapy room, is one of Rescuer and Persecutor in response to a perceived Victim (Widdowson 2010). If we are to be authentically present in the therapeutic relationship, it is essential we know these positions within ourselves. We need to know and explore the times when we feel drawn to persecute, as if joining a gang in the school playground, and when we are not offered the seductive warmth of the Rescuer, but instead encouraged to find our own power, not sink into helplessness. Knowing these tugs and demands makes us better equipped for the therapy room. We learn these in group process.

It is not the intention of group process to be a shaming environment; quite the reverse. However, it is a context where, initially, we might hide parts of ourselves that have not been welcomed by those on whom we were dependent for care (Evans and Gilbert 2005). Perhaps we have been deemed too quiet, too watchful, too loud, too demanding, too bossy, too much or too little. Maybe our developmental needs (Kahn 1997; Clarkson 2003) could not be met by an overwhelmed, depressed or angry caregiver. These early experiences create our relational expectation – they teach us how to adapt in order to have some semblance of safety and belonging. They are played out in group process and are within our client–therapist relationships.

Perhaps, in the face of others, we feel ourselves to be wrong in our anger, distress, hurt, jealousy, and anxiety, or even exuberance, joy or pleasure. The wholeness of who we are may feel too big, too dangerous and the biggest relational challenge may be the shame of asking for something new and reparative in the here-and-now (Yontef 1988) of group process. It is much more familiar and comfortable to keep repeating our old scripts and behaviours. We know these. They are predictable and have served us well. Our clients know this too.

So here in group process is the invitation to bring into relationship the parts of ourselves that we find shaming – the untold fears and secrets, a fear of feeling forgotten, of needing to fight to make contact, of just not knowing how to make an impact, of our longing to belong, our protest. Here is the opportunity to reveal that which we may not have fully told ourselves, let alone another, and alongside this richness of experience is to know equally that we can survive the disappointment of what is not possible in the time and relationships that are available.

Teaching about the relationship from a Gestalt relational perspective

In approaching the question of which four concepts are most figural for me in my approach to training and therapy, my brain goes into meltdown. Everything I (George) reflect upon is interconnected. No one part of the field is separate from the rest; the whole is greater than the sum of its parts. An impasse ensues. Tension builds; inwards, then outwards . . . a breakthrough – a solution emerges; an answer appears – field theory! I feel suddenly enthusiastic and ready to embrace my project . . .

In this section, I explain the nature of my vision for my relational Gestalt psychotherapy training course through four key concepts stemming from Gestalt theory: field theory, dialogic contact, inclusion and presence, story and story structure. Each of these can be similarly applied to our therapeutic relationships.

Field theory is a *gestalt* notion derived from the work of Kurt Lewin (1938) and other Gestalt psychologists (Kohler 1930; Koffka 1935). We are our others. Experience is co-created and in the moment-to-moment engagement, we are a part of the mutually influencing and interacting forces that constitute our life space. We are not separate entities bouncing off of each other, trapped in a cosmic pinball game. While many people behave as if getting the highest score is the ultimate goal, the playing, and the game itself, is what is most important.

Any relationship is the ultimate combination of You and I, and it is how we play the game of relationship that really matters. In the training context, our relational experience together – where we bring our unique sense of self to the encounter of group process – offers a myriad of possibilities for contact. In gestalt terms, that contact is dialogic (Hycner and Jacobs 1995). It strives towards the true meeting of two (or more) human beings, appreciating and acknowledging our similarities and our differences within the psychosocial cultural encounter of the training experience. As a trainer, I seek to raise awareness of, and support, the deepening recognition that growth is co-created in the space between us. Furthermore, I believe it is the ebb-and-flow of our meeting that reveals our patterning of relationship. In turn, these patterns reveal our culture, our history, our memories, our learning, and our choices/adaptations of how best to be in the world.

The commitment towards truthful contact, while being mindful of trainees' level of growth and internal self-support, is paramount. Expressing what is really being felt/experienced can lead to sometimes vibrant and sometimes not always enjoyable experiences, for both parties. At such times the trainer is 'barefoot in the park', offering their human-ness, vulnerability, and sometimes their 'not so nice' sides for growth and change. This is particularly pertinent when the 'contact functions' and character style of the trainees' evoke/induce responses in the other that serves to repeat 'fixed gestalts'.

The process of how this contact is achieved leads me to the third concept that underpins my relational approach: the balance of inclusion, presence, and confirmation (Hycner and Jacobs 1995). This is the process of entering empathically into another's world while holding on to oneself. Extended expression of trainees' recalled and lived experience (including the lived-out patterns/fixed gestalts, or enduring relational themes in the training relationships) is encouraged and becomes the focal point of reflection. Through phenomenological enquiry, the 'what-and-the-how' of relationship between the person and their environment become evident. The environment in this case contains the real, as well as imagined, 'other' of the trainer/group member. Raising the trainees' awareness of the dynamics inherent in relationship, often through experimentation to stretch their growing edge (increasing a capacity for new behaviours) and to complete unfinished business, offers a model for skills to take into their therapeutic work.

Counterpoint to inclusion is my commitment as trainer to offer, judiciously, and with sensitive timing, the kind of contact that will enable growth of the trainees' emerging sense of self within the crucible of the group dynamic through presence. Presence, within this framework, involves my active/authentic involvement with trainees while opening to them. My role is to bear witness to how trainees experience the behaviour of each other and encourage new ways to engage. This also challenges me, as trainer, to hear how I am experienced and together we negotiate the uniqueness of our relationship.

As a Gestalt therapist who totally believes in the transformative power of creativity and the performing arts, and the universal container of story (I am also a drama therapist, actor, and performance storyteller), I also draw on the notion of story and story structure (Yorke 2013). Training is focused on raising awareness of the dramatic scene that is being created between us and to reflect upon its origins within our life story. This may be a process that emanates from the trainee's past, or indeed my own.

Once insight is gained by both parties, the relational task is then to explore what the 'missing scene' is – that is, what the trainee needed from the other but the need was never met, or in retrospect what they needed to do differently, and then find ways to support the trainee in completing that need. In Joseph Campbell's (1949) extensive writing and research on myth, and his development of the idea of the monomyth (a meta-story), there will always be a 'Call to Adventure'. In story structure this call is often viewed as an 'Inciting Incident', where something happens that propels us forward, challenges us to change our life. Whether this is loss, negative events within relationships, or abuse in all its many forms, it is time to do something different. We enter a new space (therapy) and meet a helper (the therapist), we go into the forest (the therapeutic journey) and encounter adversaries and challenges (internalized oppressors both real and imagined). Striving for victory (experiencing oneself in new ways) and willing to risk defeat (turning away from the challenge), we claim our 'prize' and return to our lives with insight, wisdom, and strength.

Intrinsic to both story structure and the framework of the monomyth are, as I see it, the philosophical and theoretical position of enquiry into the client's/trainee's awareness and understanding of their stance or 'bottom line' in terms of their values and principles in life. Such an enquiry encourages a therapeutic focus upon their intentional states (White 2007) in their actions – what they are trying to achieve, in their behaviour that expresses the essence of what they hold dear. By extension, this engagement models what they may offer to their clients.

While this description may reflect similarities with therapeutic practice, the emphasis in training is upon the learning that can be gained by the trainees from the experience. By my modelling as well as teaching the relational theory and process-based skills for therapeutic work, the trainees are immersed in the Gestalt approach, and are able to respond reflexively (Finlay and Evans 2009) and reflectively to the moment-by-moment encounter with another human being.

Summary

In this chapter, we have sought to present our vision of group process as an essential element of relationally based training and suggest that this approach enables neophyte therapists to work at relational depth with their clients. Inevitably, our approaches with regard to the three courses are different, as a result of the unique stamp of each trainer. But we are joined in an overarching philosophy, committed to a relational-developmental process-based way of working, and through this philosophy attention is paid to what we all convey relationally, as we engage in the reparation of past developmental deficits.

There are many facets of psychotherapy training that play a part in preparing us for what awaits us in the therapy room. Group process is the key in our relational-developmental model of therapy on which the SCPTI training is based. The challenge and containment of group process asks us to bring more and more of who we are into relationship and increasingly experience the comfort of being our authentic selves.

This grounds us for the work with clients and gives us the skills and awareness to create a therapeutic relationship within which each client's unique journey can unfold. We cannot expect, nor will our clients allow us, to walk with them to places that we have not been ourselves. Group process allows us to travel to many places, with witnesses that have our wellbeing at heart.

In this chapter, we have focused on the centrality of group process as an experiential training method, and have stressed the importance of living and breathing the experience of what occurs between the trainer and trainee as a means of knowing many of the dimensions that are mirrored in the space between the therapist and client. In the between of group process, all lived experience unfolds as is available in the here-and-now.

Further reading

Clarkson, P. (2003) *The Therapeutic Relationship*, 2nd edn. London: Whurr. The relational-developmental model at SCPTI grows out of Clarkson's five-relationship model, and thus this book is a core text for each of our three courses.

Erskine, R., Moursund, J. and Trautmann, R. (1999) *Beyond Empathy: A Therapy of Contact-in-Relationship*. Philadelphia, PA: Brunner/Mazel. The authors explore, both theoretically and through numerous clinical examples, how a compassionate and reparative therapeutic relationship can offer sufficient relational safety for the client's development needs to emerge and, potentially, be met.

Finlay, L. and Evans, K. (Pending) An invitation to engage in relational-centred phenomenological research, in P. Brownell and J. Melnick (eds.) *The Challenge of Creating a Research Tradition for Gestalt Therapy: The Research Conference, 2013*. CreateSpace Publications. This book chapter demonstrates how the combined presence and skills of the relationally centred therapist can be utilized in research.

References

Campbell, J. (1949) *The Hero with a Thousand Faces*. Novato, CA: New World Library.

Clarkson, P. (2003) *The Therapeutic Relationship*, 2nd edn. London: Whurr.

Clarkson, P. (2004) *Gestalt Counselling in Action*, 3rd edn. London: Sage.

Delisle, G. (2011) *Personality Pathology: Developmental Perspectives*. London: Karnac Books.

Evans, K. and Gilbert, M. (2005) *An Introduction to Integrative Psychotherapy*. Basingstoke: Palgrave Macmillan.

Finlay, L. and Evans, K. (eds.) (2009) *Relational-centred Research for Psychotherapists: Exploring Meanings and Experience*. Chichester: Wiley-Blackwell.

Hycner, R. and Jacobs, L. (1995) *The Healing Relationship in Gestalt Therapy: A Dialogic Self Psychology Approach*. Gouldsboro, ME: Gestalt Journal Press.

Kahn, M. (1997) *Between Therapist and Client*. New York: Henry Holt.

Klein, R. (2010) *On Becoming a Psychotherapist: The Personal and Professional Journey*. Oxford: Oxford University Press.

Koffka, K. (1935) *Principles of Gestalt Psychology*. London: Kegan, Paul, Trench, Trubner.

Kohler, W. (1930) *Gestalt Psychology*. London: Bell.

Lewin, K. (1938) Will and need, in W. Ellis (ed.) *A Source Book of Gestalt Psychology*. London: Routledge and Kegan Paul.

Mearns, D. and Cooper, M. (2005) *Working at Relational Depth in Counselling and Psychotherapy*. London: Sage.

Stern, D. (1998) *The Interpersonal World of the Infant*. London: Karnac Books.

Wallin, D. (2007) *Attachment in Psychotherapy*. New York: Guilford Press.

White, M. (2007) *Maps of Narrative Practice*. New York: W.W. Norton.

Widdowson, M. (2010) *Transactional Analysis: 100 Key Points and Techniques*. London: Routledge.

Wilkinson, H. (2008) *The Muse as Therapist: A New Poetic Paradigm for Psychotherapy*. London: Karnac Books.

Yontef, G. (1988) *Awareness, Dialogue and Process*. Gouldsboro, ME: Gestalt Journal Press.

Yorke, J. (2013) *Into the Woods*. London: Penguin.

11 Dimensions of the coaching relationship

Geoff Pelham

Introduction

The word 'coach' has its origins in the fifteenth century, from the small Hungarian town of Kocs, which became famous for producing a small light vehicle for travelling, commonly called a 'coach'. These origins provide a lovely metaphor for the essence of coaching: enabling someone to journey from one place to another; a 'vehicle' for travelling to a self-chosen destination.

Sport coaching has a long history and provides a vital context and resource for all forms of coaching. However, the form of coaching that is the focus of this chapter is commonly called life, business or organizational coaching, where the focus is on improving performance in a personal or work setting. This form of coaching has appeared on the scene much more recently, during the 1990s, though it has expanded hugely in its short history, such that as an approach to management and leadership it is now embedded in the majority of large national and multinational organizations. Indeed, it's fair to say that it is the 'corporate' interest in coaching that has made it so successful and popular while also shaping many of its practices.

There is a challenge in writing about 'the coaching relationship' because there is an implication that there is one integrated approach that can be laid out, which is not the case. Coaching draws on a number of traditions, such as clinical and occupational psychology, organizational development, and theories of leadership and management. However, having acknowledged the significance of other traditions, therapy has had a huge impact on coaching. For example, in any book that provides an overview of coaching (e.g. O'Connor and Lages 2007; Cox et al. 2010), you will find approaches that have their origins in therapy: cognitive behavioural therapy, person-centred therapy, transactional analysis, psychodynamic, and so on. Also, practitioners from therapeutic backgrounds have had a major impact on the formation of the coaching profession. For example, recently all the main professional bodies agreed that supervision is a requirement for ethical practice – something that was initially seen as unnecessary by many practitioners from non-therapeutic backgrounds.

Foundations of theory and practice

Given that there are many approaches to coaching, most agree that Timothy Gallwey's (1974) book, *The Inner Game of Tennis*, is a founding text. Gallwey was a sports coach and also involved with the Esalen Institute, the home of the human potential movement and humanistic psychology. He was a tennis coach for Werner Erhard, the founder of EST. In his book, Gallwey said the player has two opponents, the person on the other side of the net and the opponent 'in their head', and the latter is often the most significant. The 'inner game' refers to the psychological processes that affect performance. Drawing upon the fundamental paradigm of humanistic approaches, Gallwey argued that the mind has two aspects, which he called self 1 and self 2. Self 2 is the natural self, which can be trusted, acts spontaneously, creatively and skilfully, and is the source of high performance in sport. Self 1 is the critical, judgemental inner voice that is often present, undermining Self 2 confidence and performance. Gallwey (1974) captured all this in his formula 'performance equals potential minus interference' $(p = P - I)$. His coaching approach was to quieten Self 1 to enable Self 2 to more fully express itself and thereby enhance performance.

Gallwey's ideas were brought to the UK and Europe in the 1990s by John Whitmore, a former racing driver and pioneer of business coaching. His *Coaching for Performance* (Whitmore 2002) is probably the most widely read book on coaching, and the model he presents, GROW (Goal, Reality, Options, Wrap-up), the most widely used model.

The relationship

It will be useful in our discussion of the coaching relationship to present a 'case study' to more concretely grasp what is involved. The example is written to illustrate some of the basic features of coaching. The situation can, however, be more complex than laid out below, and I shall introduce some more of that complexity in the 'Challenges' section that follows.

Case vignette

I receive a call from an inner-city Academy that would like me to provide coaching for one of their staff. The school has seen significant improvements over the past years, but are under considerable pressure to meet government targets for A–C GCSE grades in English and maths. Failure to meet these targets could have a catastrophic consequence for the school and particularly the senior leadership team. The maths department in particular has been a concern and a new head of department has been appointed, as an internal promotion within the school. It is this newly appointed head of department who has been offered coaching to support her in this very challenging, pressured role.

Claire is a well-respected, hard-working specialist in maths and an excellent teacher, and has risen through the department on this basis. She hasn't had a great deal of experience in management and leadership, and the coaching is focused on helping her make this step. Her way of managing, since taking on the role, has been doing what she knows best as an expert in her subject, getting more and more involved in the detail of colleagues' work but in the process becoming overworked, stressed, and creating resentment in colleagues who feel that she does not quite trust them and is micromanaging instead.

> *Claire is quite a reserved person but in our first session she opens up more and speaks in a feelingful way about her lack of confidence in her new role and her fear that she will be a failure and let the school down. She is quite critical of colleagues and does not trust them to do a good job but at the same time recognizes that she's not a 'people person', so her way of dealing with problems and managing her own anxieties is to do the work herself rather than enabling others. She also struggles somewhat with the community the school serves. Her own background is white middle-class whereas the community is ethnically very mixed, with a high percentage of children on free school meals. In particular, she is concerned about the presence and impact of children from families from Eastern Europe who have recently moved into the area. There is considerable prejudice in the community against these recent arrivals, and that prejudice is apparent in the school too. She has the added anxiety that these children often have a poor grasp of English, which impacts their learning and so threaten her GCSE results.*

As in any professional relationship, building trust is fundamental, so in our first session I check with Claire that she wants to engage in coaching (that she is not coming because she has been 'sent' by her manager); once clear about that, we contract around confidentiality, number of session, place to meet, etc. I also take time to ensure she has an understanding of coaching, particularly that it is about her finding her own way forward: I'll not be offering advice or guidance. You have probably noticed that the motivation for the coaching is not primarily personal as it might be in therapy, but about her performance in her key role in an organization. Although the context frames the agenda, I contract with Claire about her specific agenda, what she would like to get out of the six two-hour sessions we have agreed to.

She wants to talk first about her style of leadership. She knows she is too 'hands-on', interfering, and takes responsibility for others' work, and in our conversation comes to realize it is her anxiety that drives her current behaviour: she fears they won't do the job properly and results will suffer. She realizes her strengths as a specialist in maths and an excellent teacher have got her to her current position but have become a trap when something new is needed. In our discussion she comes to realize that leadership is around influencing others and she wishes to do so to help colleagues develop their own personal and professional capability.

My background in therapy is helpful in the work we do together as I help her explore:

- her 'relationship with herself', i.e. her anxiety and how her current behaviour defends against it;
- her relationship with others, i.e. her repeating patterns of behaviour and how these interfere with the leadership style she wishes to adopt;
- her relationship with me – the transference – as she treats me as the expert whom she wants answers from;
- her relationship with the organization – how the culture and pressure of the organization permeate her thinking, feeling and behaviour, and relations throughout the school;

- how she can prepare for and try out new behaviours that align with her emerging view of leadership (e.g. 'ask not tell' to help colleagues think things through for themselves).

We also talk through her concerns about the recent arrivals in her classes from Eastern Europe. We realize together that there is a pervasive prejudice against this community nationally (in politics, in the newspapers) and locally, and that the children and parents have a different cultural background and are likely to be struggling in the new and often hostile environment, where even speaking the language can be a barrier. We explore the issue from the perspective of her *leadership* – how is she going to influence the situation? I invite her to connect with her fundamental values, beliefs, and ethics to grasp hold of her vision for these children and she realizes she wants to ensure they get the best possible education, and this is more important than meeting targets imposed by government. We explore what needs to happen to implement her vision, beginning with her own prejudices and anxieties, and then how she can work with the senior leadership team to explicitly address the prejudice in the school and the wider community.

Challenges

This account of working with Claire will, I hope, give a flavour of a coaching approach. Coaching can, however, be more complicated, primarily because it usually takes place within an organizational setting, which throws up significant relational challenges. To illustrate this, I will retell the story with some additional common challenges included.

Who is the client and whose agenda is it?

In therapy, it is obvious who the client is and whose agenda to address – it's the person you meet in the session. In coaching, it's not so clear because the sponsor for the coaching is the organization: they are paying for it, and often they want to have a say in what the coaching is about. There are three parties involved: the coach, the organization, and the person being coached.

In our example, the school invited me to coach Claire but left it to Claire to decide upon what to talk about, and our conversation remained confidential. It is common practice in organizations, however, for the sponsor of coaching to take a view of what the coaching is to be about and to be updated about how it's going. Indeed, the sponsor is likely to want to set up some way of evaluating the effectiveness of the coaching.

So who is the client, the person being coached or the sponsor? People from a therapeutic background are mostly likely to say the client has to be the person being coached. For the coaching to be effective, the client has to be fully involved with the process and have ownership of the coaching agenda. Any sense that the coach is primarily serving the needs of the organization will fatally undermine trust and be ethically dubious. On the other hand, people from an organizational background are more likely to argue that the client is the organization. It is the organization that is paying for the coaching, and the coaching is only taking place because of the organizational relevance of the agenda. People argue passionately for both positions, each with good reason. No doubt you'd like an answer to this question, but there is no definitive answer; rather, we have to work with the tension that is always present. This question, however, is fundamental to the coaching relationship and it generates a tension throughout the work that can surface in many ways.

What actually happens in practice? How does the coach manage the triangular relationship? Good practice is three-way contracting, where the sponsor, the person to be coached, and the coach meet together to agree the coaching agenda (I'm simplifying matters here somewhat – in reality, there may be more parties who have a stake in the work). Ideally, all parties come to an agreement about the coaching agenda and other important issues such as confidentiality and arrangements for reporting back to the organization progress and outcomes of the sessions. This can work well and be a good basis for the subsequent coaching. I say 'ideally' because the process is often much more messy than the ideal. It may not be possible to get the three parties in the room together, or the sponsor and coachee may not be entirely candid and may later seek to privately tell the coach what they really believe. For example, Claire might say that she does not trust her manager, that her so-called difficulties are the result of poor leadership above her, and she only agreed the agenda because it was 'politically' risky not to do so. What's more, her true intention is to leave the school at the end of the year. The coach has the challenge of acting with integrity and ethically managing the various tensions between all parties with a stake in the coaching.

Gathering 'data' for the coaching

In therapy, it is normal practice for the therapist to work with the client on the basis of what the client brings into the room: we work with the client's 'story', their account of events. In coaching, it is normal practice to seek other sources of information about the client so that the coaching is not based only on the coachee's account of the situation. For example, it is common practice to use 360-degree assessment tools (e.g. around leadership capability or emotional intelligence) to provide feedback from people who are involved with the coachee and can give a view as to how they perform in their role. Or the process may be less formal. For example, the coach may meet with some of the coachee's key colleagues, to get feedback on their experience of the coachee in relation to the coaching agenda. The coach would then report back to the coachee on what colleagues have said, probably in an anonymized thematic way rather than comments attributed to individuals.

In our example, it might be that I agree with Claire that I would speak informally to key people she is involved with (more senior colleagues, people she manages, peers, other members of staff, maybe members of the governing body), explaining I am working with Claire to support her development in her role, and have a discussion around questions and topics agreed beforehand with Claire.

The additional perspectives gained from other sources about the coachee can be very valuable and help set the context and direction of the work. For example, emotional intelligence 360s often demonstrate that senior people in organizations are very good at driving performance and strategic thinking but less good at the 'soft skills' of relationship building such as empathy. It is these latter capabilities that are more and more prized in organizations, as they seek to increase the quality of leadership. It can come as quite a surprise to the coachee to hear the consistent messages coming back from people they work with, and this can often be a prompt for self-reflection and help form the coaching agenda.

While a source of valuable information, such 'data gathering' can have a significant impact on the coaching relationship, so it is a process that has to be carefully managed. The coach will normally receive the feedback from assessment tools before the coachee so that they are ready to take the coachee through the results. The coach can feel themselves to be in the role of a quasi-expert, the deliverer of the information, and likely to find themselves thinking beforehand about how to manage the feedback, particularly if there are some difficult messages for the coachee. Though anonymized, the coachee often has a good idea of who said what about them, and this can have an impact on the conversation that follows.

The challenge can be even greater if the coach has used the less formal process of asking colleagues about the coachee. Inevitably, the coach will hear a great deal about the coachee, their relationships with people, and probably a lot of other background about the organization. It is likely there will be a variety of views, often conflicting and the coach then has to decide how to feed all this back to the coachee. The process of interviewing these people will have an impact on how the coach views the coachee, as well as the coachee's colleagues and the organization. We cannot 'unhear' what we have heard and this will impact on the relationship with the coachee. So, in our example, I might hear a consistent theme that colleagues find Claire critical, that she has her 'favourites', and is out of her depth as a head of department. What do I do with such information? From Claire's side she is likely to be wondering about what I've heard, what else I may have heard that I'm not saying, whether I'm still 'on her side' or not.

Managing multiple boundaries

Therapists take boundary management very seriously and for good reason. The very possibility of effective work is rooted in the provision of a safe, confidential space, speaking to a person who has no relationship with others involved in the work, and no personal or professional interests other than the wellbeing of the client and the effectiveness of the work they do together. The therapist has a sense of 'where things begin and end' in that they work on what the client brings into the session; mostly they are not being affected by information from sources outside the therapeutic relationship.

Coaching can be very different: typically coaches are involved in a web (sometimes a very tangled web) of relationships that extend beyond the relationship with the coachee, and this can create some of the greatest challenges for the coach, the coachee, and the coaching relationship. I have already indicated some of these boundary issues; indeed, the discussions above about 'who is the client', the coaching agenda, and 'data' gathering are all, at heart, issues of boundaries and boundary management. But the situations described so far are just a foretaste of some of the boundary issues that are likely to be encountered.

The main 'clients' for coaches are organizations and once commissioned it is likely that the coach will be invited to work with more than one person in the organization. It is common practice for a coach to be asked to work with a number of people in the same organization, people who often know and work with each other. In our example, it may be that I am already coaching the head teacher and other members of the senior leadership team.

Take a moment to consider the implications of such a situation; the kind of issues and dynamics it creates. Here are some of them:

- What do I do with the information I am hearing about Claire from Jayne, the head teacher and Fiona, head of the English department, both of whom I am also coaching? Indeed, as they work in the same team, each will frequently refer to the other and have their own particular views on the shared work they are doing together. I am likely to hear information about what is going on that Claire has not told me. Perhaps even more problematic, I may hear things about Claire and her role that Claire does not yet know – perhaps the head teacher has more doubts about her than she has openly expressed and is actively considering replacing her. How do I manage all of this? I'm quite likely to lose a sense of 'where things begin and end': who told me what; did Claire tell me that or did someone else? What do I do with information that is pertinent to my work with Claire, but I heard it from Fiona and cannot share it with Claire without breaking confidentiality with Fiona?
- The people in the team know I am coaching their colleagues. How does this affect the work we are doing? Those from a therapeutic background will immediately see the kind of dynamics, conscious and unconscious, such a situation is likely to evoke. What have others been saying about me? Who do you believe – me or them? Who is the favourite? Whose side are you on? I have found myself wondering about the ways I am 'used' as a conduit for sending messages to others. For example, Claire knows I'll be coaching Jayne later that same day and we are talking about her relationship with Jayne. I find myself wondering after the session whether, perhaps unconsciously, perhaps not, Claire had been 'positioning' me to take a certain point of view into the forthcoming coaching with Jayne.

I'm sure you'll have a sense of the complexity of these coaching relationships and the challenges posed to the coach. And I've left one question hanging in the air – how does the coach manage all this complexity? Part of the reason for leaving it hanging is there is no clear answer. The ethical framework, particularly around confidentiality provides some guidance, but doesn't really address the experience, for example, of knowing that the coachee's plan of action is about to be derailed by forthcoming organizational changes that have yet to be announced. I think that in the main coaches' draw upon their tacit background understanding of how to manage complex relationships that we learn in everyday life, such as how to be trustworthy and act with integrity with family and friends, when we are already involved, have our own interests, hear differing points of view, and seek to act in a way that helps others find their way forward.

Where is the line between coaching and therapy?

This is a question often asked by people training to be coaches, particularly if they come from a therapeutic background, as the coaching and therapeutic skill set seem very similar. The difference arises from the intention of the practitioner. In therapy, the focus of the work is primarily on the 'self' of the client, and the intention is to seek a deeper understanding of the client's relations with their own self and with others as the source and 'solution' to the issues they bring. In coaching, the focus is on improving performance in a task or project and the intention is to seek a deeper understanding of what is involved to achieve that goal. The coach works with the psychological aspect enough to enable the client to get some understanding and freedom of movement to address their specific coaching agenda, but no more. For Claire, we explored how she could psychologically get more freedom of movement around leadership and that was enough, we were not interested in a deeper exploration of other aspects of her 'self'. If it became apparent that there were deeper issues at play, for example depression or experience of abuse, then the possibilities of referral to a therapist would be discussed. An interesting question is whether the client could work with a therapist and coach at the same time or whether coaching should be suspended while the therapeutic issue is dealt with. My view is that the client could work with both at the same time.

New developments

Coaching is a rapidly evolving profession and, as indicated in the introduction, many of the developments will be in this area, particularly around the processes of accreditation, paralleling the development of counselling and psychotherapy some decades ago. Organizations have played a vital role in the development of coaching and this will continues to be the case. Increasingly, organizations in the public and private sector, such as the NHS and large multinationals, are seeking to develop their own internal coaching capability and this is sure to drive further developments in coaching. For example, the kind of issues described here around managing multiple stakeholders and boundaries will need to be addressed more directly. Also, although not discussed in this chapter, the significance of the organizational culture, the systemic aspect, though already recognized, will surely become an increasing area of focus. Lastly, organizations are investing more and more in developing 'coaching cultures, whereby coaching as a style of management (as with Claire in our case study) is taking centre-stage.

Summary

This chapter has focused on coaching in organizational settings. It has only appeared on the scene in the past twenty years but is having an enormous impact on organizations, particularly in the area of leadership and management.

The primary intention of coaching is to improve performance but to do so by enabling the client to find their own way forward. The 'mantra' for the coach is 'ask not tell'. The 'psychological dimension' is a significant aspect of any coaching agenda, with the coach addressing both the 'inner' and 'outer' aspects of the client's situation.

Coaching in organizations brings a complexity around a variety of issues that are, in essence, about boundary management. This complexity poses huge challenges and though ethical frameworks provide some guidance, there is still much to do to think through and become clear about how to manage the boundaries. In many ways, coaches navigate their way by drawing upon the tacit understanding of managing complex relationships that they have learned in other areas of life.

Further reading

The following key texts provide a good overview of the fundamentals of the theory and practice of coaching.

Bluckert, P. (2006) *The Psychological Dimension of Executive Coaching*. Maidenhead: Open University Press.

Gallwey, T. (1974) *The Inner Game of Tennis*. New York: Random House.

Rogers, J. (2012) *Coaching Skills: A Handbook*. Maidenhead: Open University Press.

Whitmore, J. (2002) *Coaching for Performance*. London: Nicholas Brealey.

It is also worth looking at the websites of the main coaching professional bodies:

- Association for Coaching [http://uk.associationforcoaching.com]
- European Mentoring and Coaching Council [http://www.emccouncil.org/uk]
- International Coach Federation [http://www.coachfederation.org/]

References

Cox, E., Bachkirova, T. and Clutterbuck, D. (2010) *The Complete Handbook of Coaching*. London: Sage.

Gallwey, T. (1974) *The Inner Game of Tennis*. New York: Random House.

O'Connor, J. and Lages, A. (2007) *How Coaching Works: The Essential Guide to the History and Practice of Effective Coaching*. London: A&C Black.

Whitmore, J. (2002) *Coaching for Performance*. London: Nicholas Brealey.

SECTION 3

Group Therapies, Systemic Therapies, Couples/Marital and Family Therapy, and Sex Therapy

12 The relationship in group therapy

Stephen Paul and Divine Charura

We all live in relation to others. Our self-concept is formed as a result of our experiences with others. We learn to value ourselves in relation with others.

(Paul 2012)

Introduction

For several decades, group theory has had an enormous influence on therapeutic practice. Group psychotherapy or group therapy as it is commonly known is a therapeutic intervention widely used in different modalities. In generic interpersonal group psychotherapy theory, sessions are held with individuals presenting with the same psychological problem or individuals who come together for therapy with similar goals or objectives. A broad theoretical assumption is that group therapy helps an individual to relate their experiences to that of the others in the group (Charura 2012). In a way, it could be argued that as we are born in relationship, our families and networks are some kind of group, which impact and influence us in different ways. The statement above by Stephen Paul (2012) highlights this. In a one-to-one therapeutic relationship, the relationship is co-created by both client and therapist within a particular context. When working with groups, however, a different set of dynamics is at play, as there are a number of people involved in the process. In this chapter, we review research that concludes that cohesiveness is the agent for therapeutic change in groups. We identify the therapeutic components for establishing a cohesive and effective group. We have worked with different groups and from experience are aware that the relationship in group therapy is not without its own challenges and we outline some of these challenges. To end, we present some of the new developments within group psychotherapy practice.

Foundations of theory and practice

Group therapy developed around the beginning of the twentieth century. In the early stages of practice, it was used with people who could not afford individual therapy. It is considered to have first started with the work of Pratt, who set up groups with people suffering from tuberculosis. He developed a combination of support, education, and practical information through using sufferers who were managing their illness to act as examples to others. The approach was basically didactic. After the First World War, with the need to work with large numbers of war veterans, Lazell worked with groups of mentally disturbed combatants using a similar approach. Marsh developed group methods with people suffering from chronic mental health problems in a psychiatric setting.

In the 1920s, the influence of Freud and psychoanalytic theory led to the use of transference (Wender 1936) and free association (Schilder 1936) in groups. Burrow (1927) developed the concept of 'group analysis'. He observed that in groups, people behaved in ways they believed others wanted them to. They developed social images, virtually masks through which they presented themselves to others. This impeded spontaneity and led to rigid ways of behaving.

At the same time Freud was working in Vienna, Moreno developed psychodrama, a method of working with individuals in groups to resolve repressed feelings by re-enacting past experiences using role play and action methods, which were literally played out on stage and then processed. Moreno introduced the term 'group psychotherapy'. Adler (1958) developed an approach that worked on social empowerment. These approaches were precursors to humanistic ways of working in therapy.

Many European therapists came to the UK and USA as Nazism spread. Klein was central to the development of object-relations theory, while Bion (1959) developed classical group analysis. Foulkes (1964) founded the British school of group analysis, while Perls created Gestalt therapy (Perls et al. 1959).

Goldstein (1939), whose research was instrumental to the development of humanistic psychology, noted that individual neurons always function as part of a network. This led Foulkes to formulate the notion that each individual functions as a meeting – or nodal – point within a network of relationships in groups and that analysis needs to work with all the relationships the individual is involved in. He proposed that there are no fixed boundaries between the individual and their environment, the inner and the outer.

During the 1950s, Rogers' person-centred approach was developed to work with groups. He created encounter groups as a means of enabling authentic communication and psychological growth. He believed that the desire for change is the healthy result of inner incongruence. Maslow (1964) formulated the concept of synergy: that an individual has more potential for growth in a healthy group than on their own, literally $1 + 1 = 11$.

Family therapy developed during the 1960s (Slipp 1993), with the disturbed family member being seen as a symptom of dysfunction in the family itself. Laing (1985) proposed it was not a person's perception of the world that was problematic but that social pressures led to a distortion of how they experienced and acted in the world. So-called ill behaviour was, in his view, a sane response to an insane situation. The therapeutic community enabled the reparation of these early family traumas.

Cognitive behavioural therapy approaches to group work have been developed in recent years, often with a formulaic approach. In the 1980s, Yalom developed an existential approach to group therapy, which he later reformulated into an interpersonal approach. This approach and versions of it are used commonly in a wide variety of settings worldwide, by therapists of different professional backgrounds who work more in relationship with their clients.

Group therapy today has moved a long way from the early group work of Pratt, Burrows, Moreno, and others. As well as psychoanalytically oriented group therapy, we now have cognitive behavioural, humanistic, eclectic, and self-help therapy groups. All of these have quite different approaches towards effecting change in their members. Research inspired by social psychologists gives insights into the outcomes of interpersonal interaction in all such settings.

What the research says

Research by social psychologists into groups has been instrumental in informing professionals about the behaviour of people in a wide range of group settings, not simply therapy groups. This research provides real insights into group dynamics not seen through the potentially opaque lens of a theoretical model.

In a classic study, Bales (1958) identified two necessary functions for a group leader:

- *Instrumental task function*: initiating action, keeping members focused on the task, organizing the group, and emphasizing the need to meet original aims.
- *Socioemotional function*: meeting expressed needs of the group, being sensitive to members' feelings, mediating disputes, encouraging and supporting other members, using humour to relieve tension.

(Paul 2012: 620)

An effective therapist needs to be aware of the task of the group, its aims and goals, and socioemotional factors, mindful of the need for members to feel secure and supported. Additionally, the therapist will pay attention to both dimensions of their own behaviour in the group. The research further indicates that it might be better for a therapist to change the model of practice to his or her own leadership style rather than faithfully try to follow ways of behaving. Rigid adherence to chosen ways of behaving may actually cause harm to group members.

Cohesiveness is probably the most important factor in group performance. A group with low cohesiveness will perform less well than a highly cohesive group. A person in a group with low cohesiveness may not benefit as much as someone in a highly cohesive group. A new member of the group might find themselves scapegoated or alienated. Furthermore, members of a highly cohesive group may attack members who threaten the group's perceived cohesiveness, which may then lead to the blocking of potential therapeutic change.

Festinger et al. (1950) proposed that cohesiveness could be considered as attractiveness to members of the group and to the group as a whole. Attraction within the group, therefore, is a key factor in group cohesion: group cohesion can thus be said to occur when group members have positive feelings towards each other.

Three bases of attraction to the group itself have been identified (Secord and Backman 1964):

1　The basis of attraction is in the group itself.
2　The activities of the group are inherently rewarding.
3　Membership is a means to an end.

A group with high cohesiveness is considered to have the following advantages:

1　The behaviour of group members is under greater normative control.
2　The group boundary is better defined.
3　Communication is freer and more efficient.
4　Members are more likely to report a sense of security and high self-esteem;
5　There is a freer and more wide-ranging expression of opinions.

Frank (1957) identified eight key factors for high cohesive groups: shared issues, instrumental value, prestige, reward structure, attainable goals, limited alternatives, exclusivity, absence of coercion and democratic leadership.

Cohesiveness is now considered a central factor in the effectiveness of group therapy (Bednar and Kaul 1994). Research has indicated that the relationship is the most important factor for in-session change in individual therapy (Paul and Haugh 2008). In their summary of group therapy research, Burlingame et al. (2004: 683) identified cohesiveness as 'the therapeutic relationship in group psychotherapy'.

Too much cohesiveness, however, and the group becomes too comfortable and secure; too little cohesiveness and it becomes an unsafe place to work in. Cohesiveness may be considered to have two dimensions in therapy groups (Burlingame et al. 2011): relationship structure and relationship quality. Relationship *structure* refers to the form of the relationship. In the structure of cohesiveness, *vertical cohesion* may be considered to refer to a member's perception of the therapist's competence, genuineness, and warmth. *Horizontal cohesion* describes a member's relationship with other members of the group and with the group as a whole. Relationship *quality* describes how members feel towards the leader and other members (positive bonds) and the tasks and goals of the group (positive work) (Burlingame et al. 2011). A lack of empathy with the leader and conflict in the group (negative relationship) will lead to decreased cohesion and thus less positive outcomes (Johnson et al. 2005). See Box 12.1.

Box 12.1　Group cohesion

- Cohesion is positively associated with a reduction in symptom distress and/or an improvement in interpersonal functioning.
- All therapists need to foster cohesiveness in all its elements in the group.
- Cohesion is positively associated with outcome in groups using a cognitive behavioural, psychodynamic or interpersonal orientation.
- Group leaders who focus on member interaction, irrespective of theoretical orientation, achieve higher cohesiveness–outcome links compared with groups without this focus. Thus, it is important to encourage member interaction.

- Group cohesiveness builds over time. It is strongest when a group runs for over twelve sessions and has five to nine members.

Source: After Burlingame et al. (2011)

The individual-in-context

Owing to the complexity of group dynamics compared with the dynamics of one-to-one therapy, the factors impacting on the therapeutic arena are diverse. Fielding and Llewelyn (1986) among others have indicated different dimensions in groups that impact on interaction and participation:

- Intra-group factors: relations between different factions in the group.
- Inter-group factors: relations between the therapy group and other groups, for eample in a hospital setting.
- Interpersonal factors: relations between individual members.
- Intrapersonal factors: internal tensions each member brings.

This research can assist the therapist in their understanding of the behaviour of individuals in groups. Clarkson and Fish (1988) and Tudor (1999) explored the client-in-context. Each member is accompanied by their family, work, and social networks, all of which are elements of the lens through which individuals view the therapist and the group. The group therapist needs therefore to be open to and aware of the different and unique dimensions potentially present in the group. All of these factors therefore impact on relationship and the multiplicity of relationships in group therapy.

The therapeutic relationship: models of therapy

Psychoanalytic group therapy

Psychoanalytic group therapy can be said to have developed in three stages:

Psychoanalysis in the group
This classical approach to psychoanalysis in the group setting places little emphasis on group dynamics. The group therapist works with each client in the group in turn. Individual intra-psychic dynamics remain the focus. Classically trained individual therapists often adopt this approach. The therapist is expert, perceiving him or herself as a blank screen working with resistance, transference, and interpretation and does not engage relationally with members.

Psychoanalysis of the group
Developed by Bion (1959) after the Second World War, in this approach the task of the analyst is to interpret group phenomena. The group learns as the analyst identifies what is happening to the group. The analyst works with the resistances and

transferences in the group and not individual group members. Ezriel (1952) developed this way of working – the Tavistock model – with its focus on the 'here-and-now' interactions in the group. The therapist relates not to individuals but to the group as a whole, in which members are component parts.

Psychoanalysis through the group

Foulkes (1964) saw the individual as a social being whose psychological disturbances are founded through relationships. Self-perceptions, often faulty, are developed based on these relationships. People always seek to behave in ways that reduce the anxieties they feel in relations to themselves and others. As a result, they take up roles in groups to manage the 'group tension' resulting from the conflicting needs of individual members and the group as a whole. The focus here is more explicitly relational. The role of the therapist is as conductor, an empathic member of the group who works both with the 'group tension' and the individual difficulties members express. Group members also make important contributions.

Existential therapy

From a traditionally existential perspective, the focus of an existential group is on the subjective experiencing of group members working with how to respond to life's limitations. The intersubjectivity of living, temporality, acceptance of the givens of life, and the focus on authenticity are all central tenets (Paul 2012).

The existential therapist works through therapeutic relationships to help members reassess their emotional experiences (Corey 2003). Therapy is a partnership and change comes about though relationships. The therapist works to foster meaningful and authentic relationships between members of the group as well as working with members in confronting and working through existential, universal life issues. The aim is to help members work towards living more authentically and meaningfully.

Person-centred therapy

As developed through the encounter groups of Rogers, the aim of therapy is the breaking down of false incongruities and the emergence of personal power. In line with the person-centred tradition, group therapy in this modality is non-directive. The group facilitator's role is to communicate, and thus model, empathy, congruence (genuineness), and unconditional positive regard for group members. These conditions are seen as central for the facilitation of the therapeutic process. An underlying assumption in person-centred therapy is that through authentic relational encounters, transformational change occurs (Rogers 1951, 1961). Where the 'original group' (i.e. the client's family) may have contributed to psychological distress, the person-centred group contributes a template for relating. The person-centred group therapist is present in the group, is willing to take part as an equal member of the group, and to share their struggles with group issues as appropriate. Typically, the focus is on intra-psychic and interpersonal dynamics and not on interpretation or the dynamics of the group.

Gestalt therapy

Gestalt therapy, as developed by Perls (Perls et al. 1959; Hinksman 1988), aims to enable group members to overcome the blocks and unfinished issues that prevent the individual from being fully alive and fulfilled in the here-and-now, and to enable the individual to take personal responsibility. Group members are actively encouraged to make contact with others in the group to work towards full contact with self and others. The group is the medium for therapy; it is the 'therapeutic field' all members are located in.

The approach of Perls was direct and engaging in which he used his personal power as a catalyst with group members. Techniques (e.g. two chair work) and methods developed from Moreno (1958), the founder of psychodrama, were used as the therapist considered them useful.

A more recent development is more relational, with less emphasis on techniques or the authority of the therapist. The therapist aims to be in relationship with members and work with them on their boundaries and defences, which impede them from making contact with themselves and other group members.

Cognitive behavioural therapy (CBT)

Cognitive behavioural group therapy was first used to enable the treatment of individuals in groups. The therapist's task is to assess and treat group members using therapeutic programmes. However, the importance of a good working relationship is emphasized (Meichenbaum 1985; Lazarus 1989). While CBT programmes are psycho-educational and didactic in nature, research indicates the therapeutic relationship is pivotal in relation to successful outcome.

Characteristics associated with successful therapists include respect for their clients, a non-judgemental attitude, warmth, humour, genuineness and authenticity. Some group therapists now recognize and work with the dynamic processes of the group (White 2000).

Group therapy research

Recently, individual models of therapy have embraced research findings into effectiveness of therapy. Meta-summaries of research clearly demonstrate that members of therapy groups who report experiencing acceptance, belonging, and support, irrespective of therapeutic model, improve (Burlingame et al. 2002). Attributes experienced in groups such as warmth, openness, and empathy are associated with increased cohesiveness and better outcomes. Research into person-centred group therapy unsurprisingly corresponds with these outcomes (Paul 2008). In their development of a relational paradigm in which the focus of therapy is relational, Paul and Pelham (2000: 110) propose the therapeutic relationship itself is 'central to change'.

Paul (2012: 620) noted that while there is some evidence to suggest that different modalities may be directly linked with effective outcomes with some client groups (see Johnson 2008; Burlingame et al. 2013), research findings can be summarized thus:

- Group therapy works as a whole.
- There is no significant evidence to suggest that one modality is better than any other.
- Modality-based intervention may potentially pathologize normal behaviours.
- Therapists should check recent research into group therapy with the client group they are working with.
- The therapist may be more effective working in a way which they are comfortable with rather than trying to 'fit' into a modality.
- Cohesiveness is central to group therapy and the therapeutic relationship is central to outcome.
- Many social factors can affect group members. Therapists should not pathologize them and be mindful of the human rights of members of therapy groups.
- A group leader is in a position of power and needs to be mindful of this.

Relationships in group and individual therapy

Table 12.1 summarizes differences in approach between practitioners of individual and group therapy.

Table 12.1 Summary of differences between individual and group therapies

Group	Individual
Wide range of relationships possible	Therapist–client relationship central
Process issues may be more central	Content issues may predominate
Group can replicate the dynamics of external experiences	One relationship processes all outside material
Therapist trained in interpersonal dynamics	Therapist trained typically in intra-psychic dynamics
Plethora of interactions within the group that the therapist has to work with	Therapist may implicitly or explicitly hold expert power and have more influence over interactions
Therapist may have less personal influence or power as expert	
Therapist open to feedback at any time from any member about any thing	Feedback to therapist only from one person
Research indicates group cohesiveness most important factor across modalities	Research indicates therapeutic relationship most important in-therapy factor

Source: After Paul (2012)

Key factors in the therapeutic relationship

The therapeutic or curative factors developed by Yalom (1975, 1985; Yalom and Leszcz 2005) have been recognized as a virtual benchmark in group therapy (Burlingame et al. 2004). The therapist has a key role in relation to group members to facilitate the effectiveness of these factors as they emerge. See Table 12.2 for a summary of what makes an effective group therapist.

Box 12.2   What makes an effective group therapist

An effective group therapist need attend to the following in order to maximize their potential to work effectively:

1   A training in working in groups within a coherent theoretical model
2   Significant experience as a member of a therapeutic group
3   To have explored personal issues relating to groups
4   An ability to work at a number of dynamic levels
5   An ability to manage own personal material in group settings
6   An awareness of group dynamics and how to work with them
7   An awareness of how to work anti-oppressively and to work with oppressive behaviour of group members towards others in the group
8   To be able to consistently offer warmth, openness, and empathy
9   To manage clear group boundaries
10   To have clearly contracted goals (even if not task focused)

Source: Paul (2012)

Table 12.2 Yalom's curative factors and therapist functions

Interpersonal input	Group members learn through the input of others in the group. Group therapist facilitates members' contributions and contributes own understanding
Catharsis	Letting out feelings in the group. Group therapist facilitates catharsis and ensures group boundary is safe
Cohesiveness	A sense of belonging and feeling accepted in the group. Group therapist communicates warmth, openness, and empathy
Self-understanding	Linking past experiences to present thoughts and feelings. Group therapist works with members to process accordingly
Interpersonal output	Learning how to behave in relation to helpful advice from others in the group. Group therapist models authentic behaviours
Existential factors	Coming to terms with the fact that some things cannot be changed but have to be faced up to, and that everyone is in the same life situation and can find mutual support in this. Group therapist is transparent in relation to own experiences and facilitates sharing of other group members
Instillation of hope	The realization that as others in the group can improve, so the group member can. Group therapist models and facilitates sharing of other group members
Altruism	The gains to self-esteem through helping others in the group. Group therapist models and facilitates sharing of other group members
Family re-enactment	The group somehow recreates the family experience and can help members to understand behaviour patterns from their past. Group therapist highlights and processes as appropriate
Guidance identification	Getting helpful advice from others in the group. Group therapist models and facilitates sharing of other group members

Source: After Yalom (2005)

The limitations, challenges, and complexities of maintaining a therapeutic relationship across this range of life issues

Coulson (1994, quoted in Lago and Macmillan 1996) has suggested that the issue of group facilitation is problematic insofar as no one can predict who is going to do or say something that is facilitative for another. One of the challenges of the group therapeutic relationship is that there is no control over what individuals may say to each other. Charura (2012) noted that resistance in group therapy is a complexity that needs to be acknowledged and challenged in order for group therapy to be helpful. Resistance can be evidenced by individuals retreating from problems that are disclosed or minimizing the significance of other group members' experiences. It may also be evidenced by denial or the minimization of the destruction that one may be causing to the group therapeutic process. Furthermore, it can be evidenced by avoiding meaningful interpersonal contact or responses that are closed and brief in a way that makes exploration difficult.

Paul (2012: 617) summarizes significant challenges in working with the therapeutic relationship in group therapy:

1 The therapist–client relationship is not central. There is a multiplicity of relationships taking place in the therapy group. Focus on a uni-dimensional therapeutic relationship may lead the therapist to some degree to be blind to the many other communications that take place in a group.

2 The group has a unique pattern of dynamics related exponentially to the number of members. Complex process issues may predominate and the group therapist needs to be able to work with process issues at both individual and group level.

3 There may be different levels of intra-psychic, interpersonal, and intra-group relationships in play at any one time. The therapist needs to be aware of and competent to work with them.

4 Boundary issues are often of added importance as the therapist works with the group. Members may test boundaries and challenge the therapist in quite different ways to individual therapy.

5 There are particular social phenomena that occur in groups that are not necessarily pathological or interpretable psychotherapeutically (e.g. groupthink, conformity, influence, cognitive dissonance). There is a real potential for stereotyping to take place in groups, which a therapist needs to be aware of and able to work with. It is facile to sit within a therapeutic model and ignore such occurrences.

6 There are a number of 'experts' who may question the therapist or offer their own therapeutic and other support to each other.

New developments

Interpersonal

While traditionally professionals trained as group therapists have worked within a clear model, it is apparent that many therapists and helping professionals work relationally. The work of Sullivan and of Yalom, who moved from an existential to an interpersonal way of working, is important in the development of an interpersonal approach to group therapy. This approach is widely used (Ratigan and Aveline (1988) but with little common, conceptual methodology.

The underlying assumptions of an interpersonal approach are threefold:

1   Existential factors (Yalom 1985, 2005). These involve the facing up to and acceptance of life's givens and moving towards self-determination, free choice, and personal responsibility.
2   Interpersonal and social psychology and the notion that *I define and limit myself through my relations with others* (Lewin, Rogers, and Buber).
3   Group analytic theory (Ezriel 1952). Group members behave normatively (the required relationship) because if they said and did what they really wanted to (the avoided relationship), something terrible would happen (the calamitous relationship).

Sullivan (1953) proposed that personality is developed by social forces and is neither innate nor determined in childhood. Psychopathology is based on maladaptive interpersonal experience. Therapy works by interpersonal learning (see Yalom's curative factors), the group as microcosm of family and society, and the here-and-now focus of the group. The therapist works to translate presenting complaints into intrapersonal symptoms, process past issues and presenting problems in the here-and-now, and with their own authentic behaviour in the group.

The therapist works with three levels of relationship:

- relationships between members and the therapist;
- relationships between group members themselves; and
- relationships between group members and the group.

The therapist processes individual (intra-psychic), interpersonal, and group as a whole phenomenon. The therapist avoids zero-sum (generic) responding and responds using the facilitative conditions, as pioneered by Rogers, empathically to all dimensions of relationship that present.

Relational group process

A development of the work of Foulkes and others, relational group process (RGP) emphasizes interpersonal contact, and the processes of intersubjective relating between group members. The focus of both the group therapist and group members is on the interplay between the present moment and the emergence of unconscious relational patterns (Erskine 2013). Erskine has suggested that RGP is an implementation of Buber's (1923/1958) I-Thou philosophy. The group therapist does not interpret or work individually with group members. Instead, focus is on facilitating authentic encounter and relationships between group members.

This way of working with group therapy is also in line with more recent developments in psychology, for example. Owusu-Bempah and Howitt (2002) suggest an increasing awareness of non-Eurocentric ways of being with a movement away from the focus on the self and more emphasis on the person-in-the-group.

Practice-based evidence

It is evident that cohesion is a central factor in the group therapeutic relationship. In a meta-analytic study, Burlingame et al. (2011) reviewed the literature from forty studies published over the last forty years to examine cohesion and found a positive relationship between cohesion and group psychotherapy outcome. Despite the modality differences and developments of different ways of working with groups, it is clear from the research presented in this chapter that the efficacy of group psychotherapy often has been shown to lie in the 'process' that occurs in the room; yet capturing, understanding, and accurately interpreting each member's experience is a task that requires skill and therapist competence. As a result of this need to show therapist competency, practice-based evidence of group therapy outcomes is increasingly considered.

Summary

Cohesiveness is considered the primary factor in group therapy effectiveness. Research has indicated that the relationship is the most important factor for in-session change in individual therapy regardless of the therapeutic model used. Similarly, the therapeutic relationship is now regarded as central to change in group therapy. Cohesiveness is identified as *the* therapeutic relationship in group psychotherapy. The therapist can help build cohesiveness in a group by communicating warmth, empathy, and openness, by having clearly agreed goals with group members and by maintaining clear boundaries.

Further reading

Corey, G. (2008) *Theory and Practice of Group Counseling*, 7th edn. Belmont, CA: Wadsworth/Thomson. A generic text that reviews the theory and practice of the different modalities.

Yalom, I.D. with Leszcz, M. (2005) *The Theory and Practice of Group Psychotherapy*, 5th edn. New York: Basic Books. A classic exposition. Every group therapist should have a copy.

References

Adler, A. (1958) *What Life should Mean to You*. New York: Capricorn Books.

Bales, R.F. (1958) Task roles and social roles in problem-solving groups, in E.E. Maccoby, T.M. Newcomb and E.L. Hartley (eds.) *Readings in Social Psychology*, 3rd edn (pp. 437–47). New York: Holt.

Bednar, R.L. and Kaul, T. (1994) Experiential group research, in A.E. Bergin and S.L. Garfield (eds.) *Handbook of Psychotherapy and Behavior Change* (pp. 631–63). New York: Wiley.

Bion, W.R. (1959) *Experiences in Groups*. New York: Basic Books.

Buber, M. (1923/1958) *I and Thou* (trans. R.G. Smith). New York: Scribner.

Burlingame, G.M., Fuhriman, A. and Johnson, J. (2002) Cohesion in group psychotherapy, in J.C. Norcross (ed.) *A Guide to Psychotherapy Relationships that Work* (pp. 71–87). New York: Oxford University Press.

Burlingame, G.M., Mackenzie, K.R. and Strauss, B. (2004) Small-group treatment: evidence for effectiveness and mechanisms of change, in M.J. Lambert (ed.) *Bergin and Garfield's Handbook of Psychotherapy and Behavior Change*, 5th edn. New York: Wiley.

Burlingame, G., McClendon, D. and Alonso, J. (2011) Cohesion in group psychotherapy, in J. C. Norcross (ed.) *A Guide to Psychotherapy Relationships that Work*, 2nd edn. (pp. 110–31). New York: Oxford University Press.

Burlingame, G., Strauss, B. and Joyce, A. (2013) Change mechanisms and effectiveness of small group treatments, in M.J. Lambert (ed.) *Bergin and Garfield's Handbook of Psychotherapy and Behavior Change*, 6th edn. (pp. 640–89). New York: Wiley.

Burrow, T. (1927) *The Social Basis of Consciousness*. New York: Harcourt Brace.

Charura, D. (2012) Demystifying the curative factor of group psychotherapy in rehab, *Addiction Today*, 23 (135): 22–3.

Clarkson, P. and Fish, S. (1988) Systematic assessment and treatment considerations in TA child psychotherapy, *Transactional Analysis Journal*, 18: 123–52.

Corey, G. (2003) *Theory and Practice of Group Counseling*, 6th edn. Belmont, CA: Wadsworth.

Erskine, R.G. (2013) Relational group process: developments in a transactional analysis model of group psychotherapy, *Transactional Analysis Journal*, 43 (4): 262–75.

Ezriel, H. (1952) Notes on psychoanalytic therapy, II: Interpretation and research, *Psychiatry*, 15: 119–26.

Festinger, L., Schachter, S. and Back, K. (1950) The spatial ecology of group formation, in L. Festinger, S. Schachter and K. Back (eds.) *Social Pressure in Informal Groups*. Stanford, CA: Stanford University Press.

Fielding, R.G. and Llewelyn, S.P. (1986) Applying the social psychology of groups in clinical settings, *British Journal of Psychotherapy*, 2 (4): 281–91.

Foulkes, S.H. (1964) *Therapeutic Group Analysis*. New York: International Universities Press.

Frank, J.D. (1957) Some determinants, manifestations and effects of cohesiveness in therapy groups, *International Journal of Group Psychotherapy*, 7: 53–63.

Goldstein, K. (1939) *The Organism: A Holistic Approach to Biology Derived from Pathological Data in Man*. New York: American Book Co.

Hinksman, B. (1988) Gestalt group therapy, in M. Aveline and W. Dryden (eds.) *Group Therapy in Britain* (pp. 65–87). Milton Keynes: Open University Press.

Johnson, J. (2008) Using research-supported group treatments, *Journal of Clinical Psychology: In Session*, 64 (11): 1206–24.

Johnson, J.E., Burlingame, G.M., Olsen, J.A., Davies, D.R. and Gleave, R.L. (2005) Group climate, cohesion, alliance, and empathy in group psychotherapy: multilevel structural equation models, *Journal of Counseling Psychology*, 52: 310–21.

Lago, C.O. and Macmillan, M. (1996) The facilitation of large groups: participants' experience of facilitative moments, in R. Hutterer, G. Pawlowsley, P. Schmid and R. Stipsits (eds.) *Client-Centred and Experiential Psychotherapy: A Paradigm in Motion*. Frankfurt: Peter Lang.

Laing, R.D. (1985) *Wisdom, Madness and Folly: The Making of a Psychiatrist*. London: Macmillan.

Lazarus, A.A. (1989) Multimodal therapy, in R.J. Corsini and D. Wedding (eds.) *Current Psychotherapies*, 4th edn. Itasca, IL: F.E. Peacock.

Maslow, A.H. (1964) Synergy in society and the individual, *Journal of Individual Psychology*, 20: 153–64.

Meichenbaum, D. (1985) *Stress Inoculation Training*. New York: Pergamon Press.

Moreno, J.L. (1958) Fundamental rules and techniques of psychodrama, in J.H. Masserman and J.L. Moreno (eds.) *Progress in Psychotherapy*. New York: Grune & Stratton.

Owusu-Bempah, K. and Howitt, D. (2002) *Psychology Beyond Western Perspectives*. Chichester: Wiley-Blackwell.

Paul, S. (2008) The relationship in group therapy, in S. Haugh and S. Paul (eds.) *The Therapeutic Relationship: Perspectives and Themes*. Ross-on-Wye: PCCS Books.

Paul, S. (2012) Group counselling and therapy, in C. Feltham and I. Horton (eds.) *The Sage Handbook of Counselling and Psychotherapy*, 3rd edn. London: Sage.

Paul, S. and Haugh, S. (2008) The relationship not the therapy? What the research tells us, in S. Haugh and S. Paul (eds.) *The Therapeutic Relationship: Perspectives and Themes*. Ross-on-Wye: PCCS Books.

Paul, S. and Pelham, G. (2000) A relational approach to therapy, in S. Palmer and R. Woolfe (eds.) *Integrative and Eclectic Counselling and Psychotherapy*. London: Sage.

Perls, F.S., Hefferline, R.F. and Goodman, P. (1959) *Gestalt Therapy: Excitement and Growth in the Human Personality*. Harmondsworth: Penguin.

Ratigan, B. and Aveline, M. (1988) Interpersonal group therapy, in M. Aveline and W. Dryden (eds.) *Group Therapy in Britain*. Milton Keynes: Open University Press.

Rogers, C.R. (1951) *Client-Centered Therapy*. Boston, MA: Houghton Mifflin.

Rogers, C.R. (1961) *On Becoming a Person*. New York: Houghton Mifflin.

Schilder, P. (1936) The analysis of ideologies as a psychotherapeutic method, *American Journal of Psychiatry*, 93: 601–15.

Secord, P.F. and Backman, C.W. (1964) *Social Psychology*. New York: McGraw-Hill.

Slipp, S. (1993) Family therapy and multiple family therapy, in H. Kaplan and B. Sadock (eds.) *Comprehensive Group Therapy*. Baltimore, MD: Williams & Wilkins.

Sullivan, H.S. (1953) *The Interpersonal Theory of Psychiatry*. London: W.W. Norton.

Tudor, K. (1999) *Group Counselling*. London: Sage.

Wender, L. (1936) The dynamics of group psychotherapy and its application, *Journal of Nervous and Mental Disease*, 84: 54–60.

White, J. (2000) Introduction, in J. White and A. Freeman (eds.) *Cognitive-Behavioural Group Therapy for Specific Problems and Populations*. Washington, DC: American Psychological Association.

Yalom, I.D. (1975) *The Theory and Practice of Group Psychotherapy*, 2nd edn. New York: Basic Books.

Yalom, I.D. (1985) *The Theory and Practice of Group Psychotherapy*, 3rd edn. New York: Basic Books.

Yalom, I.D. with Leszcz, M. (2005) *The Theory and Practice of Group Psychotherapy*, 5th edn. New York: Basic Books.

13 The therapeutic relationship in the systemic therapies

Phil Arthington and Paula Boston

Introduction

As an approach, systemic therapy attends to relationships between members of couples or families. The therapist's focus is on simultaneous multiple relationships – the problematic relationships between clients, and the development of an alliance with each individual client and the family system as a whole. Furthermore, the therapy may include other systemic therapists who observe the session and offer the reflecting team intervention (Andersen 1990). This technique requires the team to have a mid-session conversation in front of the family about key themes. The team offers re-descriptions aimed at promoting positive change and, in doing so, must make accommodation to their assumptions about how the family members will hear what is said. So, this approach focuses a highly complex layering of individual, family as-a-whole, and team relationships. The significance of this unique aspect of the therapeutic relationship in family and couple therapy has been under-represented in the original descriptions in service of differentiating systemic therapy from other models of therapy by emphasizing new theoretical and technical aspects. In contemporary systemic practice, reflecting upon and maintaining the therapeutic relationship has become central in guiding the therapist's choices and actions.

Systemic therapists draw on a number of theoretical principles that provide a framework for working with therapeutic relationships. The primary task of the systemic therapist is to help families to overcome problems by engaging in particular kinds of conversations conducive to change. Ethical engagement requires the therapist to consider their use of professional knowledge, subjective experience and position, and to attend to issues of power and cultural difference.

Systemic therapy can thus be a highly complex, subtle, and challenging business. At the same time, we feel that when a therapist brings family members together in a room and begins to negotiate the politics of family life and relationships, they have the privilege of engaging in a lively, creative, and emotionally enriching experience.

Systemic therapies

'Systemic therapy' is an umbrella term for a number of distinct models of practice. These include structural family therapy, brief strategic therapy, Milan systemic therapy, solution-focused therapy, functional family therapy, collaborative-dialogical therapy, and narrative therapy. We will offer brief descriptions with greater emphasis on contemporary practice in the UK, which has been influenced by postmodern and post-structuralist theories.

Bateson, the theoretical founder of much of systemic practice said, 'Without context, there is no meaning' (Bateson 1972). This phrase has profound consequences for a view about the nature of selfhood and what it means to be human. Problems are conceptualized as located between people, rather than within the individual. Emotions, personality traits or psychiatric symptoms are understood as expressions of relationship. While systemic therapists most commonly work with families, the recognition of the role of specific social contexts means that they will work with whichever members of a social system are suitable for creating change, such as involved professionals or important friends. It is recognized that 'family' is culturally defined and the traditional picture of the two-parent, two-generation cohabiting unit is frequently one that does not fit with how families construct themselves (Singh 2009). Systemic work with individuals also places relationships with others and attention to context as central to the process.

Viewing the family as a system leads to the appreciation of circular patterns between family members rather than cause-and-effect processes. For example, rather than identifying 'who is to blame' for an argument, the therapist is interested in the problematic communication family pattern, with its constituent elements that escalate or decrease the degree of reaction and effects on members and the group as a whole. Alliances and attempts to keep the peace would be understood as part of the pattern under scrutiny.

Families, as systems, function to maintain stability, while also adjusting to internal and external pressures to change. Clinical problems may arise at points of transition in the *family life cycle* (e.g. following a bereavement or when an adolescent leaves home) when a change in established relationship patterns is demanded. For Watzlawick et al. (1974), problems could be seen as the result of the family system's failure to adapt; either by rigidly persisting in patterns more appropriate to an earlier life cycle stage or failure to create appropriate new responses.

An influential team of therapists working in Milan (Selvini-Palazzoli et al. 1980) ushered a shift in focus to emphasize change at the level of personal meaning rather than behaviour. The therapist's circular questions were not merely used for information-gathering, but specifically designed to help the family members to develop new perspectives. The therapist's ideas are evaluated on the basis of usefulness in promoting change, rather than a claim to objective truth. This reflects a move towards a constructivist theory of knowledge in which our perception of the world is viewed as subjective and influenced by multiple factors – our historical context, family history and values, professional training, organizational culture, and so on.

Family therapists had critiqued traditional psychotherapies for isolating the individual from their context. In the mid 1980s, systemic therapists came to see that they, too, had made a false dichotomy, isolating the family from the wider context of cultural and political domains. This led to a further development into postmodernism and social constructionism, philosophies that placed emphasis on the role of language and the interplay of discourses and values within cultures and societies. Social constructionism holds that language does not merely reflect reality, but that it actively creates and shapes it (Gergen 2009). While narrative and collaborative approaches are both based on social constructionism, they make use of this theory of knowledge in different ways.

Narrative therapy is centred on the idea that we live in a world of language, where social discourses influence how we make sense of our experienced reality. Our social identities are constructed within a context of culturally available possibilities that have been created by significant others, family of origin, institutions, and local and wider culture. Often, clinical problems are maintained by language that locates the problem as intrinsic to the person. One foundational premise of the narrative approach is that the person is not the problem – the problem is the problem (White and Epston 1990). The therapist holds a belief that the roots of change already exist within a client's repertoire and do not need to be invented through the process of therapy. By exploring stories about the problem and its place in family life, problem-saturated stories may be deconstructed while preferred stories, such as existing but neglected stories of strength and resilience which stand out as exceptions, may become more dominant in the family's on-going conversation. The therapist may use therapeutic letters to augment these emerging stories of hope and strength. Reflecting team members or communities of people with similar experiences to the client may act as witnesses to the therapy conversation, reflecting in a way that honours and embeds the client's developments.

Collaborative approaches draw on similar philosophies of knowledge, assuming that our conceptions of self and reality are continually constructed as they are played out in the on-going conversation that characterizes human life. This premise has a number of implications for the therapeutic relationship: the therapist and family form a unique system that is organized around a problem and that will engage in therapeutic conversations in which the language and meanings used will evolve until the problem becomes dis-solved. In this way, therapy is cast as a linguistic event in which change takes place through the process of dialogue. The therapist acts as a conversational artist, where expertise is based on the therapist's capacity to facilitate a healing conversation rather than to unilaterally provide their understanding. Anderson and Goolishian (1992) conceptualized the therapeutic relationship as one of mutual inquiry in which the clients are experts in their own lives and the therapist is a curious learner, asking questions and sharing thoughts in order to better understand. Anderson describes the therapist as being both a welcoming host to the client and a guest in their lives, a metaphor that captures the quality of respectfulness which characterizes this way of working. These ideas have been developed into a view of therapy as an unfolding dialogue between persons who are themselves engaged in a constantly unfolding internal dialogue. Ideas about the problem may be offered by the therapist in response to the family's words and mediated by an inner conversation, or they may emerge in a more shared way through the reciprocal exchange of ideas (Rober 1999; Bertrando and Arcelloni 2006).

The therapeutic relationship

Examples from systemic models

Many ideas surrounding how systemic therapists approach the therapeutic relationship can be considered in terms of the therapist's use of self. A primary task is to engage the family sufficiently enough to develop a therapeutic alliance as a foundation from which to work. Salvador Minuchin (1974), whose structural approach required the therapist to establish a particularly influential position in the therapy room, described how the therapist must *join* with the family by accommodating themself to their patterns of communication, emotional connection, and initial presentation of family power dynamics as a prerequisite to promoting change. The therapist shows respect for the family in its current state of being, using questioning and observations to become better acquainted with the family's communication patterns. The therapist adapts features of their communication such as pace, humour or emotional expressiveness to match that of the family. For example, if the most reluctant client is also seen as highly influential to the system, the therapist may intentionally develop a seemingly irrelevant conversation as a means of creating a stronger affective bond. After successful 'joining' activities, the therapist has a sufficiently strong relationship to offer therapeutic challenges to problematic patterns and support new types of behaviours and family organization.

While the structural approach places emphasis on joining through intentional activity strategically aimed at specific family members, the Milan method offered the concept of *neutrality* as an alternative therapist stance (Selvini-Palazzoli et al. 1980). Neutrality invited the therapist to engage all family members to an equal degree. The therapist would have achieved this position if, afterwards, each participant was unable to state who the therapist had supported or sided with. Later reconceptualized as *curiosity*, the emphasis is on exploration and creativity in generating different explanations, while holding a sceptical attitude towards any sense of finality in understanding. For Cecchin (1987), curiosity and neutrality support each other in a recursive process; for if the therapist loses their curiosity, they will settle on an explanation that invites limited and linear descriptions that are characterized by a lack of neutrality. A stance of respectful curiosity allows a more systemic point of view, by orienting the therapist towards embracing the complexity of human interactions with multiple descriptions and explanations. There has been much thinking in the field about how the therapist can maintain the therapeutic relationship while also retaining the ability to address issues of safety and risk that might require the input of additional professionals (e.g. Lang et al. 1990).

Social constructionism has had a profound influence upon how the therapeutic relationship has come to be viewed. Since knowledge is seen as subjective and context-bound, the therapist must reflect upon their sense-making and the influence of their prejudices, values, and preferred ways of thinking upon the family. The emphasis on language means that the therapist and client(s) can approach their relationship in an active and transparent way; the way we talk about our relationship will shape how we experience it (Burnham 2005). The therapist might ask about particular meanings of words to aid better communication, or openly discuss the experience of therapeutic relationship and what the client(s) want from the therapist. This *relational reflexivity*, or 'talk about the talk', can be a vital part of improving the therapeutic alliance and bringing a sense of presence and collaboration. It may also give license for the therapist to take more risks in the relationship, such as adopting a more challenging position or utilizing expert knowledge in contexts of uncertainty, while also retaining an ethical posture in which the family may provide feedback about how they experience this stance (Mason 1993, 2005).

A useful framework for thinking about the therapist's use of self is to think of the therapist as both *embedded* and *embodied* in the therapeutic relationship (Hardham 1996). The therapist, family, and indeed the therapeutic relationship itself can be considered as being embedded in a sociocultural context, which to some extent determines what takes place. For example, an adolescent client might assume that some topics are not appropriate for discussion, or wouldn't be understood and so edit them from the conversation. The therapeutic relationship developed between the therapist and client will be influenced by factors such as the organizational setting or cultural or familial beliefs regarding professionals. In addition, the embodied nature of selfhood highlights the therapist as a discrete individual with a felt reality that affects their experience and actions within the therapeutic encounter. These aspects of selfhood can influence how the therapist positions themself within the therapeutic relationship and vice versa.

Ethical conduct is central to systemic therapy. It has been argued that the postmodern philosophies that underlie contemporary systemic practice lead the therapist to a localized, bottom-up ethics centred around each specific family, rather than a top-down set of moral values applied to every situation (Freedman and Combs 1996). For some, postmodernism brings a concern that if there are no single identifiable truths, the therapist may be rendered unable to challenge injustices or state a strong opinion, as if 'any truth goes'. In contrast, the postmodern therapist can be seen as being in a position that requires a much more active concern with ethics and power in the therapeutic relationship. If they cannot rely on the comfort of certainty offered by one particular value or principle, then they must constantly engage reflexively in thinking about the ethics of their actions. Karl Tomm describes an ethical posture of empowerment based upon the therapist seeking to foster change by acting through sharing knowledge and aiming to increase the family's options (Bernstein 1990). These principles would be encouraged over interventions based on secret 'professional' knowledge or which close down options, although specific circumstances may call for a different ethical posture (e.g. some situations of risk may call for the closing down of options or for the therapist to act in the absence of full disclosure of facts). These concepts are a useful guide for the therapist to locate herself and consider the impact of her positioning within the relationship.

Case vignette

A very brief episode of initial discussions in the early stages of therapy will be offered as an example of systemic thinking and negotiation of therapeutic relationship. Two adult sisters (Anne 38 and Jane 43), who were raised in Scotland, sought therapy with the second author (P.B.) to resolve their conflicted relationship. There was a fracture in their relationship some years back as a result of a disclosure by Anne to Jane about their father's inappropriate sexual behaviour in their childhood. According to Anne, Jane had failed to be adequately supportive when she disclosed their father's sexualized behaviour towards her. They had stopped communicating as a result.

In the first meeting, we spent some time discussing my approach, professional background, therapy and what they wanted from it. Anne said she wanted Jane to more fully appreciate how damaged she had been by the abuse and by Jane's continued relationship with their father following the disclosure. Jane said that she wanted to support Anne in the therapy, whom she saw as more vulnerable. The systemic need to hold a therapeutic relationship with each individual in the face of their conflicted relationship emerged within the first few moments.

One of the central concerns expressed by Anne was that privacy of the content of the therapy would be transgressed by Jane's communication with their mother. Anne wanted to be able to discuss their shared and separate past without any reverberations in their current relationships with their parents. Anne had severed all contact with her father (who was now divorced from their mother) and had minimal contact with their mother. I could see this as an issue of great significance to the therapeutic contract, the on-going process of therapy, and to the origins of the story of the difficulties. We spent a good deal of time attending to the context that would be surrounding the therapy, boundaries, how trust could be established between them, and what Jane could discuss with their mother without betraying Anne's wish for privacy. Working carefully with these issues was essential for engagement and alliance. It also represented the beginnings of therapeutic change, as my questioning supported the sisters in negotiating the rules around their relationship. Informed by the narrative and collaborative emphasis on the importance of 'lived experience' and detail, the therapeutic relationship was supported by listening to each person's fears, preferences, and dilemmas without moving too quickly to a plan. I was active in helping each of them to avoid making demands that would be experienced as unreasonable. Anne would really like to have insisted that Jane also sever all ties with her parents, but at some level appreciated that this would be asking too much. I shared an idea that this was not being mentioned out of 'sisterly respect'. Here, I was positively supporting the adult sibling relationship, creating a boundary around them while also actively scaffolding the development of a shared understanding and agreement between them. It was important for me to form an emotional connection with each of them, appreciating their perspectives as based on very different childhood experiences. I reflected on how I would try my best to hear both of their experiences and reactions in therapy, and how although I might appear to be favouring the needs of one sister over another at times, I would be balanced overall. Stating my intentions openly helped me to position myself on the side of their hopes for a renewed relationship: my primary alliance was with their relationship. We prepared for the difficult discussion of the historical episode of child abuse by exploratory discussions of the effect of what was referred to as the 'elephant in the room' or 'The Conversation' before they actually spoke specifically of the toxic past events. It seemed that Anne needed to feel safe enough about the capacity to manage the resurrected feelings of abuse and disappointment, while Jane needed to be ready to hear it without feeling defensive and have the confidence that this time around she could respond in a confirming and sensitive way.

This provides a small sample of the more detailed workings of systemic thinking about the therapeutic relationship. The factors that contributed to the therapeutic relationship were the negotiation of safety and timing of important conversations, the commitment to the sister relationship as opposed to one or the other individual, a transparent effort to be balanced in my connections to each while attending to different emotional needs, the ability to grasp signs of movement, and finally to appreciate the wit and humour of these women despite difficulties. The concepts of joining, neutrality, relational reflexivity, and risk-taking all applied to this work. The ten-month therapy was successful in terms of having done sufficient work to enable them to end therapy with a post session lunch together, sharing humour and renewed out-of-session contact.

Challenges

Working competently with issues of social difference is a vital component of establishing a therapeutic relationship with the family. The therapist is mindful of how areas of social difference can shape the relationship, either through hidden assumptions and prejudices, or through actively reflecting upon and talking about such differences in therapy and supervision. Therefore, it is not unusual for systemic therapy to include conversations about issues such as gender, race, religion, social class, and sexuality, and to consider their impact upon the therapeutic relationship (Burnham et al. 2008). Waldegrave et al. (2003) argue that many psychotherapists ignore issues of inequality and injustice which are often the basis of clients' problems and that to marginalize such issues in therapy is irresponsible. Questions have also been raised about the degree to which the therapist has a responsibility solely to the clients in the room, or if they carry a sociopolitical responsibility to challenge wider societal injustices (Monk and Gehart 2003).

One longstanding challenge for systemic therapists has been how to approach the issue of power in the therapeutic relationship. This has centred around theoretical differences about the nature of power in systems, and how the therapist ought to make use of the power afforded to them by their status and role in the therapeutic relationship. There may be tensions between a preference for the aesthetics of exploration and understanding on the one hand, and pragmatically pursuing change on the other (Keeney and Sprenkle 1982). This is a longstanding issue that speaks to some of the differences between narrative and collaborative approaches, and is likely to continue to reverberate through future developments in systemic practice.

New developments

Supervision, attunement, and research on alliance

Systemic supervision has moved in parallel with the thinking that has been developing in relation to the practice of therapy. Systemic supervisors are concerned about the influence of power in the supervisory relationship. As part of this, there will be transparency about the context in which the supervisory relationship takes place, such as whether it is part of an assessed training, an aspect of line management, or private post-qualified supervision or consultancy (Boston 2010). The systemic supervisor considers the goals of the supervisee and their preferences for learning. Depending on the experience of the trainee, supervision is aimed more at supporting the needs of the therapist in establishing the therapeutic relationship than the offering of advice or expertise.

One of the central aims of systemic supervision is to enhance the therapist's capacity to be the therapist required for this particular family and their concerns. This may mean an exploration of 'trigger issues' or resonances from the therapist's own family if they seem to impede the development of working engagement and support in adapting to different age ranges or cultural differences.

Systemic therapy has embraced 'live supervision' as well as the review of visual recorded material. This direct exposure of the client and therapist and their working partnership offers very rich material for the supervisor. One particular benefit is that micro-moments in therapy can be explored between supervisor and therapist. This can help systemic supervisor and therapist be more attentive to subtle shifts of meaning or turns in therapy through mutual observation.

Systemic therapy is open to influences from many directions. While contemporary systems approaches have highlighted the significance of language, there have also been prompts to renew attention to unarticulated felt experiences or bodily expressions. Dialogic theory and its associated phrase *withness-thinking* highlight a humanizing way-of-being. The therapist is emotionally connected, highly responsive, and spontaneous in the therapeutic moment, in contrast to objectifying *aboutness-thinking* (Shotter 2010). There has been growing interest in the role that mindfulness and acceptance can play (Gehart 2012; Lord 2012) as a method for the therapist to maintain a sense of presence and attunement to each moment in the process. This interest in mindfulness can be considered part of a broader interest in integrating systemic concepts with those of other theoretical models. Integrations with other models, most notably with attachment theory, have become well established and can more commonly be seen in modern systemic practice (e.g. Johnson 2004; Dallos 2006). It remains to be seen how such integrations might come to influence systemic thinking about the therapeutic relationship in the future.

The important role played by research has increasingly become accepted within the systemic therapy profession. Empirical research on outcome points to the importance of a positive therapeutic relationship in psychotherapy (Hubble et al. 1999) and family therapy is no exception. A positive therapeutic alliance developed in the early stages of therapy is a strong predictor of subsequent success in therapy (Castonguay et al. 2006). Building a relationship based on warmth, trust, and informality is important, as is the value of creating a balanced alliance in the eyes of the family members (Blow et al. 2007). Friedlander et al. (2006) emphasize engagement in the process, emotional connection, safety, and a shared sense of purpose as key factors in determining the quality of the alliance. While these findings reflect the importance of many of the principles discussed in this chapter, there remains a challenge for systemic therapists to have their practice be informed by the nuances of research on therapy process in addition to the broader findings about the effectiveness of systemic therapy.

Summary

The therapeutic relationship is a central component of systemic therapy. Tasks include engaging the family by building numerous therapeutic alliances, showing curiosity about each individual's unique perspective, holding a degree of neutrality but with attention to inequalities of power, and considering issues of social difference and their potential for influencing (and indeed enhancing) the therapeutic relationship. Families are micro-political cultures that require reflexive thinking and a well-developed capacity for making emotional connections and to take positions in relationships with intention. We believe that systemic therapy offers a wealth of concepts and techniques to benefit practitioners using various therapeutic models.

Further reading

The following two books will enable the reader to understand more about the complex dynamics of the therapeutic relationship.

Flaskas, C. and Perlesz, A. (eds.) (1996) *The Therapeutic Relationship in Systemic Therapy*. London: Karnac Books.

Fredman, G. (2004) *Transforming Emotion: Conversations in Counselling and Psychotherapy*. London: Whurr.

References

Andersen, T. (1990) *The Reflecting Team*. New York: W.W. Norton.

Anderson, H. and Goolishian, H. (1992) The client is the expert: a not-knowing approach to therapy, in S. MacNamee and K. Gergen (eds.) *Therapy as Social Construction* (pp. 54–68). London: Sage.

Bateson, G. (1972) *Steps to an Ecology of Mind*. New York: Ballantine.

Bernstein, A. (1990) Ethical postures that orient one's clinical decision making, *AFTA Newsletter*, 41: 13–15.

Bertrando, P. and Arcelloni, T. (2006) Hypotheses are dialogues: sharing hypotheses with clients, *Journal of Family Therapy*, 28 (4): 370–87.

Blow, A., Sprenkle, D. and Davis, S. (2007) Is who delivers the treatment more important than the treatment itself? The role of the therapist in common factors, *Journal of Marital and Family Therapy*, 33 (3): 298–317.

Boston, P. (2010) Three faces of supervision: individual learning, group learning and supervisor accountability, in C. Burck and G. Daniel (eds.) *Mirrors and Reflections: Processes in Systemic Supervision* (pp. 27–48). London: Karnac Books.

Burnham, J. (2005) Relational reflexivity: a tool for socially constructing therapeutic relationships, in C. Flaskas, B. Mason and A. Perlesz (eds.) *The Space Between: Experience, Context and Process in the Therapeutic Relationship* (pp. 1–18). London: Karnac Books.

Burnham, J., Palma, D.A. and Whitehouse, L. (2008) Learning as a context for differences and differences as a context for learning, *Journal of Family Therapy*, 30: 529–42.

Castonguay, L.G., Constantino, M.J. and Holtforth, M.G. (2006) The working alliance: where are we and where should we go?, *Psychotherapy: Theory, Research, Practice, Training*, 43: 271–9.

Cecchin, G. (1987) Hypothesizing, circularity, and neutrality revisited: an invitation to curiosity, *Family Process*, 26 (4): 405–13.

Dallos, R. (2006) *Attachment Narrative Therapy: Integrating Systemic, Narrative and Attachment Approaches*. Maidenhead: Open University Press.

Freedman, J. and Combs, G. (1996) *Narrative Therapy: The Social Construction of Preferred Realities*. London: W.W. Norton.

Friedlander, M.L., Escudero, V. and Heatherington, L. (2006) *Therapeutic Alliances in Couple and Family Therapy: An Empirically Informed Guide to Practice*. Washington, DC: American Psychological Association.

Gehart, D. (2012) *Mindfulness and Acceptance in Couple and Family Therapy*. New York: Springer.

Gergen, K. (2009) *An Invitation to Social Construction*, 2nd edn. London: Sage.

Hardham, V. (1996) Embedded and embodied in the therapeutic relationship: understanding the therapist's use of self systemically, in C. Flaskas and A. Perlesz (eds.) *The Therapeutic Relationship in Systemic Therapy* (pp. 71–89). London: Karnac Books.

Hubble, M.A., Duncan, M.L. and Miller, S.D. (1999) *The Heart and Soul of Change: What Works in Therapy*. Washington, DC: American Psychological Association.

Johnson, S. (2004) *The Practice of Emotionally Focused Couple Therapy: Creating Connection*. New York: Routledge.

Keeney, B.P. and Sprenkle, D.H. (1982) Ecosystemic epistemology: critical implications for the aesthetics and pragmatics of family therapy, *Family Process*, 21 (1): 1–19.

Lang, P., Little, M. and Cronen, V. (1990) The systemic professional domains of action and the question of neutrality, *Human Systems*, 1: 39–55.

Lord, S.A. (2012) Meditative dialogue: tuning into the music of family therapy, *Journal of Family Therapy* (DOI: 10.1111/j.1467-6427.2012.00594.x).

Mason, B. (1993) Towards positions of safe uncertainty, Special Issue of *Human Systems*, 4 (3/4): 189–200.

Mason, B. (2005) Relational risk-taking and the therapeutic relationship, in C. Flaskas, B. Mason and A. Perlesz (eds.) *The Space Between: Experience, Context and Process in the Therapeutic Relationship* (pp. 157–70). London: Karnac Books.

Minuchin, S. (1974) *Families and Family Therapy*. Cambridge, MA: Harvard University Press.

Monk, G. and Gehart, D. (2003) Sociopolitical activist or conversational partner? Distinguishing the position of the therapist in narrative and collaborative therapies, *Family Process*, 42 (1): 19–30.

Rober, P. (1999) The therapist's inner conversation in family therapy practice: some ideas about the self of the therapist, therapeutic impasse, and the process of reflection, *Family Process*, 38 (2): 209–28.

Selvini-Palazzoli, M., Boscolo, L., Cecchin, G. and Prata, G. (1980) Hypothesizing- circularity-neutrality: three guidelines for the conductor of the session, *Family Process*, 19 (1): 3–12.

Shotter, J. (2010) *Social Construction on the Edge: 'Withness-Thinking' and Embodiment*. Chagrin Falls, OH: Taos Institute.

Sinclair, S.L. and Monk, G. (2005) Discursive empathy: a new foundation for therapeutic practice, *British Journal of Guidance and Counselling*, 33 (3): 333–49.

Singh, R. (2009) Constructing 'the family' across culture, *Journal of Family Therapy*, 31 (4): 359–83.

Stratton, P. (2011) *The Evidence Base of Systemic Family and Couple Therapies.* AFT Report [http://www.aft.org.uk/SpringboardWebApp/userfiles/aft/file/Training/Evidence-BaseofSystemicFamilyandCouplesTherapies(Jan2011).pdf].

Waldegrave, C., Tamasese, K., Tuhaka, F. and Campbell, W. (2003) *Just Therapy – A Journey: A Collection of Papers from the Just Therapy Team, New Zealand.* Adelaide, SA: Dulwich Centre.

Watzlawick, P., Weakland, J.H. and Fisch, R. (1974) *Change: Principles of Problem Formation and Resolution.* New York: W.W. Norton.

White, M. and Epston, D. (1990) *Narrative Means to Therapeutic Ends.* New York: W.W. Norton.

14 The therapeutic relationship in couples/marital and family therapy

Anne Burghgraef and Divine Charura

Introduction

The relationship between couples/marital and family therapy to systemic theories is complex. It has been argued that couples therapy has never been fully integrated into the family therapy field, as the focus has tended to be on the wider family system rather than on couple work (Lebow 2013). Couples have often been reduced to being a 'subsystem' of the family without recognizing their unique nature. In this chapter, we focus on the couple relationship and use the terms couple and family interchangeably. While traditionally couples therapy was assumed to be marital therapy, in today's arena, couples may be from a wide range of sexual orientations, cultural or socioeconomic contexts. We have maintained use of both terms to ensure inclusivity but also to recognize that for many a distinction between marriage and couples therapy remains (Wolska 2011).

While we situate couples therapy within a family and systemic framework, we acknowledge that other theoretical frameworks have practice models for working with couples. Due to the evolving nature of marriage/couples therapy with its myriad theoretical influences, and various clinical methods, any attempt to generalize will fail to do justice to this complexity. Family and systemic therapists, however, have been quick to theorize the implications of contemporary philosophical ideas for human relationships and therapeutic practice (Rivett and Street 2005). This is evident through the many strands of family and systemic therapy that have developed, which we will now outline as a foundation upon which the way we work with couples rests.

Foundations of theory and practice

Since family therapy first emerged in the 1950s, it has metamorphosed in diverse ways, which has significantly altered the role of the therapist and the nature of the therapeutic relationship. Originally, it grew out of the child psychiatry movement, when the individualistic, psychodynamically informed approach proved to be insufficient to address the mental health problems of children and adolescents. Researchers and clinicians who were experimenting by working with whole families came together (Gurman and Kniskern 1981) and began publishing the influential family therapy journal, *Family Process*, in 1962. Research informed by general systems theory and cybernetics shifted the focus from individual, intra-psychic pathology rooted in the past to an interpersonal perspective centred upon current patterns of interaction and communication (Dallos and Draper 2003). Early family therapy practice focused on context and relationship patterns, viewing the couple relationship and individuals as 'sub-systems' of the larger family system. Little attention was given to individual thoughts, beliefs, and personal agency or the unique nature of the couple relationship.

In the 1980s, the nature of change was explored, and the distinction between first- and second-order change emerged. The former addressed patterns of interaction while the latter engaged with the beliefs and values of the family members that informed these patterns. Rather than seeing families as dysfunctional structures maintained by symptoms, they were now viewed as comprising members who actively co-created meanings together (Dallos and Draper 2003).

While the first generation of family therapists were clearly 'experts', imbued with power and authority, in this new context the therapist's role changed to become more collaborative. Therapist and clients were explorers who worked to develop and co-create more fruitful ways of understanding their situations. Therapists retained an active role and utilized such techniques as circular questions and positive connoting to enable new ways of seeing to emerge. Therapists were encouraged to become reflective about their own beliefs, values, and perceptions, and to recognize they formed a part of the 'therapeutic system' with the family.

In the late 1980s, couples and family therapy became profoundly influenced by postmodern social constructionist approaches, which emphasized the role of language in creating reality. Carmel Flaskas noted that post 1990s family therapy consisted of four different models, while recognizing the mutual influence and overlap between them.

The Milan model, which was the first to change focus from behaviour to meaning, no longer used questions simply to gain information to formulate interventions, but transformed them into the means to engage families in exploring their beliefs, values, and stories. The therapist was expected to be skilful in asking reflexive questions to draw out the contours of relationships while maintaining a relationship of respectful curiosity. This therapeutic system and way of working included referrers, the family, and the therapist with his or her own organizational framework, and hence evolved into 'systemic therapy'. While feminist and postmodern thought challenged the hierarchical nature of the therapeutic relationship, ecosystemic structural family therapy (ESFT) ideas have remained foundational to the model with the therapist maintaining a position of expertise and responsibility for the therapy (Flaskas 2011).

Narrative therapy, which was inspired by cultural anthropologists Geertz and Myerhoff, emphasized re-membering and re-authoring stories. Michael Foucault's ideas about knowledge and power as well as dominant and subjugated discourses challenged family therapy to recognize and address the broader socio-political context, especially the power of social practices that shaped gender and racial identities. The therapeutic relationship in narrative therapy is even more collaborative, as therapists work with their clients towards their preferred future story. Like the Milan model, the therapist retains the responsibility to be mindful of the socio-cultural influences and for scaffolding the therapeutic conversations (Dallos and Draper 2003).

Flaskas (2011) described a further development in family and systemic therapy, that of solution-focused therapy – a hybrid modernist/postmodernist therapeutic approach. Rather than looking at problems and failed attempts to solve them, this approach attends to a positively imagined future to guide the therapeutic work. It is pragmatic and focused upon change, emphasizing the client's/couple's expertise and utilizing techniques that have emerged out of practice. The therapist establishes a positive working relationship, without any particular concerns for therapist reflexivity in the use of self, as it is the family's/couple's goals and the necessary steps to achieve them that drives the therapy.

Flaskas (2011) further identified dialogical therapy as aiding the evolution of major family therapy and systemic ideas. Dialogical therapy is seen as a postmodern therapy that begins with the premise that humans in relationships form 'linguistic systems'. Dialogical therapy is construed as a linguistic event, conducted as a collaborative conversation with the family/couple. In this way of working, many writers and practitioners have followed the lead of Anderson and Goolishan, who postulated the importance of the therapist adopting a 'non-expert' stance in the therapeutic encounter (Rober 2008). The therapist's expertise is primarily that of managing therapeutic conversations, with problems being constructed and then 'dis-solved' in language. Although the 'non-expert' view of the therapist has stirred up controversy between the modernists and the postmodernists, it has very helpfully focused attention upon the therapeutic relationship. At the core of this way of working is valuing clients' views and reiterating the importance of listening and witnessing as therapist and clients together co-construct meanings. New meanings that emerge of the client's/couple's experience/story may be seen as a useful corrective to the earlier emphasis upon the power and authority of the therapist to initiate change.

Dialogical therapists endeavour to engage respectfully and sensitively with clients working with connections while acknowledging difference within the therapeutic relationship. Like other postmodernist therapeutic models, there is a concern for the use of the therapist-self, which recognizes the uniqueness of each therapist who will vary in a range of ways according to their social graces (gender, race, religion, age, ability, culture, class, education, employment, spirituality, and sexuality).

With increasingly pluralistic cultures, it cannot be assumed that therapists share the same world-view and fundamental beliefs of the families/couples they see, or even that family members have shared beliefs and expectations about family life. These differences may be more obvious in cross-cultural work but will also be present in families/couples in more hidden ways. Good practice requires therapists to be aware of what they personally and professionally bring to the therapeutic context, and to have the capacity to acknowledge and work with these differences.

The therapeutic relationship

Recently, the therapeutic relationship between the therapist and family members has been highlighted as important for effective therapeutic outcomes (Friedlander et al. 2011). This fits with general psychotherapy research, which suggests that 30 per cent or more of a successful therapeutic outcome is attributed to the strength and quality of the therapeutic bond (MacFadzean 2000; Carr 2005; Friedlander et al. 2011). Paradoxically, it appears that family and systemic therapy focuses upon a theoretical understanding of family functioning along with the techniques used to initiate change, with little attention being paid to feelings. However, Harari (1996: 55) argued that 'systemic models rely on empathy and attend to the emotional states and to the therapeutic relationship to a greater degree than has hitherto been recognized by critics of family therapy'.

Within family and systemic therapy, while such qualities as warmth, trust, and sincerity are essential they are insufficient in themselves to form an effective therapeutic alliance. The therapist also needs to be attuned to the clients'/couple's view of the therapeutic relationship, work collaboratively towards shared goals, and be geared to the clients'/couple's readiness to change. Developing a therapeutic alliance with a couple is complex, as there is one therapeutic relationship on the individual level (self-with-therapist) and another on the couple level (couple-with-therapist) (Friedlander et al. 2011). Multiple factors may impact the success of a therapeutic relationship with couples, including the degree to which the couple feel safe and comfortable with each other in the therapeutic context, how they feel about the therapist, and their alliance and shared sense of purpose in working on their problems (Friedlander et al. 2011). In research on working with couples, Thomas et al. (2005) have shown that both men and women had a stronger bond with the therapist when their partners self disclosed but felt more distant from the therapist when their partners challenged or made negative comments about them.

Attachment

Within couples therapy, the focus on patterns of communication, problem-solving, and negotiation has been deepened by attachment theories that recognize the unique nature of a relationship, which is characterized by 'emotional bonding'. While there has been recognition of the need for children to be securely attached, it has become more widely appreciated that attachment styles impact couple relating and that adults continue to need emotional security to flourish.

According to Bowlby (1969), in childhood the primary caregiver acts as a prototype for future relationships via the internal working model. This internal model governs how the child feels towards their parents, towards their self, how the child expects to be treated, and plans for their own behaviour towards others. The main features of the internal working model relate to how much the individual can trust other people, values their self-worth, and interact with others. An infant who experiences frequent abuse may develop a negative internal working model that tells them, 'No one cares about me, I am unlovable, people who I hope will love me only hurt or reject me, I am not good enough.' If this 'attachment model' of self, others, and the world is not changed as the child grows, they may develop low self-esteem, be overly dependent or independent, and sabotage friendships or relationships (Paul and Charura 2014). Adults' interactions with others are therefore guided by memories from their internal model, which influence and help evaluate their contact with others (Bretherton and Munholland 1999).

Sue Johnson (2008), the founder of emotionally focused therapy, pointed out that as couples understand their need for emotional attachment and are enabled to recognize their ways of protecting themselves from vulnerability, they can begin to take steps towards positive change. The fear of loss of connection can be so great that when the relationship is threatened, one or both partners may panic and go into 'fight of flight' mode. If they go into flight, they may withdraw emotionally, whereas if they fight, they may become hostile and aggressive towards their partners. Someone with an ambivalent attachment pattern may send confusing messages of 'come close' and then 'go away'. Couples can learn to recognize each other's attachment mode and become attuned to each other's needs and be sensitive in response. Johnson's attachment-based emotionally focused therapy has a reported success rate of around 75 per cent in helping couples get their relationship back on an emotionally satisfying track (Johnson 2008: 7).

Love

In working with couples, we believe that it is also very important for the therapist to be aware of love theories, and how the dynamics of love interplay in the therapeutic relationship. Different authors have proposed different styles of love in relationships. For example, Lee (1973) proposed six basic styles of love, namely: Agape, Eros, Philia, Storge, Ludus, and Mania. Sternberg (1998) hypothesized a duplex theory of love that has two sub-theories – the triangular theory of love and the theory of love as a story. In the triangular theory of love, he suggested there are three components of love, namely: intimacy, passion, and commitment. From this theoretical perspective, Sternberg argues that there are different kinds of love created as a result of different combinations of the components of love. In the theory of love as a story, Sternberg postulated that in order to understand a loving relationship, one should understand the stories/experiences that influenced its development and the perspective of each person in the relationship. Fisher (2004, 2009; Fisher et al. 2005) explored love from psychological, social, and biological perspectives. She further asserted that four neural systems are regularly associated with a constellation of personality traits that influence partner choice. Lago and Charura (2012) explored the nature of love and hate from various transcultural perspectives. They outlined ten points that highlight the complexity of love, and its interconnectedness to different cultures and their different views on intimacy, partnership/marriage, relationship/s, sex, power, shame, hate, life cycles, and death. The therapist's knowledge of attachment and love patterns/styles and how they manifest in relationships and in the therapy room is essential. In relation to practice, Paul and Charura (2012) viewed love as reparative within the therapeutic relationship. They argued that love is the agent for change in successful psychotherapy and the essence of contact.

Challenges to the therapeutic relationship in working with couples

To consider the challenges, it is necessary to understand why couples present to therapy. There is evidence that clients may seek therapy because they want to communicate more effectively and improve their relationship (Lebow 2013). From our experience, however, such cases are limited. Often couples seek therapy when in severe crisis and their relationship's stability is under threat, or as a last resort (Friedlander et al. 2001; Wolska 2011). Often one partner may be less willing to engage, which is a challenge in itself from the start. Individuals may shift the blame for the crisis on their partner, another family member, or even someone else, while at the same time expecting the therapist to take the role of their ally, solicitor, advocate, judge (Wolska 2011).

Quarrelling or further ruptures may ensue as couples begin to narrate their reason for attending therapy and each individual expects the therapist to agree with their view and prove their partner wrong. Attachment styles may make it more difficult if, for example, one partner with an anxious attachment style clings to the therapist for security when feeling rebuffed by his or her partner.

Figure 14.1 presents a model to explore some of the dynamics and challenges of working with couples. The figure shows the different dynamics that interplay in couple

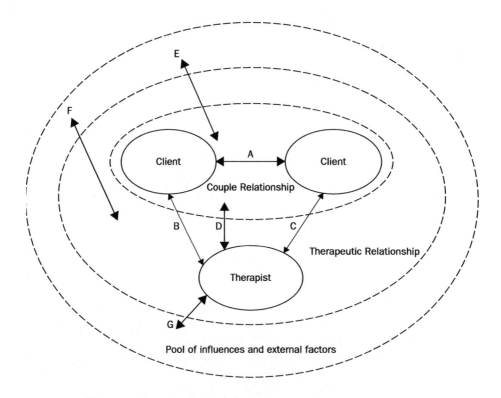

A = Couple communication and dynamics. (Often this is the reason to come for therapy)
B = Communication and dynamics between therapist and individual client
C = Communication and dynamics between therapist and the other individual client in the couple unit
D = Communication between therapist and couple as a unit
E = Influence of external forces onto the couple as individuals and as a system
F = Influence of external factors on the Therapeutic Relationship i.e. family of origin values, beliefs, environment, society etc.
G = Influence of external factors on the Therapist

Figure 14.1 Therapeutic relationship dynamics and influencing factors in couple work

work. The complexity of working with two individuals raises many challenges. We outline here some of the dynamics that therapists working with couples may face.

- In each individual there is also an intra-psychic internal psychological process.
- The therapy setting also has an impact on the therapeutic relationship.
- In dynamics B, C, D as noted in Figure 14.1, it is important for the therapist to be aware of attachment styles as well as the psychodynamic notions of projection, transference, and countertransference. The following questions may help practitioners to think about their work with couples:
  - What might each individual be projecting onto the therapist?
  - What might the couple as a unit be projecting onto the therapist?
  - What is the therapist experiencing and feeling about each individual and about the couple as a unit?
  - What am I as a therapist projecting onto the couple?

There are many challenges that emerge when working with couples. Those from our experience are shown in Box 14.1.

Box 14.1 Challenges of working with couples

- Dealing with the couple's way of relating to each other and their attachment patterns.
- The therapist's own unresolved relational and attachment patterns.
- Parallel process, such as when working with a distressed couple and the therapist is experiencing their own relationship difficulties.
- Transference and countertransference in the therapeutic relationship.
- Working with couple/family secrets.
- Dealing with abuse that may emerge in therapy.
- The therapist's own inner conversation about what's right or wrong or what the couple could do.
- Working with difference and diversity.
- Self-disclosure.
- Working with blame from the couple about why their relationship has not worked.
- Dealing with a couple's decision to end their relationship.

The list in Box 14.1 is not conclusive, but it does identify some key areas that may be challenging for therapists.

To illuminate aspects of the therapeutic relationship when working with couples, we will explore the dynamics of working with couples.

Case vignette

Ben attended for therapy with his fiancée Amy. They got engaged after dating for six months having met at a speed-dating event in London. After Ben's contract ended in

> *London they moved to the North of England to live with Ben and his parents. They attend for therapy because Amy feels they have grown apart. She states that she also feels very isolated. Ben states he has had enough because they just don't see things the same way. He states that they are just different cultures (Ben says he sees himself as 'a working-class Yorkshire lad'). Amy states that Ben blows hot and cold, stating that sometimes he 'loves her to bits and wants her' and is very needy, and at other times appears indifferent. Amy made the referral and Ben has attended hesitantly. Ben states they have been to therapy before and it was a waste of time. However he states to the therapist he does not 'want it all to end'.*

As can be seen from the case vignette above, from the moment a couple presents the therapist is faced with the opportunity as well as challenge of forming a therapeutic relationship. There is also the obvious question of how she or he will work with the couple.

Reflection question

In the case vignette example, Ben and Amy explore the challenges to the couple's relationship and to the therapeutic relationship using attachment pattern theory perspectives and views of love. What skills could you use and how may you work with this couple?

Circular questioning

One approach from a systemic therapy perspective may be to ask 'circular questions' (Dallos and Draper 2003). Important concepts include circularity, neutrality, and hypothesizing.

- Circularity constitutes asking questions to stimulate multiple perspectives enabling the couple to make new connections and think differently about their situation.
- Neutrality helps to protect therapists from being forcibly drawn into a family's system, or from taking sides and trying to rescue a family member (Schwartz and Nichols 2006).
- Hypothesizing refers to the therapist's formulation of alternative tentative explanations or thoughts regarding the presenting problems. It is derived from information available from the couple about their problem, behavioural and dynamic observations in the room, and the therapist's past clinical experience. Hypothesizing enables the therapist to make connections and a full exploration of all aspects of the story that the couple or family brings, thus guiding the direction of the therapy (Schwartz and Nichols 2006).

From the case vignette, different questions could be asked.

Therapist: I understand how frustrating it must be for you both to come here when Amy you feel you have to force Ben to come and Ben you feel it's a waste of time. But I also realize that you have both got to this point because you don't want it all to end. Bearing that in mind, if we could start somewhere to work through how each of you is feeling where you each would like to start?

In exploring feelings, the therapist could ask:
Amy how do you feel when Ben 'blows hot and cold'?

Ben what is happening for you when you feel what you described as 'not being bothered about the relationship'?

Later in the session in establishing the couple's goals, the therapist may ask questions like:
If you could each have three things you would want for your relationship to work, what would they be?

Challenges of working with difference and diversity

Case vignette

Shamim and Salim attend for therapy. They have been married for two years. They state that they are on the verge of divorce because they had an arranged marriage in their home country and feel they did not marry for love. Salim had an affair that Shamim recently found out about. Shamim says she wants to separate but feels that religious, cultural, and societal expectations would mean serious consequences and personal struggles for her. Salim states he wants to make it work.

This vignette illustrates the challenges of working with difference, in this case of religious and cultural diversity. The therapist needs to consider who to include in the marital or couple subsystem. When working across cultures in particular, extended family, religious or community leaders may be very influential in their internal processes as a couple (Lebow 2013). Therapists need to be aware of client views of self and family/couple organization, as well as be sensitive to race, religion, sexuality, and so on. Therapists also have to be aware of different cultures and love perspectives (Lago and Charura 2012).

Challenges of working with secrets and physical, mental or chronic illness

> ## Case vignette
>
> *Kelly and Jo attend for therapy. Kelly made the referral. In consultation it emerges that Jo has been living with cancer for just under a year and undergoing treatment and has kept it away from Kelly, and their families. She has recently been told she has a few months to live and Kelly only found out when she opened an appointment letter addressed to Jo from the oncology department. Kelly feels betrayed, but Jo states that she did not want anyone to know because she did not want anyone to be distressed. Jo also has two teenage children from a previous marriage. Although she states she has a good relationship with them, she does not want them to know yet. Kelly states she is struggling with this decision and that a part of her wants to end the relationship, but a part of her feels she loves her and has to stay 'until the end'. She also wonders if Jo is 'going into depression again', as she was diagnosed with bi-polar depression a few years ago and withdrew from their relationship when she started to experience depression. In the session there is a lot of silence.*

Sometimes couples access therapy to process the impact of physical, mental or chronic ill health and even death in their families. Individual members will experience different emotional reactions, including shock, confusion, numbness, denial, anger, anxiety, guilt, self-blame, fear, helplessness, depression, as well as inner resentment towards the sick person, spouse or children (Rao et al. 2004). Studies have shown that couples with chronically ill family members/spouses report greater marital/relationship distress compared with samples of matched couples with healthy family members (Ellenwood and Jenkins 2007).

Reflection questions

- As the therapist, how might you progress in working with this couple?
- What may be the challenges?
- Recognizing that both the person with the illness and significant others will have a relationship to the illness, how might you address that?

Working with couples and families experiencing such distress is complex. Rober (2008) offers a helpful way of working with the impact of such dynamics. He postulated that when therapists are sensitive and tuned into the emotional needs of the family/couple, they will experience emotional and bodily responses which he describes as 'inner experiencing'. He asserts that when this inner experiencing is attended to and reflected upon, this 'inner conversation' can help to guide and move the therapy along, particularly when both the family and therapist appear to be stuck.

Rober describes this knowing as knowledge of a third kind, as distinct from a theoretical knowledge (knowing that) or a skill-based knowledge (knowing how), which has to do with our knowledge of social situation and enables us to anticipate the movements of others and coordinate our movements with it. This implicit knowing is not dependent upon conscious reflection or deliberation but is a form of relational knowing that can be observed in relationships (Rober 2008).

Here we believe Rober is making explicit and validating what many effective therapists do as they engage therapeutically with families/couples in distress. They do not necessarily think explicitly about the application of theories at the moment of their therapeutic encounter but have over time metabolized their theoretical knowledge and clinical experience so that they can respond 'spontaneously'. Thus this implicit knowledge should not simply be conceptualized as 'intuition' but can be construed as a form of 'tacit knowledge' as articulated by the philosopher Michael Polanyi, who used the word 'indwelling' to describe the application of tacit knowledge to the understanding of people (Polanyi 1966). By drawing upon this notion of tacit knowledge, the therapist can have a clinically enriched 'inner dialogue' that honours their skill and expertise without the trappings of the power and authority of the 'expert' position. It enables them to break out of the false dilemma of being an expert versus a non-expert, and to make explicit the unique combination of personal and professional experience that the therapist contributes to the therapeutic relationship.

As seen from the case vignettes, not all couples have the same needs, issues or problems that they want to address. Thus there may be a time when families/couples need to speak together and there may be a time when they need to be silent because words are inadequate to address a depth of grief or trauma. Perhaps the best they can do is to acknowledge that these issues are real and present in their lives even if they can't be spoken of together (Rober 2011).

While all humans are social beings who live in relationship with others, couples and family therapy is not a 'one-size-fits-all' therapy. Humans are multi-dimensional, thus it may be that individuals need to access other forms of therapy that can address issues that are more personal to them such as bereavement or trauma or that they need to be addressed in a non-verbal modality such as through art or drama.

One of the strengths of couples therapy is that it has a broad conceptual base and can integrate insights from other theories such as attachment theory, which enriches the work. It has also developed so that it can work with families even when they aren't physically present or alongside other therapies as part of a treatment plan, as in a residential setting.

The task for any therapist in working with couples therefore is in ensuring that they maintain neutrality and avoid falling into the trap of imposing one's own convictions about gender roles in relationship, perceived cultural/moral values or beliefs. On the one hand, therapists should form a collaborative partnership with families/couples in which the family/couple members are experts about the particulars of their own family/couple problems. On the other hand, the therapist brings a body of clinical and scientific knowledge relevant to family development and dynamics (Carr 2005). In this way, the therapist straddles a 'knowing and not knowing position'. As therapists often work in teams, multiple perspectives can help to prevent hasty conclusions or imposing cultural stereotypes.

Key factors with the therapeutic relationship in working with couples/families are as follows. Therapists need to:

- Be aware of the overall dynamic within the couple/family system while at the same time being aware of and tending to the therapeutic relationship with each individual.
- Have an awareness of how attachment patterns and perspectives on love/relationships inform couple dynamics and how they interplay and manifest in the therapeutic relationship.
- Have an awareness of difference and diversity in relation to issues of race, gender, class, sexual orientation, disability, religion, and age, and their impact on the family/couple system.
- Be able to work alone or collaboratively with a reflecting team in hypothesizing, formulating, and deconstructing what couples/families present, and at the same time be open to sharing his or her formulations or hypotheses with the family/couple.
- Convey that she or he has a shared sense of purpose with the couple, a particularly important dimension of the alliance. (Where the therapist is working in a reflecting team, if unsure of what direction to take, members of the reflecting team can help by suggesting ways in which the therapist can intervene with the couple in order to move from a position of impasse. For those who work in individual practice, supervision is essential in ensuring best practice.)
- Be able to collaborate with the couple as a unit creating a safe and secure base in which each individual can bring their views and experiences. At the same time, the therapist should be able to work collaboratively as well with each member in formulating goals and tasks to achieve the desired therapeutic outcome.
- Have the ability and competence to work with 'unbalancing', yet ultimately remain neutral when family members attempt to entice the therapist to take sides.
- Be able to work to conflict resolution or in supporting the couple to explore the decision of staying together or separating – a decision that lies exclusively with the couple (Wolska 2011).
- Be able to maintain curiosity, neutrality, and the position of not knowing, yet at the same time drawing from specific therapeutic skills and family therapy and allied theories on working with couples.

Summary

This chapter has focused on the couple as a subsystem within marital and family therapy/couples work. In most cases, couples seek therapy because of difficulties in relating to each other. There are therefore many modalities and interventions that can be adopted in working with couples. Many challenges may emerge, including managing the therapeutic frame when the couple are withdrawn from each other, or are quarrelling, or when working with complex dynamics such as the impact of physical/ chronic illness. Central to the therapist's role is the ability to help the couple make sense/define the rules of functioning of their relationship, fulfilling roles, defining the limits of internal boundaries (individual) and external boundaries (separating the relationship from the rest of the world) (Wolska 2011). There are also limitations in offering couple therapy where, for example, there is an intention to put a partner or their own life at risk or if abuse or violence emerges in the therapy room.

It is important to work with and acknowledge difference and diversity and the impact of their internal/individual factors as well as external influences. The emphasis in couples therapy is on developing a collaborative approach, ensuring that therapist and clients work together to determine the goals of therapy and shape the therapeutic bond (Dallos and Draper 2010).

Further reading

Dallos, R. and Draper, R. (2010) *An Introduction to Family Therapy: Systemic Theory and Practice* 3rd edn. Maidenhead: Open University Press. This book will help the reader understand the basic principles of family and systemic therapy.

Flaskas, C., Mason, B. and Perlesz, A. (eds.) (2005) *The Space Between: Experience, Context and Process* in *the Therapeutic Relationship*. London: Karnac Books. This book addresses the dynamics of the therapeutic relationship in family therapy.

References

Bowlby, J. (1969) *Attachment and Loss* (Vol. 1). New York: Basic Books.

Bretherton, I. and Munholland, K.A. (1999) Internal working models revisited, in J. Cassidy and P.R. Shaver (eds.) *Handbook of Attachment: Theory, Research, and Clinical Applications* (pp. 89–111). New York: Guilford Press.

Carr, A. (2005) Research on the therapeutic alliance in family therapy, in C. Flaskas, B. Mason and A. Perlesz (eds.) *The Space Between: Experience, Context and Process in the Therapeutic Relationship*. London: Karnac Books.

Dallos, R. and Draper, R. (2010) *An Introduction to Family Therapy: Systemic Theory and Practice* 3rd edn. Maidenhead: Open University Press.

Ellenwood, A. and Jenkins, J. (2007) Unbalancing the effects of chronic illness: non-traditional family therapy assessment and intervention approach, *American Journal of Family Therapy*, 35 (3): 265–77.

Fisher, H.E. (2004) *Why We Love*. New York: Henry Holt.

Fisher, H.E. (2009) *Why Him? Why Her?* New York: Henry Holt.

Fisher, H., Aron, A. and Brown, L.L. (2005) Romantic love: an fMRI study of a neural mechanism for mate choice, *Journal of Comparative Neurology*, 493: 58–62.

Flaskas, C. (2011) Frameworks for practice in the systemic field: Part 2 – Contemporary frameworks in family therapy, *Australian and New Zealand Journal of Family Therapy*, 32 (2): 87–108.

Friedlander, M.L., Escudero, V., Heatherington, L. and Diamond, G.M. (2011) Alliance in couple and family therapy, *Psychotherapy*, 48 (1): 25–33.

Gurman, A.S. and Kniskern, D.P. (eds.) (1981) *Handbook of Family Therapy*. New York: Brunner/Mazel.

Harari, E. (1996) Empathy and the therapeutic relationship in systemic-oriented therapies: a historical and clinical overview, in C. Flaskas and A. Perlesz (eds.) *The Therapeutic Relationship in Systemic Therapy*. London: Karnac Books.

Johnson, S. (2008) *Hold Me Tight: Seven Conversations for a Lifetime of Love*. New York: Little, Brown.

Lago, C. and Charura, D. (2012) Transcultural perspectives on love and hate: the yin and yang of relationships, within and without therapy, *The Psychotherapist*, 52: 28–9.

Lebow, J. (2013) Editorial: Couple therapy and family therapy, *Family Process*, 52 (1): 1–4.

Lee, J.A. (1973) *Colours of Love: An Exploration of the Ways of Loving*. Toronto, ONT: New Press.

McFadzean, D. (2000) *What Really Matters: The Foundation of Effective Counselling and Psychotherapy* [http://talkingcure.co.uk/articles/whatreallymatters.pdf].

Paul, S. and Charura, D. (2012) Accepting the therapeutic relationship as love, *The Psychotherapist*, 52: 22–3.

Paul, S. and Charura, D. (2014) *An introduction to the Therapeutic Relationship in Counselling and Psychotherapy*. London: Sage.

Polanyi, M. (1966) *The Tacit Dimension*. Garden City, NY: Doubleday.

Rao, P., Pradhan, P.V. and Shah, H. (2004) Psychopathology and coping in parents of chronically ill children, *Indian Journal of Paediatrics*, 71: 695–9.

Rivett, M. and Street, E. (2003) *Family Therapy in Focus*. London: Sage.

Rober, P. (2008) The therapist's inner conversation in family therapy practice: struggling with the complexities of therapeutic encounters with families, *Person-Centred and Experiential Psychotherapies*, 7 (4): 245–61.

Rober, P. (2011) The therapist's experiencing in family therapy practice, *Journal of Family Therapy*, 33: 233–55.

Schwartz, R.B. and Nichols, M.P. (2006) *Family Therapy: Concepts and Methods*, 7th edn. Boston, MA: Pearson/Allyn & Bacon.

Sternberg, R.J. (1998) *The Triangle of Love*. New York: Basic Books.

Thomas, S.E.G., Werner-Wilson, R.J. and Murphy, M.J. (2005) Influence of therapist and client behaviours on therapy alliance, *Contemporary Family Therapy*, 27: 19–35.

Wolska, M. (2011) Marital therapy/couples therapy: indications and contraindications, *Archives of Psychiatry and Psychotherapy*, 3: 57–64.

15 Sex and relationship therapy: therapeutic relationship perspectives

Jacob Jacobson and Andrew Mirrlees

Introduction

Sex and relationship therapy explores the dynamic between the physical, psychological, and relational aspects of people's lives. Relationship therapy addresses relationship problems not necessarily linked to sexual dissatisfaction. The individual or couple hope to restore relationship wellbeing even though they may enjoy a robust sexual life. Sex therapy, however, targets specific sexual dysfunctions brought about by physical or psychological conditions or a combination of the two. Physical factors include the effects of illness, disease, medication, surgery or substance abuse. Psychological and combined factors include relationship breakdown, age, impaired sexual knowledge, sexual abuse, and mental distress such as anxiety and depression. The sex therapist must possess a working knowledge of anatomy, the brain, and sexual functioning and how these interplay with psychological processes. When a couple presents for sex therapy, it is the therapist's role to assess need and consider all potential contributing factors before recommending a task-centred intervention plan.

Most clients that present in our practice report a variety of sexual dysfunction due to physiological conditions. These include diabetes, cardiovascular conditions, hypertension, spinal injury, HIV, cancer, and endocrine imbalances. A common characteristic of sexual problems, in our experience, is that couples often defer seeking treatment due to the sensitive nature of the dysfunction. When self-help fails, the sexual problem acutely impacts on their psychological wellbeing. Dysfunctions such as impaired desire, vaginismus, dyspareunia, premature ejaculation, erectile disorders, and inability to orgasm often result in sexual frustration, self-loathing, and relationship breakdown. Referrals are usually made by general practitioners, consultants or specialized clinics. Sex therapists work in medical settings, charitable agencies, and independent practice, often liaising with general practitioners and medical consultants during the course of treatment.

Foundations of theory and practice

Although sex therapy is a task-centred intervention, it shares similar therapeutic challenges found in more general relationship therapy. Both often result in a therapeutic triangulation of couple and therapist (Malan 1995: 102–4). Equally, there is a need to understand possible unconscious dynamics impairing couple intimacy (Middleberg 2001: 341–3; MacKenzie 2005: 4–5) as well as the systemic mechanism of couple 'actions and reactions' driving unhelpful behaviour (Nichols and Schwartz 2006: 108). Sex therapy therefore requires a skill and expertise to address blocks not only which present within the couple's system of conscious and unconscious dynamics but also those borne of the therapeutic triangle. When conflict arises, alliances within the triangle are prone to ruptures (Malan 1995: 165). The sex therapist must be able to negotiate the complexities of this triangulation to resist ruptures and restore trust and collaboration in the therapeutic process. In doing so, the sex therapist has the opportunity to model healthy collaboration and change to restore wellbeing in the couple.

The ability of the sex therapist to convey empathy and genuineness without blame during therapeutic ruptures challenges the couple to resolve conflict. Exploring how the couple experiences the therapeutic relationship can be useful in offering a model to their own relationship. Westbrook et al. (2007: 45) suggest that, where ruptures have been identified, the role of the therapist is to use 'the therapeutic relationship to provide the client with a corrective emotional experience'. This is done in collaboration, discussing alternative perspectives and not viewing the therapist's own system of beliefs as a starting point from which to offer internal reflections of judgement (Newman 1994: 55–6). The sex therapist must attend to the therapeutic relationship in a way that respects the couple and their autonomy while revisiting agreed goals for change. The therapeutic relationship is therefore central to change.

The stages of the practice of sex and relationship therapy outlined in this chapter reflect the Relate model of working with sexual dysfunctions (Litvinoff 2001: 6–10). The Relate model is an integrative approach that adapts Masters and Johnson's original sensate focus exercises as the framework for treatment (Masters et al. 1988: 488–92). The Relate model of sex therapy includes three main ingredients: graded, task-centred homework which is presented throughout therapy, couples counselling to deal with blocks, and sexual education which is usually the focus of a specific treatment session.

The therapeutic relationship

The initial interview

Sex and relationship therapy begins with an initial interview. There is often an overwhelming sense of powerlessness as the couple face a problem they cannot fix. When sexual dysfunctions present as the primary problem, the couple often view the sex therapist as they would a medical clinician. This is particularly relevant in a medical setting. An accelerated form of trust in the therapeutic relationship is easily built on a medicalized perception that the couple may hold of sex therapy. The authority of the sex therapist therefore creates a therapeutic relationship more akin to the medical model of the clinician and their patient.

The early creation of focused collaboration between couple and sex therapist is essential for change to occur. This begins at the first meeting by working together on the mutually identified 'problem-focused' goals to restore sexual wellbeing in the couple. The sex therapist listens to the story, asks appropriate and relevant questions, and offers recommendations for change. Working in collaboration is central in sex therapy, even at the early stages because it builds confidence and trust within the therapeutic process. The outcome of the initial meeting might be a referral back to the medical consultant or other professional, continued assessment or relationship therapy.

Case vignette: An initial interview

Mary, 24, and Joe, 26, both work in finance and have been together for six years. The couple presented with loss of sexual desire on Mary's part. Mary was from a strong Catholic background. Five months ago, Mary agreed with Joe that cohabitation was a better alternative to marriage at this point of their careers, but she felt uneasy about telling her family of her decision. Mary lost interest in sex shortly after moving in together.

Therapist:	*Aside from the sexual problem, how is your general relationship?*
Mary:	*Great. But I feel angry a lot of the time and hold back.*
Therapist:	*What do you mean?*
Mary:	*[glancing at Joe nervously] I don't know. Just that, I hate living a lie. I feel that Joe forced me into this situation of having to lie to my parents.*
Therapist:	*[turning to Joe] Is that how you see the situation, Joe?*
Joe:	*I never forced Mary. I don't know. My parents got divorced when I was young. My brothers are divorced. My sister is going through a rough patch. What's the point?*
Therapist:	*Have you said this, Joe, to Mary?*
Mary:	*No, he never said that.*
Therapist:	*[looking at both] What would you like to see happen?*
Mary:	*For us to be happy again.*
Joe:	*Yeah. That's what I want.*
Therapist:	*In my experience, it's not uncommon to lose our sexual drive during stress and anxiety. If I understand you correctly, you, Mary, feel that you are living a lie because your parents don't know about your situation. That creates a lot of stress. You, Joe, have a history of witnessing marriages breaking down. I guess we bring a lot of our past into our relationships. Does that make sense?*

Both nod in agreement.

After hearing and reflecting upon their story, the therapist decided to offer relationship therapy for seven sessions plus a review of progress. The couple agreed providing they could access sex therapy if necessary. If sexual dysfunctions have persisted for less than six months, relationship therapy often restores the sexual wellbeing. After seven sessions, Mary and Joe set a date for their wedding and disclosed their decision to her parents. Sexual functioning was restored by the third session. Talking openly about their sexual problem fostered intimacy and communication, thus reducing anxiety and allowing sexual functioning to return (Bancroft 2009: 305–6).

The formulation

If the couple problem requires sex therapy, continued assessment over several sessions followed by a brief account of the nature of their problems further strengthens the collaborative relationship between couple and sex therapist. The formulation of the sexual problem identifies likely contributory factors. Each contributing factor is viewed in relation to its place within the underlying aetiology, which helps establish a rationale for the treatment approach. Exploration of the couple's story thus becomes a shared experience with the sex therapist.

The formulation contextualizes the couple's history and offers an initial focus on how to better understand the way in which their problem has developed. The formulation also provides the couple with an alternative way of perceiving their prior experience. During formulation, the sex therapist demonstrates sensitivity to the couple's perceptions of self while gently challenging maladaptive behaviours. The provision of structure and guidance for change in the formulation reinforces the alliance between couple and sex therapist. In sex therapy, the formulation is followed by mutually identifying goals for treatment, which further strengthens the therapeutic alliance. Setting realistic goals builds the couple's trust and confidence not only in the therapist but in the treatment itself (Leiblum 2006: 144–5).

> ### Case vignette: The therapeutic relationship and sex therapy formulation – working with erectile dysfunction
>
> *Gordon, 68, and Gerry, 57, have been experiencing erectile difficulties. Gerry was admitted to hospital two years previously after a sudden cardiac arrest. Ever since then, he has been unable to sustain his erections. Twelve months later, Gordon also began experiencing erectile dysfunction. Both are retired and have been a couple for 22 years. The therapist was given permission to contact Gerry's cardiologist and referred Gordon for a full medical check-up. Particular consideration was placed on the sexual diversity of the couple to reflect their experience (Simon 1996: 102). After a detailed historical assessment exploring contributing factors, both psychological and physiological, the therapist offered psychosexual treatment.*
>
> Therapist: *[towards the end of the formulation] Ultimately, I assess how strong a couple is to find out if sex therapy is best for them. I was very impressed by what you both told me at the history-taking. Gordon, you said that there's no one like Gerry. He's what gets you up in the morning. And what gets you in bed at night! [all laugh] And Gerry, you said that you love Gordon to bits. That he's the best, the very best thing that has ever happened to you. It's that depth of a relationship which profoundly impressed me. I hope I got everything right. That's how I understand what is going on from what you both told me. Did I get that right?*
>
> Gerry: *Yes. [tears well up in his eyes as he is smiles]*
>
> Gordon: *That was spot on. [glances at Gerry]*
>
> Therapist: *As I said at the beginning of our meeting today, I believe that you both would benefit from sexual therapy. We are basically going to work on*

> *the behaviours which you identified to be detrimental to your relationship and replace them with a different set of behaviours. I will always give you a rationale for why I want you to do something, so please never hesitate to ask if you don't understand the relevance. If it doesn't make sense, then we can talk about it and maybe come up with something else. Is this ok with you both?*

Together with the sex therapist, Gordon and Gerry listed goals for treatment and embarked on this process. Gordon had hidden concerns that any type of sexual activity could kill Gerry. Creating a safe space to discuss Gerry's health status enabled Gordon to overcome his fears. Both looked at the role of sex in their lives and devised strategies to manage their health and wellbeing. Sexual functioning was restored by week twelve.

The therapeutic process and treatment

Within a presentation of the complex inter-relational processes in sex therapy, there is a need to therapeutically hold the couple as they reflect on the internal psychological processes and feelings that relate to their particular form of sexual dysfunction. Treatment consists of graded homework assignments, which the couple do privately and report back to the sexual and relationship therapist through detailed feedback. The process of discussing and agreeing to the tasks builds the collaboration between the couple and the sex therapist.

Treatment restores the relationship the couple have with their sexual functioning and helps model sexual autonomy through participation in assigning tasks. There is always a rationale given when introducing tasks but couples often question the efficacy of what they are offered to do or sometimes come up with their own modification of the original task. The sex therapist will sometimes have to revisit the formulation when giving rationale to help guide the couple towards their overall goal of sexual wellbeing. Enabling the couple to create their own pace towards achieving their goal reinforces the therapeutic relationship.

The importance of collaboration in sex therapy

Case vignette: Collaborative aspect in the therapeutic process and treatment

David, 47, and Lucy, 45, have two children. Two years previously, Lucy was diagnosed with early stages of uterine cancer. She underwent a hysterectomy and received a short course of radiotherapy. Lucy had been diagnosed with diabetes at the age of 35. Both reported being obese, although this was less apparent when meeting them. Lucy had a reduced sex drive and reported pain on intercourse. They were eventually referred to sex therapy by her medical consultant after many failed attempts to treat the problem medically. The sex therapist immediately promoted a sense of committed partnership with the couple to better understand and resolve the problem. The collaboration successfully helped the couple towards their own wellbeing. Impaired collaboration often results in poorer outcomes to treatment (Hawton 1985: 145–59). After ten weeks in treatment there was a noticeable shift in how the couple approached the sexual dysfunction.

Therapist:	Well done with your homework! Something's changed. [smiling at both David and Lucy] What's going on?
Lucy:	I'm feeling a whole lot better. After the last session I thought, 'To hell with this. I'm not going to let cancer take my sex life as well.'
Therapist:	Great! We all have the right to a healthy sex life. Well done, both of you, for wanting that.
Lucy:	Well, I thought about what you said last time and it makes sense to me. It's my body and I can allow myself to have pleasure with it instead of hating it. Looking at my vulva made me connect the dots if you know what I mean?
David:	[smiling] I also found it useful. I never really knew what went on down there with women.
Therapist:	As I said last week, arousal is a complex dynamic and the more we know about it the better we are at understanding ourselves.
Lucy:	Yes. But I never could realize how the surgery and radiotherapy doesn't have to rule my life. They told me about lubrication but it was so much and I don't think I took it all in.
Therapist:	Was there a reason you didn't ask your doctor to explain again?
Lucy:	[blushing] I just felt so stupid for asking.
David:	More like embarrassed!
Lucy:	Yeah, it was that too.

David and Lucy were able to regain their sexual life. Increased sexual knowledge, especially regarding the impact of surgery and radiotherapy, was reinforced by Lucy's own exploration of her genitalia. Both also became more aware of the effects of diabetes on sexual functioning and made lifestyle changes to help them lose weight and be more active. They were also able to speak openly about sex with each other without embarrassment.

The use of feedback in the therapeutic relationship

A key component of sex therapy is the use of feedback. The mechanism of feedback for task-centred homework continually integrates the view of the couple, thereby strengthening mutuality and collaboration. Feedback exists as an 'equalizing factor' within the therapeutic process. Discussing the feedback reinforces the sense of collaboration within the therapeutic relationship by offering the couple the opportunity for ownership of the problem and thereby regaining a sense of control. Feedback also creates a dialogue between couple and sex therapist. As the couple provides feedback, the sex therapist may modify treatment plans based on the feedback. A more personal resonance within the couple develops and the sense of collaboration with the sex therapist strengthens the therapeutic alliance (Miller and Donahey 2012: 204).

Taking feedback also permits issues that relate to social, cultural, religious or other ethical considerations to be acknowledged within the course of treatment, as they may play an integral role in the sexual problem. The sex therapist's own culture or beliefs, however, often inform the way in which they view or understand the feedback of their clients. Reese et al. (2009: 418–21) state that our personal, social, moral or cultural beliefs may cause us to fail to acknowledge the feedback received, and thus to apply it within the therapeutic relationship in such a way that is not congruent to the feelings expressed by the couple.

Feedback allows a sense of equality to exist. The way in which it is acknowledged by the sex therapist offers the couple a sense of control over the progression of therapy. It allows the couple to reflect on their own experience, thereby placing them as central within the therapeutic process of change. Feedback also allows the sex therapist to reflect on how well or not the couple believe the treatment plan is working.

Case vignette: How feedback allows for alternative sexual scripts

Mercy, 28, and Johnson, 29, met while studying at university. Johnson reported lifelong premature ejaculation, which he had managed by masturbating prior to any sexual intercourse. The couple had not had penetrative sex before because Mercy's faith prohibited premarital sex and masturbation. On their wedding night, Johnson ended up 'spilling his seed', and they did not have sex. Mercy also held the belief that men only had a finite number of sperm, so considered male masturbation as a waste. Mercy was furious and was referred to sexual and relationship therapy by her minister. Although premature ejaculation is best treated by a structured masturbation programme, we had to adjust treatment to respect her faith and culture. Therapy should always respect an individual's sexual value system (Brauner 2000: 20).

Therapist:	*Welcome back. So how did homework go?*
Mercy:	*I don't know. It was strange touching Johnson like that, you know. I mean, I never did anything like this before!*
Johnson:	*Well, I ejaculated at first. I could not help myself.*
Therapist:	*[smiling at both] What do you mean?*
Mercy:	*[laughing] Like I said. It was strange doing that!*
Therapist:	*What exactly happened?*
Johnson:	*We were doing the touching homework and things as you said and then it came time for Mercy to touch me down there.*
Mercy:	*I just looked at it and thought, 'What am I to do with that!' You said to pleasure him until he was hard but he was hard right away. And he spilled his stuff all over the place!*
Johnson:	*Yes. I was trying to be cool, you know. But she's too sexy!*
Mercy:	*[laughing] Well, I told him to go and wipe himself clean before I do that again.*

> *Johnson:*   I was okay. We started again. This time she did it right.
> *Mercy:*   You should speak for yourself. I did everything right. You need to behave!
> *Therapist:* So how did it go after that?
> *Mercy:*   Oh, wonderful. I stopped when he told me he was close to the point of inevitability. And I told him, 'No misbehaving you!'
> *Therapist:* [turning to Johnson] Did you feel you had control then?
> *Johnson:*   Yes.
> *Therapist:* So what's different about this experience and what was it like before, Johnson?
> *Johnson:*   Now she is doing it!

Although Johnson still ejaculated before sex, he did not masturbate himself out of respect for Mercy. The couple decided it would be acceptable for Mercy to masturbate him. With Mercy's help, Johnson learned to take control of his ejaculation. Mercy still did not accept masturbation as a sexual practice. However, sexual education during treatment led to her developing a deeper understanding of the male anatomy, which challenged her previous belief regarding sperm count. Mercy no longer believed that Johnson was 'wasting his seed' when he ejaculated prematurely. Two months later, the couple reported a healthy sexual life.

Challenges

The collection of beliefs, experiences, and rules that direct or inform patterns of behaviour and thoughts offer specific considerations for how blocks within the therapeutic relationship can occur. If a couple holds beliefs that involve mistrust of others, there might be limits to self-disclosure that adversely impact on the work. Any internalized guilt or shame associated with particular aspects of their sexual history, for example, could lead to the creation of blocks, ruptures or collusions within the therapeutic relationship.

The therapeutic triangulation of the couple and the sex therapist might also pose a challenge in maintaining the therapeutic relationship (Malan 1995: 14). Ruptured alliances in the couple relationship during the treatment process are not uncommon. Couple ruptures, where one blames the other, often lead to ruptures in the therapeutic relationship or to real or imagined collusions within the triangle. The couple thereby distance themselves from the therapeutic process through blame or negative interpretations. The act of restoring intimacy causes heightened anxiety in some couples who unconsciously wish to disengage emotionally (Daines and Perrett 2000: 142–7). When this happens, it is often after long periods of time in which the couple have attempted to resolve the issue themselves but consistently met with failure. As a result of possible anxiety generated by failure, the couple may unconsciously seek to attribute failure of the therapy to the sex therapist or to the treatment itself. Maintaining an empathic attitude without blame helps the sex therapist revisit goals for treatment and heal ruptures in the therapeutic alliance.

Working with therapeutic ruptures

Case vignette: working with a ruptured therapeutic relationship

Judy, 36, and John, 36, self-referred for couples therapy after a major row the previous month. Both work in sales, often working long hours with the occasional business trip. Judy's mother minds their two small children and helps manage the family home. John is resentful of Judy's career success because he feels she should be at home more. After three sessions, John said he thought couples therapy was 'useless' and announced he was not planning on attending further sessions.

John: I don't see the point of continuing. Nothing seems to be changing.

Therapist: What do you mean?

Judy: [turning to John] You don't want to change. You expect me to change but aren't willing to discuss anything that I want.

John: That's not true. I told you, you need to get your priorities in order. Why did you want to get married and have kids anyway? You couldn't give a toss about the kids.

Therapist: [turning to Judy] You said, Judy, that [turning to John] you, John, don't want to change. [turning back to Judy] What do you mean?

Judy: John just wants things exactly the way they are for him but I'm supposed to make all the sacrifices.

Therapist: Such as what?

Judy: Giving up everything and being a housewife while he has the life doing whatever he wants. Drinking, his mates, just doing what he wants.

Therapist: [turning to John] Is that how you see things, John?

John: There's nothing wrong with what I do. And anyway, if I go out drinking it's work related. I don't need to change. The children need their mother. End of.

Therapist: Was that what you had growing up?

John: No. Maybe that's why I want it for my kids. Otherwise forget it. There's no point to anything. I knew I shouldn't have come.

Therapist: [pause] As I said when we first met, there is no right or wrong way to be in a relationship. At least that's what I believe. If it works, then it works. Why fix it if it ain't broke. But if there is a problem, as the two of you said when we first met, then maybe it's good to go back to the drawing board. What we do know in my profession is that healthy communication is a key ingredient to a good relationship. You, John, told me when we first met that you felt you couldn't talk to Judy anymore. That you felt you weren't being heard. You, Judy, said that you felt you were being strangled by the relationship. I remember that you said at our first visit, John, that you didn't believe in therapy, yet you did come and that's commendable. As I said in the beginning, my job is to enable effective dialogue so that we have choices. And again, I think it's commendable that you both are here. You both invested a lot into this relationship, so it makes sense that you take some time to explore what your options are. I don't know if that makes sense.

John: Yeah it does.

Judy and John continued relationship therapy for the agreed seven sessions plus review. During the review, both acknowledged the value of having continued and returned for a further seven sessions. At the second review, the couple had re-evaluated their expectations of marriage and family life through reflection on their own upbringings and their unspoken anxieties of intimacy and abandonment. John feared re-enacting his childhood dynamics of an absent mother while Judy craved independence from her enmeshed family of origin. They remained in the relationship after renegotiating expectations and were able to develop a plan for shared responsibilities in the family home.

Summary

Sexual and relationship therapy addresses couple dissatisfaction, sexual dysfunction or a combination of both. Central to the role of the sexual and relationship therapist is holding and containing the anxiety within the relationship and offering a safe space to explore alternative patterns of cognition, behaviour, and emotional response. As with most psychological therapies, the therapeutic relationship underpins the efficacy of treatment.

Psychosexual work further complicates the work. The medical model requires the sex therapist to make diagnoses of sexual dysfunction and this potentially creates an accelerated relationship similar to that of the clinician and their patient. There is an initial expectation that the symptoms will be treated and wellbeing restored. Working in a medical setting further emphasizes this dynamic. Although this is advantageous initially, task-centred homework often uncovers therapeutic blocks that must be handled with care.

Challenges in maintaining a therapeutic relationship in sex therapy often centre on the dynamics of the therapeutic triangulation inherent in couples work (Crowe and Ridley 2000: 235–93). Ruptures occur through real or imagined collusions as an attempt by the couple to disengage emotionally from the process through blame or negative interpretations. Maintaining empathy and respect for the couple enables the sex therapist to revisit goals for treatment and help heal any ruptures in the therapeutic alliance.

Reported feedback from the couple reinforces the collaborative nature of sex therapy and builds a bridge towards couple autonomy. As the couple grow stronger, the therapeutic relationship is enhanced and alliances are often quite powerful. Perhaps, given the intimate nature of working with sexuality and sexual dysfunctions, it is the sense of vulnerability that must be embraced by the couple and sex therapist, which, paradoxically, may enhance the therapeutic relationship.

Sex and relationship therapy offers unique challenges in creating and maintaining therapeutic relationships with couples who present for treatment. Sex therapy targets specific sexual dysfunction in the couple that may be a result of physiological or psychological factors. It is a task-centred intervention that requires thorough assessment and diagnosis before collaborative work with the couple work begins. The therapeutic relationship in sex therapy promotes collaboration and autonomy and is therefore central to change.

Further reading

Bancroft, J. (2009) *Human Sexuality and its Problems*, 3rd edn. Edinburgh: Churchill Livingstone Elsevier. Provides a thorough analysis of the psychological, socio-cultural, and neurophysiological aspects of human sexuality.

Harper, F.D. and McFadden, J. (2003) *Culture and Counselling: New Approaches*. Boston, MA: Allyn & Bacon. An informative resource examining theoretical models of counselling practice in relation to multicultural perspectives.

Hawton, K. (1985) *Sex Therapy: A Practical Guide*. Oxford: Oxford University Press. A practical guide to assessing and treating common sexual problems.

References

Bancroft, J. (2009) *Human Sexuality and its Problems*, 3rd edn. Edinburgh: Churchill Livingstone Elsevier.

Brauner, R. (2000) Embracing difference: addressing race, culture and sexuality, in D. Davies and C. Neal (eds.) *Pink Therapy: Issues in Therapy with Lesbian, Gay, Bisexual and Transgender Clients*. Buckingham: Open University Press.

Crowe, M. and Ridley, J. (2000). Therapy with Couples: A Behavioural-Systems Approach to Couple Relationship and Sexual Problems, 2nd edn. Oxford: Blackwell Science.

Daines, B. and Perrett, A. (2000) *Psychodynamic Approaches to Sexual Problems*. Buckingham: Open University Press.

Hawton, K. (1985) *Sex Therapy: A Practical Guide*. Oxford: Oxford University Press.

Leiblum, S.R. (2006) *Principles and Practice of Sex Therapy*, 4th edn. New York: Guilford Press.

Litvinoff, S. (2001) *Sex in Loving Relationships*, 3rd edn. London: Vermilion.

MacKenzie, A.A. (2005) *Object Relations Theory and Implications in Couples Therapy* [http://works.bepress.com/alan_mackenzie/8/; accessed 8 December 2013].

Malan, D.H. (1995) *Individual Psychotherapy and the Science of Psychodynamics*, 2nd edn. Oxford: Butterworth-Heinemann.

Masters, W.H., Johnson, V.E. and Kolodny, R.C. (1988) *Masters and Johnson on Sex and Human Loving*, 2nd edn. New York: Little, Brown.

Middleberg, C.V. (2001) Projective identification in common couples dances, *Journal of Marital and Family Therapy*, 27 (3): 341–52.

Miller, S.D. and Donahey, K.M. (2012) Feedback-informed treatment (FIT): improving the outcome of sex therapy one person at a time, in P.J. Kleinplatz (ed.) *New Directions in Sex Therapy: Innovations and Alternatives*, 2nd edn. New York: Routledge.

Newman, C.F. (1994) Understanding client resistance: methods for enhancing motivation to change, *Cognitive and Behavioural Practice*, 1: 47–69.

Nichols, M.P. and Schwartz, R.C. (2006) *Family Therapy: Concepts and Methods*, 7th edn. Boston, MA: Allyn & Bacon.

Reese, R.J., Norsworthy, L.A. and Rowlands, S.R. (2009) Does a continuous feedback system improve psychotherapy outcome?, *Psychotherapy: Theory, Research, Practice, Training*, 46 (4): 418–31.

Simon, G. (1996) Working with people in relationships, in D. Davies and C. Neal (eds.) *Pink Therapy: A Guide for Counsellors and Therapists Working with Lesbian, Gay and Bisexual Clients* (pp. 101–15). Buckingham: Open University Press.

Westbrook, D., Kennerly, H. and Kirk, J. (2007) *An Introduction to Cognitive Behaviour Therapy: Skills and Applications*. London: Sage.

SECTION 4

The Therapeutic Relationship in the Helping and Mental Health Professions

16 The therapeutic relationship in the helping professions

Sally Read

Introduction

Which are the 'helping professions?' This chapter is aimed at any health or social care professional who spends time thinking about the relational aspect of their roles. It will also help counsellors and psychotherapists working in multidisciplinary teams, particularly those for whom at least some colleagues are working to a 'medical model'. There is no scope here for a detailed examination of any one professional group. However, as a former general practitioner and doctor working in drug addiction, now an integrative psychotherapist, I have observed the challenges of working in teams: balancing the needs of clients, managers, and service, all while striving to maintain effective therapeutic relationships.

To explore how therapeutic relationships are shaped by our professional roles, this chapter focuses on those relationships, as it were, from the inside out. Examples of a wider range of professionals involved in engaging in therapeutic relationships are considered. There is then an examination of goals and values of professional teams, and, finally, the boundaries of different professionals within society.

Foundations of professional practice and ethics in the therapeutic relationship

I work alone in private practice, and as part of a team at a homeless hostel. Therapists working in teams may find themselves alongside others carrying out 'listening' roles. Teams vary enormously – multidisciplinary or uni-professional, statutory or voluntary sector, primary or secondary care, and so on. Often, workers from different disciplines may work with the same clients. There may be working across teams, for example with children's social care or criminal justice. All these settings bring challenges to relationships that need to be considered, particularly by those working psychotherapeutically. I want to address just two issues here, confidentiality and therapist self-disclosure.

Whatever your profession, you will be used to its codes of confidentiality. It cannot be assumed, however, that practices are universally shared. As a doctor I thought that I *knew* about confidentiality. And, in a medical sense, I did. But therapists I met were doing things differently; and this could perhaps best be summarized as *thinking* much more carefully about the effects of disclosure. Healthcare teams are likely to think in more concrete ways about who 'needs to know', without much consideration of the psychic impact. This is a generalization, I know, but it is true to my experience. Wherever we work, it is worth thinking about who we 'take with us' into the therapy room and what we share outside it. For example, do we share notes with other professionals? If so, what do we do with information gained from reading the notes, rather than from our client directly? What do we write in our notes if they are going to be seen by others? At the hostel where I work, my meetings with residents are confidential (with the usual caveats), but there are times when I need to consider carefully the impact of not sharing *some* information with keyworkers. I need to think about what the recipient of this information will do with it, and what codes *they* are bound by. Professional guidance leaves room for manoeuvre. For example, the Code of the Nursing and Midwifery Council (NMC 2010) states, 'You must respect people's rights to confidentiality' (p. 2), but that members must share information with colleagues (p. 4). Guidance for social workers (BASW 2012) recognizes that problems arise, and encourages professionals to 'identify dilemmas about confidentiality and seek support to address these issues' (p. 14).

It is usually held as self-evident in both health and social care that 'joined-up working' is a good thing. However, my psychotherapy training has taught me the importance of thinking about the *meanings*, for our clients and colleagues, of sharing information.

Just as we differ in our thinking about client confidentiality, attitudes to *how much of ourselves* we bring to our work also vary. Many family doctors disclose, occasionally, information from their private life. Surgeries announce such things as forthcoming weddings of their staff, and some patients seem to enjoy this sense of involvement. Psychotherapists *may* differ, and wonder about the effect of such information on their clients. Allan (2009) wrote that knowing nothing about her social worker meant that she 'never had to worry about' her. She concludes, 'I cannot emphasise enough how valuable this was to my recovery' (p. 1). Conversely, many workers might have been trained to withhold their *feelings* from their work, whereas most psychotherapists consider it vital to pay attention to countertransferential feelings and sometimes to share them (Maroda 2004). You may want to reflect on your own practice in the sharing of 'information' about yourself, or whether you ever find it helpful to tell a client, for example, that you feel moved by what they have told you, or angry about their behaviour.

The therapeutic relationship: who are we helping, and who not?

Unless you are a GP or primary care nurse, it is likely that your team will have 'entry criteria' for clients, and that you are, therefore, working only with people who fulfil these criteria. Clearly, this is pragmatic and, at times, essential; but it also means that, sometimes, people are excluded from treatment. Rizq (2013) suggests that some of the most difficult, complex human suffering is denied by the prevalent culture of providing only that which can be demonstrated worthwhile by quantitative scores. I know from long, bitter personal experience, as a doctor working with marginalized people, that such complex suffering renders my former patients unsuitable for treatment across primary and secondary care, even by specialist personality disorder services. So while we think about the ways in which our various workplaces might dictate who we see and what sort of relationships we can develop, we should also think about whom we cannot see and what is happening to them.

Teams, their goals and values

In this section, we will consider how the goals towards which we work, and our underlying values, affect the quality of our relationships. Implicit in this discussion is the question of how much the therapeutic relationship is *itself* recognized as valuable, and the pursuit of it an important goal.

The range of *goals* across the 'helping professions' is enormous and it would be fruitless to try and list them all here: from managing high blood pressure, to achieving abstinence from illicit drugs, to securing move-on accommodation – the range is enormous. Our *values* may be less variable between professions, but between teams they may vary greatly and be influenced by setting, resources, and individual commissioners, managers, and colleagues.

Goals and their measurement in the relationship

In GP training, I learned about goals of the consultation, which included listening to my patients' concerns, involving them in management, and attempting to achieve a shared understanding. In short, I was taught that I needed to nurture therapeutic relationships. Medical students still learn this. But the reality for many healthcare staff is that this 'patient-centredness' is threatened by the need to achieve targets, follow guidance, and practise only that which adheres strictly to the evidence base. All of these are important but, if followed without reflection, risks practice becoming 'tyrannical, hierarchical, controlled, intolerant, and dogmatic' (Spence 2012).

Most health and social care professionals will be members of a professional council that falls under the aegis of the Professional Standards Authority (PSA). Others work in services that are on the voluntary register of the PSA, or applying for voluntary registration. Many services are subject to inspection by the Care Quality Commission (CQC). The goals of registration and inspection are laudable. The CQC expects services to be safe, efficient, caring, well-led, and user-focused. However, I suggest that, at times, the pursuit of these goals may challenge our therapeutic relationships.

How is the 'target culture' affecting the world of counselling and psychotherapy? With the next re-tendering exercise looming, under increasingly rigorous financial constraints, teams work hard to prove their effectiveness to commissioners. What impact does this have on the relationship between counsellors and their clients? Rizq's (2013: 23) view is clear: 'attention to targets, outcomes, protocols and policies is consistently privileged over attention to the patient's need for a confidential psychotherapeutic relationship with an experienced, consistent and thoughtful clinician'. I believe there is an urgent need for therapists working in teams taking on NHS contracts to find spaces to talk about how their work, their relationships, and their morale are being affected.

Outside of statutorily funded services, many in the private or charitable sectors monitor outcomes too. They use quantitative scores such as CORE and PHQ9, or more qualitative measures that, perhaps, stay closer to the clients' experience. One example of such a tool is the Outcomes Star (www.outcomesstar.org.uk), which allows client and worker to assess progress together, across a range of variables. Evidence of effectiveness is essential, clearly, but equally important is how we incorporate monitoring into our clinical practice and the effect it has on our relationships with clients.

Values

However we measure effectiveness, professionals from many fields have long known that the quality of the relationship has profound effects on their efficacy. For psychotherapists, across the modalities, the quality of the therapeutic relationship is a good indicator of therapeutic success. Paul and Haugh (2008) provide a thorough summary of research that demonstrates the importance of therapeutic alliance across most therapeutic traditions. This is notwithstanding what is at times a heated debate between modalities about *how* the relationship is valued. Following the announcement of IAPT money in 2007, along with NICE's endorsement of cognitive behavioural therapy and related therapies, a debate ensued between Andrew Samuels (UKCP) and David Veale (BABCP) (Samuels and Veale 2007). One of the points of contention between the protagonists is the importance of the relationship. If you are one of the many therapists or nurses undertaking cognitive behavioural therapy, you will undoubtedly view relational factors as important; perhaps recognizing that therapist warmth, genuineness, and empathy create the setting in which cognitive techniques can be most effectively applied (Gilbert and Leahy 2007). However, this is a different emphasis from either the humanistic or analytical traditions where the relationship, in different ways, is considered as the 'vehicle of cure'. Evans and Gilbert (2005) suggest workers across these traditions are recognizing this increasingly, at the same time as growing neurobiological knowledge demonstrates the fundamental importance of interpersonal interactions in influencing brain function.

In medicine, Balint (1957, in Gomez 1997) developed thinking and practice around the use of the 'drug doctor'; or the efficacy of the doctor's *personal presence* and his ongoing therapeutic relationship with his patient. A huge body of literature has built upon Balint's work. For example, Neighbour (1987) has written extensively about relational consulting styles for GPs and Tasman (2002) demonstrates how the use of empathy, meaning, and the doctor–patient relationship, in contrast to a working style based only on DSM diagnosis, improves psychiatrists' effectiveness.

In social work, Hennessey (2011) provides an effective argument for the centrality of therapeutic relationships. Ingram (2013) argues that emotional intelligence in social work has much to offer professional and client. And Bach and Grant (2011) provide both a practical handbook on communication and interpersonal skills for nurses and a summary of evidence for its efficacy.

While most healthcare professionals agree that the relationship is of central importance, it is tragic that many are being asked to work as if this were not the case. Such denial is making the daily working lives of many doctors, nurses, psychotherapists, and others frustrating and leading to the loss of dedicated staff. The threat appears greatest to those working in team settings – in the statutory sector to a large extent, but increasingly for those in non-statutory settings who receive statutory funding.

The pressure to work mechanistically, without sufficient attention to the building and maintenance of a strong therapeutic alliance has been around for a very long time. Rizq (2013) cites Menzies-Lyth's (1959) study of nurses who were forced to work in depersonalized, task-focused ways and left the profession as a result. I have worked in teams where 'attachment' was seen as unhealthy, not able to be thought about, and unnecessary to reach team targets. Staff were confused, angry, and demotivated as a result.

However, I have found that even in the most goal-driven services, it is possible to take time to think about our relationships, if we value this. One of the 'tools' I have found most helpful for this is Karpman's drama triangle (Widdowson 2010). Staff with relatively little experience can understand the concepts of victim, persecutor, and rescuer quickly and to great effect. At one team meeting, a worker recalled a conflict that arose when she was trying to help her client find housing. Having found herself feeling like a persecutor, by thinking about her client's 'victimhood', she gained some insight. By then thinking instead about her client's vulnerability and her own power, she was able to find creative potential in the situation.

The power dynamic within relationships can be overlooked in any setting, but perhaps particularly within a strongly goal-driven service, where specific outcomes are required. To disavow our power puts us in danger of exerting it. Larner (1999: 41) writes: 'therapists can be powerful, but sacrifice themselves for the sake of the other (and this) allows the power of the other to emerge'. You might want to consider how possible this is for you in your workplace setting. How far are you able to allow your clients' voices to be heard? This may entail a struggle – for therapist, client, and the wider service. Totton (2009: 19) suggests the struggle is healthy and necessary: 'the client and therapist can negotiate, argue, wrestle together over how to understand their experience of each other'. Such openness can bring about deepening of trust and important advances in therapeutic progress. Sometimes the 'struggle' results in what amounts to a rupture in relationship. But such ruptures are opportunities for growth. Safran et al. (2011) conducted two meta-analyses of ruptures and subsequent interventions. Attempts to repair therapeutic strains may include, they suggest, a revisiting of therapeutic rationale, changes to therapeutic goals or styles, surface clarifications, and an examination of the relational themes and history associated with the rupture. DeYoung (2003: Ch. 5) provides an in-depth exploration of how a therapeutic rupture came to be understood in transferential terms as a repetition of an earlier relational rupture, which could be explored and understood, albeit painfully, through the therapeutic relationship.

Therapeutic relationships in society

In this section, I consider how our health and social care systems are situated within society. I will start by looking at boundaries of time and place, and then at where we are placed, in a conceptual sense, in society's power structures.

Time boundaries

Most readers who work within statutory services will be used to being very busy, working under challenging time demands. Appointments overrun or are cut short; people get called away on emergencies. Time boundaries are moveable, even loose. We know that this affects relationships but we may feel powerless, indeed *be* powerless, to change the system.

These looser boundaries may even extend to times outside of work, as expected of us by society at large. When we bump into patients or clients in the street, it may be considered acceptable to have a brief chat, or at least to acknowledge each other. Some patients will think nothing of consulting in the post office! Many workers are resigned to this; others choose to live some distance from their workplace in order to avoid such encounters. Psychotherapists tend to think carefully about unplanned meetings with clients in public places, appreciating both the intra-psychic and interpersonal implications. Many will prepare clients for the possibility of such encounters, but find that they can still cause difficulties.

In the longer term, there is an 'ebb and flow' of some work in health and social care, with periods of frequent contact interspersed by absences of months or years. This results in many professionals (social workers, nurses, and some doctors) knowing their clients for years, or even families of several generations. For others, interventions occur over well-circumscribed periods with a clear beginning and end. Society sometimes has different expectations from professionals. This can also be the case among professionals themselves, such as the tension that exists between those who see drug addiction as a chronic condition requiring long-term open-ended treatment, and the current expectation that addictions can be cured in single defined 'treatment episodes'.

I have been interested to notice the different rhythms of a psychotherapist's life. The predictability of the therapeutic frame (Clarkson 2003) is one that psychotherapists learn provides safety. Clarkson suggests that adherence to the contractual working alliance crosses all therapeutic boundaries and is an essential foundation of therapeutic efficacy. These stricter time boundaries may not sit easily within the more chaotic setting of, for example, a primary healthcare centre. For counsellors working in such a team setting, the looser time boundaries of other professionals (e.g. doctors running late) may have an impact on their own, and challenge the working alliance.

However, some therapists will deliberately, if cautiously, allow a relaxation of strict boundaries occasionally. This might be understood as a temporary benign regression (Balint 1968, in Gerrard 2011), an attempt to repair very early relational damage. While private practitioners are able to offer an extra session, for example, this may not be possible in statutory settings, which are likely to offer time-limited contracts with strict criteria on discharge for non-attendance. The variation in contracts offered by counselling services is a debate that I will not enter into here, but which I mention to encourage readers to consider their own position, and that of their service.

Working with homeless people challenges many boundaries, including those of time. Homeless people may find it hard to arrive or to finish on time; and there are many reasons for this, but therapists working with them are finding effective ways of working. Brown et al. (2011) describe a project to engage the most socially excluded clients and consider the implications of the flexibility that is necessary.

And finally, endings. Unlike the lifelong relationships enjoyed or endured by some healthcare workers, or the very brief encounters for others, many therapists enter into what could be called medium-term relationships that need to be ended carefully (see, for example, Holmes 2001). In my previous professional roles it would often not have been possible for workers to plan endings, and unusual for workers to allow themselves time to process the countertransferential effects of successful discharges, unplanned disappearances or deaths. Your services may be better at this, or you may want to think about how they could be improved.

Physical boundaries

We tend to take for granted that therapy occurs within safe, quiet rooms. Holmes (1992) wrote of the impact on transference relationships and therapeutic process when NHS psychotherapy was moving from hospitals into the community, with consultations sometimes taking place in patients' homes. If you work in both clinic and community, you too will notice the different 'feel' to the relationship you have with patients in different settings.

Alternatively, our clinical spaces, whether treatment or therapy rooms, are sometimes felt to be oppressive (Read 2011). I have observed this for those who spend their lives on the streets, and for clients who have been imprisoned and tortured. I am helped to understand it by Adlam and Scanlon (2005), who describe the state of internal 'unhousedness' that develops as a result of disorganized attachment histories and may contribute to the unwillingness of some homeless clients to enter *our* spaces. Hare-Mustin (1994) suggests that the therapy room contains society's dominant discourses, obscuring the view of the marginalized discourses outside.

This leads us to a consideration of the *conceptual* space occupied by psychotherapy and to some extent by all health and social care in society today. Bound by our professional standards and committed to working towards our service targets, we occupy a place within the *centre* of society. We are, as it were, in the mainstream. Blackwell (2005) suggests our registering bodies retain vestiges of empire in their ideologies. But many of our clients come to us in states of distress that take them closer to the *edges* of society; whether sick, abused, bereaved, divorced, jobless, or homeless. How do we respond to this potential dislocation? Do we stay within the secure centre of our professional registration, teams, outcome measures, and evidence base? Or does time spent with people on the margins leads us to vicarious experiences of our clients' powerlessness and distress? And if we do find ourselves out on the margins alongside our clients, how do we relate to the power at the centre? All of us, whatever our profession, have a duty to work in a way that does not oppress our clients, but know this can be difficult. We struggle with the oppression that arises from systems apparently outside of our control – benefits systems, housing regulations, and staff shortages are just a few examples, but many more encountered on an all-too-frequent basis contribute to an environment in which professionals from all sorts of backgrounds are uncomfortably aware of being part of a society that oppresses. McFarlane (2012) makes a strong case *against* indifference to oppression, and *for* the adoption of a loving stance in our work; one that never ceases to be aware of the personal, political, and social aspects of our encounters. Could it be that love might help provide an answer to the challenges of trying to bridge the gaps between centre and margins?

Paul and Charura (2012) offer a history and analysis of the presence of love in the therapeutic relationship. They recognize that the use of the word 'love' engenders fear of erotic transference or malpractice. I think that in many of our workplace settings, talk of love raises fears of being woolly-minded, and not evidence-based. Sometimes it feels safer to talk about compassion, and there are signs of professions reclaiming this quality. Nurses have launched a three-year strategy, Compassion in Practice (CBCNO/ DHCNA 2012), following a large consultation with both professionals and patients. In social work, Bilson (2007) reflects on the role of love in addressing ethical issues. One of the great champions of a human, compassionate face to medicine is Iona Heath. In her 2012 lecture; *Love's Labours Lost*, she made a plea for the freeing of all professionals from some of their present straitjackets, and for a commitment to living with the uncertainty arising from loving therapeutic relationships.

As a psychotherapist, I understand love, in part, in terms of two concepts: *presence and acceptance*. The therapist who is fully *present* is one who, while maintaining optimal intra-psychic contact (or awareness of his own responses), stays fully available for the client. Paul and Charura (2012) describe presence as authenticity, and Yontef (2002) agrees that presence implies a way of being that is authentic, interested, patient, and humble, enabling the client to discover and accept himself before he can begin to change. Rogers' (1992) unconditional positive regard describes an attitude that is at one with the concept of non-possessive love, or agape (Rogers 1962, in Paul and Charura 2012). And as the therapist accepts and values the client, so the client has a chance to develop *self-love* and acceptance. Thus accepting his current condition, he can slowly begin to change; this being the basis of Beisser's paradoxical theory of change (Beisser 1970, in Joyce and Sills 2010: 39): 'change occurs when one becomes what he is, not when he tries to become what he is not'. This marvellous phrase sums up, for me, the attitude of love available to all in the helping professions who wish to make it their own, but which can be so difficult to hold on to when change is demanded through target-chasing, rather than hoped for with compassion.

Summary

I have ended this chapter with some thoughts about love. Having endeavoured to think about issues addressing a range of 'helping professionals', it is perhaps fitting to finish with a quality and aspect of our practices that surely unites us more than any other.

By thinking about ourselves and our clients, the values of our workplaces and professional structures, and our boundaries of time and place within society, as professionals, wherever we work, we will be helped to think about our therapeutic relationships. Through such reflection, we continue to challenge and enrich our working lives, and the lives of our clients.

As we have seen, the challenges to our therapeutic relationships are many. However, with developments such as nursing's Compassion in Practice (CBCNO/

DHCNA 2012) and the UKCP devoting an issue of its journal (*The Psychotherapist*, issue 52, Autumn 2012) to love, perhaps there is room for hope that those who wish to can continue to develop their practice with relationships in mind.

Further reading

The following books are an 'essential read' for not only psychotherapists but also those in the helping professions who want to understand more about the therapeutic relationship.

Clarkson, P. (2003) *The Therapeutic Relationship*. London: Whurr. Considers the relationship across a range of fields.

DeYoung, P.A. (2003) *Relational Psychotherapy: A Primer*. Hove: Brunner-Routledge. An engaging account of working relationally in psychotherapy.

References

Adlam, J. and Scanlon, C. (2005) Personality disorder and homelessness: membership and 'unhoused minds' in forensic settings, *Group Analysis*, 38 (3): 452–66.
Allan, C. (2009) *My Brilliant Survival Guide* [http://www.guardian.co.uk/society/2009/jan/14/mental-health-clare-allan-social-worker; accessed 26 July 2013].
Bach, S. and Grant, A. (2011) *Communication and Interpersonal Skills in Nursing*, 2nd edn. Exeter: Learning Matters.
Beisser, A. (1970) *The Paradoxical Theory of Change* [http://pioneersofchange.net/library/articles/Paradoxical%20Theory%20of%20Change.pdf; accessed 13 December 2007].
Bilson, A. (2007) Promoting compassionate concern in social work: reflections on ethics, biology and love, *British Journal of Social Work*, 37 (8): 1371–86.
Blackwell, D. (2005) *Counselling and Psychotherapy with Refugees*. London: Jessica Kingsley.
British Association of Social Workers (BASW) (2012) *The Code of Ethics for Social Work: Statement of Principles* [http://cdn.basw.co.uk/upload/basw_112315-7.pdf].
Brown, G., Kainth, K., Matheson, C., Osborne, J., Trenkle, A. and Adlam, J. (2011) An hospitable engagement? Open-door psychotherapy with the socially excluded, *Psychodynamic Practice*, 17 (3): 307–24.
Clarkson, P. (2003) *The Therapeutic Relationship*. London: Whurr.
Commissioning Board Chief Nursing Officer and DH Chief Nursing Adviser (CBCNO/DHCNA) (2012) *Compassion in Practice* [http://www.england.nhs.uk/wp-content/uploads/2012/12/compassion-in-practice.pdf; accessed 13 October 2013].
DeYoung, P.A. (2003) *Relational Psychotherapy: A Primer*. Hove: Brunner-Routledge.
Evans, K.R. and Gilbert, M.C. (2005) *An Introduction to Integrative Psychotherapy*. Basingstoke: Palgrave Macmillan.
Gerrard, J. (2011) *The Impossibility of Knowing: Dilemmas of a Psychotherapist*. London: Karnac Books.

Gilbert, P. and Leahy, R.L. (eds.) (2007) *The Therapeutic Relationship in the Cognitive Behavioral Psychotherapies*. Hove: Routledge.

Gomez, L. (1997) *An Introduction to Object Relations*. London: Free Association Books.

Hare-Mustin, R.T. (1994) Discourses in the mirrored room: a postmodern analysis of therapy, *Family Process*, 33 (1): 19–35.

Heath, I. (2012) *Love's Labours Lost: Why Society is Straitjacketing its Professionals and How We might Release Them*. International Futures Forum; Michael Shea memorial lecture [http://www.internationalfuturesforum.com/u/cms/Iona_Heath_Lecture2012.pdf; accessed 14 October 2013].

Hennessey, R. (2011) *Relationship Skills in Social Work*. London: Sage.

Holmes, J. (1992) Psychiatry without walls: some psychotherapeutic reflections, *Psychoanalytic Psychotherapy*, 6 (1): 1–12.

Holmes, J. (2001) *The Search for the Secure Base: Attachment Theory and Psychotherapy*. Hove: Brunner-Routledge.

Ingram, R. (2013) Locating emotional intelligence at the heart of social work practice, *British Journal of Social Work*, 43 (5): 987–1004.

Joyce, P. and Sills, C. (2010) *Skills in Gestalt Counselling and Psychotherapy*. London: Sage.

Larner, G. (1999) Derrida and the deconstruction of power as context and topic in therapy, in I. Parker (ed.) *Deconstructing Psychotherapy* (pp. 39–53). London: Sage.

Maroda, K. (2004) *The Power of the Countertransference: Innovations in Analytic Technique*. Hillsdale, NJ: Analytic Press.

McFarlane, K. (2012) Love: taking a stance, *The Psychotherapist*, 52: 24–5.

Menzies-Lyth, I. (1959) The functioning of social systems as a defence against anxiety, *Human Relations*, 13: 95–121.

Neighbour, R. (1987) *The Inner Consultation*. Lancaster: Kluwer.

Nursing and Midwifery Council (NMC) (2010) *The Code: Standards of Conduct, Performance and Ethics for Nurses and Midwives* [http://www.nmc-uk.org/Publications/Standards/The-code/Introduction/; accessed 12 October 2013].

Paul, S. and Charura, D. (2012) Accepting the therapeutic relationship as love, *The Psychotherapist*, 52: 22–4.

Paul, S. and Haugh, S. (2008) The relationship not the therapy? What the research tells us, in S. Haugh and S. Paul (eds.) *The Therapeutic Relationship: Themes and Perspectives* (pp. 9–22). Ross-on-Wye: PCCS Books.

Read, S. (2011) *Tougher than ever before? What is the experience, both professional and personal, of humanistic psychotherapists working with destitute asylum seekers?* Unpublished MA dissertation.

Rizq, R. (2013) The language of healthcare, *Therapy Today*, 24 (2): 20–4.

Rogers, C.R. (1992) The necessary and sufficient conditions of therapeutic personality change, *Journal of Consulting and Clinical Psychology*, 60 (6): 827–32.

Safran, J.D., Muran, J.C. and Eubanks-Carter, C. (2011) Repairing alliance ruptures, *Psychotherapy*, 48 (1): 80–7.

Samuels, A. and Veale, D. (2007) *Correspondence between Dr David Veale, President of BABCP and Professor Andrew Samuels, UKCP* [http://ipnosis.postle.net/pages/IAPTCBTdebate.htm; accessed 26 July 2013].

Spence, D. (2012) What happened to the doctor–patient relationship?, *British Medical Journal*, 344: e4349.

Tasman, A. (2002) Lost in the DSM-IV checklist: empathy, meaning and the doctor–patient relationship, *Academic Psychiatry*, 26 (1): 38–44.

Totton, N. (2009) Power in the therapy room, *Therapy Today*, 20 (7): 16–19.

Widdowson, M. (2010) *Transactional Analysis: 100 Key Points and Techniques*. Hove: Routledge.

Yontef, G. (2002) The relational attitude in Gestalt therapy theory and practice, *International Gestalt Journal*, 25 (1): 15–34.

17 Working with diagnosis within psychiatric settings: about diagnosis, evolution, and paradigm shift

João Hipólito, Odete Nunes and Rute Brites

Introduction

The practice of diagnosis has been a subject of debate and controversy, even in the psychiatric setting. That is, some theoretical and clinical perspectives consider it as a starting point for their intervention, while others believe this evaluation process to be useless or even counterproductive. The antagonism between the various stances has sparked reflection on the preponderance of diagnosis, leading to some changes in the way it is applied, especially in terms of the appropriateness of treatment.

The notion of psychiatric diagnosis, currently based on psychopathological classifications such as the DSM-V (American Psychiatric Association 2013) and the ICD-10 (World Health Organization 1992), has been undergoing reformulation, at times profound. The concept of a biomedical diagnosis is defined as the process that aims to place the disease/disorder within a given knowledge system, structuring it according to a set of common and 'universal' terms. It stems from an understanding of physiological and pathological processes that have evolved progressively based on the natural sciences (Clyne 1998). However, the underlying biomedical model remains unchanged.

According to such an analysis, psychological problems are examined in a manner analogous to physical problems with regard to identification, in an attempt to find a treatment specific to each situation (Joseph and Worsley 2005). Thus, diagnosis and treatment emerge as notions that are intertwined. In the words of Strawbridge and Woolfe (2003), diagnosis 'assumes that if the "symptoms" can be properly categorized (diagnosed) this will lead to the application of a "treatment" (. . .) to target the symptoms in predictable, measurable ways' (cited in Fletcher 2012: 2). On this point of view, disease-centred biomedical diagnosis underpins the proposed treatment of the patient. The divergence with other perspectives lies in the disagreement about the systemization of the treatment as a result exclusively of the diagnosis.

In 1977, Engel attempted to demonstrate the inadequacy of the biomedical model, replacing it with what he called the bio-psychosocial model. According to Kaplan et al. (2006), this model presupposed a more systemic and integrated understanding of the disease and respective treatment, taking into account the interrelation between the systems that are a part of ourselves, namely the biological, psychological, and social systems. However, from our point of view, this perspective does not represent a real paradigm shift, rather an enhancement of the traditional biomedical model of linear causality.

It should be noted that the many perspectives on the value of diagnosis and its application are aligned with the philosophical principles of the models of therapeutic intervention. These range from those anchored in an essentialist stance (e.g. psychoanalytical model; Rycroft 1973) to those based on an existentialist perspective (e.g. client-centred approach, existential therapy).

We now examine three models of psychotherapeutic intervention whose diagnostic process is in line with the philosophical ideal that underpins the approach to the person in distress.

Foundations of theory and practice

Classical approaches and evolution of the practice of diagnosis

Since its early days, psychology's main approaches have developed ways of conceptualizing and implementing diagnosis that are closely associated with the intervention plan. The change that has occurred gradually results from consensus that the efficiency of the therapeutic relationship is conditioned by the good decoding of patients' individual needs. However, this 'gluing' to the biomedical model still persists, which, in our view, is manifestly insufficient to understand human behaviour.

Psychoanalytical approach

Regardless of the specificity claimed by models that follow the psychoanalytical trend, we believe that they base their therapeutic intervention largely on diagnosis. The difference may ultimately lie in the type of diagnosis used. From a historical perspective, psychoanalysis has contributed markedly to the development of psychiatric diagnosis. However, as emphasized by Bornstein (2001: 6), 'in the span of a few decades, the official psychiatric diagnostic system shifted from being predominantly psychoanalytic to being determinedly atheoretical and nonanalytic'.

Despite the use, whenever necessary, of psychiatric diagnosis, the focus of psychoanalytical practice has been on the patient's analysability, i.e. on their potential to develop a transference relationship and its quality. The diagnosis allows us an idea of the type and quality of the transference that the patient will be 'able' to do, even if a reflection on the practice leads to the conclusion that 'clinicians' ideas about the capacity of different kinds of patients to form transference relationships have varied according to their own personal experiences' (Wolfe 1989: 188).

Contemporary psychoanalysis has relinquished Freud's fundamentally intra-psychic perspective and embraced the 'two-person psychology' that emphasizes the importance of lifelong bonding relationships (Nelson-Jones 2006). This contemporary perspective examines the notion of diagnosis in association with the therapeutic relationship co-constructed between the patient and the psychoanalyst, including the formulation of the diagnosis. McWilliams (2011) warns of the care one must take in this formulation, because when the psychoanalyst is 'observing something, s/he is part of what is being observed'; diagnosing individuals involves taking a 'one person perspective of trying to understand what is consistent about the patient in any relationship' (p. 95).

The expectations developed by the psychoanalyst about a patient based on his diagnosis may lead him to overvalue certain aspects of his discourse and to undervalue others (considered as resistance), while simultaneously laying bare his weaknesses/ fears about the evaluation that the patient may undertake of him, whether consciously or unconsciously (McWilliams 2011).

Thus, this is a relational approach that depends on the diagnosis and which, despite distancing itself from the biomedical model, is still based on an essentialist approach in so far as the diagnosis leads to a particular behaviour that has been established *a priori* by the psychoanalyst.

Cognitive behavioural approach

In the context of cognitive behavioural therapy (CBT), diagnosis has always been the main determinant of treatment. As stated by Scott and Sembi (2006), CBT treatments have been developed with respect to specific diagnoses. Treatment interventions are based on the initial diagnosis evaluation, with treatments appropriate to each diagnosed disorder being described. They address the identified symptoms – target behaviours (behaviour) and the erroneous thoughts and beliefs that underlie them (cognition), seeking to remove the systematic pre-conceptions (systematic biases) of patients' thoughts (Nelson-Jones 2006).

According to Boswell (2013: 381), 'over several decades, there has been a proliferation of treatment manuals that prescribe narrowly defined techniques aimed at narrowly defined problems', which denotes a systematic (methodical) concern in deepening the study of the effectiveness of treatment according to the patient's psychiatric diagnosis. Historically, CBT itself was developed by Beck to address a specific problem – depression. Simultaneously, the proliferation of procedures and variations in treatment to some extent submerged professionals, highlighting the need for change. In 1980, Goldfried presented a set of change principles, or intervention strategies, that cut across theoretical and diagnostic boundaries.

These principles, which in terms of the therapeutic relationship underpinned the development of an integrative perspective, also gave substance to the subsequent emergence of the so-called cognitive behavioural transdiagnoses (Boswell 2013), in line with those who considered that 'relying on a particular clinical manual for a specific psychological disorder often does not work in the real world' (Beard and Björgvinsson 2013: 281). Transdiagnoses objectify the integration of common principles of human functioning in core treatments and intervention strategies that cut across several diagnostic approaches and categories. Underlying this is the idea of the existence of a core pathology that is present in several individuals suffering from different emotional disturbances, such as anxiety and depression, among others (Norton and Philipp 2008; Boswell 2013). They aim to become more effective, reliable, and comprehensive methods with regard to patients (McManus et al. 2010).

Moreover, individualized forms of case analysis (case formulations) are becoming increasingly used and systemized, providing the basis for choosing the most appropriate treatments instead of those proposed by the 'textbook'. Described by Mumma (2011: 29) 'as an idiographic theory of the person and his or her life situation (the person-situation), which includes problems as well as triggering and maintaining variables, including cognitions (thoughts and beliefs), that have relevance for treatment planning for a particular individual', the case formulation aims to reduce the unpredictability associated with individual idiosyncrasies and lack of rigour in diagnosis, in addition to bringing the planned intervention closer to the needs of each patient.

Although some psychotherapists uphold the incompatibility between diagnosis (centred on pathology) and case formulation (centred on the individual), Scott and Sembi (2006) argue that these two practices complement each other, the first acting as a focus bringing to the fore emerging cognitions, the second highlighting environmental and psychosocial factors that may influence the course and success of treatment. Even though they go beyond the treatment proposed in the 'textbook', the model supporting these two alternative ways of analysing cases continues to be the biomedical model developed from associated symptoms, signs, and beliefs.

Client-centred approach

Regarding the client-centred approach, despite the widespread belief that Rogers opposed diagnoses, a careful and in-depth examination of the evolution of his thinking points to a different conclusion. Rogers was not against the biomedical diagnosis system; instead, he considered the suitability of different diagnostic methods according to the specificity of (psycho) therapeutic settings. Rogers changed his view on this matter over his clinical path, 'from a young "diagnostic-prescriptive" clinical psychologist to one who had come to trust the great potential residing within the individual for self-understanding and self-direction' (Rogers 1977/1986: 23–4).

Initially, the position of Rogers was in line with the prevailing biomedical model. The book[1] that followed his PhD, of a psychometric nature,[2] reflects his adaptation to the biomedical diagnosis of a classifying and quantitative nature. In his 1939 work, *The Clinical Treatment of the Problem Child*, the diagnosis theme is advanced as a prior condition of the intervention plan anchored in a biomedical approach.

In 1940, at a conference titled *New Concepts in Psychotherapy*, Rogers' talk was met with surprise and perplexity. This impact, probably unexpected, struck a chord in the author, to the point that he later said: 'It would seem quite absurd to suppose that one could name a day on which client-centred therapy was born. Yet I feel it is possible to name that day and it was December 11, 1940' (Rogers 1964, cited by Kirschenbaum 2007: 109). In 1942, he published a book on the fundamental notion of this conference (*Counselling and Psychotherapy*), presenting the premises of a new psychotherapeutic relationship model which he expressed as follows: 'effective counselling consists of a definitely structured permissive relationship which allows the client to gain an understanding of himself to a degree which enables him to take positive steps in the light of his new orientation' (p. 18).

In this book, Rogers enunciated a set of principles that defined the distinctive essence of this new approach to psychotherapy and which simultaneously required a new type of specific and suitable diagnosis that was different from the biomedical one. It represents a 'cutting off' from psychotherapeutic models deemed to be effective both from a diagnostic viewpoint and from a relational-therapeutic perspective.

These principles emphasize the client's active role at various levels, namely: his capacity to be the 'therapeutic resource', in that he has a drive for growth and adaptation; the importance of the emotional dimension of the client, without underestimating the cognitive element; the emphasis on the present, expressed in the 'here-and-now' of the therapeutic condition, which replaces the (psychodynamic) focus on the client's past; and an interest in the actual therapist–client interpersonal experience as a facilitator of growth (Rogers 1942).

The psychotherapeutic intervention, grounded on an interpersonal relationship, indicates the need for experience, on the client's part, of a certain degree of tension, while maintaining, at some level, the ability to manage the stress of daily life. The relationship is an opportunity for the client to express his tension, and have the ability to do so verbally or by any other means. He should be reasonably independent, physically and emotionally stable, mainly from an organic viewpoint, enjoying a level of intelligence that enables him to manage his own life. Finally, he should be old enough, preferably between 10 and 60 years of age (Rogers 1942).

In this description, it is possible to note the influence (albeit residual) of the dominant psychodynamic model, particularly the requirement for certain specific personal characteristics. We believe that this is to do with the insight process and its relevance in the new model being developed. This was one of the last concepts to be 'waived' by Rogers.

Although Rogers was in the process of going 'against the flow', his theoretical model was not yet fully structured. Even though Rogers stressed the importance of the client's emotional conditions, valuing the present and the relationship itself for the course of the psychotherapy, the indications he proposed have a more cognitive weight (intelligence and age), associated with the constraints of a historical, individual, and/ or familiar (stability and independence) nature. This can also be noted in the contraindications to the client being involved in non-directive therapy: factors related to maladaptation; inaccessibility to the process; age, instability or slowness/intellectual disability of the client; realizing that an environmentally based treatment would be easier and more effectual (Rogers 1942).

The 1946 book *Counseling with Returned Servicemen* (Rogers and Wallen 1946) represents an attempt to operationalize the principles set out: at the same time, Rogers formally suggested the term 'client-centred' as being equivalent to the concept of a non-directive approach, denoting an effort to replace the term due to the misunderstandings and misinterpretations it raises.[3]

The 1951 book *Client-Centered Therapy* (CCT) systematizes Rogers' theoretical-therapeutic conceptualization. In this work, Rogers provides answers to some criticisms made by professionals using other models, such as transference issues and indications for therapy. One of the innovative aspects was the application of the principles of CCT to other therapeutic settings. Specifically, the designated core conditions may be developed in any form of relationship (professional or not), in a wide range of contexts, while safeguarding the need to resort to other techniques or procedures. In this book, Rogers stated that: 'psychological diagnosis as usually understood is unnecessary for psychotherapy, and may actually be a detriment to the therapeutic process' (Rogers 1951/2003: 220). This statement allows us to introduce a 'new' concept that is fundamental to understand this 'radical' stance: relational diagnosis.

As he addressed the issue of diagnosis, Rogers stated that such knowledge is unnecessary in therapy. However, he stressed, albeit with minimal emphasis, that '(. . .) there is no intent here to maintain that diagnosis evaluation is useless. We have ourselves made heavy use of such methods in our research studies of change in personality. It is this usefulness as a precondition to psychotherapy which is questioned' (Rogers 1957: 95). From then on there was a significant change in his thinking, which we consider to constitute a paradigm shift: the emergence of a holistic approach based on self-organization and on the body's potential for self-healing, which are the premises of current positive psychology. However, we emphasize that it is only within the setting of CCT that biomedical diagnostic evaluation loses its meaning and appropriateness.

In his 1957 article, Rogers reformulated the conditions that must be present in therapy, in particular, the six necessary and sufficient conditions for therapeutic change of personality to occur. These conditions inform the new paradigm proposed and developed by Rogers, constituting the only diagnostic system/indication of psychotherapy that can be used in the setting of CCT. The indispensability of insight, on the client's part, definitely disappears and loses its purpose in an approach intended to be experiential. According to Rogers, the ownership of these conditions is shared between the client and the psychotherapist, the result, according to Tudor (2011), of a co-creation. They reflect an evolution resulting from the deepening of his intervention model, inasmuch as the system he proposed in 1942 was based almost exclusively on the client.

Through therapy practice, Rogers wove a thread of his own ideas that enabled him to make an epistemological leap, i.e. he stopped valuing the causes expressed through symptoms and started to stress the importance of the body's self-healing potential. Thus, from a diagnostic point of view, a paradigm characterized by a holistic and circular approach arises, which, however, does not waive the need to use a biomedical and linear method when the situation so requires.

For Rogers, the psychotherapist's first approach with regard to the likely help he is faced with should follow the holistic paradigm, whose basic essence is the quality of the relationship; in the absence of the necessary and sufficient conditions for therapeutic change to occur, and of the resources to create them, the biomedical paradigm is to be used again. However, it is assumed that the clinician will, in his practice, continue to include the internalized conditions that characterize the philosophy of the person-centred approach.

The therapeutic relationship

The co-existence of two paradigms in the therapeutic relationship

The therapeutic relationship with clients within a psychiatric setting or in contact with psychiatric settings can be a challenging one. Their experience of being medicated, injected, held against their will or labelled can in itself contribute to further psychological distress. One may then ask in which specific situations a diagnosis, or type of diagnosis, is justified or paramount.

In this chapter, we do not intend to revive the anti-psychiatry movement (see Laing and Cooper 1964; Cooper 1967; Szasz 1979) or call for the relinquishment of psychiatric diagnosis when its advantages are clear and referred by professionals from different approaches. In particular, it facilitates communication between the various health professions, especially in psychiatric settings in which the biomedical model is dominant (Sommerbeck 2003, 2012; Joseph and Worsley 2005; Wilkins 2005; McWilliams 2011); it is efficient as a classification system, helping to enable statistical and epidemiological applications (Clyne 1998), to deepen knowledge about the relationship between symptoms, complaints, and causes (Wolfe 1989), and 'to investigate the genetic, familial and social correlates of various disorders' (McWilliams 2011: 495); it makes the client feel safe by 'making him' part of a group which he can identify with (Fletcher 2012); it is a form of sharing, since a sick person has something in common (a diagnosis) with others (Sommerbeck 2003); and it is a potential means to access the client's process (Wilkins 2005). Wolfe (1989: 187) also stresses the importance of diagnoses in that 'they can be an integral part of the effort to discover the best means of helping individuals who suffer and of preventing crippling emotional disease'. Finally, it can be a tool to ensure the safety of professionals (Fletcher 2012).

However, there are others who highlight that diagnosis has its limitations. For instance, a patient may start having anxiety bouts, feelings of loneliness and discrimination by not identifying with other individuals who are not part of the same diagnosis group; the therapeutic decision based on diagnosis may not meet individual needs; it may be a limited way of addressing the suffering of others (Fletcher 2012). According to Clyne (1998), diagnosis is the designation of an abstract process (disease), but it does not describe the person suffering from it.

A continuous challenge for therapists is what we do when faced with two paradigms within the therapeutic relationship, one being the psychiatric diagnostic biomedical model and the other the psychotherapeutic holistic non-medical model. Professionals must have knowledge and skills to be able to use the most suitable 'diagnostic' approach depending on the specific clinical situation, in order to make decisions in terms of treatment, including cases of involuntary commitment. Working with clients who may be referred to psychotherapy or counselling services therefore requires therapists to be aware of the impact the psychiatric system may have on clients. We propose that within such therapeutic relationships, a paradigm shift is necessary for all modalities, from a position of focusing on diagnosis, labelling, and treating to the co-development of a therapeutic relationship that is, in itself, a facilitator of change and can reduce the suffering of patients.

As a psychiatrist and psychotherapist, Hipólito offered a way to understand this paradigm shift.[4] He stated that:

> psychopathology can be understood through the combination of traumas that took place throughout life, both with regard to the individual's strengths and with regard to acting upon those strengths, on the premise that self-healing forces start to act, which, in themselves, are reflexes of the trend for hyper-complexity[1] acting upon the individual.
>
> (Hipólito 2011: 159)

This means that if we consider that each human being has in himself the internal resources to grow, to become more complex as a being through his capacity for self-organization, to upgrade his potential for self-healing and for self-fulfilment (hyper-complexity) within his reference framework, there is no longer a place for a label that smothers and crystallizes instead of promoting cure. Client-centred therapy is the only approach in which this paradigm shift has occurred, despite the fact that most professionals with different approaches are aware that the therapeutic relationship extends well beyond biomedical diagnosis.

From a diagnosis point of view, a paradigm characterized by a holistic and circular approach arises. However, it does not waive the need to use a biomedical and linear method when the situation so requires. For example, some clients may be in serious distress or florid states of psychosis and could be a risk or danger to themselves or others. We argue, however, that even in such cases our approach should be centred on the client as a person, not on a diagnostic tool and 'manualized' guidelines of treatment. The psychiatrist, psychotherapist, psychologist or any other professional working in therapeutic relationships with such clients also has to be aware of their role power and use it in a way that promotes healing/fosters change.

Summary

In psychiatric or psychological settings where the biomedical paradigm is used, it is important that as professionals working with clients, we offer a relationship that not only draws from the person-centred facilitative conditions of empathy, unconditional positive regard, and congruence but that also helps clients to work through their experience of diagnosis. This creates an opportunity within the therapeutic relationship for a co-creation of meaning and self-understanding of the client's subjective experience that goes beyond applying a label and offering 'treatment'.

It is thus paramount that technicians have personal and professional training to use each type of assessment according to the needs they experience in each specific intervention. Nevertheless, in general terms, their intervention should be guided by coherence and honesty, reflecting the internalization of the 'way of being' proposed by Rogers.

Notes

1 *Measuring Personality Adjustment in Children Nine to Thirteen Years of Age* (Rogers 1931/1972).
2 *Rogers' Test of Personality Adjustment* (Rogers 1931, as cited by Burchinal et al. 1958).
3 In this book's bibliography, Rogers refers to the work *Counseling and Psychotherapy* as 'a more complete presentation of the nondirective or client-centred approach to counselling' (Rogers and Wallen 1946: 153).
4 Rogers (1977/1986) defined the more complex process inherent to the universe as a formative trend. In life terms, this process speeds up into what Rogers called the 'actualizing tendency', which, in Hipólito's (2011) theory, is the tendency for hyper-complexity.

Further reading

Milton, M. (ed.) (2012) *Diagnosis and Beyond*. Ross-on-Wye: PCCS Books. Maintaining a person-centred approach, the contributors reflect on how the diagnosis may interfere with the therapeutic process.

McWilliams, N. (2011) *Psychoanalytic Diagnosis: Understanding Personality Structure in the Clinical Process*, 2nd edn. New York: Guilford Press. In this book, the author discusses, from a psychoanalytic perspective, the problems that may arise in the therapeutic relationship, after diagnosis.

Scott, M. and Sembi, S. (2006) Cognitive behaviour therapy treatment failures in practice: the neglected role of diagnostic inaccuracy, *Behavioural and Cognitive Psychotherapy*, 34 (4): 491–5. From a cognitive behavioural perspective, the authors discuss the problems that can stem from improper diagnosis, both in terms of therapeutic outcomes and development of the therapeutic process.

References

American Psychiatric Association (2013) *Diagnostic and Statistical Manual of Mental Disorders*, 5th edn. Arlington, VA: American Psychiatric Publishing.
Beard, C. and Björgvinsson, T. (2013) Psychological vulnerability: an integrative approach, *Journal of Psychotherapy*, 23 (3): 281–3.
Bornstein, R. (2001) The impending death of psychoanalysis, *Psychoanalytic Psychology*, 18 (1): 3–20.
Boswell, J. (2013) Intervention strategies and clinical process in transdiagnostic cognitive-behavioral therapy, *Psychotherapy*, 50 (3): 381–6.
Burchinal, L., Gardner, B. and Hawkes, G. (1958) A suggested revision of norms for the 'Rogers test of personality adjustment', *Child Development*, 29 (1): 135–9.
Clyne, M. (1998) O diagnóstico (Diagnosis), in E. Balint and J.S. Norell (eds.) *Seis Minutos para o Doente. Interações na consulta de clínica geral*, 2nd edn. (*Six Minutes for the Patient: Interactions in General Practice Consultation*). Lisbon: CLIMEPSI.
Cooper, D. (1967) *Psychiatry and Anti-Psychiatry*. London: Tavistock.
Engel, G. (1977) The need for a new medical model: a challenge for biomedicine, *Science*, 196 (4286): 129–36.
Fletcher, R. (2012) Introduction: dealing with diagnosis, in M. Milton (ed.) *Diagnosis and Beyond* (pp. 1–12). Ross-on-Wye: PCCS Books.
Goldfried, M.R. (1980) Toward a delineation of therapeutic change principles, *American Psychologist*, 35: 991–9.
Hipólito, J. (2011) *Auto-organização e complexidade: Evolução e desenvolvimento do pensamento rogeriano*. Lisbon: Ediual.
Joseph, S. and Worsley, R. (2005) Psychopathology and the person-centred approach: building bridges between disciplines, in S. Joseph and R. Worsley (eds.) *Person-Centered Psychopathology: A Positive Psychology of Mental Illness* (pp. 1–8). Ross-on-Wye: PCCS Books.

Kaplan, H., Sadock, B. and Grebb, J. (2006) *Compêndio de Psiquiatria. Ciências do Comportamento e Psiquiatria Clínica*, 7th edn. Porto Alegre: Artmed.

Kirschenbaum, H. (2007) *The Life and Work of Carl Rogers*. Ross-on-Wye: PCCS Books.

Laing, R.D. and Cooper, D.G. (1964) *Reason and Violence: A Decade of Sartre's Philosophy*, 2nd edn. London: Tavistock.

McManus, F., Shafran, R. and Cooper, Z. (2010) What does a 'transdiagnostic' approach have to offer the treatment of anxiety disorders?, *British Journal of Clinical Psychology*, 49: 491–505.

McWilliams, N. (2011) *Psychoanalytic Diagnosis: Understanding Personality Structure in the Clinical Process*. Abingdon: Guilford Press.

Mumma, G. (2011) Validity issues in cognitive-behavioural case formulation, *European Journal of Psychological Assessment*, 27 (1): 29–49.

Nelson-Jones, R. (2006) *Theory and Practice of Counselling and Therapy*. London: Sage.

Norton, P. and Philipp, L. (2008) Transdiagnostic approaches to the treatment of anxiety disorders: a quantitative review, *Psychotherapy Theory, Research, Practice*, 45 (2): 214–26.

Rogers, C. (1939) *The Clinical Treatment of the Problem Child*. Boston, MA: Houghton Mifflin.

Rogers, C. (1942) *Counseling and Psychotherapy: Newer Concepts in Practice*. Boston, MA: Houghton Mifflin.

Rogers, C. (1957) The necessary and sufficient conditions of therapeutic personality changes, *Journal of Consulting Psychology*, 21 (2): 95–103.

Rogers, C. (1972) *Measuring Personality Adjustment in Children Nine to Thirteen Years of Age*. New York: AMS Press (original work published 1931).

Rogers, C. (1986) *Carl Rogers on Personal Power* (original work published 1977). London: Constable.

Rogers, C. (2003) *Client-Centered Therapy*. London: Constable & Robinson (original work published 1951).

Rogers, C. and Wallen, J. (1946) *Counseling with Returned Servicemen*. New York: McGraw-Hill.

Rogers, C., Gendlin, E., Kisler, D. and Truax, C. (1967) *The Psychotherapeutic Relationship and its Impact*. Madison, WI: University of Wisconsin Press.

Rycroft, C. (1973) *A Critical Dictionary of Psychoanalysis*. London: Penguin Books.

Scott, M. and Sembi, S. (2006) Cognitive behaviour therapy treatment failures in practice: the neglected role of diagnostic inaccuracy, *Behavioural and Cognitive Psychotherapy*, 34 (4): 491–5.

Sommerbeck, L. (2003) *The Client-Centred Therapist in Psychiatric Contexts*. Ross-on-Wye: PCCS Books.

Sommerbeck, L. (2012) Being nondirective in directive settings, *Person-Centered and Experiential Psychotherapies*, 11 (3): 173–89.

Strawbridge, S. and Woolfe, R. (2003) Counselling psychology: origins, developments and challenges, in R. Woolfe, S. Strawbridge, B. Douglas and W. Dryden (eds.) *Handbook of Counselling Psychology* (pp. 3–20). New York: Sage.

Szasz, T.S. (1979) *Schizophrenia*. Oxford: Oxford University Press.

Tudor, K. (2011) Rogers' therapeutic conditions: a relational conceptualization, *Person-Centered and Experiential Psychotherapies*, 10 (3): 165–80.

Wilkins, P. (2005) Assessment and 'diagnosis' in person-centred therapy, in S. Joseph and R. Worsley (eds.) *Person-Centred Psychopathology: A Positive Psychology of Mental Illness* (pp. 128–45). Ross-on-Wye: PCCS Books.

Wolfe, B. (1989) Diagnosis and distancing reactions, *Psychoanalytic Psychology*, 6 (2): 187–98.

World Health Organization (1992) *The ICD-10 Classification of Mental and Behavioural Disorders: Clinical Descriptions and Diagnostic Guidelines*. Geneva: WHO.

18 Psychiatry and young people

Pallab Majumder

Introduction

In the UK, a child and adolescent psychiatrist usually works within a multidisciplinary children and adolescent mental health team. Use of medication in the treatment of psychiatric disorders in young people is surprisingly low considering the magnitude of the problem. Non-pharmacological therapeutic modalities have been the main method of treatment. However, the unconscious processes in these therapies mostly remain unrecognized (Podobnik and Podobnik 2006). In this chapter, I discuss my perspective as a psychiatrist, and working also as a therapist with young people, many with psychiatric diagnoses. I present the theoretical, clinical, and research bases of different modalities of medical psychotherapy, especially when working with young people. Examples of therapeutic interventions will be discussed, highlighting the key relational components of the approaches, and the development and management of the therapeutic relationship within these models. It is important in our work as professionals to be competent in working transculturally as our communities become more diverse. I therefore also include my work with refugee and asylum-seeking young persons with mental health difficulties within the mainstream western psychiatric service, as they are representative of a varied and diverse population. A hypothesis on the ways to reinvent the therapeutic relationship for young people, in a context-specific and culturally sensitive manner, will be offered. The limitations, challenges, and complexities of maintaining a therapeutic relationship for psychiatrists, especially when working cross-culturally, will also be explored. New developments within therapeutic practice in psychiatric settings with young people will also be highlighted.

Foundations of theory and practice

The assessment and care of young people with mental health issues involves specialized knowledge and skills. In this section, I discuss different psychological interventions for mental health problems in this population, and their theory and practice. These include family therapy, cognitive behavioural therapy, psychodynamic therapy, and group therapy. Depending on the specific needs of the young person, a variety of different psychological interventions, in different settings, including individual, group, and school-based interventions can be used.

Meaning systems and their influence on shaping interactions have always had their place in family therapy. More recent developments have placed narratives at the centre of several therapy approaches, in particular narrative therapies. This approach has been the most overtly embedded in a social constructionist understanding, which emphasizes the relativity of observed reality and sees language and narratives as the vehicle through which one acquires one's definitions of self. Individual problems are understood to be the result of the filtering of experiences through narratives that people have about themselves. These individual narratives are seen as being embedded in wider cultural, political or educational systems. This means listening not just to young people's stories about themselves, but also adults' stories about their childhood, as well as the stories of parents, grandparents, other family members, teachers, clergy, professionals, and lay helpers. This may also mean listening to the stories the clinicians tell when psychosocial interventions are designed. These stories can form the basis for the social construction or reconstruction of childhood (Henderson et al. 2010).

During the last twenty years, family therapy has become established as a supplementary or alternative therapy to individual therapy within child and adolescent psychiatry. Together with the development and change of concepts of family therapy, there has been a greater interest in the interrelationships within the triad of patient–family–therapist. In the training of family therapists, the meaning of the family of origin has been recognized (Buddeberg-Fischer 1998). In family therapy, the best predictors of outcomes were described by Karver et al. (2006) as the counsellor's interpersonal skills, therapist's direct influence skills, young person's and parents' willingness to participate, and young person's and parents' actual participation in treatment. Parental therapeutic alliance is seen to be a predictor of child outcome independently of age and pathological child status (Kabuth et al. 2005).

Cognitive behavioural therapy (CBT) is an expanding and empirically supported treatment for a range of child and adolescent mental health problems. The principles of this modality are based on the premise that cognitions or thoughts can influence emotions and behaviours across a variety of circumstances, thus altering maladaptive, distorted or deficient cognitions can be effective in treating various forms of psychopathology (Lochman and Pardini 2008). Although cognitive therapies are theoretically distinct, there is also a clear overlap with a narrative approach, both at a conceptual level and in practice. For example, both approaches view meanings and beliefs attached to problems as central treatment targets. They also borrow from each other's intervention techniques, such as the use of behavioural scaling techniques by narrative therapists or the use of externalization in some CBT approaches (Eisler and Lask 2008).

Psychodynamic therapies aim to strengthen patients' capacity to understand the motivations and meanings of their own and others' subjective experiences, behaviour, and relationships. Psychodynamic therapists strive to understand the organization of the young person's mind in its full complexity, the social influences on the emotional experience, and the ways in which the young person's subjectivity has adapted to internal and external pressures. The therapist aims to expand the young person's conscious awareness of these mechanisms and influences, so that they are more able to use their increased emotional awareness to manage continuing pressures. However, comprehensive reviews of outcome studies of psychodynamic approaches in child and adolescent populations are limited, and there are fewer randomized controlled trials of psychodynamic psychotherapy. Those few trials are underpowered and suffer from other methodological limitations (Fonagy and Target 2008). Psychodynamic principles have been used with vulnerable groups of young people through different indirect expressive techniques, such as play, art, drawing and drama, rather than through 'talking' (Fazel and Stein 2002).

There is enough evidence to show that group work is effective in treating psychological problems in children and young people (Kymissis and Halperin 1996). A group setting is the closest one can get to a young person's natural way of being. Group interventions give young persons a chance of sharing their experiences as well as benefiting by interacting with others who share common or similar narratives. Social activities reinforce group cohesion and support, and promote cultural identity. Based on evidence of group therapies, this appears to be an effective way of helping vulnerable young people develop a sense of mastery and share ways of solving common problems (Fazel and Stein 2002).

The therapeutic relationship

Case vignette: Building a therapeutic alliance

A.J. is a 16-year-old boy from Somalia who reported that he couldn't sleep, had nightmares, aches and pains all over his body, headaches, forgot things, and did a lot of 'thinking' all the time. He arrived in the UK after a one-year journey through parts of Africa, the Middle East, and Europe. He had experience of being tortured, incarcerated, and living in a detention centre during that time. He also witnessed his father, uncle, and many other people being killed in the village during the civil war. He very strongly expressed his reluctance to commence therapy for post-traumatic stress syndrome after this treatment was introduced to him following a period of assessment. He stated, 'I don't want to talk about myself; I don't want to talk about the past. I will cry and get worse if I do that. I have to think about my life, my immigration, job, money. I got lots to sort out.' The psychiatrist accepted A.J.'s view, but focused mainly on relationship-building over the next few sessions by discussing emotionally neutral topics and being genuinely curious about what A.J. wanted to talk about. This led to the gradual development of trust between therapist and patient. Soon A.J. felt less distressed and was able to gradually bring up more emotionally significant contents, eventually resulting in much improvement in his symptoms.

The vignette above highlights themes that will now be explored in relation to forming an effective therapeutic relationship.

Therapeutic alliance refers broadly to the quality of the relationship between client and therapist, the nature of collaboration on treatment-related tasks and goals, and the personal bond that emerges in treatment. Cruz et al. (2011) showed that psychiatrists devoted much of their time to relationship-building while maintaining a focus on symptoms or psychosocial issues. The success of this approach is highlighted in the case vignette. It has been suggested that a strong alliance may be particularly important for successful treatment with youths. Predictors for health gain seem to lie in the variables of therapeutic alliance and family functioning rather than presenting symptoms (Green et al. 2001). Early therapeutic alliance (DiGiuseppe et al. 1996) and therapist collaboration (Creed and Kendall 2005) may be especially important in therapy with children. Young people do not typically volunteer to come to treatment and are usually brought to the psychiatrist by parents. They can be referred by a school, social service or court for treatment of problems that they often do not believe they have. Building a positive relationship may be the key to increasing motivation for therapy, retention in treatment, engagement in tasks, protection against premature attrition, and better outcomes (Kendall et al. 2009).

Setting the appropriate therapeutic tone for young people involves using the decor of the office, therapist's personality, humour, and a myriad of other strategies to facilitate successful therapeutic alliance (Jansen 2011). In his research review, Crenshaw (2008) proposed the therapeutic use of symbols, drawing, and storytelling to create portals of entry to reach disconnected children. Bostic and Pataki (2000) used a shared knowledge of popular heroes and celebrities and an ever-changing 'pop' culture as an approach to foster effective therapeutic alliance. Therapist-guided exposure tasks for children with anxiety disorders may lead to alliance ruptures, as the therapist encourages the child to confront anxiety-provoking situations. Alternatively, such exposure tasks may strengthen the therapeutic relationship, as transient alliance ruptures are repaired within the session (Kendall et al. 2009). Motivational interviewing is also an efficient collaborative style of clinical interaction that can boost the effectiveness of the therapeutic alliance by enhancing three major elements: empathy that is true to their experience, patient's confidence in their ability to improve, and positive expectations from the treatment. These strategies show promise in augmenting young people's adherence to treatment (Dilallo and Weiss 2009).

In patients with a severe and enduring mental illness, a supportive therapeutic alliance allows the psychiatrist to gain essential information about the patient to develop trust in the psychiatrist and a desire to cooperate with treatment. Identifying the patient's goals and aspirations and relating these to treatment outcomes fosters the therapeutic relationship and thereby treatment adherence (Lehman et al. 2004). Interestingly, many young patients are generally supportive of conditions of treatment that can potentially restrict their liberty, such as a community treatment order. Many value this because of access to services and the sense of security obtained, and attribute improvements in their health to treatment under 'order'. This dynamics can have a positive effect on the quality of therapeutic relationships between the young person and the psychiatrist (Gibbs et al. 2005). Clinicians are sometimes reluctant to resort to compulsory admission because of a fear of damaging the therapeutic relationship with their patients. Clinical observations, however, point to the converse being the case. Compulsory treatment may in fact be an act of compassion. It shows that professionals recognize the severity of the illness, and often the patients and their families are immensely relieved to hand over the responsibility, temporarily, to the professional team (Russell 2001). Although children often come into treatment against their will, they usually can make use of the therapeutic relationship that is negotiated over time. This experience leads to the recognition that many seemingly coercive treatment contexts may in fact turn out to be effective interventions.

Transcultural dimensions

In working with refugee children, the gender of the mental health professional appeared to be a factor that influenced some young persons' engagement in the treatment process. The strong cultural expectation that the female gender should be protected from any exposure to trauma, adversities, and harsh realities of life appears to act against young persons trusting female therapists with their own painful memories and emotions.

The race of the therapist can play a significant role in the manifestation of transference and countertransference phenomena in inter-racial psychotherapy. References to the race of the psychiatrist involved in therapy may be the first sign of a developing transference relationship. Failure to appreciate the impact of racial difference can impede therapeutic progress while sensitive confrontation may be a valuable tool in the recognition and communication of emotionally charged feelings (Varghese 1983). This means that, during the session, the therapist may bring up the unexpressed feelings about the difference between him or her and the young person. This should, however, be sensitively timed and balanced against the comfort level from both sides, and the stage of transference reaction in the therapy. The cultural constructs of shame and privacy may contribute to the difficulties in talking about personal aspects of life and sharing emotions in young persons from certain cultural backgrounds. These observations have implications for the influence of the therapist on the process of therapeutic alliance.

By being supportive to their young patients, psychiatrists help to underpin an illusion that has been created by the patient and help to overcome his or her gradual disillusionment. This is a way of handling transference and countertransference. Being supportive implies gratifying the patient's pre-oedipal needs within the boundaries of the psychiatrist's professional role. The psychiatrist in the process of being supportive plays three different roles, which are, looking after the 'child' element in the patient, encouraging the 'adult' element, while watching over the therapeutic alliance, and surviving attacks from tyrannical elements by facing up to them and setting boundaries (Hebbrecht 2004).

Melzak (2009) reported that refugee children often need time and help in sharing their stories, which initially emerge as a series of fragments that may be unspeakable and shared non-verbally. The psychiatrist doing therapy must build a relationship of trust with each young person and hold their experiences for an extended period, before gradually reprocessing and returning them. The young person thus slowly becomes able to take ownership of these experiences. In my work with refugee children, suppressing the past trauma appeared to operate as a coping mechanism, as described in the case vignette above. They tend to prefer their contact with clinicians to be more about addressing current needs. Young persons stated that the ideal help should be prompt, and should offer immediate relief and solutions. This possibly helps explain their reluctance to engage in long-term psychological therapies. This reluctance to talk about the 'past' reflects a belief that locates the problem and the solution not only externally, but also in the here-and-now, and does not link the current problem with past events. This seems to be at odds with the principles proposed by psychodynamic psychotherapy frameworks (Fonagy and Target 2008).

Challenges

There are many challenges to building up an effective therapeutic relationship with young persons. These are even more marked in engaging youths from other cultures. In general, young persons can be particularly avoidant of talking about past events and revisiting their memories of adversities, and instead favour focusing the intervention on solving current problems. They often perceive a quick and hands-on resolution of their present difficulties to be the ideal intervention. In my own experience, young refugees' perceptions of 'talking treatment' ranges from being ineffective to being harmful. Lynch (2001) argued that some young people originate from cultures where perceptions of mental illness are markedly different to western constructs. For them, the suggestion of talking therapy can be quite meaningless. This, however, does not mean that their distress should not be acknowledged.

Young persons often do not engage well with mental health services, thus there is a need to explain the benefits of treatment to them. Lack of exposure and limited knowledge of the system can lead to an information gap and, therefore, potential suspicion of the psychiatrist and other professionals working in a seemingly complex multi-agency environment. This issue of trust can negatively affect the therapeutic relationship, leading to a poor treatment outcome. In my clinical and research experience, young refugees generally struggle to trust professionals, partly due to their own personal histories with authorities and partly due to the formal manner in which the process of healthcare is run in our current system. Unfortunately, without establishing a trusting therapeutic relationship, it is less likely that any treatment will succeed or even complete its full course.

Lustig et al. (2004) stated that cultural understanding of mental illness and treatment are often limited by the use of western diagnostic symptoms and instruments, and by the complications inherent in the westernized medicalization of what elsewhere may be viewed as religious or social issues. Therefore, traditional western mental health approaches may not be equally effective with children from other cultures, who consequently under-utilize mental health services. A lack of clinicians who speak the young persons' language can be a barrier to optimum engagement. It is also important for the therapist to acknowledge that, even for young persons who speak English, there may be specific terms or expressions used by the therapist that need further exploration to aid their understanding. Kennedy et al. (1999) reported that the availability of appropriate interpreting services helped the successful completion of the mental health assessment with young persons who didn't speak English. In contrast, Huemer and Vostanis (2010) argued that the presence of interpreters may affect children's ability or willingness to share difficult feelings. This debate was reflected in the findings of my own research with refugee children. The presence of interpreters in the clinical sessions was perceived to facilitate their communication, and hence engagement. It was, however, also perceived to restrict communication of complex or sensitive personal information by creating inconvenient commotions in the therapeutic alliance.

Although there is limited literature on direct activity-based treatments, a number of case series and single case studies reported positive outcomes for modalities associated with activity and creativity that can be helpful in facilitating engagement and therapeutic relationship through play, art, music therapy, and storytelling (Miller and Billings 1994; Fazel and Stein 2002). These approaches can be effective through distraction and suggestion, and facilitate social interaction, therapeutic engagement, and social integration. Successful engagement in therapy programmes emphasizes the role of cross-cultural teams who can work in an extended outreach model. Some approaches with young persons from different cultures also try to integrate traditional healing methods, which may be more culturally acceptable to some young people (Fazel and Stein 2002).

New developments

There have been promising ongoing developments in the area of therapeutic work with young people in psychiatric settings.

Rothe (2008) revealed that negative, long-term mental health outcomes are related to autonomic dysregulation and distorted narratives of events, which result from exposure to overwhelming stress. The proposed role of the therapist in his therapy model involved: (a) intervening to decrease hyper-arousal and protect the young person's neuroendocrine integrity; (b) helping them construct a cohesive narrative of the events during the peri-traumatic period; and (c) becoming an advocate for them, helping them to attain mastery and control over the forces that threaten their coping capacities.

Therapists should be open to whether children from non-western cultures can utilize 'talking therapies', or whether other means may be better. Ehntholt and Yule (2006) proposed a phased model of intervention for young refugees in the context of a holistic framework. They detected promising findings from studies of cognitive behavioural therapy, testimonial psychotherapy, narrative exposure therapy, and eye movement desensitization and reprocessing, and suggested that interventions should include a combination of different modalities of treatment, depending on the young person's individual, psychosocial, and mental health needs.

My work with young refugees suggests that greater efforts should be made to explain and educate young persons about the mental health care system; and to address any potential biases in the initial phase, even before the therapy begins. Immigration status and a stable base are their highest priorities, which need to be tackled before any meaningful engagement in therapy is to be expected. Sometimes psychological intervention that requires verbal skills may need to be deferred until the young person's English has improved. Locations other than clinics, such as at their home, youth centres or school are proposed. Although there has been limited research on the efficacy of such treatment sites, policy has recently focused on schools as potential venues for mental health interventions (Fazel and Stein 2002; Lustig et al. 2004; Kia-Keeting and Ellis 2007).

I also found that young persons prefer to receive 'help' when they perceived the need rather than when it was offered. They wanted shorter waiting time, and responsive, flexible, and open-ended appointments as and when required. What I am proposing is a dynamic, client-led therapy and a user-led service. Surprisingly, however, many young persons also expected to receive a prescriptive treatment from professionals, with them being a passive recipient. These apparently paradoxical findings can possibly be explained by a gradual shift in the young person's perceptions of being a passive subject, whose fate is decided by others, to a more active player who is able to make decisions and assert rights.

This research also found that these young persons' engagement is able to be facilitated by building a trusting relationship, sharing apparently neutral activities, and being flexible in therapeutic contacts. Strategies to develop trust include befriending, making genuine attempts to know the young person, and meeting and interacting with them within their own comfort zones. Engagement of communities and families can help diminish the power differentials and facilitate clients' trust.

Summary

Regardless of theoretical orientation, in any effective intervention the emphasis should be on how to acquire ways of becoming more empathic, flexible, non-prejudiced, and open-minded when listening to the narratives of young people; and cultural attributes must be integrated into psychodynamic, family, group, cognitive, and behavioural approaches. However, addressing their needs can often appear overwhelming to those involved. Therefore, cultural training for professionals and education of young persons is essential to enhance engagement from both sides. Establishing relationships, sharing activities, and demonstrating flexibility are useful ways of facilitating trust and engagement. The role of the child psychiatrist and their relationship with the young person is a dynamic one that is shaped by the ever-evolving response of society, law, and the medical profession. As psychiatrists, we seem to be focusing increasingly on the practical guidelines for treating psychiatric disorders and are thereby in danger of losing sight of the importance of our therapeutic relationship with patients. More attention, therefore, needs to be given to the relational aspect of psychiatric practice by medical professionals.

Further reading

Crenshaw, D. (2008) *Therapeutic Engagement of Children and Adolescents: Play, Symbol, Drawing, and Storytelling Strategies*. Lanham, MD: Jason Aronson. This book will help those interested in further study of the ways to engage young persons in therapy by creative means.

Lewis, M. (1991) Intensive individual psychodynamic psychotherapy: the therapeutic relationship and the technique of interpretation, in M. Lewis (ed.) *Child and Adolescent*

Psychiatry: A Comprehensive Textbook (pp. 796–805). Baltimore, MD: Williams & Wilkins. This chapter is recommended for readers interested in underlying dynamics of therapeutic relationships and psychodynamic approaches in the treatment of young people.

Rutter, M., Bishop, D., Pine, D., Scott, S., Stevenson, J., Taylor, E. and Thapar, A. (2011) Part V: Approaches to treatment, in *Rutter's Child and Adolescent Psychiatry*, 5th edn. (pp. 971–1206). Oxford: Blackwell. Useful for further study of the general principles of different treatment approaches for children and adolescents with mental illness.

References

Bostic, J. and Pataki, C. (2000) All the world's a stage, *Journal of the American Academy of Child and Adolescent Psychiatry*, 39 (12): 1565–7.

Buddeberg-Fischer, B. (1998) The development of family therapy – interrelationship between the patient's and the therapist's family, *Praxis der Kinderpsychologie und Kinderpsychiatrie*, 47 (3): 174–85.

Creed, T.A. and Kendall, P.C. (2005) Therapist alliance-building behavior within a cognitive– behavioral treatment for anxiety in youth, *Journal of Consulting and Clinical Psychology*, 73: 498–505.

Crenshaw, D. (2008) *Therapeutic Engagement of Children and Adolescents: Play, Symbol, Drawing, and Storytelling Strategies*. Lanham, MD: Jason Aronson.

Cruz, M., Roter, D., Cruz, R.F., Wieland, M., Cooper, L.A., Larson, S. et al. (2011) Psychiatrist– patient verbal and nonverbal communications during split-treatment appointments, *Psychiatric Services*, 62 (11): 1361–8.

DiGiuseppe, R., Linscott, J. and Jilton, R. (1996) Developing the therapeutic alliance in child–adolescent psychotherapy, *Applied and Preventive Psychology*, 5: 85–100.

Dilallo, J. and Weiss, G. (2009) Motivational interviewing and adolescent psychopharma- cology, *Journal of the American Academy of Child and Adolescent Psychiatry*, 48 (2): 108–13.

Ehntholt, K.A. and Yule, W. (2006) Practitioner review: Assessment and treatment of refugee children and adolescents who have experienced war-related trauma, *Journal of Child Psychology and Psychiatry*, 47 (12): 1197–1210.

Eisler, I. and Lask, J. (2008) Family interviewing and family therapy, in M. Rutter, D. Bishop, D. Pine, S. Scott, J. Stevenson, E. Taylor and A. Thapar (eds.) *Rutter's Child and Adolescent Psychiatry*, 5th edn. (pp. 1062–78). Oxford: Blackwell.

Fazel, M. and Stein, A. (2002) The mental health of refugee children, *Archives of Disease in Childhood*, 87 (5): 366–70.

Fonagy, P. and Target, M. (2008) Psychodynamic treatments, in M. Rutter, D. Bishop, D. Pine, S. Scott, J. Stevenson, E. Taylor and A. Thapar (eds.) *Rutter's Child and Adolescent Psychiatry*, 5th edn. (pp. 1079–91). Oxford: Blackwell.

Gibbs, A., Dawson, J., Ansley, C. and Müllen, R. (2005) How patients in New Zealand view community treatment orders, *Journal of Mental Health*, 14 (4): 357–68.

Green, J., Kroll, L. and Anson, R. (2001) Health gain and outcome predictors during inpatient and related day treatment in child and adolescent psychiatry, *Journal of the American Academy of Child and Adolescent Psychiatry*, 40 (3): 325–32.

Hebbrecht, M. (2004) The psychiatrist as supportive object: a psychoanalytic approach [De psychiater als steunfiguur: Een psychoanalytische visie], *Tijdschrift voor Psychiatrie*, 46 (3): 157–66.

Henderson, S.W., Baily, C. and Weine, S. (2010) Child refugee mental health, in E. Garralda and J.-P. Raynaud (eds.) *Increasing Awareness of Child and Adolescent Mental Health* (pp. 93–119). Lanham, MD: Jason Aronson.

Huemer, J. and Vostanis, P. (2010) Child refugees and refugee families, in D. Bhugra, T. Craig and K. Bhui (eds.) *Mental Health of Refugees and Asylum Seekers* (pp. 225–42). New York: Oxford University Press.

Jansen, S. (2011) Review of 'Therapy with young men: 16–24 year olds in treatment', *Journal of Child and Adolescent Mental Health*, 23 (1): 61–2.

Kabuth, B., De Tychey, C. and Vidailhet, C. (2005) Alliance thérapeutique avec les mères et évolution clinique des enfants d'un hôpital de jour, *Annales Médico-Psychologiques*, 163 (6): 486–92.

Karver, M.S., Handlesman, J.B. and Fields, S. (2006) Meta-analysis of therapeutic relationship variables in youth and family therapy: the evidence for different relationship variables in the child and adolescent treatment outcome literature, *Clinical Psychology Review*, 26 (1): 50–65.

Kendall, P.C., Comer, J.S., Marker, C.D., Creed, T.A., Puliafico, A.C., Hughes, A.A. et al. (2009) In-session exposure tasks and therapeutic alliance across the treatment of childhood anxiety disorders, *Journal of Consulting and Clinical Psychology*, 77 (3): 517–25.

Kennedy, J., Seymour, D.J. and Hummel, B.J. (1999) A comprehensive refugee health screening program, *Public Health Reports*, 114 (5): 469–77.

Kia-Keating, M. and Ellis, B.H. (2007) Belonging and connection to school in resettlement: young refugees, school belonging, and psychosocial adjustment, *Clinical Child Psychology and Psychiatry*, 12 (1): 29–43.

Kymissis, A. and Halperin, D.A. (1996) *Group Therapy with Children and Adolescents*. Washington, DC: American Psychiatric Press.

Lehman, A.F., Lieberman, J.A., Dixon, L.B., McGlashan, T.H., Miller, A.L., Perkins, D.O. and Kreyenbuhl, J. (2004) Practice guideline for the treatment of patients with schizophrenia, 2nd edn., *American Journal of Psychiatry*, 161 (2 Suppl.): 1–56.

Lochman, J.E. and Pardini, D.A. (2008) Cognitive behavioural therapies, M. Rutter, D. Bishop, D. Pine, S. Scott, J. Stevenson, E. Taylor and A. Thapar (eds.) *Rutter's Child and Adolescent Psychiatry*, 5th edn. (pp. 1026–45). Oxford: Blackwell.

Lustig, S.L., Kia-Keating, M., Knight, W.G., Geltman, P., Ellis, H., Kinzie, J.D. et al. (2004) Review of child and adolescent refugee mental health, *Journal of the American Academy of Child and Adolescent Psychiatry*, 43 (1): 24–36.

Lynch, M.A. (2001) Providing health care for refugee children and unaccompanied minors, *Medicine, Conflict and Survival*, 17 (2): 125–30.

Melzak, S. (2009) Psychotherapeutic work with children and adolescents seeking refuge from political violence, in M. Lanyado and A. Horne (eds.) *The Handbook of Child and Adolescent Psychotherapy: Psychoanalytical Approaches*, 2nd edn. (pp. 381–405). Hove: Routledge.

Miller, K.E. and Billings, D.L. (1994) Playing to grow: a primary mental health intervention with Guatemalan refugee children, *American Journal of Orthopsychiatry*, 64 (3): 346–56.

Podobnik, J. and Podobnik, I.F. (2006) Countertransference problems in psychopharmacology of children and adolescents, *Socijalna Psihijatrija*, 34 (4): 183–9.

Rothe, E.M. (2008) A psychotherapy model for treating refugee children caught in the midst of catastrophic situations, *Journal of the American Academy of Psychoanalysis and Dynamic Psychiatry*, 36 (4): 625–42.

Russell, G.F.M. (2001) Involuntary treatment in anorexia nervosa, *Psychiatric Clinics of North America*, 24 (2): 337–49.

Varghese, F.T. (1983) The racially different psychiatrist – implications for psychotherapy, *Australian and New Zealand Journal of Psychiatry*, 17 (4): 329–33.

19 Psychotherapy for disorganized attachment, dissociation, and dissociative identity disorder

Jo Ringrose

We accept the love we think we deserve.

(Stephen Chbosky 2012: 27)

Introduction

The therapist's consistent love and care is the bedrock to the formation of a strong therapeutic relationship. Having a close relationship is vital because it forms the basis of trust that encourages the client to bring their entire self, not simply what they see as their 'acceptable' self. In addition, in cases of clients with attachment problems, the therapist's consistent nurturance challenges clients' assumptions about relationships. Yalom (2008) describes how the therapy relationship provides the process material in the therapy work. It is the dissection of the process (i.e. the interactions between client and therapist) that provides key clues as to how the client relates outside the therapy room, thus providing an invaluable source of information on how to help the client. Psycho-education strategies and techniques offer content which in itself is valuable but on its own limiting.

In the case of clients with dissociative identity disorder (DID), the therapy relationship is arguably even more important because these clients have developed a disorganized attachment style, where caregivers were a source of comfort as well as terror. These clients thus anticipate being hurt in relationships. In addition, clients with DID have multiple identities, one of which is often a child self, typically aged about five. Therapists need to form a secure relationship with these identities, relate to each identity in an age-appropriate manner, as well as foster relationships among them. In this respect, therapy with clients with DID can resemble family therapy more closely than individual therapy.

Foundations of theory and practice

Development and presentation of dissociative identity disorder

Case vignette: Presentation of DID

Sally is thirteen and lives with her father and mother. Her father is an alcoholic. Sally doesn't know why but she is scared in his presence, even when he is sober and being pleasant. However, she knows that she loses time. Sometimes she can lose days and have no idea where she has been or what she has been doing. On several occasions she has come to in a strange place and not known how she got there.

As a very young girl Sally realized that when her father was sexually abusing her she could pretend things were not really happening to her, that they were happening to someone else. This became such a practiced way of coping that whenever her father was abusive she would dissociate,[1] which meant she could retreat from the limelight for a while. At these times, an alter personality, Mandy, would take over. It was Mandy who bore the brunt of their father's abuse.

Tabatha also knows why Sally gets scared when their father is around because she comes along whenever their father is shouting at Sally and forcing her to sit and listen to his tirade of how she is 'a waste of space' and 'will never amount to anything'.

Tabatha and Mandy know each other as well as Sally but Sally is only vaguely aware that she is not always herself. She has clues to the others' presence because she has heard her alter personalities talking to one another, which she experiences as whispering in her head. She becomes scared at these times because she fears she has schizophrenia, so tells no-one. Also sometimes when she has been out, someone has called her Tabatha or Mandy and swore they knew her but Sally does not recognize the other person.

Mandy coped with the sexual abuse by cutting and burning herself. She explains that she does this to try and stop running inside; she spends a lot of time in a high state of anxiety. On other occasions, she harms herself in order to try and convert her psychological angst into something physical because this means it is somehow easier to contend with.

Tabatha has spells of binge drinking and has anorexia. Both are used as a means to blot out the flashbacks of abuse. She has realized that if she is hungry she is less prone to thinking about the abuse, as her thoughts can focus on what she is eating and when. Being hungry is also one of her many forms of punishing herself. She deprives herself of drinks when thirsty, sleep when tired, and even warm clothing when cold – these are her ways of punishing herself for being born bad. She has been told so many times that her father's abuse of her is her fault for being bad, that she now believes it.

The above is typical for someone with DID. We call the part of the personality who first presents to therapy and the one in control most of the time (in this example, Sally) the host, and the emotional parts who tend to be the ones who carry the emotional trauma, alter personalities (in this example, Mandy and Tabatha).

The criteria for dissociative identity disorder

The above case vignette provides a fictitious clinical example of the main features of DID as outlined in DSM-V (APA, 2013). For a diagnosis of DID, clients need to report, or therapists need to observe, two or more separate identities or personality states within the one individual. Each identity has its own individual way of perceiving and relating to the world. Two (or more) of the identities recurrently are seen to take control of the person's behaviour. This means that when one identity is in control, the other retreats to the background. This results in there being considerable gaps in the recall of everyday events as well as memory difficulties around the traumatic experiences.

Presenting issues of clients with DID

When some clients with DID first present to therapy the therapist could be forgiven for thinking the client is ambivalent. This is because although the host is wanting to engage in therapy, one or more alter personalities often do not. This makes initial engagement complex and multi-layered, as each alter personality's viewpoint warrants consideration and attention. When first entering therapy, the client is usually living a very chaotic lifestyle where they are able to do little. They tend to spend most days battling past demons using ritualistic behaviours to try and manage flashbacks (often there will be a drink, food or drug problem). Clients frequently articulate they cannot cope, yet currently there is little that you would see as challenging, it is their past that overwhelms them (except in cases where the abuse is ongoing). The main other symptoms these clients express are anxiety and depression along with a collection of somatosensory (body felt) symptoms that typically relate to the abuse they experienced. These are varied but may include experiences of pain, problems swallowing, and feeling sick. Frequently there are sleep problems either due to nightmares or alters wanting time in the limelight. Usually related to an anxiety response, clients may report they sometimes cannot move, or talk, or only in a whisper. Suicide attempts and self-harm are commonplace.

Dissociative experiences in clients without DID

Dissociative identity disorder is the extreme end of a continuum, hence there are many clients who do not present with all the symptoms of DID but nonetheless have dissociated trauma experiences. The main difference between someone diagnosed with DID and someone with dissociated trauma experiences is that with the former, there is not one identity who is in control all of the time but many, whereas in the latter case there is only one. This means that people with DID have a discontinuity of existence as their parts vie for control over the body, which results in the host experiencing this as lost time. Clients with dissociated experiences are nevertheless similar to clients with DID in that they have trauma experiences that are stuck in the time frame they were first experienced. These trauma experiences can be described as developmental blockages that arise when traumatic incidents have never been fully acknowledged, accommodated, and worked through (cathected) either at the time, or since. This results in the person responding to the current situation based on what is happening now, as well as to other similar incidents from their past that have remained unresolved.

An example of a client who does not have DID but who nonetheless has a younger self stuck at an earlier developmental age, may be evident in the client who repeatedly fails to have a long-term intimate relationship with a partner. Bowlby (1973) theorized we develop an internal working model, a representation of how we expect relationships to be based upon our earliest attachment experiences. While often not known at a conscious level, clients tend to expect their partners to behave in a similar manner to how a parent behaved when they were small. The original childhood relational experiences have transferred onto subsequent relationships. Therefore, a client may report their father was inconsistent in his parenting, in that he would be loving and brutal. The adult from this background may be waiting for their partner to be brutal in the same way their father was. Just as in this example the client is having problems in their personal relationship outside of the therapy room, a parallel process within the therapy relationship often occurs too. This may be observed when the client finds reasons not to attend weekly and this coincides with the therapist beginning to sense the client getting closer. Lastly, clients may go to some lengths to push the therapist away only to then draw them back in close.

Disorganized attachments

Without exception, clients with DID have a disorganized attachment style (Ringrose 2011, 2012). This arises when parents (or main carers) are a source of comfort as well as fear. As children, these clients wanted to approach their parents for comfort but they also wanted to run from them because they were fearful. The result of this is confusion and dissociation (Main and Hesse 1990).

In addition, clients typically learn from their parents what is ruled in and what is ruled out when relating (Wallin 2010). Therefore, parents (and other influential figures such as teachers and priests) teach us what we can safely feel, say or do and what is unsafe or unacceptable to share with them and consequently other people (Wallin 2010). Hence, the child born of a depressed mother may find happiness hard to express. The child sexually abused by a parent tends to have learnt to remain silent about it. Clients may also have learnt in childhood not to cry. Old ways of behaving and thinking guide behaviours in new situations. Hence, the child who learns not to cry in childhood often remains stoically holding it all together in therapy.

The therapeutic relationship

These clusters of symptoms demonstrate that therapy needs to focus on three main areas: the client's attachment problems, their multiplicity, and usually their trauma. In cases where clients are not multiple but nonetheless have dissociated trauma experiences, the work is usually very similar. As mentioned above, clients with dissociative experiences may have attachment problems in addition, although this problem is by no means seen in everyone with dissociative experiences and the attachment problems tend to be less severe.

The attachment relationship and boundaries

During their childhood, the relationships of clients with DID were typically riddled with broken boundaries. The child will normally have had to parent at least one of their parents; they will commonly have witnessed or participated in sexual behaviours with a parent and or other children or adults and they may have witnessed or experienced physical abuse, emotional abuse, neglect or torture. Thus boundaries were essentially absent for this group of clients. Therefore, role modelling clear and consistent boundaries in the therapy relationship is essential in order that the client can learn they have boundaries too and can learn how to protect themselves from harm as adults.

Working with multiplicity: fostering cooperation, collaboration, and communication

One of the main initial focuses in therapy needs to be on the client's relationship with their dissociated alters. I teach clients the concept of dissociation and where appropriate DID. This is because whether the client has DID or dissociated trauma experiences, they need to be encouraged to work with their younger hurt self (selves) (Ringrose 2012). I encourage clients to dialogue, verbally or on paper, with their child selves as a means to working out what the different sides to them are thinking and feeling and work out how an equilibrium between opposing parts can be reached. Dave Mearns (1999) writes about the client's multiple selves and the importance of attending to each. Without this attention, he notes it is not always possible for the therapist to value the whole client. I also talk to clients about inner boundaries. Initially, the main goal of therapy with clients with DID is to foster cooperation, collaboration, and communication within the whole system (Ringrose 2010). For years these clients will have been pulled in a multitude of directions dependent upon which alter is in charge. This can result in a great deal of time being wasted. For example, if the host has decided they want to go to college to study but one child alter wants to stay in bed because they are feeling depressed, then the system will invariably grind to a halt. In the beginning stages I want the host to absorb my way of nurturing her and use this to nurture her inner identities. The host needs to act like the matriarch of her family, listen and attend to her younger selves' needs but provide strict boundaries stating what is safe and acceptable behaviour and what is not.

Repairing attachment problems and the core conditions

The therapist will need to become one of the client's main attachment figures. Patterson and Hidore (1997) present a sample of the extensive evidence from research over several decades detailing how insufficient love in childhood is 'the source of much, if not most, psychosocial disturbance and disorder' (p. 15) as well as the healer. Similarly, Guntrip (1953) used the term 'agape' to describe the kind of parental love psychotherapists need to offer clients, particularly when what they received from their own parents was insufficient to meet their needs. The relationship needs to serve as a safe place for clients to try out relating in a way that begins to challenge their childhood assumptions of how relationships work. My offering and them receiving the core conditions of client-centred psychotherapy – empathy, congruence, and unconditional positive regard, irrespective of what clients tell me – is demonstration that relationships do not have to be based on conditions (Rogers 2002). They come to learn that I accept them irrespective of what they have said, done or feel ashamed about, that the depth and breadth of their own and their alter identity's feelings, desires, views, and behaviours are acceptable (Wallin 2010). In so doing, the therapist accepts experiences the client's original attachment figures couldn't tolerate, or accommodate. This is crucial, particularly when faced with young alter identities who fear the therapist will reject them when they speak about what they experienced.

This work is also imperative if the client wants to stop dissociating. In the vignette, I described the function of the alters as a means of taking the trauma away from the host in order that the host can more easily carry on with daily living. However, the alter identity also carries the feelings which relate to the trauma incident. These feelings will be ones the host believes are too risky to take on board or to express. The most common are anger, anxiety, and despair. Often there are one or more alters who carry these feelings for the whole system. By fostering an acceptance and tolerance of all emotions, this limits the need for the host to dissociate and switch to the alter who expresses the emotion because they can then express the emotion themselves.

'Now moments'

The most powerful elements in therapy in terms of fostering the client–therapist attachment relationship are what Daniel Stern (1998) calls 'now moments'. This is a moment when in relation with someone, no words need to be spoken, when two minds and hearts are working in perfect harmony and together produce an outpouring of love. It is the moments in therapy when client and therapist look at each other and without speaking there is a shared understanding and warmth that flows between the two. In that moment there is a deep sense of connection and intimacy. It is these moments of one-ness that offer the greatest potential for change and growth (Stern 2004).

Challenges

The above notwithstanding, attachment relationships pose many problems to clients with DID who may avoid intimacy sometimes because to an alter it may be equated with abuse. Hence, a further key area I look at with clients is their defences to becoming attached.

A potential barrier to building a strong client–therapist relationship is a by-product of one of the symptoms of DID, depersonalization. Where parents of clients were physically available but not emotionally so, or where clients learnt not to express their emotions, they may present unanimated and with a blank expression irrespective of what is said. This demonstration of a flattening of affect can have a significant impact on the client's relationships, as they often appear unmoved and or bored when relating. Therapists who are unaware of this condition may find it hard not to have an emotional reaction to these clients. A colleague who was working with such a client said that she wanted to grab the client by the shoulders and shake them, a little like a frustrated parent may do if they think their child has not got the significance of the message they are trying to convey. In these cases, I will explain the potential effect the client's behaviour may have on me and on relationships outside the therapy room.

A further possible obstacle that can hamper a strong therapist–client relationship may ensue when child alters telephone or text incessantly. Most clients with DID have a very young alter identity who is scared and as a consequence repeatedly requests reassurance between sessions. This can be irritating for therapists, which may be detected by clients. Also, the young identity may similarly become irritated or distressed if their incessant demands are not met and interpret this as a sign the therapist doesn't care. These problems can lead to the therapy relationship ending in instances where practitioners have become burnt out (Warner 1998) or if the client feels insufficiently held and leaves. This highlights the importance of stipulating clearly the boundaries to the therapy relationship in respect to time and contact limitations and ensuring they are adhered to.

In the beginning sessions, it is not uncommon to have one or more alters who are highly suspicious of anyone wanting to help. This can mean there is an identity who is awkward, unpleasant or who simply instructs the host to remain silent. For example, I had one alter personality who wanted to commandeer the entire session and say nothing but 'I dunno', 'don't care', and 'sod off'. This type of behaviour can be infuriating especially for the therapist ignorant of the condition. In this case, this was precisely the alter's aim – they wanted to keep people at a distance. On a similar note, some clients will use sarcasm as a means to convey their anger and frustrations and perhaps sometimes to try and push therapists away. For example, I had one client who became very irritated with me for confusing the order of their previous partners and as a consequence said to me, 'do keep up, you can be dreadfully slow'. While this type of response may be a demonstration of the client's anger or irritation, these exchanges may also be used unwittingly, or wittingly, to push the therapist away. Whatever their purpose, I talk to the client about my feeling response to their words and deeds and how other people the client relates to may feel similarly. Using my felt response in this way is one of the key ways I have adopted Wallin's (2010) theory of making the client's 'unknown known'.

Different theoretical approaches: attachment theory, cognitive behavioural therapy, and challenging cognitive distortions

While I view a strong therapy relationship (based on Rogers' core conditions) as absolutely vital, I do not hold that the core conditions alone are sufficient. The most effective way of working with all clients but with clients with DID in particular, necessitates the use of a number of theoretical approaches and the adoption of a wide variety of strategies and techniques (Ringrose 2010).

Above I discussed how I use John Bowlby's concept of an internal working model to understand how our early childhood experiences guide our selective attention and information processing in new situations. Hence, the child who has learnt they are bad will search out evidence to confirm this belief and play down, or ignore, information that contradicts it. This maintains and strengthens negative messages developed previously. Encouraging clients to look at the totality of their experience – the good, the bad, and the indifferent – is the beginning stage to helping them to challenge faulty childhood beliefs. Cognitive behaviour therapists call these beliefs cognitive distortions and in clients with DID these are numerous. In addition to the common belief they were born bad, the alter personalities of clients with DID frequently have magical thinking and believe in witchcraft or such like. For example, they often believe that their abusers have special powers, in that they think their abusers will know if they share their abuse histories and in sharing will burn in hell or suffer some horrific fate. Talking to the alter identities either directly, or indirectly through the host is usually necessary in order to begin the breakdown of this indoctrination, which can resemble brainwashing.

Working through the trauma

Where appropriate, working through the client's trauma needs to be taken slowly and only begin when all identities are ready. In some cases, it is not appropriate to undertake trauma work at all. This is because some clients have insufficient adult ego strength to cope with the feelings trauma work may unleash. I have also documented elsewhere the problems that can ensue if this work is performed without unanimous agreement on all parts (Ringrose 2011). Suffice to say that if this is inappropriate or mistimed, one or more identities may harm the body as a result (Warner 1998; Ringrose 2011).

Material from the client's past life intrudes on their current living because the material was never fully acknowledged and the feelings relating to it remain unresolved. This results in the client continuously being propelled back into their past life. I use the BASK model first developed by Braun (1988) to work through the key trauma events. This acronym stands for Behaviour, Affect, Sensation, and Knowledge and I tend to attempt to look at the key trauma incidents each alter holds from these four perspectives. For example, I will look at how the client behaved and what they felt but most importantly the client needs to express the emotions attached to each trauma incident. I will also explore the sensations involved at the time. These are often body felt and we will attempt to try and find a knowledge or understanding of those sensations and their relationship to the incident as a whole.

New developments

One of the major shortcomings of my research in 2010 was to discover that although researchers and practitioners in the field all reported these clients have attachment problems, little theory had been developed on how this work can evolve in the therapy sessions with this client group. This chapter aims to begin the process of redressing that imbalance. Psychotherapists are so accustomed to hearing a good therapy relationship is central that they think that once the client opens up in therapy this is demonstration that the relationship is good and this may be where the relationship work ends. However, it is vitally important to take advantage of a strong relationship by 'making the unknown known' (Wallin 2010) and by capitalizing on 'now moments' through verbalization of the meaning of them for client and therapist.

Summary

All clients with DID and many with multiple dissociative experiences will also have a disorganized attachment style. Aside from providing a nurturing and secure safe base, the therapist plays a central role in demonstrating their acceptance of the thoughts, feelings, and behaviours the client was previously unable to express for fear of rejection. It is the therapist's love and acceptance of all aspects of the client, including the dissociated parts, that can result in the client accepting these parts of themselves too, thereby making the cause for dissociation redundant. Clients who have DID will also require their therapist to assist them in learning how their parts can work together in order that the system doesn't keep grinding to a halt. Lastly, therapy will typically involve the client working through their trauma incidents that were too toxic for them to fully process at the time.

Note

1   Dissociation is a form of trance-like state that occurs automatically and is experienced by everyone sometimes. Perhaps the most common form occurs when we are driving a car and realize we are nearly at our destination but do not recall part of the journey. In clients with trauma histories, they have often learnt to dissociate as a way of not fully taking on board the trauma experience.

Further reading

Caine, L. and Royston, R. (2004) *Out of the Dark*. London: Corgi. A story of one woman's journey in therapy viewed through her trauma history.

Putnam, F.W. (1989) *Diagnosis and Treatment of Multiple Personality Disorder*. London: Guilford Press. Although now a little dated, it still provides an easy-to-read comprehensive text on DID/MPD.

Ringrose, J.L. (2012) *Understanding and Treating Dissociative Identity Disorder (Or Multiple Personality Disorder)*. London: Karnac Books. A beginner's guide containing practical suggestions of how to work with this condition.

Wallin, D.J. (2010) *Attachment in Psychotherapy*. New York: Guilford Press. Makes excellent reading for those wanting to know more about how the client–therapist attachment relationship can facilitate change in therapy and how to capitalize on this.

References

American Psychiatric Association (APA) (2013) *Diagnostic and Statistical Manual of Mental Disorders*, 5th edn. Washington, DC: American Psychiatric Press.

Bowlby, J. (1973) *Attachment and Loss, Vol. 2. Separation*. New York: Basic Books.

Braun, B.G. (1988) The BASK model of dissociation. Part II. Treatment. *Dissociation*, 1 (2): 16–23.

Caine, L. and Royston, R. (2004) *Out of the Dark*. London: Corgi.

Chbosky, S. (2012) *The Perks of being a Wallflower*. London: Simon & Schuster.

Guntrip, H. (1953) The therapeutic factor in psychotherapy, *British Journal of Medical Psychology*, 26: 115–32.

Main, M. and Hesse, E. (1990) Parents' unresolved traumatic experiences are related to infant disorganised attachment status: is frightened and/or frightening parental behaviour the linking mechanism?, in M.T. Greenberg, D. Cicchetti and E.M. Cummings (eds.) *Attachment in the Preschool Years: Theory, Research and Intervention* (pp. 161–82). Chicago, IL: University of Chicago Press.

Mearns, D. (1999) Person-centred therapy with configurations of self, *Counselling*, May, pp. 125–30.

Patterson, C.H. and Hidore, S.C. (1997) The primary prevention of psychosocial disorders: a person/client-centred perspective, *Person-Centered Journal*, 4 (1): 8–17.

Putnam, F.W. (1989) *Diagnosis and Treatment of Multiple Personality Disorder*. London: Guilford Press.

Ringrose, J.L. (2010) *Working psychotherapeutically with the dissociative disorders – an exploration of contemporary theory and practice*. Unpublished doctoral thesis, Metanoia Institute.

Ringrose, J.L. (2011) Meeting the needs of clients with dissociative identity disorder: considerations for psychotherapy, *British Journal of Guidance and Counselling*, 39 (4): 293–305.

Ringrose, J.L. (2012) *Understanding and Treating Dissociative Identity Disorder (Or Multiple Personality Disorder)*. London: Karnac Books.

Rogers, C.R. (2002) *Client-Centered Therapy*. London: Constable.

Stern, D.N. (1998) The process of therapeutic change involving implicit knowledge: some implications of developmental observations for adult psychotherapy, *Infant Mental Health Journal*, 19 (3): 300–8.

Stern, D.N. (2004) *The Present Moment in Psychotherapy and Everyday Life*. New York: W.W. Norton.

Wallin, D.J. (2010) *Attachment in Psychotherapy*. New York: Guilford Press.

Warner, M.S. (1998) A client-centred approach to therapeutic work with dissociated and fragile process, in L.S. Greenberg, J.C. Watson and G. Lietaer (eds.) *Handbook of Experiential Psychotherapy* (pp. 368–87). New York: Guilford Press.

Yalom, I.D. (2008) *Staring at the Sun: Overcoming the Dread of Death*. London: Piatcus.

20 Making the invisible visible: the relationship when working with people with learning disabilities

Zenobia Nadirshaw

Introduction

The lives and careers of people with learning disabilities have undergone significant change, from institutional care to care in the community, from the medical model to a social care model. Furthermore, we have seen the introduction and implementation of personal and citizen advocacy and a person-centred planning system. Many people with learning disabilities experience discrimination and disadvantage in many aspects of their lives, in education, housing, employment, and health services. They are limited in their choice of different lifestyles and are subject to racism, discrimination, and poverty. This is further reinforced by poor housing, high levels of unemployment, low pay, minimal pension rights, reduced benefits, and inadequate education. This chapter explores the importance of the therapeutic relationship when working with people with learning disabilities. The focus in particular is on individuals from minority ethnic backgrounds with learning disabilities.

There is a history of abuse and maltreatment of people with learning disabilities. They are vulnerable to exploitation, forced marriages, personal violence, bullying, sexual, physical, and financial abuse. They are at risk due to their difficulties understanding and communicating their concerns. Living in a group home with staff members who are often locum agency paid carers, raises even more concern for this group. Relationship and attachment issues are also known to be prevalent among persons with learning disabilities. Experience of social and personal rejection may begin with adverse early attachment relationships, leaving the person with bonding and interpersonal issues and affective disturbances. Regular interpersonal difficulties and social interactions can perpetuate depression. Furthermore, multiple relationship-based losses are also common (adoptions, multiple bereavements, unstable living arrangements, lack of reciprocal relationships) and can reinforce the perception of their stigmatized learning disability identity.

The Mental Health Foundation (1996) estimates that 2 per cent of the UK population, over one million people, have a learning disability. There is no definitive record of the number of people with learning disabilities in England. It is estimated that in 2012, 1.14 million people had a learning disability, including 236,000 children and 908,000 adults aged 18+, of whom 199,000 (22 per cent) were known to general practitioners and 404,000 (44 per cent) were receiving disability allowance.

Three core criteria define learning disability and its classification:

1   Significant impairment of intellectual functioning
2   Significant impairment of adaptive/social functioning
3   Age of onset before adulthood (18 years)

Psychological and emotional distress often goes unrecognized because services often place a greater emphasis on whether individuals meet the eligibility criteria. It is well known that learning disability is a social construct, the presence of which may be difficult to determine in the absence of learning disability associated syndromes, or a significant history of developmental delay, or educational history. Among black and minority ethnic communities, the language barriers, lack of education and healthcare opportunities in their country of origin, and incomplete or uncorroborated histories make assessment especially complicated (Royal College of Psychiatrists 2011).

Foundations of theory and practice

Britain is a multi-ethnic, multicultural society with nearly 10 per cent of the English and Welsh population coming from black and minority ethnic (BME) communities, with a concentration in London and other inner-city areas. Evidence on the prevalence of learning disabilities in BME communities is not consistent. Conceptual and practical difficulties with the definition of learning disability make prevalence data across ethnic groups and from communities around the world difficult to establish.

Nadirshaw (1997) alerts us to the double discrimination and double disadvantage that people with learning disabilities from BME backgrounds experience. She warns of the 'victim blaming' as well as the colour blind approach within the system by powerful professionals who do not acknowledge the fact that mental health and psychological needs are affected by social and political stances – leading to people of a BME background being viewed – and treated – as of less value than their white counterparts, resulting in the denial of a positive black racial and cultural identity. In addition, it is important for the helping professions to note that many BME parents believe that religion has something to say about their child's learning disability and that their religious faith or spirituality has helped them to cope (Fatimilehin and Nadirshaw 1994).

Azmi et al. (1996) reported similar results. The lack of social services and interpreting services coupled with social attitudes of discrimination at the point of delivery appear to be major obstacles to service users. In addition, emotional and psychological distress may not be recognized by GPs who often identify somatic problems with this group.

There is responsibility in the helping professions to ensure that they are equipped to work within an equal opportunity perspective that will prepare them to work in a multi-racial, multicultural context. Improving access to psychotherapy (IAPT) is a NHS initiative to improve the psychological health care of people living in England.

The helping professional provides a service that is diverse, clinically and culturally, in today's Britain. They must accept this responsibility and work towards building a more inclusive society and respond by having the appropriate understanding of problems faced by an invisible segment of British society, whose needs for psychological services and input may be expressed differently. Theoretical frameworks for psychotherapeutic practice must move away from dealing with concepts that are central to middle-class white populations and provide teaching and training about a population that is culturally and ethnically diverse. Widespread silence and indifference is preventing the problem from getting the attention it deserves.

There are significant barriers to psychotherapy for people with learning disabilities (Royal College of Psychiatrists 2004). For example, there is a reluctance to engage with people with learning disabilities. And a person with a learning disability may be afraid to talk to their GP when they are physically ill or distressed for fear of being labelled a trouble-maker. There is an apparent widespread lack of understanding between professionals and persons with learning disabilities. Beail (1995) and Dagnan and Chadwick (1997) highlight that psychotherapists remain reluctant to engage with people with learning disabilities, citing inappropriate supervision and a lack of confidence as the reasons for this. Helping professionals believe that psychological therapies are better reserved for people with more cognitive abilities; therapeutic 'disdain' has become 'institutionalized in the profession', with therapeutic work with people with learning disability being perceived as unrewarding.

People with learning disabilities suffer from mental health problems as well as being vulnerable to exploitation. Mental health problems in people with learning disabilities have largely been neglected, with widespread under-diagnosis and under-reporting of mental health conditions. The Royal College of Psychiatrists (2004) identify several reasons for this. It has generally been believed that people with learning disabilities do not have the cognitive abilities to experience mental health problems, and the behavioural difficulties shown by this group have been attributed to their learning disability. Fortunately, there is now a belief that people with learning disabilities do experience mental ill health, just as the general population do, but they are the most vulnerable in society (Smiley 2005). The definition and identification of mental health problems in learning disability are varied and includes such terms as mental illness, mental disorder, psychiatric illness, psychiatric disorder, emotional problems, and behavioural disorder.

Life events similar to those of the general population can also affect people with learning disabilities. Adults with learning disabilities experience at least as many life events and are at least as vulnerable to these as adults without a learning disability but who suffer from affective or neurotic disorders. There is evidence that people from minority ethnic communities are more likely to be diagnosed with psychiatric illness, especially psychosis, than the white Caucasian population.

The therapeutic relationship

Helping professionals must be aware of their clients' ethnic, cultural, and religious background so as to develop an understanding of how these factors can impact on the assessment and formulation process in therapy and interpretation of mental health.

Psychotherapy and counselling have engaged with issues of gender, class, and ethnicity, but not with people with learning disabilities from BME backgrounds. Their unspoken emotional and psychological distress remains unaddressed. Helping professionals need to embrace new therapeutic approaches and adapt them to a more diverse, multicultural society. They need to discuss their feelings of guilt, fear of addressing black issues, and belief they may be singled out as 'racist', as well as discussing and working through and beyond their cultural, social, ethnic, and class differences.

Building a strong therapeutic relationship takes time. Asking the client to make changes to things that are easy to change within the home environment and which are easy to observe makes the engagement process in therapy much easier. It is important to nurture the therapeutic relationship and focus on the therapeutic alliance, allowing the client to talk about their feelings at the end of each session. Helping professionals need to be patient and not worry they think the client to be 'non-compliant' during the session. Defences and projective identification on the part of the therapist also need to be reflected upon.

When working with people with learning disabilities, it is important to reflect on their attitude towards seeing themselves as disabled or coming from a BME background. They want to be seen as 'ordinary' people with ordinary problems and difficulties like their non-disabled and/or white friends. This should have an impact on the working alliance and therapeutic relationship. Helping professionals must raise the double discrimination agenda with their tutors and supervisors and ensure that BME people with learning disabilities are not seen as 'childlike', powerless, and dependent on others, with passivity and incompetence as the main features of their personality/ identity. The focus should be on the social model rather than the medical model of disability, with access to counselling and related therapeutic work viewed as a right rather than a second thought. Advice on the different therapies needs to be discussed openly with the person and his or her carers (if necessary). An equal partnership also needs to be developed, the client should feel comfortable within the therapeutic space, and there should be harmony between the therapist's world views and the 'other' world view.

Therapeutic relationship and therapeutic alliance are the cornerstone in any form of therapy with the BME population, with the disabled person at the centre of services. Bordin (1979) writes on the working alliance theme, which can be conceptualized as having three components:

1 Task (the manner in which therapy is conducted)
2 Goal (the agreed purpose and final objective of therapy)
3 Bond (the trust and confidence a person has in their therapist)

Empathy on the part of the therapist will lead to the client feeling understood and valued. Being seen in a safe place can also go a long way in developing a collaborative, honest, open, and equal partnership.

A therapeutic alliance incorporating the following components resulted in a positive outcome for the client, Imran, and his family.

- Using interventions that were meaningful to Imran and providing advice on different therapies.
- Being sensitive to the cultural variation and cultural bias of my approach, being committed to working within an approach that reflects the cultural, religious, and spiritual needs of Imran and his family.
- Having a sound cultural knowledge of Imran, including experiences of racial discrimination, the stigma attached to mental health problems, and the role of alternative help-seeking behaviours.

In my view, the attitude towards people with learning disabilities from BME communities, the interpersonal skills and ability to show genuine empathy, concern, and respect that is meaningful to the client, far outweighs the type of therapy used. Meaningful contact leading to a positive relationship between the helping professional and the BME client with learning disabilities goes a long way to achieving a positive outcome.

Working within an anti-oppressive, proactive relationship, assessing the quality of Imran's relationship with myself led to a cooperative therapeutic alliance in which he developed confidence in me and feelings of security arising from the constructive, genuinely compassionate approach that I adopted towards him. The helping professional's support for the status quo and being socialized to work within the system and rarely challenge the negative racist stereotype needs to be identified and worked through so that a person with a learning disability from the BME community will achieve his or her potential.

Wilberforce (2004) identifies common factors among these psychological approaches, irrespective of the approach/intervention used. They are:

- The relationship between client and therapist
- The working alliance between client and therapist
- The support provided and reassuring manner shown to the client
- The insight that is developed in the client following therapeutic work
- The reinforcement of healthy and adaptive responses following positive change in the client.

From a psychoanalytical perspective, Sinason (1992) suggests that a person with a learning disability may adopt secondary handicaps, such as compliant exaggeration of the original handicap to keep others happy, and appearing submissive, acquiescent, and eager to please, as a defence against their stigmatized identity.

Therapeutic and working alliance

Case vignette

Imran, 20, came to the notice of the learning disability services via the mental health service, as well as his GP. Both were concerned about his eating disorder (bulimia) for the past four years and his negative reaction to treatment. His mother provided the following history for Imran.

Imran was born in Kuwait and is one of three children. He arrived in England with the family when he was four years old. His mother described him as a hyperactive child displaying difficult behaviours at home. Marital discord between the parents resulted in a divorce. Imran's mother took sole custody of the children, living in isolation and poverty. She was very fearful of the health and social services believing that if she complained or asked for help and support, Imran would be taken away from her. Imran went to an ordinary school for three years, after which he was moved to a special school following identification of his learning difficulties and intellectual impairment. He took time to settle into the new school environment due to his limited language skills in English. He did not make any friends and the school children made fun of him. He was called names and was bullied by some children. He started to eat a lot over the growing years resulting in weight gain that was difficult to shed. Feelings of rejection led to a negative belief about self and others ('I am no good, something is wrong with me, I am not liked, I am worthless, people are not to be trusted') leading to low mood, anxiety, and loss of control within his external world. To combat the dysfunctional assumptions, a vicious cycle of thinking, feeling, and behaviour triggered off binging reactions. Imran believed this to be the only way to exert control in his life.

Assessment and treatment undertaken in English with Imran and his family addressed Imran's background, including his early experiences, identification of emotionally arousing situations both within and outside the home, his coping and other behavioural responses, his and his family's thoughts, expectations, and appraisal of events, his motivation to change, and ability to follow the treatment plan. Treatment adopted the ideas from a number of sources, including psychoanalysis, cognitive behavioural therapy, rational emotive therapy, social skills training, anger management via applied relaxation training techniques, problem-solving techniques, and art therapy/drawing.

Integration of internal factors, such as emotion, perception, and cognition with social, environmental, and cultural factors played a key part in Imran adopting a normal eating pattern. From a dejected and isolated young man, Imran was transformed into a person full of confidence and energy. He stopped his binge eating and began going to the gym and eating at specialist restaurants with his family. Combining work with Imran and his family resulted in a competent, less anxious, and trusting young man. Advocating a social rather than a medical model of disability, promoting anti-discriminatory practice, and developing a multi-disciplinary and multi-agency approach in the treatment plan, involving different health and social service staff led to a successful resolution to Imran's eating disorder. Imran was able to regain power and control via change in his own behaviour and the development of self-advocacy, which facilitated a new self and identity. He said he was proud to be Kuwaiti and from a Muslim background.

Drawing from a variety of therapeutic approaches – behavioural, psychodynamic, cognitive, humanistic, and alternative therapies – combined with clinical skills and knowledge, I was able to work with Imran towards a successful outcome. Therapy consisted of approaches with some common factors. These were:

- A working alliance between Imran and myself in which a positive working partnership was fostered, and a shared understanding of goals and aims was established.
- A trusting relationship characterized by mutual respect and genuine trust in which Imran felt secure, understood, and heard.
- Increasing insight into his emotional problems of identity confusion and eating disorder.
- A considered approach to providing reinforcement, support, reassurance, and safety in a calm and relaxed atmosphere and relationship.
- Placing Imran at the centre of therapy and focusing specifically on his unique experience and needs.
- Offering more than the usual time to Imran and working to his rhythm and pace of change.

Other contributing factors that guided my thinking included:

- Understanding learning disabilities and challenging behaviour and identifying emotional problems associated with the label.
- Listening to Imran and his family and working with them in joint partnership.
- Designing the intervention around Imran and focusing on achieving the same life outcomes as for other citizens and having skilled support in place to assist him.
- Ensuring effective and collaborative team working, with members supporting each other in working sensibly, planning risk, sharing responsibility/resources.
- Having a real partnership and a 'no blame' approach between clinical staff, his family, and managers.

Based on my own experience of work with this client group, it would be useful and informative if helping professionals reflected on their experience of the therapeutic alliance with their clients, and explored what it would be like to create a therapeutic alliance and therapeutic bond. What would be the tensions and challenges in working with this group and how would that impact on the therapist's personal and professional development? For example, attending to power issues, transference and countertransference issues, tackling social injustices, looking at multiple roles within learning disability settings, boundaries versus bonds and being connected with the client, satisfaction relating to the empowered position of this group, adapting around disability. Such reflections could contribute to an increased understanding of the therapeutic alliance and decrease the perceived difficulties in creating a therapeutic alliance and relationship. Little has been written about the therapeutic process with people with learning disabilities – including the alliance and relationship from a helping professional's perspective. Roth and Pilling (2008) consider therapeutic alliance as a core competence in cognitive behavioural therapy. Therapeutic alliance with BME people with learning disabilities needs to be addressed, which will inform clinical practice and policy on the provision of an equitable psychotherapy service.

Challenges

Helping professionals need to:

- Examine their own beliefs, their stereotyped prejudiced attitudes and feelings when faced with somebody who is different.
- Look at their own personal attitudes and history when working with people who have been subjected to oppression, discrimination, devaluation, and disadvantage.
- Develop a critical view of the profession and question whether it acts as a neutral science with a range of westernized assumptions and beliefs of diagnosing, labelling, and working with mental health or mental ill health issues.
- Understand disability, including such conditions as autism, Asperger's syndrome, and cerebral palsy.
- Work within the systems that people with learning disability experience (health service, social services, and educational services) and understand the challenges facing traditional therapeutic work and therapeutic boundaries.
- Develop communication skills, including interpreting skills, when working with clients with severe learning disabilities and their careers.
- Coordinate the equality and personalization agenda with a view to reducing the health and social inequalities faced by this client group.
- Make clinical and managerial changes, including having professional support and supervision for counsellors and therapists.
- Be mindful of the fact that the therapeutic approach (e.g. cognitive behavioural therapy) used for bulimia needs to be modified in the light of learning disabilities and motivational obstacles, particularly those relating to meals, normalizing body weight, and working constructively with the family.

Ways forward

Inequity in psychological care can no longer be justified. Steps that need to be taken to ensure that BME clients with learning disabilities receive their fair share of care include:

- Use visual media such as videos, DVDs, and radio and television stations popular with ethnic communities, provide information about local services (e.g. community learning disability teams, psychological/counselling services) and how to access them.
- Work with community leaders at cultural centres to disseminate information and reduce the stigma of learning disabilities and mental health.
- Develop a workforce that is culturally competent and has a positive understanding of BME client groups within their local communities. This includes learning about mental health, disability, stigmatization, acceptance of a world-view interpretation of mental health and emotional disorders,

acceptance of religious and spiritual understanding of mental health and learning disabilities.

- Work with voluntary organizations to organize events whereby services and BME persons with learning disabilities and their carers come together.
- Develop a 'one-stop-shop' model whereby a specialist liaison worker visits or telephones the families on a regular fortnightly basis about the availability of services.
- Work with a professional interpreting service that is knowledgeable about learning disabilities and related communication and cognitive deficits.
- Develop a person-centred approach that takes into account a person's linguistic abilities, cultural and religious beliefs and attitudes as part of the person-centred plan that is developed.
- Identify the prevalence of learning disabilities in BME communities to help assess the psychological need within this group.
- Ensure that a senior member of staff is responsible for services to this group.
- Helping professionals should familiarize themselves with the diversity and range of religious and cultural practices that exist within local communities. Learn to understand and respect those diverse needs.
- Determine the number of languages spoken and the dialects used.
- Employ professionally trained workers who understand the emotional and psychological problems of this group. Helping professionals need to examine their racial biases and prejudices and work through these so that they can offer therapy and counselling objectively, without anxiety, shame, and/or guilt. They need to be culturally competent.
- Address the reality of a learning disabled person from a BME background, acknowledge the Eurocentric bias of western models, and explore the role of religion/spiritual beliefs in work with such clients.

New developments

There is a need to develop workforce skills via training and clinical placements for students of psychotherapy in order to help them to understand the double disadvantage faced by BME people with learning disabilities and to work with the system and support network in a collaborative way. Training must take into account the needs of marginalized, disadvantaged, and oppressed groups and ensure a deeper understanding of the social, political, and ethical issues in providing therapy. The relevance and consequences of oppression, discrimination, personal and institutional racism, and personal power and privileges enjoyed by the dominant sections of the counselling/therapy world needs to be highlighted in all training courses. Difference and diversity needs to be explored in a positive light for black and minority ethnic people with learning disabilities.

Training courses must develop practice supported by research and theory that is inclusive of disability, gender, class, and sexual preference/orientation. Theories of psychological models and counselling must provide evidence of understanding of the complex ways in which BME persons with learning disabilities experience multiple oppressions and disadvantages. The stereotyped, historical, and biomedical model of therapy and counselling needs to be replaced, so that helping professionals can examine at the outset their deep-seated prejudices and biases towards physical disability and/or intellectual disability and 'race' issues.

The proper and appropriate psychological care must be provided with services adapting to meet the need of this group who remain segregated from mainstream society. The helping professions need to address shortcomings in current training and develop models with an emphasis on the individual and his or her cognitive structures together with the cultural, family, and political contexts.

Such therapies as dialectical behaviour therapy, cognitive analytical therapy, and interpersonal therapy need to be developed in conjunction with other behavioural, cognitive, and family therapy and systemic therapies. Some research on these therapies has been conducted (Sinason 1992; Beail 1995; Baum and Lynggaard 2006; McKim 2013). An intensive interaction approach that facilitates two-way communication with people with severe or profound learning difficulties and/or autism should also be made available within health and education services.

Anger management interventions for people with a wide range of cognitive and communication abilities, primarily in a group setting using a cognitive behavioural approach, have shown promising results. Pictures and symbols, progressive muscle relaxation, and imagery – appropriately modified – have also been used. These need to be developed further.

Summary

Black and minority ethnic persons with learning disabilities remain invisible to therapeutic helping professionals. They have other people's values imposed on them so as to fit into existing service provision through the adoption of a colour blind, victim-blaming approach. This needs to be carefully dealt with within the therapeutic process and in the development of the therapeutic alliance. Helping professionals must accept responsibility and work towards building a more inclusive society and respond to people whose needs are expressed differently. Attention is required by the training community/colleges and professional organizations to address the widespread silence and indifference that exists regarding this client group.

Further reading

Epstein, N., Schlesinger, S.E. and Dryden, W. (eds.) (1988) *Cognitive Behavioral Therapy and Families*. New York: Brunner/Mazel. A good read on working with families using cognitive behavioural therapy.

Wilberforce, D. (2004) Psychological approaches, in B. Gates (ed.) *Learning Disability: Towards Inclusion*, 2nd edn. London: Churchill Livingstone. This book provides a sound basis of understanding the different aspects of learning disabilities, including the different psychological approaches and therapeutic interventions for people with learning disabilities.

References

Azmi, S., Emerson, E., Caine, A. and Hatton, C. (1996) *Improving Services for Asian People with Learning Disabilities and their Families.* Manchester: Hestor Adrian Research Centre/The Mental Health Foundation.

Baum, S. and Lynggaard, H. (eds.) (2006) *Intellectual Disabilities: A Systemic Approach.* London: Karnac Books.

Beail, N. (1995) Outcome of psychoanalysis, psychoanalytic, psychodynamic psychotherapy with people with intellectual disabilities: a review, *Changes*, 13: 186–91.

Bordin, E. (1979) The generalizability of the psychoanalytical concept of the working alliance, *Psychotherapy: Theory Research and Practice*, 16 (3): 252–60.

Caine, A.D. and Hatton, C. (1998) Working with people with mental health problems, in E. Emerson, C. Hatton, K. Dickson, R. Gone, A. Caine and J. Bromley (eds.) *Clinical Psychology and People with Intellectual Disabilities*, 2nd edn. Chichester: Wiley.

Dagnan, D. and Chadwick, P. (1997) Cognitive behaviour therapy for people with learning disabilities: assessment and intervention, in B. Kroese, D. Dagnan and K. Loumidis (eds.) *Cognitive Behaviour Therapy for People with Learning Disabilities.* London: Routledge.

Fatimilehin, I. and Nadirshaw, Z. (1994) A cross-cultural study of parental attitudes and beliefs about learning disability, *Mental Handicap Research*, 7 (3): 202–27.

McKim, J. (2013) Developing the use of intensive interaction in the Oxfordshire Learning Department NHS Trust (Ridgeway Partnership), *Clinical Psychology and People with Learning Difficulties*, 11 (1/2): 12–19.

Mental Health Foundation (1996) *Building Expectations: Opportunities and Services for People with a Learning Disability.* London: Mental Health Foundation.

Nadirshaw, Z. (1997) Cultural issues, in J. O'Hara and A. Sperlinger (eds.) *Adults with Learning Disability: A Practical Approach for Health Professionals* (pp. 139–53). Chichester: Wiley.

Roth, A.D. and Pilling, S. (2008) Using an evidence-based methodology to identify the competences required to deliver effective cognitive and behavioural therapy for depression and anxiety disorders, *Behavioural and Cognitive Psychotherapy*, 36 (2): 129–47.

Royal College of Psychiatrists (RCPsych) (2004) *Psychotherapy and Learning Disability.* Council Report CR116, March. London: RCPsych.

Royal College of Psychiatrists (RCPsych) (2011) *Minority Ethnic Communities and Specialist Learning Disability Services.* Report of the Faculty of the Psychiatry of Learning Disability Working Group. London: RCPsych.

Sinason, V. (1992) *Metal Handicap and the Human Condition: New Approaches from the Tavistock.* London: Free Association Books.

Smiley, E. (2005) Epidemiology of mental health problems in adults with learning disability: an update, *Advances in Psychological Treatment*, 11: 214–22.

Wilberforce, D. (2004) Psychological approaches, in B. Gates (ed.) *Learning Disabilities: Towards Inclusion*, 2nd edn. London: Churchill Livingstone.

SECTION 5

Further Dimensions of the Therapeutic Relationship

21 Transcultural and diversity perspectives: the space between us

Colin Lago and Val Watson

Introduction

It is a basic truism of any endeavour in counselling and psychotherapy that the quality of relationship between the therapist and client is of fundamental significance to the therapeutic task and outcome. Therapeutic relationships span the spectrum of connectedness: from what is described as 'relational depth' (Mearns and Cooper 2005), where therapist and client experience 'a state of profound contact and engagement in which each person is fully real with the other, and able to understand and value the other's experiences at a high level' (p. 12), through relationships described as being 'good-enough' to those possessing minimal 'relationality'.

Pearce and Sewell (2013) provide a case example of this latter category, defining this as 'tenuous contact'. A therapist concluded that they had failed to develop some sort of psychological contact with their client – assessing that despite their efforts, the client seemed to be unaffected by the therapist or the therapeutic relationship. It was only some years later that this perception was revised, at a chance meeting between the two, when the client told the therapist that they had realized the therapist had been someone who, at some level, must have valued and loved them! From this latter perspective, we have to acknowledge that we often do not know what impact we are having as therapists – and indeed may never know! Something had passed in the space between this client and counsellor, which, for the client, was not fully accessible until much later when therapy had ended.

In a discussion on the subject of inter-subjectivity, a friend and colleague of one of the authors, Dot Clark (2013), asserted that the dynamics of relationship exist intra-personally as well as inter-personally. She hypothesizes that relationship is inherent in the way we relate to existence itself. From this perspective, 'being' takes on a unique and inescapable form, or set of 'conditions', in every individual. The challenge we face, both in relation to 'being' itself and in relation to other people, is to be as compassionately aware as we can be of the specifics of our identity because such acceptance softens its limits and expands the space available for encountering the other, internally and externally. The transcultural perspective pays close attention to this dynamic in negotiating difference, especially to the socially embedded power differences which human beings create around minority and majority groups. Clark links her ideas with Rogers' (1951: 520) eighteenth proposition in his theory of personality, which attests to the power and positive impact of self-acceptance and non-defensive integration of all of our sensory and visceral experiences, arguing that 'the most personal is also the most universal and vice versa; "being" flourishes when witnessed fully without fear'.

In our consideration of the complexities of the transcultural therapeutic relationship, it is worth acknowledging that our understanding of 'being' could be said to comprise the value we place on the multiplicity of our identities (Moodley and Murphy 2010), and lived cultural frameworks that might be relevant and available for attention in a therapeutic relationship. Some of these are visible, such as minority or majority status, ethnicity, gender, and disability. Others may be hidden, such as sexuality, disability, health concerns, faith, and socio-economic status. When the client and counsellor are able to bring the whole of their 'being' into the relationship, this increases the likelihood of a positive therapeutic outcome.

Foundations of theory and practice

The 'transcultural relationship'

From the research literature, we note Cooper's (2008) excellent review of findings related to the therapeutic relationship. He highlights the considerable discrepancies in the estimation of the extent to which relational factors account for variance in outcome. Compare, for example, Assay and Lambert's (1999) figure of 30 per cent with the significantly lower estimates by Beutler et al. (2004) of 7–17 per cent and by Chambless and Ollendick (2001) of only 9 per cent. He also notes the complexity of the multiplicity of elements that constitute and contribute to the overall theme of 'relationship'. These include therapeutic alliance, goal consensus and collaboration, therapist interpersonal skills including empathy, positive regard, and congruence, management of counter-transference, self-disclosure, feedback, repairing alliance ruptures, and transference interpretations.

It would appear we are unable to say, with any great accuracy, how significant relationship is, and neither can we narrow down the wide range of relational elements, each of which can interrupt and disrupt the therapeutic process.

Within 'transcultural therapy', we are additionally confronted by further challenges to the successful creation of 'good enough' working relationships. These are summarily listed below:

1   The statistical evidence of ongoing oppression and discrimination in society and how this overall societal pattern may be re-enacted in and impact upon the everyday, specific, moment-to-moment unfolding of a therapeutic relationship (see, for example, Lago 2006, 2011; Lago and Smith 2010). Alleyne (2011) offers nine examples of how (subtle) racism and hidden racial prejudice are exhibited by practitioners of counselling and psychotherapy. One example is where the practitioner assumes that all members of a racial group adhere to all its cultural tenets and norms, ignoring the client's individuality and unique cultural identity.

2   'Multicultural' or transcultural counselling was delineated as the fourth force
     in psychology after the theoretical schools of analytic (first force), cognitive
     behavioural (second force), and humanistic approaches (third force) by the
     American Psychological Association in the 1990s. 'Transcultural therapy' may
     be delivered by counsellors and psychotherapists of all psychotherapeutic
     theoretical orientations. While there are some indicators of what constitutes
     'good, sensitive' practice (Moodley and Lubin 2008; Lago 2010), these are not
     equated or made explicit in the various theoretical paradigms. Transcultural
     and diversity-aware therapeutic practice demands that counsellors and
     psychotherapists not only require knowledge of and sensitivity towards a
     wide range of others occupying different diversities, but need to address the
     nature of their own 'identity' within society.

                                                                    (Carter 1995)

In the case of the first point above, if patterns of oppression and discrimination exist
within every aspect of sociocultural life, then what reassurance and evidence is there,
as therapists, that we will not repeat such patterns in our work? Secondly, it is likely
that the relational components that are a feature of one's predominant theoretical style
will be relied on by the therapist within a transcultural relationship. Sadly, working
successfully with difference and diversity in therapy raises many sociological
implications related to identities that are often barely, poorly or never addressed in
counselling/psychotherapy training in ways that encourage and support trainees to
celebrate rather than problematize the realities of the multiplicity of identity.

The therapeutic relationship and its 'transcultural' challenges

Most writers over recent decades addressing this field of application in counselling
and psychotherapy have repeatedly asked the question: Can therapists from differing
origins to their clients truly accept and understand the complete panoply of differences
represented by the 'other'? There are a multitude of texts that strive towards enhancing
therapist knowledge, skills, awareness, and sensitivity in this arena (e.g. D'Ardenne
and Mahtani 1989; Lago and Thompson 2006; Haugh and Paul 2008; McKenzie-Mavinga
2009; Lago and Smith 2010; Ryde 2011; D'Ardenne 2013; Lago 2013).
    We have simultaneously used various terms (such as 'transcultural', 'multicultural',
'difference', and 'diversity') to denote this area of therapeutic activity. While there are
important differences accorded to differing terminologies, our overall concern is to
address the significant disruptions to the therapy process across difference, rather
than debate the nuances of difference between interpretations of title. However, we do
not wish to ignore the increased complexity and challenge added to the therapist's task
when the North American derived notions of 'multicultural counselling' of the 1970s
(which addressed differences related to cultural origin, ethnicity, and race) were
extended to incorporate the 'seven stigmatized identities' (Moodley and Lubin 2008)
with the use of the term 'diversity' attracting common usage around the turn of the
century. Moodley and Lubin's conceptualization included gender, sexual orientation,
dis-ability, ethnicity, age, class, and religion. The considerable range of human

difference, as presented by clients coming for therapy, is a challenge and opportunity to create a sensitive, empathic, genuine therapeutic relationship.

One potentially complex relational phenomenon within therapeutic relationships of difference is that between persons who reside within the 'majority group' in society and those from a 'minority group', be that ethnic, religious, disabled, and so on. Based on extensive research, Robert Carter (1995) explored the therapeutic relationship implications between participants who not only originated from majority and minority groups, but were also at differing stages of what is termed 'identity development'. His research revealed considerable evidence to suggest that therapists whose own sense of ethnic identity was more developed than the clients that they worked with were much more likely to have more effective therapeutic outcomes. It is proposed that the extent to which the therapist is sufficiently knowledgeable and grounded in their own identity has implications for their ability to work comfortably with the differences of their clients, their social situatedness, their projections onto the therapist and their stories.

Within the focus of this chapter, that is, the therapeutic relationship, we are reminded of Rogers' specific conviction (and later assertion by leading researchers such as Cooper 2008) in the primacy of the client's perception of the therapist and their relationship to the therapist. Within diverse settings, one can only appreciate the sheer enormity of this single criterion. If the client does not experience the relationship with the therapist as 'good enough', then the work is not likely to be of therapeutic value; the client is judge!

Practice

We offer two anonymized case examples demonstrating some challenges to practice.

Case vignette: Transcultural practice

Daniel, 32, was referred for short-term counselling (a maximum of eight sessions) by his manager aimed at addressing problems with anxiety that had resulted in three consecutive periods of sick leave absence. In his first session with his counsellor, Bridget, Daniel described himself as confident, easy going, and happily married for six years with a four-year-old son whom he and his wife doted on. Daniel expressed guilt and worry that his recent difficulties were having a negative impact on family relationships and his self-esteem. His stated goal was to end 'bouts of panic' and develop strategies to manage his anxiety. Daniel wanted to get to the 'root of the problem' so that he could return to 'normal'. He explored and worked on the triggers of recent panic and anxiety attacks that occurred mostly when travelling to work. Daniel and Bridget generated and customized a range of coping strategies that he experimented with, reporting a high degree of success.

Bridget's enthusiastic reports in clinical supervision indicated that the therapeutic relationship with Daniel was working well and moving towards a positive conclusion. They had noted their cultural differences and highlighted the ways in which open discussion about their ethnic and gender difference was a positive factor enabling them to build trust. Daniel remarked that Bridget's sensitivity contrasted with his usual experience where White colleagues and acquaintances often made negative assumptions about him as a Black man, father, and employee.

Bridget was shocked when in his penultimate session Daniel spoke of his disappointment with counselling, claiming that 'things' were unchanged. He questioned her training, qualifications, and competence. Distressed and breathing with difficulty, Daniel dismissed Bridget's offer to help with his impending panic attack mimicking her attempt to empathically reflect on his experiencing. Bridget emphasized that she wanted him to feel free to say and be what he wanted without her interruptions. After ten minutes of silence, Daniel slumped to the floor. Bridget responded, telling Daniel that she 'heard him'. He replied: 'But that's impossible, I only whispered it to myself once two months ago.'

Daniel said later that in the silence he felt Bridget had moved closer to him and that he was now able to speak openly about what was troubling him rather than continually whisper it only to himself. Geller (2013) describes therapeutic presence as the way in which the attuned therapist reaches out to touch the depth of the client with the positive intent of healing. Bridget's attuned state and her openness to being vulnerable and available to Daniel to take a risk meant that he too could take risks to be more of how he felt in the moment without fear of judgement.

This intense interaction between client and counsellor could be understood as an example of the contested concept of relational depth (Mearns and Cooper 2005) in which the client's and the counsellor's development is facilitated by their willingness to deepen and 'change the quality of their psychological contact' (Wyatt 2013). This 'change' enabled Daniel to envisage and experience the possibilities of hearing and seeing himself as a whole person rather than a series of valued, discarded, hidden, undeveloped parts. Wyatt (2013) advances the notion that the development of enhanced quality of psychological contact and Rogers' concept of the therapist's 'presence' are significant factors in the potential for social and global change. Schmid (2013) asserts that 'We are not only *in* relationships – as persons, we *are* relationships.' Client and therapist bring the sum of all their experiences and other relationships; acknowledging this and our inter-relatedness enriches the relationship and can transcend cultural difference.

In the remainder of the seventh and his eighth sessions, Daniel disclosed experience of childhood abuse and discussed with Bridget his options for further therapy and support.

Case vignette: Client choice of therapist

Michelle, 36 (a White, British heterosexual woman), was convinced that a middle-aged male Asian would not understand her or her situation. Her counsellor, Narinder, acknowledged her doubts in the early stages of their relationship remaining optimistic and positive about the relationship and therapeutic outcomes. Michelle had been referred by her GP because she was suffering from persistent low mood, anxiety and insomnia, the symptoms of which were only partially relieved by medication. Michelle told Narinder that her relationships with her children (aged 14, 12, and 8) and husband were tense and that she was being bullied at work. A ten-year history of conflict with other close and extended family members had led to her avoiding contact with them. She had no close female friendships but had a confiding relationship with Adam, a male friend of the family with whom she attended community and social events. Michelle stated that Adam had been particularly supportive when she had post-natal depression eight years previously after the birth of her third child. At that time she was prescribed anti-depressants and had some counselling which was helpful and effective.

Michelle and Narinder found a relational meeting point through their use of metaphors and symbols to describe and communicate feelings, thoughts, and experiences. One area they returned to time and again was their love of gardening, nature, and the challenges of the weather! Born and educated in Britain, Narinder was familiar with Christian beliefs and responded knowledgeably, to Michelle's surprise, to biblical references recalled from her childhood. Although Michelle was not a practising Christian, she frequently referred to its tenets in therapy, contrasting these with her growing understanding of Narinder's faith principles while aligning herself along Pagan belief systems.

At her fourth session Michelle stated that she was sure her husband was being unfaithful. She described her relationship with her husband, Neville, as always being difficult and verbally volatile. They had little in common and had diverging views about domestic life, finance, parenting, and their plans for the future. Early in their marriage Neville had pushed and hit her a few times but this had stopped just before she was pregnant. Empathizing with Michelle, Narinder reflected on Michelle's expression of confusion, powerlessness, and betrayal. Internally, he noted confidently and, in hindsight, with an element of certitude that this would not occur in his marriage because of an adherence to the traditions and norms of marriage related to his faith beliefs and culture.

In her fifth session Michelle reported that Neville had threatened divorce if she did not end her relationship with Adam. In Neville's view Adam's overt and visible expressions of homosexuality were a bad influence on Michelle and had a negative impact on her parenting. For the first time in counselling she cried and was angry. Narinder heard how Michelle was torn between the competing tensions of exercising her inclination towards assertiveness, and submission in favour of preserving her family life and current conditions. Narinder witnessed her struggle to retain an important and regulating attachment figure in her friendship with Adam (Schore and Schore 2008) and her desire for harmonious family relationships and improved sense of wellbeing. This was a 'moral moment' for Michelle and Narinder exploring the dilemma together – recognizing the tensions, feelings, and implications of her decisions and possible actions beyond the therapy room.

In clinical supervision, Narinder expressed frustration and indecision, feeling caught between two opposing frames of reference. One supported his education, socialization, and westernized focused training, which valued the importance of self-determination, choice, and authenticity; the other was rooted in his original family values and faith, *prioritizing collective responsibility, the sacred, and relegation of will in favour of traditional observance and compliance. While practitioners may be convinced of the rectitude and universality of their preferred counselling/psychotherapy orientation, these theoretical paradigms can be experienced as inadequate and insufficient in transcultural therapeutic relationships. Narinder wanted to find a way of engaging in an honest encounter with Michelle that would not confirm her original doubt in his ability to understand her. He concluded that the effects of cultural encapsulation including bias towards his frame of reference and his orientation as a therapist had affected his ability to recognize that by prioritizing Michelle's needs (for an advocate) in the 'now' of their relationship, she was more likely to feel supported to make a decision, which would be of benefit to her and her family.*

A turning point occurred when Narinder revisited his own cultural codes, spiritual observances, prejudices, and guiding principles as a therapist. He identified diverging views, assumptions, and experiences as well as points of contact with Michelle that he had previously overlooked. It was as if he had re-set the dial, and was anchored in his culture and spirituality, but not rigidly so; aware of the challenges and conflicts of managing multiple identities. He could accept Michelle and appreciate her as separate, connected to him, and being part of a unified whole rather than feeling obliged to influence or steer her in a particular direction. 'Tuning' into himself and his identity helped Narinder to empathically attune to his client. This attitude helped to facilitate Michelle's burgeoning interest in self-understanding and ultimately the challenge of honestly advocating for herself and her family in ways that enhanced her sense of wellbeing and was reflected in the significant reduction in her original symptoms and reasons for coming to therapy.

New developments

Moodley (2003) argues that the growth of therapy practice, and the recognized demographics of diversity, is not matched with sufficient serious attention and funding being given to research in this area in the counselling and psychotherapy profession. As a general consequence of this impoverished research output within this field, new developments, informed by research outcomes, are somewhat limited in application. Also, much of the research has been and continues to be conducted within the United States (which consequently requires careful attention in its application within a British setting), though there is an increasing amount of activity now happening within the UK.

One particularly useful outcome of research has been the exploration of the concept of 'ethnic matching', where clients and therapists might be ethnically matched to enhance the potential efficacy of their work together. What this research has revealed is the complexity of creating sufficiently sophisticated systems for such matching to occur (see Farsimadan et al. 2011). Importantly, though, many therapy agencies strive to implement and evaluate client choice of therapist within their everyday working practices. The considerable body of work formerly conducted by

Carter (1995) on the influence of racial identity led to earlier speculations that the 'ethnic identity development' models developed might form the basis of an ethnic matching system. Subjected to practice analysis, Lee and GoEun Na (2011) report that while these earlier hopes were not realized, nevertheless the models constituted a very useful mechanism for therapist analysis and reflections on their work.

The many benefits of technology are accompanied by an increasing felt demand to respond speedily in our communications with each other. This contemporary *zeitgeist*, combined with decreasing financial and resource demands, has inevitably imposed considerable pressures upon therapeutic practitioners to facilitate and evidence more change, more quickly in their clients. Yet the reality is that, as human beings, we are still influenced by our earlier developmental periods of evolution. Our capacity to change at the psychological/emotional level is much slower and more individual than current surface impressions of society indicate. The case example quoted by Pearce and Sewell (2013) above is not unique. It serves to encourage the therapy profession to continually challenge the accuracy and credibility of, and quick conclusions that might be drawn from, some post-therapy outcome measurements.

Consequently, it is no surprise that there has been an increasing interest in the benefits of contemplative practices such as meditation, yoga, and mindfulness, which invites us to slow down, to wait; to integrate our experiences and communications at our own individual pace. Personal change and growth is most powerful when it unfolds experientially within the client's own experiencing. Inappropriate therapist pressure for clients to change seriously impacts the efficacy of therapeutic relationship and thus therapeutic outcome.

One particular example of this tension between society's context of speedy change and individual rates of personality change is the situation where interpreters are involved within the process to facilitate communication across language differences between client and counsellor. The very act of interpretation slows down the communication process, yet it is interesting to note how many therapy agencies do not allow for this in their imposed session limits.

While recently working in Austria, one of the authors noted just how many participants in a large group setting acknowledged the value of the use of two languages, German and English, for the communication process. As one participant reported, 'It slowed the process down enough so that I had time to really understand the issues under discussion.' New developments in this field are generally being driven by practitioners and it is reassuring that an increasing amount of literature (in terms of journal articles, book chapters, and monographs) continues to appear and will, over time, inform developing practice. These include new perspectives on: the structure of training courses and requirements for continuing professional development (Lago 2011); the implications of identity upon therapeutic practice (Tuckwell 2002; McKenzie-Mavinga 2009; Ryde 2011); language usage (D'Ardenne and Mahtani 1989); and different fields of application (D'Ardenne 2013).

Summary

This chapter has addressed the nature of relationship in order to more fully explore the challenges to the formation of transcultural therapeutic relationships. Working across difference and diversity has to take into account the continuing patterns of discrimination experienced in society by those in minority groups, with the recognition that such micro-aggressions can easily be repeated within the counselling relationship. Furthermore, we argue that therapists in transcultural settings need to understand the nature of their identity within society and how this might impact upon the client from a different background. Extended case examples are given to illustrate issues in practice. We also discussed concepts such as ethnic matching, identity development, the use of interpreters, and continuing professional development as factors that contribute strongly to the formation of successful therapeutic relations.

Recommendations

The following brief pointers are offered:

- The ecopsychology movement provides a challenge to therapists to consider the interconnectedness and impact of nature, global events, and personal crises.
- The uses of creative arts are well known and growing in therapeutic settings and may have particular value within transcultural relationships.
- Investigate the increased use of online therapeutic resources. These may not supersede the need for direct human contact but can be a lifeline and/or a starting point for many people.
- Training ideas and suggested recommendations for transcultural therapy practice may be found in: Patel et al. (2000), Alleyne (2011), and Lago and Hirai (2013), who list 26 practice recommendations.

Try to:

- Take an active interest in local, national, and international news events presented from differing cultural and political perspectives.
- Read literature, watch films, and find ways of making contact with others with different culture and/or orientation than your own. This extends to attending training events in modalities you are unfamiliar with.

Get out of your comfort zone or place of familiarity so that you can see things from different perspectives and remind yourself of the experience of 'not-knowing'. It sharpens understanding of transcultural issues when we as therapists try to translate the language of our modality or culture into or out of the one we are trying to understand.

References

Alleyne, A. (2011) Overcoming racism, discrimination and oppression in psychotherapy, in C. Lago (ed.) *The Handbook of Transcultural Counselling and Psychotherapy* (pp. 117–29). Maidenhead: Open University Press.

Assay, T.P. and Lambert, M.J. (1999) The empirical case for the common factors in therapy: qualitative findings, in M. Hubble, B.L. Duncan and S.D. Miller (eds.) *The Heart and Soul of Change: What Works in Therapy* (pp. 33–55). Washington, DC: American Psychological Association.

Beutler, L.E., Malik, M., Alimohamed, S., Harwood, M.T., Talebi, S., Noble, S. et al. (2004) Therapist variables, in M.J. Lambert (ed.) *Bergin and Garfield's Handbook of Psychotherapy and Behavior Change*, 5th edn. (pp. 227–306). New York: Wiley.

Carter, R. (1995) *The Influence of Race and Racial Identity in Psychotherapy: Towards a Racially Inclusive Model*. Westport, CT: Greenwood.

Chambless, D.L. and Ollendick, T.H. (2001) Empirically supported psychological interventions: controversies and evidence, *Annual Review of Psychology*, 52: 685–716.

Clark, D. (2013) *Reflections on the nature of relationship*. Personal communication with Colin Lago, 25 October.

Cooper, M. (2008) *Essential Research Findings in Counselling and Psychotherapy: The Facts are Friendly*. London: Sage/Rugby: BACP.

D'Ardenne, P. (2013) *Counselling in Transcultural Settings: Priorities for a Restless World*. London: Sage.

D'Ardenne, P. and Mahtani, A. (1989) *Transcultural Counselling in Action*, 2nd edn. London: Sage.

Farsimadan, F., Khan, A. and Draghi-Lorenz, R. (2011) On ethnic matching: a review of the research and considerations for practice, training and policy, in C. Lago (ed.) *The Handbook of Transcultural Counselling and Psychotherapy*. New York: Open University Press.

Geller, S. (2013) Therapeutic presence, in M. Cooper, M. O'Hara, P.F. Schmid and A.F. Bohart (eds.) *The Handbook of Person-centred Psychotherapy and Counselling*, 2nd edn. (pp. 209–22). Basingstoke: Palgrave Macmillan.

Haugh, S. and Paul, S. (eds.) (2008) *The Therapeutic Relationship: Perspectives and Themes*. Ross-on-Wye: PCCS Books.

Lago, C. (2006) *Race, Culture and Counselling: The Ongoing Challenge*, 2nd edn. Maidenhead: Open University Press.

Lago, C. (2010) On developing our empathic capacities to work inter-culturally and inter-ethnically: attempting a map for personal and professional development, *Psychotherapy and Politics International*, 8 (1) [www.interscience.wiley.com].

Lago, C. (ed.) (2011) *The Handbook of Transcultural Counselling and Psychotherapy*. Maidenhead: Open University Press.

Lago, C. and Hirai, T. (2013) Counselling across difference and diversity, in M. Cooper, M. O'Hara, P.F. Schmid and A.F. Bohart (eds.) *The Handbook of Person-centred Psychotherapy and Counselling*, 2nd edn. Basingstoke: Palgrave Macmillan.

Lago. C. and Smith, B. (eds.) (2010) *Anti-Discriminatory Counselling Practice*, 2nd edn. London: Sage.

Lago, C. and Thompson, J. (2006) *Race, Culture and Counselling*, 2nd edn. Buckingham: Open University Press.

Lee, C.C. and GoEun Na (2011) Identity development and its impact upon the therapy relationship, in C. Lago (ed.) *The Handbook of Transcultural Counselling and*

Psychotherapy, 2nd edn. Maidenhead: Open University Press.

McKenzie-Mavinga, I. (2009) *Black Issues in the Therapeutic Process*. London: Palgrave Macmillan.

Mearns, D. and Cooper, M. (2005) *Working at Relational Depth in Counselling and Psychotherapy*. London: Sage.

Moodley, R. (2003) Double, triple and multiple jeopardy, in C. Lago and B. Smith (eds.) *Anti-Discriminatory Counselling Practice*, 2nd edn. (pp. 120–34). London: Sage.

Moodley, R. and Lubin, D. (2008) Developing your career to working with multicultural and diversity clients, in S. Palmer and R. Bor (eds.) *The Practitioner's Handbook: A Guide for Counsellors, Psychotherapists and Counselling Psychologists*. London: Sage.

Moodley, R. and Murphy, L. (2010) Multiple identities and anti-discriminatory counselling practice, in C. Lago and B. Smith (eds.) *Anti-Discriminatory Counselling Practice*, 2nd edn. (pp. 137–48). London: Sage.

Patel, N., Bennett, E., Dennis, M., Dosanjh, N., Mahtani, A., Miller, A. et al. (eds.) (2000) *Clinical Psychology, 'Race' and Culture': A Training Manual*. Chichester: Blackwell.

Pearce, P. and Sewell, R. (2013) Seminar presentation of their doctoral research findings on 'Working with young people in groups in school settings', University of Keele Counselling Conference – 'Counselling and the Emotional Life', 16/17 March.

Rogers, C.R. (1951) *Client-Centered Therapy*. London: Constable.

Ryde, J. (2011) Issues for white therapists, in C. Lago (ed.) *The Handbook of Transcultural Counselling and Psychotherapy* (pp. 94–104). Maidenhead: Open University Press.

Schmid, P.F. (2013) The anthropological, relational and ethical foundations of person-centred therapy, in M. Cooper, M. O'Hara, P.F. Schmid and A.F. Bohart (eds.) *The Handbook of Person-centred Psychotherapy and Counselling*, 2nd edn. (pp. 66–83). Basingstoke: Palgrave Macmillan.

Schore, J.R. and Schore, A.N. (2008) Modern attachment theory: the central role of affect regulation in development and treatment, *Clinical Social Work Journal*, 36: 9–20.

Tuckwell, G. (2002) *Racial Identity, White Counsellors and Therapists*. Buckingham: Open University Press.

Wyatt, G. (2013) Psychological contact, in M. Cooper, M. O'Hara, P.F. Schmid and A.F. Bohart (eds.) *The Handbook of Person-centred Psychotherapy and Counselling*, 2nd edn. (pp. 150–64). Basingstoke: Palgrave Macmillan.

22 Spirituality in the therapeutic relationship

Stephen Paul and William West

There is the experience of the transcendent, that is to say of two people being linked into something greater than themselves . . . in this transcendent state there is an overpowering sense of energy, well-being and healing.

(Thorne 1991: 183)

Introduction

In this chapter, we consider the nature of what may be called spirituality in therapeutic relationships. We examine religious spirituality, individual spirituality, working with the human spirit, psychological growth, and working with spiritual crisis. We clarify the difference between religion and spirituality and the importance of spirituality in health and wellbeing for individuals. We identify ways of working with spirituality in therapeutic relationships and address some of the challenges in this area of practice.

This chapter will be of interest to those with religious beliefs and those whose approach is purely psychological. It will be of equal use to theists, atheists, and agnostics.

Foundations of theory and practice

During the latter part of the twentieth century, there was a general decline in traditional religious attendance in many populations, particularly among younger people. On the other hand, belief in something higher and a personal spirituality has remained steady for the vast majority of people in the UK (Hay and Hunt 2000). A poll of Americans (Gallup Poll, 5–8 May 2011) found 92 per cent believed in 'God or a universal spirit', 37 per cent had been to a religious service in the previous 7 days, while 71 per cent thought religion was losing its influence on society.

There has been a corresponding development of what may be called a pluralistic approach to individual spirituality (with more attention being paid to different religions, modern variants or what are called new religious movements) and psycho-spiritual approaches to personal growth. Roof et al. (1995) cite five characteristics of the new developments in religious pluralism:

- A 'cafeteria' approach (a pick and mix of preferred elements)
- Mixing of codes from the different religions
- Mixing of old and new religious practices
- The individual experience is predominant
- Indifference to religious institutions.

With the increasing interest in a personal spirituality in Eurocentric cultures and a more individual approach to religious exploration, spirituality is seen as a possible contemporary alternative to religion (Wulff 1997). A glance around any bookshop illustrates the wide range of popular literature in the field.

In an increasingly secular society, spiritual issues are increasingly brought to the attention of health care professionals (Post et al. 2000). Paradoxically, many professionals are not taught how to work with issues of spirituality, even though they may have been advised to do so. For example, with regard to end of life care in the UK, the National Institute for Health and Care Excellence (NICE) has produced a quality statement on 'Holistic support – spiritual and religious', which states 'Health and social care workers offer, facilitate and provide (including sign-posting and referral) spiritual and religious support to people approaching the end of life that is appropriate to the person's needs and preferences' (NICE 2013). However, professionals may be unsure of their own values and beliefs and there may be a 'taboo' about discussing this personal subject with clients and patients (Miller 2013).

The root of the term spirituality is considered to have come from the Latin *spirare*, to breathe, and is associated with a person's personal sense of their own essence and their relationship to it and their everyday lives. It is an essentially individual and unique point of reference. A personal spirituality is not specifically associated with an organized religion – it can only be defined by the individual (Koenig 2008).

It is quite possible to have a personal spirituality and have no belief in any higher power or life after death. For some people, there is a sense of inner spirit, a source of inspiration and strength with no religious meaning. We propose spirituality to have some or all the following components:

- A sense of something greater than the individual self or ego
- A felt sense
- Values or a belief system congruent to the individual
- The living core of being of the individual
- A sense of meaning.

Psychological perspectives

Psychology has a poor track record in the realm of the spiritual and religious. Lowenthal (2000) intimates that the following were major factors in an almost indifferent attention paid by mainstream psychology to religious experience other than social psychological studies that focused on external, observable factors:

1   The influences of Freud who postulated that:
    - Religion is a 'universal obsessional neurosis'.
    - God is a projection of the father.

2   The later predomination of empirical psychology and its seeming incompatibility with religion.

In an increasing materialistic and hedonistic society, religion and personal spirituality were marginalized by psychology. Most mainstream models of human development completely ignored spirituality in the twentieth century (West 2000).

With the decline in the religious institutions and the increasing popularity of psychological therapies, Thorne (1991) suggested that therapists are in some sense priests for a new age. Media portrayal of certain psychological practitioners as experts on the human condition and the now widespread use of counsellors for almost every human trauma reinforces the position of therapists as 'healers' and savants in modern society.

Szasz (1978: 29) maintained that therapy 'is a modern scientific-sounding name for what used to be called "the cure of the soul"'. Therapists (to include psychologists, counsellors, psychotherapists, and psychiatrists) and therapy had taken the place of religion within a new secular paradigm.

The development of humanistic psychology in the latter half of the twentieth century acknowledged the place of the unfolding potential within every individual.

Rogers moved away from religion until the very end of his life. For him the person-centred approach had two foundation blocks. 'One of these is an actualising tendency, a characteristic of organic life [and humans]. One is a formative tendency in the universe as a whole' (Rogers 1980: 114). He described a self-actualizing person, who has 'no barriers, no inhibitions, which prevent the full experiencing of whatever is organismically present. This person is moving in the direction of wholeness, integration, a unified life ... The person feels at one with the cosmos' (Rogers 1980: 128).

Maslow initially saw the goal of life to be self-actualization. He later found that for many, being part of something greater was central to their lives and he was instrumental in the development of a new transpersonal psychology:

> I should say that I consider Humanistic, Third Force Psychology to be transi-
> tional, a preparation for a still 'higher' Fourth psychology, transpersonal,
> transhuman, centred in the cosmos rather than human needs and interest,
> going beyond humanness, self-actualization and the like. We need something
> 'bigger than we are' to be awed by and to commit ourselves to in a new, natu-
> ralistic, empirical, non-churchly sense.
>
> (Maslow 1968: iii–iv)

The work of Assagioli (1993) in the development of a model of psycho-spiritual development, Wilber (1997) who mapped out an evolutionary psychological model of human development, Grof (1992) who worked with spiritual crisis, and others (e.g. Rowan 2005) has helped access psychological perspectives on spirituality.

In the training of therapists and health and social care professionals, issues of life, death, and spirituality are often still marginalized. Yet we are confronted with these issues time after time.

Spirituality and health and wellbeing

Studies have shown that having a recognized and developed personal spirituality or religious belief benefits one in times of trauma. Spirituality is thought to play a role in developing resilience. Spirituality is thought to 'fortify' the body or mind, increasing self-efficacy and other resilience characteristics (Richardson 2002).

A recognized spirituality can also be challenged by life events causing all one holds true to be threatened. Hill and Pargament (2008) found that spiritual struggles may cause distress because they challenge the most sacred aspects of life and force one to face harsh truths.

Although many aspects of spirituality include religiosity, they differ in that religiosity concerns the specific denominational characteristics of religious experiences while spirituality addresses a personal meaning of life. It includes concepts such as awe, gratitude, mercy, compassionate love, and a desire for closeness to God in whatever form one considers (Underwood 2011).

For some, this spirituality can have no religious component, no sense of life after death or a supernatural being, and may simply be a living embodiment of an existential hope or a positive energetic feeling. Whatever way spirituality is viewed, there is great potential for human wellbeing to result from an engagement with it. Like any important aspect of human life, for example sexuality, spirituality can be explored in unhealthy and destructive ways and part of the therapeutic work that clients may need to do is around the impact of their spiritual and religious belief and practices on their wellbeing.

The therapeutic relationship

Evidence shows the importance of the relationship in therapeutic practice (summarized in Paul and Charura 2014). Perhaps the relationship between practitioner and client is of even more importance when addressing issues of spirituality. Issues may be perceived as greater than or out of control of the resources of the individual.

The practitioner needs to help co-create a safe space. They need to some degree to be comfortable with their own sense of religion and spirituality and able to work with their client in a non-defensive way. This is why we consider that issues of religion and spirituality be explored in training courses of health and social care professionals. Such training must include personal reflection and exploration by the professional of their own beliefs and values.

The task of the practitioner may include facilitating their client's exploration of their own issues and helping them work towards finding their own meaning. We believe it is quite possible for an atheist to work with a believer (see Brodley 2000) and vice versa. We need to be comfortable in working with wider ranging belief systems that differ from our own.

Contexts

Religious counselling

Some people may attend religious counselling in which their personal issues and spirituality are overtly addressed in their religious context by both therapist and client, who are adherents to the same faith. This can work particularly well as long as the client's issues are not focused around belonging to their faith group (see Lyall 1995; West and Biddington 2009).

Spiritual and pastoral counselling

Many professionals are faced with life and death issues in their work. Research has indicated that the ability of the professional to work with their patient/client with such issues is rewarding for the client. The value of pastoral work including chaplaincy is highly rated. The professional, often of a particular faith, is increasingly working with clients of all religious faiths and none.

Therapeutic counselling and psychotherapy

For many people, life issues are core to their presenting problems. Finding meaning, resolving inner conflicts, and re-evaluating core values are often some of the hardest challenges. This may have, at least, an implicit spiritual aspect to it. For others who choose to work with a transpersonal therapist, spirituality may well be overtly explored (see Wittine 1993; Rowan 2005).

Working in relationship

As we have said, it is particularly important when working with issues of spirituality that the work is safely boundaried and a safe space is co-created by both parties. Maslow (1964), with his notions of synergy and the group being greater than the individual (i.e. *1 + 1 = 11*), noted the extra dimension in two people meeting collaboratively.

Other major contributors to the therapy and spirituality debate include Buber (1923), whose study of human intimacy and the I-Thou encounter pointed towards a spirituality, communion and even, for some, a sense of Divine presence which can occur in a therapeutic encounter. When working with issues of spirituality, it may be that the client is open to their own inner core or higher aspirations, and thus we need to be fully present with the client to share with them in that moment their experiencing and allow the coming into awareness of felt meaning. Some people report profound experiencing in such meetings.

Clarkson (2003) suggested that there are five levels to the therapeutic relationship, including an underlying transpersonal dimension. There is an underlying energy in the relationship that is greater than each individual's self but somehow influenced by both parties. As practitioners, we don't necessarily have to be trained to work multi-dimensionally. However, we do need to be able to meet the person with what they present to us.

We propose, therefore, the importance of meeting the other in the here-and-now in an open and non-defensive way. As we have said, we believe that each individual can with the right conditions find their own resolution. We hold this to be true with matters of the human spirit.

It is important to remain present with our clients. Mearns and Cooper (2005) introduced the term 'holistic listening' to identify relating not to only some parts of the client but to the *totality of the client*. For Rogers, the therapist's quality of presence is created through their ability to hold attention. Rogers et al. (1967) described this ability of presence as being authentically a person, fully open, living fully. Rogers (cited in Baldwin 1987: 48) stated the suitable goals for the therapist revolved around the question, 'Am I really with this person at this moment?'

Schudel (2006) suggests that presence has two faces. She believes that one of them is *professional presence*, which she practises in a therapeutic setting, and *spiritual presence*, which she experienced occasionally during therapy. She describes spiritual presence as an altered state of consciousness, a *Thou-I* encounter: 'This unique energy felt like the source of my essential aliveness, or as life itself beyond or before it takes any material form' (p. 128), which is present everywhere in the room, including her client and herself – 'defensiveness and resistance in both persons dissolve and give way to an emotional state of unconditional trust and fearlessness without the two denying their separate and different individualities' (p. 134). Thus, they feel safe, calm, and at peace with the world and trust that all is well. The therapist is 'in touch with their own core' (p. 128).

Thorne describes his experiences as similar to Rogers' *presence*, but he calls it *tenderness*, a quality he believes is essential to healing in therapy. Thorne (1998) also describes the state of being of the therapist in moments of change: 'Magic moments signify a particular intensity of relating in which a new level of understanding is achieved and sense of validating freedom experienced by both client and counsellor. The surge of wellbeing that follows such moments is almost indescribable' (Thorne 1998: 46). He, as a Christian, claims that such experiences occur in the presence of [his] God, which is the result of mutual love, openness, and acceptance of personal powerlessness in the relationship between practitioner and client.

Rogers, as a secular therapist reflected:

> When I am at my best, as a group facilitator or a therapist, I discover another characteristic. I find that when I am closest to my inner, intuitive self, when I am in a slightly altered state of consciousness in the relationship, then whatever I do seems to be full of healing. Then simply my presence is releasing and helpful. There is nothing I can do to force this experience, but when I can relax and be close to the transcendental core of me . . . At those moments it seems that my inner spirit has reached out and touched the inner spirit of the other. Our relationship transcends itself and becomes a part of something larger. Profound growth and healing and energy are present.
>
> (Rogers 1980: 129)

Wittine (1993: 166) suggests that transpersonal psychotherapy affirms:

a) the need for healing/growth on all levels of the spectrum of identity – egoic, existential, and transpersonal;
b) the therapist's unfolding awareness of the self, or deep centre of being, and his or her spiritual perspective on life as central to the therapeutic process;
c) the process of awakening from a lesser to a greater identity;
d) the healing, restorative nature of inner awareness and intuition;
e) the transformative potential in the therapeutic relationship not only for the client but for the therapist as well.

Whitmore (2004) emphasizes how important it is that techniques are not used as a substitute for relationship in therapy. The subtle skill that the therapist is required to develop is to know when to 'stay with' the client's process, in what may be very painful and despairing places. If a technique is introduced because the therapist finds the process of staying with the client's material too much to bear, it is likely to be devaluing to the frame of reference of the client (Shiers and Paul 2008).

There is also a view, particularly on the part of Buddhist influenced practitioners, that the 'transpersonal' emerges within the 'inner knowing', that a deeper wisdom can be accessed through mindful presence (Welwood 2000).

Challenges

Good therapeutic practice is rooted in a focus on the client's frame of reference, how they see their world and what challenges they face in their lives that they have brought to therapy. Therapists are often stretched as they seek to respond empathically to the client's stories. This may involve being faced with differences of gender, sexuality, class, ethnicity, religion, and spirituality. If we can let go of wanting our clients to think and feel the same or similar to us, and instead offer them the space to explore what is troubling them and what changes they need to make in their lives, then allowing the spiritual dimension to be part of our work becomes a bit easier.

Since religion is part of many people's lives and spirituality part of even more lives, it has its place within the therapeutic encounter. Jung asserted that of his clients over 35, 'there has not a single one whose problem has not been in the last resort that of finding a religious outlook on life' (Jung 1933: 164). Jung made it clear he was not talking about attending a church but about the person's engagement with religious issues that we might today regard as 'existential' or 'spiritual'.

As we have noted, the interplay between spiritual, religious, and existential is unique and personal for every individual. We as practitioners have our own, personal viewpoint; our clients' are almost certainly likely to be different, even if we purport to share the same affiliations. The task is to work, with equanimity, with this difference.

Ethics

It can be a real challenge to maintain clear therapeutic boundaries when both client and counsellor may feel boundaries are dissolving and/or experience themselves as profoundly interconnected with each other and possibly with a sense of the divine. However, the safe exploration of such experiences can be clearly of tremendous benefit to the client. So there is an ethical issue if therapists *avoid* such opportunities in their work. It is clearly helpful if therapists already have some experience of the territory perhaps in their own personal development work, and it also helps to have appropriate supervision for such work. Such experiences can, initially at least, be experienced as scary but they are surprisingly common, if relatively unspoken of. In the UK, the BACP information sheet, *Working with Issues of Spirituality, Faith or Religion* (Harbonne 2008), is a useful summary (see also West 2012).

As therapists, we need to be able to work without prejudice to whatever our client brings, regardless of our own views.

Cultural issues

There are always cultural issues even when client and counsellor share many cultural aspects. Indeed, it is important to hold a questioning attitude around any shared cultural assumptions; for example, being of the same gender, class, ethnicity, and religion. It is always important to try and understand, to hear what the client's culture means to them. This is especially important in the area of spirituality: most people have strong feelings around religion – for or against, or both. For many, some religions are seen as good and others as bad. Therapists need to be respectful of what might be very challenging experiences and attitudes in their clients.

For example, one of us was approached by a young white woman who was in distress with regard to her husband's change in his faith. They were both part of an evangelical Christian church; indeed, they had been married in the church they still attended. Her husband was beginning to lose his faith and no longer wished to attend the church. His wife was horrified and expressed deep concern that he would no longer be with her in the after life. Some of our non-religious readers might see this as ridiculous. It was a challenge to be empathic, to be open to what was real concern for this client, to allow her time and space to explore this very issue.

Working with breakdown/spiritual emergency

With the recent challenge by the Clinical Psychology Division of the British Psychological Society in the UK to the DSM-V, the debate about mental health diagnoses is hotter than ever. People regarded as having had a nervous breakdown/ crazy/ psychotic/bipolar often have spiritual and/or religious elements as part of their experience. Similarly, people having mystical or spiritual experiences can also be experiencing psychological disturbances. When spirituality and mental health problems are mixed together, then the help the person receives needs to address both (see Lukoff 1985; West 2000). Many professionals are too rigid, indeed biased (Allman et al. 1992) in their reactions to clients experiencing spiritual or mystical states. There is thus a challenge of discernment, of helping the client figure out what help they need.

In a secular society, the psychological therapist may be the only port of call for the individual struggling with psycho-spiritual issues. We need therefore to be open, fearless, and non-defensive in our approach with such issues. Individual therapists need to be clear about their own attitude to spirituality and religion. They also need to have some understanding of the differing ways people relate to and experience spirituality and religion. For example, many clients now practise yoga, meditation, Tai Chi, Qi Gong, or prayer and these can all impact on our spirituality. If as a therapist you are hesitant about asking overt spiritual or religious questions during assessment, then try asking: 'What sustains you?' This simple question can produce revealing and helpful information and be a key point of sharing for the client (see West 2012).

Working with religious content

It is always important to get a sense of what any religious content means to the client. A key question is, 'what is this doing to the client?' For example, clients who are Christians may show clear signs of guilt and a lack of self-forgiveness. It is possible to invite them to reflect on their unforgivingness. Indeed, forgiveness is a key feature of most religious traditions (West 2001). So it is possible that clients' religious beliefs may be used to help and support their healing process.

One of us worked with a client once who was a Buddhist and his connection with his Buddhist teacher has been broken due to the guilt the client was feeling. After an exploration of the key role of compassion in Buddhism, the client was at least partially reconciled to the idea that his teacher would not reject him for his actions.

It is worth exploring with religious clients what resources are available to them and how they might feel about accessing them. Many therapists might feel uneasy about sharing care of a client with a religious leader but this will often be the case. Most religious groups have some form of pastoral care available to their members, often delivered by lay members. Belonging to a close-knit religious group can be a great source of support to a religious client. However, this is not always the case and we need to consider what the client's relationship is to their religion.

The place of religion in their world-view and the space to question this may be very important to the individual. An invitation to pray or undertake religious practice may in some sense suppress an underlying need. Because spirituality and community are so important to many of us, it is possible that a spiritual or religious group could, like any other group of humans, become toxic. There is something especially shocking when a religious group does go 'off the rails' – maybe because most such groups speak of love, compassion, peace, and community. When such a group has a residential basis to it, the danger and potential damage is strong – as alluded to in the case discussed above. There are specialist sources of information around cults, for example INFORM, which offer advice and support.

Fundamentalism

Fundamentalism usually gets a bad press, though many people are inspired by the life of the founder of the religion rather than necessarily a particular interpretation of a religious text. Some people are actually moved to act out of compassionate love and forgiveness and to refuse violent acts or military service. However, most people regard fundamentalism as being about an unthinking adherence to a religious group and to a fixed interpretation of key religious texts. It is psychologically attractive to many people to have explicit answers to all of life's dilemmas and challenges rather than life with doubt and uncertainty. The key therapeutic question is, 'what is the impact of this set of beliefs on the client?'

New developments

When people connect with their sense of spirituality, it can feel new, exciting, and sometimes scary. Some like David Hay (1982) would argue that it is cross-cultural and even biological drive; that we need to feel connected to one another and creation in order to survive.

In neuroscience, elements in the brain are activated when a person has a religious experience. This has been used to denigrate such experiences, to see them as 'caused' by these brain currents rather than seeing these patterns as the effect of the experience. 'Although there is no single "God spot" in the brain, feelings of self-transcendence are associated with reduced electrical activity in the right parietal lobe, a structure located above the right ear' (Barber 2012: 1).

Many people in the West are now exploring spirituality and religious beliefs outside of traditional religions, sometimes in informal or semi-formal groupings. This is often dismissed as New Age or Do-it-Yourself spirituality. In response to such currents, some traditional religions have tried to update their image; for example, the Alpha course teaches traditional Anglican Christianity but in a more relaxed, up-to-date format.

A postmodern analysis of such developments, noting the decline in most traditional religious groups, suggests the notion that the 'grand narratives' no longer hold sway does seem something of a truth. In our modern multicultural society, there are many cultural crossovers. What is clear is that even if religion is in decline, spirituality, belief in God is not (Hay and Hunt 2000).

There is a danger in individual therapeutic work that we see our clients as having the problem; that we individualize what are often family, community or societal problems. McLeod (2001) wrote that clients do not necessarily have psychological problems, so much as problems with finding their place in society. Spirituality is often about experiencing our interconnectedness. Maybe Western societies suffer from us feeling too individualized and not interconnected. Some of the key moments of change in therapeutic practice come from and with therapist and client experiencing such connections.

Summary

Wulff (1997) proposes that all beliefs and religions are social constructs. Even in the field of the hard empirical sciences, researchers are often ideologically split and opposing parties can prove their own hypotheses. The notion of a neutral objectivity cannot be assumed in any situation.

We are reminded of the allegorical story of the blind men and the elephant. Asked what is an elephant, each man approached the elephant and felt it. One said it is like the trunk of a tree, another maintained it was like a snake, a further said it was like an awning, while the last maintained it was like a swinging branch.

Current attempts to create a holistic map of the human psyche are by their very nature incomplete, as the time and space dimension in which we operate is itself only one part of the whole and therefore limited. So how do we offer clients the therapeutic help they need, help that can encompass the varieties of spirituality that can arise today?

First, we need self-knowledge – that is, to know ourselves in relation to spirituality and religion. This usually has to involve one's own personal development. Secondly, background reading and accessing other resources relating to varieties of spirituality and religion – remembering that the client is unique. And finally, above all, we need to be ready to listen in an embodied way to our clients.

Further reading

www.INFORM.ac/: UK site for information and advice regarding cults and new religious movements.

Harbonne, L. (2008) *Working with Issues of Spirituality, Faith or Religion.* Information Sheet G13. Lutterworth: BACP. Pamphlet on professional practice.

Books on applied practice:
Cook, C., Powell, A. and Sims, A.C.P. (eds.) (2009) *Spirituality and Psychiatry.* London: RCPsych Publications.

Mathews, I. (2009) *Social Work and Spirituality.* London: Sage.

Moore, J. and Purton, C. (eds.) (2006) *Spirituality and Counselling: Experiential and Theoretical Perspectives.* Ross-on-Wye: PCCS Books. A thorough and very readable exploration of a range of person-centred approaches to spirituality.

Robinson, S., Kendrick, K. and Brown, A. (2003) *Spirituality and the Practice of Healthcare.* Basingstoke: Palgrave Macmillan.

West, W. (2000) *Psychotherapy and Spirituality: Crossing the Line between Therapy and Religion.* London: Sage. A unique and creative focus for therapists wishing to consider how spirituality may inform or shape their own practice.

References

Allman, L.S., De La Rocha, O., Elkins, D.N. and Weathers, R.S. (1992) Psychotherapists' attitudes toward clients reporting mystical experiences, *Psychotherapy*, 29 (4): 654–69.
Assagioli, R. (1993) *Psychosynthesis: The Definitive Guide to the Principles and Techniques of Psychosynthesis.* London: Thorsons.
Baldwin, M. (1987) Interview with Carl Rogers on the use of self in therapy, in M. Baldwin and V. Satir (eds.) *The Use of Self in Therapy* (pp. 45–52). New York: Haworth Press.
Barber, N. (2012) The God Spot Revisited: Spirituality as Evolved Brain Function [http://www.huffingtonpost.com/nigel-barber/the-god-spot-revisited-spirituality-as-evolved-brain-function_b_1779667.html; accessed 30 May 2014].
Brodley, B.T. (2000) Personal presence in client-centered therapy, *Person-Centered Journal*, 7 (2): 139–49.
Buber, M. (1923) *I and Thou.* Edinburgh: T&T Clark.
Clarkson, P. (2003) *The Therapeutic Relationship in Psychoanalysis, Counselling and Psychotherapy*, 2nd edn. London: Whurr.
Grof, S. (1992) *The Holotropic Mind.* New York: Harper.
Harbonne, L. (2008) *Working with Issues of Spirituality, Faith or Religion.* Information Sheet G13. Lutterworth: BACP.

Hay, D. (1982) *Exploring Inner Space: Scientists and Religious Experience*. Harmondsworth: Penguin.

Hay, D. and Hunt, K. (2000) *Understanding the Spirituality of People Who don't Go to Church*. Nottingham: Centre for the Study of Human Relations, Nottingham University.

Hill, P. and Pargament, K. (2008) Advances in the conceptualization and measurement of religion and spirituality: implications for physical and mental research, *Psychology of Religion and Spirituality*, S1: 3–17.

Jung, C.G. (1933) *Modern Man in Search of a Soul*. London: Routledge & Kegan Paul.

Koenig, H. (2008) Concerns about measuring 'spirituality' in research, *Journal of Nervous and Mental Disease*, 196: 349–55.

Lowenthal, K. (2000) *The Psychology of Religion: A Short Introduction*. Oxford: Oneworld.

Lukoff, D. (1985) The diagnosis of mystical experiences with psychotic features, *Journal of Transpersonal Psychology*, 17 (2): 155–81.

Lyall, D. (1995) *Counselling in the Pastoral and Spiritual Context*. Buckingham: Open University Press.

Maslow, A.H. (1964) Synergy in society and the individual, *Journal of Individual Psychology*, 20: 153–64.

Maslow, A.H. (1968) *Toward a Psychology of Being*, 2nd edn. New York: Van Nostrand Reinhold.

Mearns, D. and Cooper, M. (2005) *Working at Relational Depth in Counselling and Psychotherapy*. London: Sage.

McLeod, J. (2001) Counselling as a social process, in S. Palmer and P. Milner (eds.) *The BACP Counselling Reader* (Vol. 2). London: Sage.

Miller, J. (2013, July). Holistic nursing care: provision of spirituality with patients, Communication to *Sigma Theta Tau International's 24th International Nursing Research Congress*, STTI, Prague, Czech Republic.

National Institute of Health and Care Excellence (NICE) (2013) Standard for End of Life Care for Adults [www.publications.nice.org.uk/quality-standard-for-end-of-life-care-for-adults-qs13/quality-statement–6-holistic-support-spiritual-and-religious; accessed 25 May 2014].

Paul, S. and Charura, D. (2014) *An Introduction to the Therapeutic Relationship in Counselling and Psychotherapy*. London: Sage.

Post, S.G., Puchalski, C.M. and Larson, D.B. (2000) Physicians and patient spirituality: professional boundaries, competency, and ethics, *Annals of Internal Medicine*, 132 (7): 578–83.

Richardson, G. (2002) The metatheory of resilience and resiliency, *Journal of Clinical Psychology*, 58: 307–21.

Rogers, C.R. (1980) *A Way of Being*. Boston, MA: Houghton Mifflin.

Rogers, C.R., Gendlin, E.T., Kiesler, D.J. and Truax, C.B. (eds.) (1967) *The Therapeutic Relationship and its Impact: A Study of Psychotherapy with Schizophrenia*. Madison, WI: University of Wisconsin Press.

Roof, W.C., Carroll, J.W. and Roozen, D.A. (eds.) (1995) *The Post-War Generation and Establishment Religion: Cross-Cultural Perspectives*. Boulder, CO: Westview Press.

Rowan, J. (1993) *The Transpersonal: Spirituality in Psychotherapy and Counselling*, 2nd edn. London: Routledge.

Schudel, D.I. (2006) A person-centred therapist's quest for presence, in J. Moore and C. Purton (eds.) *Spirituality and Counselling: Experiential and Theoretical Perspectives* (pp. 127–35). Ross-on-Wye: PCCS Books.

Shiers, J. and Paul, S. (2008) Transpersonal dimensions on the therapeutic relationship, in S. Haugh and S. Paul (eds.) *The Therapeutic Relationship: Perspectives and Themes.* Ross-on-Wye: PCCS Books.

Szasz, T. (1978) *The Myth of Psychotherapy.* New York: Anchor Press.

Thorne, B. (1991) *Person-centred Counselling: Therapeutic and Spiritual Dimensions.* London: Whurr.

Thorne, B. (1998) *Person-centred Counselling and Christian Spirituality: The Secular and the Holy.* London: Whurr.

Underwood, L. (2011) The Daily Spiritual Experience Scale: overview and results, *Religions,* 2: 29–50.

Welwood, J. (2000) *Toward a Psychology of Awakening.* London: Shambhala.

West, W. (2000) *Psychotherapy and Spirituality: Crossing the Line between Therapy and Religion.* London: Sage.

West, W. (2001) Issues related to the use of forgiveness in counselling and psychotherapy, *British Journal of Guidance and Counselling,* 29 (4): 415–23.

West, W. (2012) Addressing spiritual and religious issues in counselling and psychotherapy, *Thresholds: Counselling with Spirit,* Winter, pp. 12–17.

West, W. and Biddington, T. (2009) Towards spiritually skilled counselling, *Thresholds: Counselling with Spirit,* Winter, pp. 11–15.

Whitmore, D. (2004) *Psychosynthesis Counselling in Action,* 3rd edn. London: Sage.

Wilber, K. (1997) An integral theory of consciousness, *Journal of Consciousness Studies,* 4 (1): 71–92.

Wittine, B. (1993) Assumptions of transpersonal psychotherapy, in R. Walsh and F. Vaughan (eds.) *Paths Beyond Ego.* New York: Tarcher/Putnam.

Wulff, D.M. (1997) *Psychology of Religion: Classic and Contemporary Views.* New York: Wiley.

23 Online text-based and video-linked relationships: holograms don't get hangovers

Jeannie Wright

You, Sam, are living in a new city where you know very few people. Your father dies, the job you moved for has gone very wrong, and your girlfriend has just decided to end the relationship. At the station you see the ad for the Samaritans. You are feeling worse than you ever thought possible and haven't any idea what to do next. You don't like talking on phones, so your attention moves on to the bar and you drink instead of going home to an empty house. Then one evening, when you're sitting eating dinner with your laptop on your knee, you find yourself looking at the Samaritans' website. You email the Jo@Samaritans.org address and when you stop telling the story, it's gone midnight. It's good to spill out the feelings and spell out how lonely you feel. Then when it's all out you feel better, briefly. Who is this Jo? You've told him or her more than anybody else, more than you've told family or any of your friends.

Im feelN realy lonely n Dpresd, I don't av d NRG 2 do Nefin, ive no Fkn lyf lft. SOS!

(Example of Txt received by Samaritans)

Introduction

More people now email the Samaritans (Jo@Samaritans.org) than use their telephone service. I am not arguing here that online relationships can be compared with a voice at the end of the phone; even more certainly there is no intention to compare presence in face-to-face relationships and relating to other people online in this chapter. The research about the relative impact of face-to-face and online relationships for clients is embryonic, although since the 1990s some researchers have begun to initiate studies that raise such questions (Cohen and Kerr 1998; Day and Schneider 2002). The crucial point is that, with a range of choices, some people who need to express how they feel and tell someone their story, like Sam in the illustration above, are choosing to use email and other online communications. Regulation, research, and policy are lagging behind online practice, which is a huge growth area in counselling and psychotherapy (Chester and Glass 2006). However, exploratory research so far offers a qualified encouragement for those considering online therapy (Reynolds et al. 2006; Richards and Vigano 2013).

In traditional face-to-face communication, we use a highly complex set of body language, tone of voice, and mutually understood words to establish rapport. This chapter is a brief overview of some research and experience of creating rapport and building therapeutic relationships between people online, using words written on some kind of electronic device. It also touches briefly on using videoconferencing (e.g. Skype). Some examples of text-based relating, using words alone, will be the core of this chapter. The much more sophisticated models, such as avatar and hologram connections are not considered here. In any case, online relationship has received limited attention to date, although tentative, early studies suggest that strong working alliances can be established via online therapy (Cook and Doyle 2002).

I will draw on the literature about establishing therapeutic relationship in conventional therapeutic contexts for maps and recipes for online rapport. Outcome research and 'common factors' studies have now indicated that it is the therapeutic relationship rather than choice of modality that contributes most to therapeutic change (Wampold 2001). Informed by recent scholarship about the unique contribution of the person-centred approach, I choose to locate this chapter within a broadly person-centred view of how to build a relationship online to help people grow and change (Cooper et al. 2013).

From different modalities and theoretical perspectives, different answers would emerge to questions about the possible factors that would create facilitative conditions in online relationships. Freud's theories of the blank screen approach notwithstanding, psychoanalytic and psychodynamic therapists seem not to be engaged in the discussion about online relationships. Some clients, however, describe finding the relative neutrality of the computer screen acceptable, even preferable to facing a 'real' person (Anthony and Nagel 2010). Several chapters could be written about how different modalities would work with text-based relationships alone, and the real challenge is to consider how trust builds in this new online environment. Peer-based self-help forums, such as the Big White Wall (http://www.bigwhitewall.com/my-account/login.aspx?ReturnUrl=%2f) are reporting that 95 per cent of users feel better after engaging with a forum. Cognitive behavioural therapy (CBT) and solution-focused approaches have moved ahead with Internet facilitated therapies, including stand-alone computerized self-help (see, for example, *Beating the Blues*). Critically, there is a lack of empirical evidence across the board. More research into such fast-growing forms of support online is urgently needed.

Attempts to prove one orientation 'better' than another in building therapeutic relationships were and remain misguided, and all approaches have their value. ELIZA, a computer program simulating non-directive therapeutic responses and designed in the 1960s quickly became emotionally engaging for those participants who worked with the experimental, computerized 'therapist'. The person-centred approach offers an easy-to-parody way of being in therapeutic relationships. Particularly challenging to the world of manualized therapy and also to those approaches that are pathologizing of ordinary human distress, theories of establishing therapeutic relationships are central to the person-centred approach (Cooper et al. 2013). The expert in the therapeutic relationship is the client (Haugh and Paul 2008). Also, it is the interest in and literature on reducing the power differentials between therapist and client that are of interest in this chapter because of the observed shift in power in online therapeutic relationships (Proctor et al. 2006).

The therapeutic relationship

Person-centred approach and the online relationship

Ironically, and because the person-centred approach emphasizes the centrality of the face-to-face relationship between client and therapist, it might appear most unlikely that a person-centred theoretical view of the online relationship is feasible or even appropriate. Yet, what I take from people's creative use of new technology to connect with another person is the actualizing tendency in action.

Carl Rogers' writings on theories of therapy (Rogers 1957) and later writings on human personality provide a clear framework for human growth in relationship. The actualizing tendency is at the core. The client knows best where this journey has started, and needs no direction from the therapist, only the facilitative conditions for therapeutic change and growth (Rogers 1974). Arguably, the three central facilitative conditions are unified in practice: 'the interrelationship of the conditions of congruence, empathy and unconditional positive regard is so high that they are inseparable in the theory' (Bozarth 1998: 83). These three central conditions are now receiving some attention in research into the relationship online, sometimes individually, rather than as a unified whole.

How appropriate are the decades of theorizing about therapeutic alliance to online counselling? Starting in the 1990s, reviews of the research into the working alliance in therapy identified three components of the working alliance between a client and a therapist that would predict good therapeutic outcomes: a focus on agreed goals, specific tasks, and an emotional bond (Bordin 1994; Hanley and Reynolds 2009). It is clear from practice-based studies that the client holds much more power in therapeutic relationships online and that agreed goals and specific tasks will only work if the client is receptive to that way of working. How to establish and maintain an emotional bond in text-based online relationships has received some research attention (for examples see www. ISMHO.org).

Building therapeutic relationships online

As in face-to-face practice, skills in pacing, empathic following, and asking questions appropriately can be learned. Presence is more elusive to define and to practise online. Tele-presence was referred to as early as 1999 in online practices and as in telephone counselling involves the feeling (or illusion) of being in someone's presence without sharing any actual physical space. What's your image of Sam in the opening vignette, for instance? Male/female? Age? Ethnicity? What about the person who sent the txt message?

One of the advantages for some people of relating via words on the screen instead of face-to-face communication is anonymity. First impressions and judgements about cultural difference based on age, race, gender, and other identifiers are more complex and possibly even transcended online. So, clients may feel 'safer', more able to disclose very personal details about themselves very quickly, and the disinhibition effect is acknowledged (Suler 2004).

The client is the agent of change, as recent research has highlighted (Duncan et al. 2004). This chapter will show that in online relationships, there are some interesting shifts of emphasis in the usual power dynamics between therapist and client. Practitioners and researchers have noted that the client tends to be more in control in online therapy, responding to questions, for example, if and when they want to (Dunn 2012). In terms of the therapeutic space, this is no longer anybody's room, with clock and tissues. How the client chooses to be in the relative privacy and anonymity of cyberspace is up to them. There are unique features in relating through written words online that have been highlighted and linked to the therapeutic potential of creative writing (Wright 2002). Recently, in studies with young people it has become clear that for a certain demographic online communication is 'normal' (Hanley 2009, 2012).

Imagination is a neglected and creative quality in counselling and psychotherapy research. At its most exciting, the Internet opens up possible options for therapy that are only limited by our imagination. The relationship with an audience, the witness/companion/blank screen depending on the theoretical modality, is always there even in writing therapy (Hunt 2004). The relationship motivates, as one interviewee who used asynchronous email counselling with me said, 'I felt I knew him from meeting him just once and wanted to continue to write to him. It was motivating.'

The person you are in relationship with online might be a therapist you've already met. It might be a therapist whose photograph you've seen online and have decided this person looks 'okay', you could trust them using email, instant messaging or video. More likely in future, an avatar or hologram will simulate human therapeutic responses. Ten years ago this might have sounded more like science fiction than any kind of therapy (Wright 2003). Now, practice has partly caught up with imagination and all we need is more research and development to investigate and protect.

Holograms don't get hangovers, and never feel tired or irritable. Holograms simulating cabin attendants now pop up at airports giving information and warning about security checks. The technology is available, but the necessary training and programming for this kind of online relationship is in its infancy.

Online therapists' training: assessing and contracting in online relationships

The need for online therapists to be trained and competent in ethical practice online has been highlighted in UK-published 'how to' texts (Evans 2009; Jones and Stokes 2009) and in the BACP's soon to be updated guidelines for online practice (Anthony and Goss 2009). The UKCP and British Psychological Society are also involved in working on policies for online work.

Research into working with adolescents online also raises questions about the specific skills and awareness training that might be necessary with this particular age group (Hanley 2006). It is clear that most therapists are already qualified in one modality or in an integration of approaches before starting training to work online. Whatever the orientation – psychodynamic, humanistic, narrative or cognitive behavioural – online relationships call for different adaptations from face-to-face guidelines; some of the taken-for-granted ways of building an alliance between therapist and client are disrupted.

Assessment and contracting in an online relationship, for example, need to be considered differently. Ethical issues are also complex. How far does the online client understand the limits of confidentiality, for example? In the 1990s in the USA, Bloom was writing about the ethical practice of 'web counselling' (Bloom 1998). The first set of guidelines for British online practice was published by BACP a few years later. These guidelines are now in their third edition (Anthony and Goss 2009), and a fourth is forthcoming. Password protection on every Word document is a necessary part of ethical, online counselling using typed text (Evans 2009; Jones and Stokes 2009). What are the time limits and boundaries of establishing relationships online? In the early days of practising online in a staff counselling service, receiving very lengthy emails and attachments from clients needed some careful discussion in supervision and then with the client – a tricky task in an email correspondence.

Metaphor and the power of figurative language online

In an email between face-to-face sessions, a client wrote to me, 'My feelings are like a volcano and I have to swallow them and they're killing me . . .'. It is clear that, as in face-to-face therapy, many clients use the poetic devices of metaphor and imagery in their writing, and so do therapists (Wright 2002). Metaphorical language is the opposite of literal language and serves to embody an experience, which is especially useful in online communication. From Greek and Latin roots, it conveys 'to carry across'. The essence of metaphor is to understand and experience one kind of thing in terms of another. Metaphor is, then, a figure of speech where two things that are unlike each other are compared and shown to have something in common. Life as a journey would be a well-known metaphorical comparison, sometimes even accused of being a cliché because it has been over-used.

Case vignette

An online client, Jasmina, wrote about going through a 'stormy' time at work and how the email counselling we were contracted to do, with an exchange of email messages weekly, acted as a kind of anchor for her. I wrote that her recent experience at work had left her feeling cast adrift and with very turbulent seas all around. We carried on with the metaphor of storms and strong winds. She reported that it helped her to picture the safety of a harbour as well as an anchor that the weekly words between us represented.

Responding to Jasmina raises some complex questions about how clients and therapists struggle to communicate, especially in the written form of language, which can only ever approximate, rather than offer accurate symbolization of the person's experience

(Charura 2014). Rogers' theory of symbolization suggests that by symbolizing – that is, both naming our feelings and experience and communicating that which may have been distorted or denied – we are accurately conveying to ourselves and to others something that may have been unrealized. This process encourages an accepting relationship with one's self as well as with others. The relationship is likely to be more open and, potentially at least, trust develops. Worsley (2009: 71) points out that Carl Rogers saw his own images and the way he used them with clients as a means of understanding as fully as he could their 'patterns . . . feelings . . . symbols . . . meanings'.

The limits of relationship through the written word

Research indicates that for some, an online relationship using written text is acceptable, accessible, and provides a re-readable form of therapeutic support. For some people, however, there is also in the use of language, and in particular written language, scope for distortion and reduction of experience (Barden and Williams 2007). Gadamer (2004) talks about the problem of no-one coming to writing's aid when misunderstandings occur.

Anyone who has ever experienced the crises in communication possible in well-intentioned email exchanges would attest to this view. There is no non-verbal communication to suggest nuance; humour is notoriously difficult and prone to misunderstanding. Some experiences are certainly unspeakable and may be outside of verbal expression, spoken or written. Words fail us. Metaphor may be one way of overcoming this failure or breakdown in communication, both with one's self and with others. Limitations are real. In his novel, *Far from the Madding Crowd*, Thomas Hardy writes about the limits of language metaphorically: 'He would as soon have thought of carrying an odour in a net as of attempting to convey the intangibilities of his feeling in the coarse meshes of language' (Hardy 1874/1974: 58). So even metaphor may not be enough, although the image of that net carrying an odour has stayed with me and gave me pause, in the way that poetical language sometimes does.

Metaphor depends on cultural and contextual factors in the relationship. The richness of some cultures' use of metaphor is the subject of another book, and cannot be considered in the limitations of this chapter.

Working through video conferencing

Using video conferencing (e.g. Skype) for supervision may in particular be necessary when geographical distance prevents face-to-face work (Lago and Wright 2007; Wright and Griffiths 2010). Clear contractual expectations are essential, both with clients and supervisees.

In client work, I find video conferencing stressful for several reasons. Technological breakdown, and anticipating sufficient backup systems should we lose connection, must be considered. There is also a lack of embodiment and presence, although we have limited visual cues. If a client is working with deep emotion and we find the Internet link 'drops' us, I feel frustrated and interrupted by what is only the vehicle for therapy. I can also start to feel very protective of the client's process.

Charura (2014) points out some of the advantages, limitations, and complexities of using secure online video platforms to continue a therapeutic relationship that had started face-to-face. He also considers working 'cross-border' with all of the potential difficulty of cross-cultural communication. Some of the advantages of having visual cues – that is, client and therapist are visible to each other – might seem obvious. Yet in my experience it is often difficult to pace the conversation, even in real-time and I can end up talking over clients and supervisees, which would be very rare in face-to-face relationships. How to manage silence using video conferencing is also problematic. However, this personal preference is not reflected in the small body of research comparing different delivery modes (Richards and Vigano 2013).

The relationship through the online therapist's lens

Day and Schneider, counselling psychologists at the University of Illinois, were among the first to report on research studies where therapists' subjective experience of face-to-face, video, and audio counselling sessions were compared (Day and Schneider 2002). Their findings show that the Internet as therapeutic vehicle made little impact on outcome and working alliance. More recent studies have tended towards the same tentative result, and there's nothing definitive as yet.

Research has suggested that, because the sense of power and 'control' is more equal online, more potential power in the relationship rests with the client than in face-to-face counselling (Cohen and Kerr 1998; Goss and Anthony 2003). Certainly, the space, the very environment in which therapy happens, is different and no longer 'owned' by the therapist: making and keeping appointments is less potentially shaming than going through the door of a high street service marked 'counselling and psychotherapy'; the therapist's office with its chosen position of furniture may be replaced by the apparent neutrality of cyberspace; the timing of the work is different too and, for some, a relationship with a therapist is not necessary at all (Tan 2008). Self-help through blogging is certainly useful for some.

Together with careful contracting and support from a university steering committee, and after ethical approval for the new initiative, I started online 'letter writing', an asynchronous email service for staff at the University of Sheffield in early 2000. The new service provided an alternative to face-to-face appointments and was used by some staff for pragmatic reasons, such as not having to travel to our offices, and by some out of choice. Reflecting on that time, some of the differences for me between face-to-face and online relationships are highlighted (Wright 2004). I missed 'presence'. It's also disconcerting, for example, when a client suddenly stops texting or emailing, just as when a client misses face-to-face appointments; questions about the client's safety and well-being might dominate. Also, self-doubt might creep in: 'What did I do that didn't meet their needs?' 'Where might they be finding help now?' In online work, the disengagement could be because the client is distracted by the television, which happens to be on and so stops the 'conversation' in the middle of emailing (Hanley 2012). I certainly experienced strong emotional bonds with clients and could sometimes work on shared 'tasks and goals'. A written record of our whole conversation online was a mixed blessing. Taking some of those 'transcripts' to supervision was sometimes embarrassing, as I noticed how much more directive I tended to be online.

In unpublished small-scale studies, experienced online counsellors who shared a person-centred orientation were asked about their experience of empathy within the online relationship. In a very small sample, most reported that they could not be 'purely' person-centred in online relationships. Participants reported that they experienced the Rogerian concept of 'psychological contact' in email counselling and tended to be tentative in their written responses, checking what had been communicated and ensuring that it had been understood. Empathic reflecting was mentioned by all of the participants.

The relationship through the online client's lens

Apparent invisibility is one of the advantages of online working for some clients. The stigma associated with seeking help can inhibit people from making a face-to-face appointment with a therapist (Wright 2007). The disinhibition effect, where clients move quickly and very openly to the heart of their distress, emerged early on in the North American literature on online communication (see, for example, www.ISMHO. org) and emerges repeatedly in research studies including the client's point of view (Dunn 2012).

   The relationship through the online client's lens was explored in a recent study in a UK university setting (Dunn 2012). Ten former email counselling clients were interviewed about their experience of asynchronous email work. The findings reinforced the emphasis of previous studies on the 'disinhibition effect'. Having 'time to think' within the asynchronous exchanges was also important for both clients and counsellors. Other factors, such as a developing realization that the person responding cares, and how this relationship might encourage accessing face-to-face therapy are cited by one client:

> As far as I was concerned I was talking to a robot with no emotions. However, after a while I began to see my online counsellor as a person, and it made me feel better. I felt she honestly cared about me and my problems and I felt better about counsellors in general which made me feel more comfortable meeting someone in person.
>
> (Dunn 2012: 323)

The key features of the online therapeutic alliance that young people reported in a UK-based study (Hanley 2012: 259) are in line with previous work (Hanley 2009) where 'telepresence' is seen as a 'central factor in . . . developing relationships of appropriate depth'.

New developments

On BBC Radio 4 in 2013, a series of programmes looked at a history of office life, documenting changes over the centuries in the office as a workspace. Lucy Kellaway's programmes are not currently available via BBC I-player, which is a pity. In paraphrasing the conclusion of the last in the series, looking at how office work might move in future, radical shifts in communication are highlighted: we have had 50,000 years of communication using speech and gesture, 5000 years of writing, 100 years of the telephone and, in the developed world, roughly 15 years of email.

If people experience congruence, empathy, and unconditional positive regard, or acceptance, in a relationship, whether online or face-to-face, they will be less conflicted in their own relationship with their experience of life's distresses. Practising in this way face-to-face is difficult enough. Carl Rogers writes:

> There can be no doubt that every therapist, even when he has resolved many of his own difficulties in a therapeutic relationship, still has troubling con-flicts, tendencies to project, or unrealistic attitudes on certain matters.
>
> (Rogers 1951: 42)

Relationships online for therapists using text-based models are difficult in different ways. The advantages and accessibility of the online counselling relationship for clients have been rehearsed (Anthony and Nagel 2010). For some, the therapeutic relationship online is accessible, less stigmatizing, and reduces inhibitions about disclosing distressing experiences. There is also that written record to review and reflect on.

We need to regularly review and evaluate where we are up to with online communication if online therapy is to thrive. Sherry Turkle, who wrote one of the first accounts of identity in the age of the Internet, *Life on the Screen*, is veering towards a more dystopic view in a recent book, where she argues that to redress the balance, we need to reclaim full attention in the moment (Turkle 2011).

Research has, however, tended to support Yalom's exhortation, 'It's the relationship that heals, it's the relationship, it's the relationship, it's the relationship . . .' (Yalom 1989: 91). Research and particularly practice-based case studies to highlight best practice are developing.

Summary

This overview is a starting point only. There is not enough scope in one chapter to do justice to the sheer scale of the growth of online therapeutic activity around the globe. Different modalities approach working with clients online in different ways, and a therapeutic alliance online can be analysed in different theoretical terms. This chapter focuses on the person-centred approach. Some key points are:

- Online therapeutic relationships are often driven by client preferences. Some people prefer the relative convenience, accessibility, and potential anonymity of the relationship mediated by the Internet. For some, it is a necessity because of shift work, geographical remoteness, disability, or other factors.
- The client can take more control in online counselling and psychotherapy, and the 'disinhibition effect' is significant in enabling some people to move quickly into working with deep feelings.
- There are serious limitations and risks in online counselling and psychotherapy. The disembodied relationship can feel impoverished. It is crucial for the therapist to provide clear and sufficient information, with careful contracting, including the appropriateness of this modality.
- Backup systems in case of technological breakdown are essential.

Further reading

The following books offer detailed theory and practice in working with different platforms online.

Evans, J. (2009) *Online Counselling and Guidance Skills: A Practical Resource for Trainees and Practitioners*. London: Sage.

Weitz, P. (ed.) (2014) *Psychotherapy 2.0: Where Psychotherapy and Technology Meet* (Vol. 1). London: Karnac Books.

Wright, J.K. (2004) Developing online, text-based counselling in the workplace, in G. Bolton, S. Howlett, C. Lago and J.K. Wright (eds.) *Writing Cures: An Introductory Handbook of Writing in Counselling and Therapy* (pp. 142–51). Hove: Brunner-Routledge.

References

Anthony, K. and Goss, S. (2009) *Guidelines for Online Counselling and Psychotherapy with Guidelines for Online Supervision*, 3rd edn. Rugby: British Association for Counselling and Psychotherapy.

Anthony, K. and Nagel, D.M. (2010) *Therapy Online: A Practical Guide*. London: Sage.

Barden, N. and Williams, T. (2007) *Words and Symbols: Communication in Therapy*. Maidenhead: Open University Press.

Bloom, J.W. (1998) The ethical practice of webcounselling, *British Journal of Guidance and Counselling*, 26 (1): 53–9.

Bordin, E.S. (1994) Theory and research on the therapeutic working alliance: new directions, in A.O. Horvath and L.S. Greenberg (eds.) *The Working Alliance: Theory, Research, and Practice*, 13–37. New York: Wiley.

Bozarth, J.D. (1998) *Person-Centred Therapy: A Revolutionary Paradigm*. Ross-on-Wye: PCCS Books.

Charura, D. (2014) Lost in translation – meeting the challenges of language and regional customs when working online, cross-border, without visual cues, in P. Weitz (ed.) *Psychotherapy 2.0: Where Psychotherapy and Technology Meet* (Vol. 1). London: Karnac Books.

Chester, A. and Glass, C.A. (2006) Online counselling: a descriptive analysis of therapy services on the Internet, *British Journal of Guidance and Counselling*, 34 (2): 145–60.

Cohen, G. and Kerr, B. (1998) Computer mediated counseling: an empirical study of a new mental health treatment, *Computers in Human Services*, 15: 13–26.

Cook, J. and Doyle, C. (2002) Working alliance in online therapy as compared to face-to-face therapy: preliminary results, *Cyberpsychology and Behavior*, 5: 95–105.

Cooper, M., Schmid, P.F., O'Hara, M. and Bohart, A. (eds.) (2013) *Handbook of Person Centred and Experiential Psychotherapy and Counselling*. Basingstoke: Palgrave Macmillan.

Day, S.X. and Schneider, P.L. (2002) Psychotherapy using distance technology: a comparison of face-to-face, video, and audio treatment, *Journal of Counseling Psychology*, 49: 499–503.

Duncan, B.L., Miller, S.D. and Sparks, J.A. (2004) *The Heroic Client*. San Francisco, CA: Jossey-Bass/Wiley.

Dunn, K. (2012) A qualitative investigation into the online counselling relationship: to meet or not to meet, that is the question, *Counselling and Psychotherapy Research*, 12 (4): 316–26.

Evans, J. (2009) *Online Counselling and Guidance Skills: A Practical Resource for Trainees and Practitioners*. London: Sage.

Gadamer, H.G. (2004) *Truth and Method*. London: Continuum Press.

Goss, S. and Anthony, K. (eds.) (2003) *Technology in Counselling and Psychotherapy: A Practitioner's Guide*. Basingstoke: Palgrave Macmillan.

Hanley, T. (2006) Developing a youth-friendly online counselling service in the United Kingdom: a small-scale investigation into the views of practitioners, *Counselling and Psychotherapy Research*, 6 (3): 182–5.

Hanley, T. (2009) The working alliance in online therapy with young people: preliminary findings, *British Journal of Guidance and Counselling*, 37 (3): 257–69.

Hanley, T. (2012) Understanding the online therapeutic alliance through the eyes of adolescent service users, *Counselling and Psychotherapy Research*, 12 (1): 35–43.

Hanley, T. and Reynolds, D.J. (2009) Counselling psychology and the Internet: a review of the quantitative research into online outcomes and alliances within text based therapy, *Counselling Psychology Review*, 24 (2): 4–12.

Hardy, T. (1874/1974) *Far from the Madding Crowd*. London: Macmillan.

Haugh, S. and Paul, S. (eds.) (2008) *The Therapeutic Relationship: Perspectives and Themes*. Ross-on-Wye: PCCS Books.

Hunt, C. (2004) Reading ourselves: imagining the reader in the writing process, in G. Bolton, S. Howlett, C. Lago and J.K. Wright (eds.) *Writing Cures: An Introductory Handbook of Writing in Counselling and Therapy* (pp. 35–43). Hove: Brunner-Routledge.

Jones, G. and Stokes, A. (2009) *Online Counselling: A Handbook for Practitioners*. Basingstoke: Palgrave Macmillan.

Lago, C.O. and Wright, J.K. (2007) Email supervision, in K. Tudor and M. Worrall (eds.) *Freedom to Practise: Developing Person-centred Approaches to Supervision* (pp. 102–18). Ross-on-Wye: PCCS Books.

Proctor, G., Cooper, M., Sanders, P. and Malcolm, B. (eds.) (2006) *Politicizing the Person-centred Approach: An Agenda for Social Change*. Ross-on-Wye: PCCS Books.

Reynolds, D.J., Stiles, W.B. and Grohol, J.M. (2006) An investigation of session impact and alliance in Internet-based psychotherapy: preliminary results. *Counselling and Psychotherapy Research*, 6 (3): 164–8.

Richards, D. and Vigano, N. (2013) Online counseling: a narrative and critical review of the literature, *Journal of Clinical Psychology*, 69 (9): 994–1011.

Rogers, C.R. (1951) *Client-Centered Therapy*. London: Constable.

Rogers, C.R. (1957) The necessary and sufficient conditions of therapeutic personality change, *Journal of Consulting Psychology*, 21: 95–103.

Rogers, C.R. (1974) *On Becoming a Person: A Therapist's View of Psychotherapy*. London: Constable.

Suler, J. (2004) The online disinhibition effect, CyberPsychology and Behavior, 7 (3): 321–6.

Tan, L. (2008) *Psychotherapy 2.0: MySpace blogging as self-therapy, American Journal of Psychotherapy*, 62 (2): 143–63.

Turkle, S. (2011) *Alone Together: Why We Expect More from Technology and Less from Each Other*. New York: Basic Books.

Wampold, B.E. (2001) *The Great Psychotherapy Debate: Models, Methods and Findings*. Mahwah, NJ: Erlbaum.

Worsley, R. (2009) *Process Work in Person Centred Therapy*, 2nd edn. Basingstoke: Palgrave Macmillan.

Wright, J.K. (2002) Online counselling: learning from writing therapy, *British Journal of Guidance and Counselling*, 30 (3): 285–98.

Wright, J.K. (2003) Future therapy stories, *Counselling and Psychotherapy Journal*, 14 (9): 22–5.

Wright, J.K. (2004) Developing online, text-based counselling in the workplace, in G. Bolton, S. Howlett, C. Lago and J.K. Wright (eds.) *Writing Cures: An Introductory Handbook of Writing in Counselling and Therapy* (pp. 142–51). Hove: Brunner-Routledge.

Wright, J.K. (2007) Online text-based counselling: reflections of a technophobe, *New Zealand Journal of Counselling*, 27 (1): 43–54.

Wright, J.K. and Griffiths, F. (2010) Reflective practice at a distance: using technology in counselling supervision, *Reflective Practice*, 11 (5): 693–703.

Yalom, I.D. (1989) *Love's Executioner and Other Tales of Psychotherapy*. New York: Basic Books.

24 The neuroscience of relationships: discovering the glia[1] of relationship or reinventing the psychotherapeutic wheel?

Andrea Uphoff

What Pari had always wanted from her mother was the glue to bond together her loose, disjointed scraps of memory, to turn them into some sort of cohesive narrative.

(Khaled Hosseini 2013)

Introduction

For over twenty years, there has been considerable excitement about neuroscience. This has presented psychological therapists with a new challenge. For the first time, it is possible to see and monitor the re-structuring of the brain that occurs with certain experiences, such as trauma (Rothschild 2002), mindfulness meditation (Kabat-Zinn 2005) or interventions such as cognitive bias modification (Fox 2012).

The terms 'interpersonal neurobiology' (Siegel 1999) and 'neuropsychotherapy' (Grawe 2007) are increasingly being used. In meeting the demand for evidence-based practice, will the future require that counsellors and psychotherapists can read functional MRI scans to determine whether they have targeted the correct brain area with their interventions and whether they are working effectively as Grawe envisions? Or is neuroscience not really telling us anything new, merely making visible and explicit what has always been known?

With the obvious constraints of this chapter, I will not attempt to revisit neuroanatomy in any detail (see Solms and Turnbull 2006; Porges 2011). Instead, I will seek overlaps in thinking and evidence by weaving together some of the developments in neuroscience and psychotherapy, while asking if and how neuroscience may enhance our practice. It is from this stance that I sketch some of the advantages of such knowledge along with inherent challenges to the profession.

Foundations of theory and practice

Increasingly, neuroscience denotes an incorporation of knowledge from diverse areas of science, psychotherapy, and philosophy. I use it here as a general term relating to any knowledge that attempts to explain the mind and human development in our embodied and relational form.

Carroll (2003; cf. Cozolino 2010) gives a brief and succinct history of the reasons why neuroscience and psychoanalysis have until recently taken separate paths of development. Freud imagined an integration of neurology, behavioural, mental, and somatic functioning. However, the studies of his era did not recognize the dynamic aspect of mind, seeking instead a correlation of clinical problems to certain areas of the brain. Dialogue between the two disciplines was very much inhibited by the difference in language used, modes and aims of research. Whittle (2000) sees this as a rift running down the middle of psychology – a rift that is now rapidly closing. Even so, looking back at early literature, one can see that great thinkers were already on to something; core concepts now being proved by neuroscience actually appeared early in psychotherapeutic theories. Both Jung (1921) and Reich (1973/1983) posited self-regulation as a basis of healing in psychotherapy, and Bowlby's (1965/1990) contribution of attachment theory has become a fundament of relational psychotherapy.

Early in the 1960s, the realization that through minute changes of input overwhelming shifts can occur (sometimes less scientifically termed the 'butterfly effect') was the pivotal idea of new science and complexity theory (Gleick 1988). The old Newtonian paradigm of linear closed systems was no longer fit for purpose and could not explain largely unpredictable phenomena, such as our eco or weather systems. This caused a shift in scientific thinking. Applied to both neuroscience and psychotherapy, central tenets of complexity theory opened up new vistas, and 'A proliferation of connections between previously separate fields is a result of the crystallization of a few core concepts, such as self-regulation, attachment, and parallel process, which are recognized and studied by many disciplines from different perspectives' (Carroll 2003: 193). But of particular importance to us, Badenoch (2008: 4) points out, is 'that there is an intrinsic push toward integration, or the subjective experience of wholeness, in our neural circuitry' (cf. Kriz 2011).

Even before the so-called 'decade of the brain',[2] it was rapidly becoming apparent that the mind could not be explained from one or two disciplines alone. The psychiatrist and psychoanalyst Daniel Stern's seminal work, *The Interpersonal World of the Infant* (1985), integrated empirical observations, use of experimental findings from people such as Ainsworth (1979), Beebe and Gerstman (1980), and Trevarthen (1979), and his clinical experience. Before technologies taken for granted today were available, he was already creating bridges across theories and emphasizing intersubjectivity as the baseline in human development. In the epilogue to his book, Stern writes,

> The value of this working theory remains to be proved, and even its status as a hypothesis remains to be explored. Is it to be taken as a scientific hypothesis that can be evaluated by its confirming or invalidating current propositions, and by spawning studies that lead elsewhere? Or is it to be taken as a clinical

metaphor to be used in practice, in which case the therapeutic efficacy of the metaphor can be determined? It is my hope that it will prove to be both.

(Stern 1985: 275)

It was not long before both of Stern's hopes were to become reality. Allan Schore (1994, 2003) had begun interpreting neurobiological evidence, taking into account not only the development of the child's brain but also its socio-emotional development. This highlighted self-organization as a system, which is changed structurally by its dynamic interaction with the environment. From 1995 onwards, innovation in neuroimaging technology allowed the study of the brain during its actual processing of external and internal information. There was a growing recognition of the crucial role the brain's right hemisphere plays in the first eighteen months of infant development. The quintessence of Schore's work is that when social and familial conditions are more right than wrong, caretaker and infant interact, attuning to each other's emotional state. This in turn fires neural connections in their separate brains, each altering the other's structural wiring. When attunement is successful, wellbeing, or regulation, is felt physiologically by caretaker and baby, promoting secure attachment.

During roughly the same period as Schore, biochemist Pert developed her molecular theory of 'mindbody', an interlinked network between systems, a 'constant exchange and processing and storage of information' with neuropeptides and receptors binding across systems (Pert 1998: 184). Her theory highlighted the internal response of one system to another with the release of hormones (positive and negative), which in turn activate gene systems responsible for programming the growth of brain regions essential to socio-emotional development. Correlating to Schore's work, Pert was positing the idea that one mindbody system might 'ignite' a psychobiological response in another person.

Limitations of any one orientation

'Caregiver/child' is potentially synonymous with 'therapist/client'.

(Schore 1994)

Evidence of the importance of right brain to right brain communication led to consensus among orientations emphasizing this type of interaction and shifting away from verbal interpretations. Different schools of thought used different language, emphasized different aspects of their approaches towards healing, but the message is clear: practitioner rigidity is unhelpful. Instead, what is transformative for the client says Schore (2000), are 'the therapist's *emotionally responsive interventions*' (emphasis added). As Fisher says, that means 'we pay less attention to the words we use and more to *how* we talk about it. Our actions, tone, and body language are used to shift the non-verbal experience of the other instead of our message' (personal communication, November 2013). This is achieved by utilizing subtle, embodied non-verbal communications of empathy and warmth – just as we instinctively do with young children or the elderly.

With the emergence of brain/mind/body data, it was becoming apparent that there was no one orientation that could have all the answers to psychotherapy, yet paradoxically all are effective (Paul and Haugh 2008: 10). The obvious solution to this is surely to combine everything we know across orientations and translate it into practice, build bridges between the research lab and the clinician's consulting room.

Verbal and somatic psychotherapies' inability to find a common language in psychotherapy caused confusion and sometimes frustration among therapists. As one philosopher describes,

> Having designated as science that which pertains to bodies, how were we supposed to think about mind? Mind was negatively defined as that which does not pertain to bodies or matter. That definition left the representation of mind with no language of its own.
>
> (Young 1994: 4)

Interpersonal neurobiology has now closed this gap to some extent, exemplified by Siegel's definition of mind as 'an embodied and relational process that *regulates* the flow of energy and information' (Siegel 2012: I–8, emphasis in original). Thinking in multidisciplinary frameworks has enabled dialogue between orientations and nowhere is this more evidenced than in traumatology.

Traumatology taught us much about how 'the body keeps the score' (van der Kolk 1994; Levine 1997; Rothschild 2002), illustrating how the events of our lives form or restructure the brain affecting its functioning and our behaviour. The interweaving of developmental neuroscience research and biological aspects of attachment theory with traumatology produced new insights and approaches to practice (see Herman 1992; Ogden et al. 2006), as well as the development of specific techniques to enable therapy without re-invoking trauma. Parallel studies from many disciplines converged on certain principles, helping us to understand ourselves, our clients, and the environment (Damasio 1994, 1999; Panksepp 1998; Totton 1998). Numerous studies now attest to the damage trauma can wreak on brains, minds, and souls, particularly in early years (see, for example, Twardosz and Lutzker 2010; Bendall et al. 2013) and the way that damage can transform into violence (De Zulueta 2008) or other disturbances. Spectacular as this evidence may be, earlier theorists (e.g. Spitz 1957; Harlow and Harlow 1965; Montagu 1971) had already taught us the correlation between absence or lack of maternal care and disturbed individuals and propensities to violence. By the same token, good caretaking of offspring resulted in resilience; the ability of the nervous system to tolerate difficult levels of affect.

It is not just the ever more increasing neuroscientific details that should be important but what those details highlight – namely, the *primacy of relationship* in all our lives. There is a clear correlation to the current DSM-V controversy. Citing and aligning himself with a number of renowned psychiatrists and articles in the *New England Journal of Medicine*, Dr Keith Ablow (2012) opines that the list of conditions with their signs and symptoms as detailed in DSM-V do not equate with a way of making sense of mental disorders unless psychiatrists make a commitment to looking at their patients as people with life stories as relevant to their disorder. Indeed, many of the additions to the DSM-V conceptualize human responses to life events as a 'disorder' rather than a natural human response to particular circumstances. He says, 'It seems strange to say it about a profession based on insight, but too many psychiatrists practicing today don't know a lot about their patients' lives; they choose diagnoses from the DSM and pick which medicines corresponds to it. That isn't treating the person.' I sense a danger here: could psychotherapists (of any orientation) become so preoccupied with or distracted by the workings of the brain, that they become prone to diagnosing a brain malfunction rather than being truly engaged in understanding the client in his or her world? Should that be the case, quality of presence would be lost, causing dysregulation and rupture in the relationship.

The therapeutic relationship

> Neurons have three sequential levels of information exchange that are called first, second, and third messenger systems. They are (1) the communication across the synapse that (2) changes the internal biochemistry of the cell, which, in turn, (3) activates mRNA (messenger ribonucleic acid, the material that translates protein into new brain structure). It is through these processes that the brain changes in response to experience.
>
> (Cozolino 2006: 5)

The task of applying this type of scientific knowledge to counselling and psychotherapy was never going to be easy. Spectacular visual images of the brain enabled through fMRI are seductive and may delude us into thinking we know something about the person by studying the scans. However, what neuroscientists can actually see is whether certain areas of the brain are active or not in certain situations and their conclusions are not explanations of the person but interpretations of what they see. It is a mistake to deduce from these that we can explain people and their inner world. Do these facts aid or influence our work, or do they actually detract from our endeavours?

The organ brain is a complex mix of genetics and lived experience, a social brain comprised of nature and nurture (LeDoux 2003), charged towards interdependence. Research shows that relationships can be either beneficial or detrimental to development, particularly in early infancy when the child is dependent on its caregiver for its psychobiological regulation. Where the relationship is more wrong than 'good enough', right brain attachment trauma may occur through misattunements or dysregulation with the significant other. The quote used at the beginning of this chapter highlights the absence of relationship to make sense of life. Pari was sold by her poverty-stricken father to a wealthy woman who wished to adopt a child. She, however, was unable to attune emotionally to Pari and their exchanges remained dysregulating and frustrating throughout Pari's life.

We experience both attunements (when we feel good with another) and misattunements (when we feel unmet or uncomfortable with another) throughout our lives. It is now evident that any meaningful relationship has the potential to change the structure of both brains. But didn't we already know that good relationships built with our clients often bring about constructive changes in both of us? My client Tim, aged 50, suffered a stroke about a year ago which left him badly paralysed on his left side, his speech slurred, and unable to care for himself. Soon after his partner left him, Tim's elderly parents became his main carers. They pressured him into coming to see me. He informed me that he would come 'just for a few sessions to keep them happy'. Tim would sit staring out of the window, not responding to me at all. Sometimes it felt as if I were alone in the room. Talking soothingly, prepared to be rebuffed, I began to empathize with what I *imagined* might be going through his mind; the shock of the stroke, not being found in time to prevent the worst of impairments, the loss of his physical sense of self, loss of his partner, and the indignity of being washed and clothed by his mother. One day he looked directly at me and began to tell me about his holidays in South Africa, how much he loved the country and how he hoped to retire there. It felt, at last, as if we had established a relationship. He talked about his childhood, which he described as one of emotional coldness. He phrased it as, 'I was washed, fed, and put out to grass.' Recently I asked Tim if he were still coming to therapy to please his parents. No, he said, 'I am coming for myself now'. Asked what had made the difference he said, 'You didn't let go'. I can only surmise that my tenacity ignited an atrophied area in Tim's brain, allowing for empathic attunement. For my part, I learned that patience is rewarded.

In their summary of research in the field of psychotherapy, Paul and Haugh (2008:19) state that regardless of paradigm, 'The relationship is the most significant in-therapy factor as related to positive outcomes', and it is not possible to consider the therapeutic relationship without referring to Rogers' work. Rogers (1959) based his thesis of a good therapeutic environment on six conditions and posited both their necessity and sufficiency for a meaningful and constructive therapeutic relationship. Rogers was an *avant-garde* thinker of his day and his theories on relationship and empathy have stood the test of time. Central to Rogers' work is the development not only of empathy, but also of *empathic understanding* for the world of the client 'as if' it were one's own.[3] This is a potent contribution to the interactive relationship. As the essence of the therapeutic relationship is a cultivated form of mutual feedback, it would be fair to surmise that Rogers was prepared himself to be changed in the process. Were he alive today, Rogers might have been intrigued and excited by the way in which interpersonal neurobiology is proving his assumptions[4] about the presence of an engaged and caring therapist, setting out to forge a connection and able to resonate with a client's world. As Paul and Haugh show in their meta-analysis, it is the relationship that makes or breaks psychotherapy independent of therapist orientation. Psychoneurobiology emphatically underlines the importance of relationship to the extent that it is creating a shift of paradigm. Even Beck, one of the founders of cognitive therapy now asserts, 'The therapeutic relationship is a key ingredient of all psychotherapies, including cognitive therapy' (Beck and Dozois 2011: 401). He also goes on to note that it is exactly those interpersonal variables originally cited by Rogers that are responsible for cognitive and symptomatic change.

Understanding the lifelong plasticity of a brain continually modifiable through experience, through relationship, gives hope but also caution to this central concept of most psychotherapies, as well as a renewed sense of responsibility, including towards future generations (Hüther 2005). Historically, scientists believed that our genes were 'set in stone' and not subject to change (Crick 1970). Recent research by Professor Tim Spector with identical twins who share identical genes at birth have played a role in disputing this view (Spector 2013). There is a growing body of evidence that the environment and experiences of early life not only shape brains, but also affect whether and how genes are expressed. This may have an enduring effect on an individual's psychological health as well as on that of their descendants. The phenomenon of the 'intergenerational template' recognizable in the way certain life 'themes' seem to be handed down through families is one familiar to many psychotherapists (Klengel et al. 2013). This brings with it a new weight of responsibility to psychotherapeutic work.

Moving into the future

Grawe (2004/2007) predicted that because of the dedication required to take command of the intricacies of theory and its implications for practice, psychotherapists would not use the new knowledge actively. Rather, they would use it only as a way of justifying their traditional ways of working, picking and choosing that which best fit the current thinking of their particular school of thought. Neurosceptics may still feel we are caught in contradiction in attempting to come up with a coherent model of psychotherapy based on neuroscience, but this seems to be the direction in which the interpersonal neurobiologists are heading. A number of practitioners help inform our understanding by deconstructing clinical features into neurobiological constructs.

Bonnie Badenoch, for example, offers a helpful chapter on diagnosis. Through the lens of neuroscience, she illustrates how depression, anxiety, dissociation, and addiction can be seen as adaptations to stress, as well as expressions of *'genetic vulnerability, alterations in neurotransmitters and hormones,* certain *deficits in brain structure and function, inner community disruption* based on internalized patterns of relating, and *social networks that often reinforce engrained neural circuits'* (Badenoch 2008: 120, emphasis in original). She maintains that, in almost all cases of trauma, regulation has failed at early stages of attachment or foetus's have been affected by the emotional-neurochemical environment *in utero*, which can cause infants 'to enter this life calm, depressed, or anxious' (p. 132). Using the relevant research sources, she explains how neuroscientifically each condition could be seen to arise. Throughout, she is firmly rooted in relationship as is another colleague, Arlene Montgomery.

Montgomery does that rare thing – she translates research into different longstanding psychotherapeutic concepts. She shows that historically we were on the right track as regards affect management in client–therapist interactions. Montgomery emphasizes that these interactions have the potential to regulate – and also to dysregulate – both parties, arousing defence mechanisms to modulate emotional arousal (Montgomery 2013: 22–3). Using a number of case studies, she retrospectively analyses session transcriptions, tracking the therapist–client interactions with reference to levels of arousal, displaying how the dyad use their right hemispheres in exchange, sometimes consciously, sometimes unconsciously. As Schore says in his foreword to her book, her goal is to 'more deeply understand the nonlinear bodily-based dynamics of the "social", "emotional" right brain, the biological substrate of the human unconscious' (Schore 2013: xv). This is an incredibly useful but time-consuming exercise. Are we up to it? It is sometimes said that a little knowledge can be a dangerous thing, and I have a concern that in the face of so much to be learned, some psychotherapists may use their limited knowledge to become 'amateur neuroscientists', possibly utilizing techniques with which they are unfamiliar and causing ruptures in their clinical relationships. Dan Siegel offers an alternative approach.

Siegel (2010a) latterly seems to refrain more and more from writing about 'how to do' psychotherapy from a neuroscientific perspective. Instead, he places more emphasis on the art of mindful being in the therapist by offering a conceptual guide with which to develop ourselves through our own neural integration. Coupled with *Mindsight* (2010b), Siegel presents a process of focusing (openness, observation, and objectivity to one's inner world), aimed at transforming the brain, forging a healthier mind and relationships. However, Neborsky (2010) is critical in his review of the book. He cites scarcity of references to psychotherapy, as well as Siegel's lack of comparison to other therapies that do not rely on his own neurological conceptualizations. His use of case studies, although interesting, does not conclude anything about the effectiveness of his approach.

All the authors cited in this section have immersed themselves in the material and contributed massively to the application of neuroscience to practice. All would agree that non-integrated systems (in therapist or client) are likely to become rigid, chaotic or both.

New developments

Neuropsychotherapy and the therapeutic relationship: help or hindrance?

Few have dared to phrase the question as to whether we actually *need* neuropsychotherapy as blatantly as Richter (2012). His valid argument is that there are epistomological contradictions between neuroscience and psychotherapy that do not make for a good match. Neuroscience is 'empirical-technical', logical in its approach, and of necessity abstract. It follows that neuropsychotherapy represents a very specific mode of augmentation and action (cause and effect thinking). But our clinical work can't be based entirely on brain imaging technology and outcomes; there is more to being human than brain activity. Psychotherapy's epistemological foundation is determined by its relation to unknown aspects of reality and must always take metapsychological premises and processes into account.

So it is with all new knowledge acquired – alongside any enhancements to practice there are inherent dangers. In Grawe's standpoint I sense a new kind of reductionism and determinism, a danger of specifically targeting brain functioning through psychotherapy (and pharmacology) at the expense of holistic relating and communication; a return to a dualism based on soma instead of psyche. Caution is required lest psychotherapists be drawn into definitive diagnoses and labelling (as seen above in the case of DSM-V) with further incentive to pharmaceutical companies to increase their profits, especially as the UK continues with its policies for cost-effectiveness.

Despite the fact that technology overtakes itself at an awe-inspiring rate, cutting-edge neuroimaging has a major limitation according to Schore (2012). He notes that *in vivo* imaging does not allow for real-time dynamics of brain function due to temporal resolution. McGilchrist sees this as a promising area but subjects it to a more stringent criticism than would a layperson:

Imaging just shows a few peaks, where much of interest goes on elsewhere. One cannot assume that the areas that light up are those fundamentally responsible for the "function" being imaged, or that areas that do not light up are not involved. And, what is more, one cannot even assume that whatever "peaks" is of primary importance.

(McGilchrist 2009: 35)

The most recent literature indicates an emerging backlash to neuroscience, suggesting much of its 'evidence' is purely speculative and highlighting our human tendency to be beguiled and deceived by the visual (Burton 2013; Satel and Lilienfeld 2013).

As yet, although contributing important information, neuroscience is not about to make psychotherapy obsolete, as it only delivers partial answers. No analysis of the brain will enable us to accurately represent or predict an 'essential' insight. It will always be the interpreter's unique interpretation of events. But in combination with what we already know, it may be a powerful tool as long as we do not reduce human beings to brain functions and focus instead on our various ways of being in the world.

The relatively new field of epigenetic enquiry is at the cutting edge of biological science and has within it a predictive element that is bothering from a neuro-ethical standpoint. If specific genes can be identified as an inherent vulnerability to a child, psychotherapists will again be challenged to re-evaluate their practice. Neuropharmacological studies are well underway in the area of epigenetics and neurodevelopmental disorders (cf. Millan 2013). Conversely, the current advances make an irrevocable case for early intervention with hard evidence available to accrue funding and develop childhood policies and programmes. An example of these are working papers of the Center on the Developing Child at Harvard University (2010, 2011) on how early experiences shape the development of executive function,[5] alter gene expression, and affect long-term development. And interest in 'brain-based' parenting is growing (Sunderland 2006; Hughes and Baylin 2012).

Summary

The sheer volume of material connected with the topic of psychotherapy when taking neuroscientific and biochemical information into account might constitute a deterent to many practitioners. Nevertheless, this topic will probably at some point likely become a requirement in training, with students studying the overarching principles of brain function along with neuropsychological strategies for intervention. While the principles can inform clinical practice, neuroscientific facts will never adequately represent the lives of our clients or the complex processes of psychotherapy.

The brain's capacity for development in terms of functionality and relational connectivity should not be underestimated, but neither should the neuroscientific contribution to psychotherapy turn into a goal to 'change the brain' or regulate gene transcription. Even providing a meta theory or developing a coherent practice of psychotherapy derived from psychoneurobiology can never be the agent for change. Although neuroscience evidences much of what we already surmised or knew by empirical observation in our practice, it also offers a different perspective on human functioning. If we are willing to engage with the material and remain at the forefront of new discoveries, poised to embrace new knowledge and continuing to ask innovative questions, we may also find new nourishment for our clinical practice.

Relationships are not built on theories, no matter how coherent, but on human contact. It will be our capacity to become the most fully present persons we can be, prepared to relate to our clients with humility and at the deepest level of humanity, that will make a difference in the face of complexity. When all is said and done, despite criticisms and flaws, neuroscience is the best evidence yet to reinforce the importance of relationship in the therapeutic endeavour.

Notes

1   Glia (Greek for glue) are tiny cells which wrap axons in myelin. They provide stability and speed connection between neurons.
2   A term given by President George Bush to the period 1990–2000 to promote inter-agency work on programmes and activities designed with the use of neuroscience, 'to enhance public awareness of the benefits to be derived from brain research'.
3   Montgomery terms this 'synchrony': the ability of the practitioner to experience a client's feelings temporarily in a way that goes far beyond mirroring and allows for the practitioner to participate in new experiences with the client.
4   Rogers may have been particularly gratified to see confirmation of the non-verbal affective mechanisms of organismic subception (1951) turn up in Porges' (2011) poly-vagal theory as neuroception, a term coined to capture 'sensory information from the environment and the viscera, continuously evaluating risk' (Porges, cited in Montgomery 2013: 95).
5   'The key functions attributed to the prefrontal regions; these include the regulation of attention, emotion, memory, behavioural response, and planning' (Siegel 2012: AI–31).

Further reading

The New Scientist [http://www.newscientist].

Jill Bolte Taylor's powerful *My Stroke of Insight* [http://www.ted.com/talks/jill_bolte_taylor_s_powerful_stroke_of_insight.html; accessed 22 December 2013].

References

Ablow, K. (2012) *Leading Psychiatrists Question Psychiatry's Diagnostic Manual* [http://www.foxnews.com/health/2012/11/05/leading-psychiatrists-question-psychiatry-diagnostic-manual/?test=latestnews#ixzz2BZiJyEQo; accessed 22 December 2013].
Ainsworth, M.D.S. (1979) Attachment as related to mother–infant interaction, in J.B. Rosenblatt, R.H. Hinder, C. Beer and M. Bushell (eds.) *Advances in the Study of Behaviour* (pp. 1–51). New York: Academic Press.

Badenoch, B. (2008) *Being a Brain-Wise Therapist: A Practical Guide to Interpersonal Neurobiology*. London: W.W. Norton.

Beck, A.T. and Dozois, D.J.A. (2011) Cognitive therapy: current status and future directions, *Annual Review of Medicine*, 62: 397–409.

Beebe, B. and Gerstman, L.J. (1980) The 'packaging' of maternal stimulation in relation to infant facial-visual engagement: a case study at four months, *Merrill-Palmer Quarterly*, 26: 321–39.

Bendall, S., Alvarez-Jimenez, M., Nelson, B. and McGorry, P. (2013) Childhood trauma and psychosis: new perspectives on aetiology and treatment, *Early Intervention in Psychiatry*, 7 (1): 1–4.

Bowlby, J. (1965/1990) *Child Care and the Growth of Love*. Harmondsworth: Penguin Books.

Burton, R.A. (2013) *A Skeptic's Guide to the Mind*. New York: St. Martin's Press.

Carroll, R. (2003) 'At the border between chaos and order': what psychotherapy and neuroscience have in common, in J. Corrigall and H. Wilkinson (eds.) *Revolutionary Connections*. London: Karnac Books.

Center on the Developing Child, Harvard University (2010) *Early Experiences can Alter Gene Expression and Affect Long-Term Development* [http://developingchild.harvard.edu/resources/reports_and_working_papers/; accessed 22 December 2013].

Center on the Developing Child, Harvard University (2011) *Building the Brain's 'Air Traffic Control' System* [http://developingchild.harvard.edu/resources/reports_and_working_papers/; accessed 22 December 2013].

Cozolino, L. (2006) *The Neuroscience of Human Relationships*. London: W.W. Norton.

Cozolino, L. (2010) *The Neuroscience of Psychotherapy: Healing the Social Brain*. London: W.W. Norton.

Crick, F. (1970) Central dogma of molecular biology, *Nature*, 227: 561–3.

Damasio, A. (1994) *Descartes' Error: Emotion, Reason, and the Human Brain*. London: Putnam.

Damasio, A. (1999) *The Feeling of What Happens*. London: Heinemann.

De Zulueta, F. (2008) Attachment research and the origins of violence: a story of damaged brains and damaged minds, in M. Blyth and E. Soloman (eds.) *Prevention and Youth Crime: Is Early Intervention Working?* (pp. 69–88). Bristol: Policy Press.

Fox, E. (2012) *Rainy Brain, Sunny Brain*. London: Random House.

Gleick, J. (1988) *Chaos: The Amazing Science of the Unpredictable*. London: Heinemann.

Grawe, K. (2007) *Neuropsychotherapy*. London: Psychology Press. [Originally published in 2004 in German as *Neuropsychotherapie*. Göttingen: Hofgrefe Verlag.]

Harlow, H.F. and Harlow, M.K. (1965) The effect of rearing conditions on behavior, in J. Money (ed.) *Sex Research: New Developments*. New York: Holt, Rinehart & Winston.

Herman, J.L. (1992) *Trauma and Recovery: The Aftermath of Violence from Domestic Abuse to Political Terror*. New York: Basic Books.

Hosseini, K. (2013) *And the Mountains Echoed*. London: Bloomsbury.

Hughes, D.A. and Baylin, J. (2012) *Brain-Based Parenting: The Neuroscience of Caregiving for Healthy Attachment*. London: W.W. Norton.

Hüther, G. (2005) *Bedienungsanleitung für ein menschliches Gehirn*. Göttingen: Vandenhoeck & Ruprecht.

Jung, C.G. (1921) Psychological types and the self-regulating psyche, in S. Storr (ed.) *The Essential Jung*. Princeton, NJ: Princeton University Press.

Kabat-Zinn, J. (2005) *Wherever You Go, There You Are: Mindfulness Meditation in Everyday Life*. New York: Hyperion.

Klengel, T., Mehta, D., Anacker, C., Rex-Haffner, M., Pruessner, J.C., Pariante, C.M. et al. (2013) Allele-specific FKBP5 DNA demethylation mediates gene–childhood trauma interactions, *Nature Neuroscience*, 16 (1): 33–41.

Kriz, J. (2011) *Chaos, Angst und Ordnung: Wie wir unsere Lebenswelt gestalten*. Göttingen: Vandenhoeck & Ruprecht.

LeDoux, M. (2003) *Synaptic Self: How Our Brains Become Who We Are*. Harmondsworth: Penguin Books.

Levine, D. (1997) *Waking the Tiger: Healing Trauma*. Berkeley, CA: North Atlantic Books.

McGilchrist, I. (2009) *The Master and his Emissary: The Divided Brain and the Making of the Western World*. New Haven, CT: Yale University Press.

Millan, M.J. (2013) An epigenetic framework for neurodevelopmental disorders: from pathogenesis to potential therapy, *Neuropharmacology*, 68: 2–82.

Montagu, A. (1971) *Touching: The Human Significance of Skin*. New York: Harper & Row.

Montgomery, A. (2013) *Neurobiology Essentials for Clinicians*. London: W.W. Norton.

Neborsky, R.J. (2010) Review of Mindsight: the new science of personal transformation, *International Journal of Group Psychotherapy*, 60 (4): 605–9.

Ogden, P., Minton, K. and Pain, C. (2006) *Trauma and the Body: A Sensorimotor Approach to Psychotherapy*. London; W.W. Norton.

Panksepp, J. (1998) *Affective Neuroscience: The Foundations of Human and Animal Emotions*. Oxford: Oxford University Press.

Paul, S. and Haugh, S. (2008) The relationship, not the therapy? What the research tells us, in S. Haugh and S. Paul (eds.) *The Therapeutic Relationship; Perspectives and Themes*. Ross-on-Wye: PCCS Books.

Pert, C.B. (1998) *Molecules of Emotion*. London: Simon & Schuster.

Porges, S.W. (2011) *The Polyvagal Theory*. New York: W.W. Norton.

Reich, W. (1973/1983) *The Function of the Orgasm*. London: Souvenir Press.

Richter, M. (2012) Do we need 'neuropsychotherapy'? A pragmatic critique from the perspective of the theory of science, *Forum der Psychoanalyse: Zeitschrift für klinische Theorie & Praxis*, 28 (1): 27–49.

Rogers, C.R. (1951/1993) *Client-Centered Therapy*. London: Constable.

Rogers, C.R. (1959) A theory of therapy, personality and interpersonal relationships, as developed in the client-centered framework, in S. Koch (ed.) *Psychology: A Study of Science, Vol. 3: Formulations of the Person and the Social Context* (pp. 184–256). New York: McGraw-Hill.

Rothschild, B. (2002) *The Body Remembers: The Psychophysiology of Trauma and Trauma Treatment*. New York: W.W. Norton.

Satel, S. and Lilienfeld, S. (2013) *Brainwashed: The Seductive Appeal of Mindless Neuroscience*. New York: Basic Books.

Schore, A.N. (1994) *Affect Regulation and the Origin of the Self*. Mahwah, NJ: Erlbaum.

Schore, A.N. (2000) Minds in the making: attachment, the self-organizing brain, and developmentally-oriented psychoanalytic psychotherapy, Paper delivered at the Seventh Annual John Bowlby Memorial Lecture at the Conference 'Minds in the

Making', 3–4 March [http://stantatkin.com/wpcontent/uploads/2012/12/import/ans/library/Bowlby%20Lecture.doc; accessed 22 December 2013].

Schore, A.N. (2003) *Affect Dysregulation and Disorders of the Self*. London: W.W. Norton.

Schore, A.N. (2012) *The Science of the Art of Psychotherapy*. London: W.W. Norton.

Schore, A.N. (2013) Foreword, in A. Montgomery, *Neurobiology Essentials for Clinicians*. London: W.W. Norton.

Siegel, D.J. (1999) *Developing Mind: Toward a Neurobiology of Interpersonal Experience*. New York: W.W. Norton.

Siegel, D.J. (2010a) *The Mindful Therapist*. London: W.W. Norton.

Siegel, D.J. (2010b) *Mindsight*. Oxford: Oneworld Publications.

Siegel, D.J. (2012) *Pocket Guide to Interpersonal Neurobiology*. New York: W.W. Norton.

Solms, M. and Turnbull, O. (2006) *The Brain and the Inner World*. London: Karnac Books.

Spector, T. (2013) The Truth about Personality. London: BBC2 Horizon [http://www.kcl.ac.uk/medicine/research/divisions/gmm/Departments/twin/about/people/spector.aspx; accessed 10 July 2013].

Spitz, R.A. (1957) *No and Yes*. New York: International Universities Press.

Stern, D. (1985) *The Interpersonal World of the Infant*. New York: Basic Books.

Sunderland, M. (2006) *The Science of Parenting*. London: DK Publishing.

Totton, N. (1998) *The Water in the Glass: Body and Mind in Psychoanalysis*. London: Rebus Press.

Trevarthen, C. (1979) Communication and cooperation in early infancy: a description of primary intersubjectivity, in M.M. Bullowa (ed.) *Before Speech: The Beginning of Interpersonal Communication*. New York: Cambridge University Press.

Twardosz, S. and Lutzker, J.R. (2010) Child maltreatment and the developing brain: a review of neuroscience perspectives, *Aggression and Violent Behavior*, 15: 59–68.

Van der Kolk, B. (2004) The body keeps the score: memory and the evolving psychobiology of post traumatic stress, *Harvard Review of Psychiatry*, 1 (5): 253–65.

Young, R.M. (1994) *Mental Space*. London: Process Press.

25 Conclusion

Stephen Paul and Divine Charura

At the start of this book, we set the scene for the exploration of the therapeutic relationship both in modalities of practice and in professional settings. Our summary of recent research in Chapter 1 concluded that:

1   The therapeutic relationship is the most important in-therapy factor.
2   There is a strong correlation between levels of empathy, positive regard, congruence, and therapeutic outcome based on clients' reporting.
3   Relationship factors of rapport and positive engagement in therapy, shared by both therapist and client, are directly linked with outcome.
4   In relation to diversity, client–therapist matching with regard to diversity *may* be linked to outcome; however, research is limited in this area.
5   Neuroscience demonstrates that through the therapeutic relationship, the provision of empathy, and other conditions that foster growth, positive therapy outcomes are achieved.

Quantitative research findings 1–3 above are largely based on meta-analyses and offer compelling evidence for the place of a positive therapeutic relationship as a prerequisite for good outcomes. These can now be virtually accepted as given.

Research in relation to diversity (ethnicity, gender, age, class, and so on) is inconclusive and there is much less research into these factors. The research in neuroscience is innovative and offers hard empirical evidence as to the direct effects of relational factors, although more rigorous studies are needed. We therefore need to be rather tentative in what we draw from this research. We will now look at the emerging themes that arise from the contributions of the experts in the different sections of this handbook.

Modalities and the one-to-one therapeutic relationship

The chapters in Section 1 explore the relationship in the traditional modalities of therapy, including person-centred therapy.

Aida Alayarian reflects on the importance of a therapeutic relationship understanding the role of empathy, genuineness, and positive regard within the psychoanalytic modality. She points to psychoanalysis as a scientific endeavour, noting the importance of the need for research into practice with an emphasis also on inter-cultural working.

Mike Thomas highlights the strong evidence base for cognitive behavioural therapy. He goes on to show how relational factors are now seen to be important in making the interpersonal aspects of therapy more equal while retaining the principle of supporting the clients in discriminating between thoughts, feelings, physical sensations, behaviour, and environment. He also discusses 'third-wave' approaches, which explore clients' relationship with their selves.

In his review of the relationship in existential, humanistic, and transpersonal therapies, John Rowan illustrates the unique importance of the relationship in each. He identifies too the difference in the place of the relationship in each approach. The relationship can be transformational and the authenticity of the therapist is requisite.

Colin Lago, Peggy Natiello, and Carol Wolter-Gustafson note the relational turn that is impacting on all approaches and revisit the person-centred approach within the context of a relationship that facilitates the client's intrapersonal relationship with themselves and their own existential reality. While revisiting the core concepts of the approach that have impacted on all therapies, they consider new relational developments, expanded from the original hypotheses towards a reworking of the approach in the twenty-first century, for example the NHS programme 'counselling for depression', which is based on key person-centred principles.

Key themes

- All of these approaches variously consider the relationship as instrumental to change.
- All have a coherent theoretical base.
- Given the evidence that no one modality is any more effective than any other, approaches that seek to take place within statutory settings will need a strong evidence base. More research is needed to evaluate process and outcomes for the more phenomenological (psychodynamic, existential/ humanistic/transpersonal, and person-centred) approaches.

Cross-modality, relational, integrative, creative, and coaching therapies

David Bott and Pam Howard assert that the vehicle for therapeutic intervention is the relationship. They are clear this needs to be located within a coherent paradigm. Effective therapy is linked to practitioner qualities and actions. A cross-modality approach respects the distinction between therapeutic modalities while valuing a dialogic pluralism. Therapy is a dramatic process where the therapist relates with the enactment of the client's dilemma and resistance is a function of the therapeutic relationship, not part of the pathology of the client.

Maria Gilbert and Ken Evans conclude that the changing focus towards the centrality of the therapeutic relationship (which has challenged the classical notions of drive theory, therapist neutrality, and 'objectivity') has been a significant change in therapy in recent years. The primary need of human beings is relational, for contact with the other.

Appropriate therapist self-disclosure, the playing out of relational patterns, and the agency of the therapist in the co-creation of the therapeutic relationship are areas currently being explored in relational therapies. Such enactments and ruptures in the therapeutic alliance are recognized as opportunities for learning and change.

Both theory and technique are central to therapy. Theory needs to be held lightly, so as to gently inform our critical refection. Theory, therefore, is like a map that helps therapists to understand the therapeutic process and evaluate their clinical interventions rather than using it to box clients into specific fixed categories.

Brian Charlesworth and Paul Nicholson propose that the shift in emphasis from technique to the personal dimension of therapy will be reflected in future training of therapists, with an increasing awareness that single-model approaches are limited in their suitability for working with the wide variety of client issues found in contemporary practice.

Relational philosophy offers a language that is more compatible with the mainstream mental health services, which adopt an evidence-based philosophy, and it provides an opportunity for integrating more qualitative approaches. Relationalism has emerged as a paradigm within an increasingly integrative landscape, presenting a platform to effectively reframe established theoretical structures and develop practice in a consistent and principled manner.

The qualities of the practitioner are essential to practice. Through a process of distillation, each practitioner draws upon their own unique relational resources in engagement with the encounter in which client and therapist co-create a therapeutic way of working. From this relational perspective, Charlesworth and Nicholson offer a model that aims to empower therapists and encourage them to be creative, courageous, and willing to access their own resources within a collaborative therapeutic relationship.

For Pam Fisher, the therapeutic alliance in the creative therapies is fostered using a wide range of media and processes. She proposes a framework within which practitioner and client can develop to work deeply through relational dimensions that may include writing, music, art, movement, role-play, play, and non-verbal peer group interaction. A therapeutic relationship can emerge in a process that may be more non-verbal than verbally based. Thus the relationship may be subtle and unspoken.

The fundamental principle of creative arts therapies is that these processes have the potential to facilitate growth and change (evidenced, too, in the humanistic principles described by Rowan in Chapter 4), and/or to support a client to be at their best. Therefore, the process may act to support a person to maximize wellness rather than be a change agent.

For George Bassett, Pete Lavender, and Lydia Noor, the philosophy of their training is founded on a relational-developmental process, and attention is paid to relational communication as we address past developmental deficits. Group process is the key to training. A therapist must have explored their own relational issues to work effectively with their clients. Exploration of self in relation to others enables the therapist to be authentic. This is both grounding and enables the therapist to develop the awareness and skills to co-create a unique therapeutic relationship: 'In the between of group process, all lived experience unfolds as is available in the here-and-now' (p. 117).

Geoff Pelham notes that the primary intention of coaching is to improve performance by enabling clients to find their own way forward. The 'psychological dimension' is a significant aspect of the coaching relationship, with the coach often working with the 'inner' and 'outer' aspects of the client's situation. Coaching approaches that have their origins in therapy (cognitive behavioural, person-centred, transactional analysis, psychodynamic, and so on) draw on relational perspectives.

Within organizations, there is often a three-way relationship in coaching: coach, coachee, and the organization itself. This brings a complexity around managing boundaries. The dynamics of coaching draws upon experiences of managing complex relationships in other areas of life.

Key themes

- For all approaches, the relationship is instrumental to change. In relationship, change happens.
- The relational approaches draw from across theory with a central premise that individuals seek relationship. The therapeutic relationship has a developmental-reparative component (see also Aida Alayarian, Chapter 2). We learn in relation to others.
- The authenticity of the therapist is cited as a requisite for effective therapy.
- Aims may differ – while coaching may be goal-oriented, the creative therapies may focus on personal growth.

Group therapies, systemic therapies, couple/marital and family therapy, and sex therapy

Stephen Paul and Divine Charura show that cohesiveness is *the* therapeutic relationship in group therapy; as with individual therapy, the therapeutic relationship is now regarded as central to change. The group therapist can help build cohesiveness by communicating warmth, empathy, and openness, by co-creating agreed goals, and by maintaining clear boundaries.

For Phil Arthington and Paula Boston, the therapeutic relationship is a central component of systemic therapy. The therapist engages the family by building numerous therapeutic alliances, seeking to understand each individual's unique perspective, maintaining a degree of neutrality but with attention to inequalities of power, and attending to issues of difference and their potential for influencing the therapeutic relationship.

Anne Burghgraef and Divine Charura note that all humans are social beings, living in relationship with other humans. Couples/marital therapy is not a 'one-size-fits-all' therapy. Recently, there has been greater recognition of the multi-dimensionality of human existence within contexts. They suggest that it is important for the therapist to have an understanding of family/systemic theory and to be aware of attachment and love styles that impact couple relating. Furthermore, they note the importance of being able to work with complex dynamics that interplay in the therapeutic relationship when working with two or more people in different social and cultural contexts. Therapist competence in helping couples make sense/define rules of functioning of their relationship is essential. Reviews of marital and family therapy literature, as with individual therapy, find that the therapeutic relationship between the therapist and family members is important for an effective therapeutic outcome.

Jacob Jacobson and Andrew Mirrlees maintain that containing and working with the anxiety within the relationship while offering a safe space to explore different ways of thinking, behaviour, and emotional response, is central to the role of the sex and relationship therapist. The therapeutic relationship underpins the efficacy of and is central to treatment.

Relationships can be complex, focusing on tasks on the one hand while working with feelings such as shame on the other. The vulnerability of clients in relation to the therapist can actually enhance the therapeutic relationship.

Key themes

- In these approaches, while relationship is central to therapy, the therapist has to work with complex relationships and relational dynamics.
- Individuals are unique and different and have learned idiosyncratic ways of coping and relating that may not be considered objectively as 'dysfunctional' but may be the ways individuals, families, and groups learn to manage best.
- Recent developments focus more on relational ways of working as opposed to classical methods.

The relationship in the helping and mental health professions

Sally Read, a general practitioner and psychotherapist, highlights the importance of Rogers' unconditional positive regard in helping relationships. She links this with non-possessive love, or agape. As the therapist accepts and values the client, so the client has a chance to develop *self-love* and acceptance. She states how the current trend for goals and targets makes this the attitude of love so difficult to hold on to.

With developments such as *Compassion in Practice* (Andrew Sims Centre 2012; NHS 2013) in nursing and the UKCP devoting an issue of *Psychotherapy* to love (Warburton and Charura 2012), there is hope that those who wish to can continue to develop their practice in this way. Read evidences the importance of empathy too in all professional relationships. She invites the practitioner boundaried by professional role, goals, limited time, and physical environment to reflect on enhancing their professional relationships.

João Hipólito, Odete Nunes, and Rute Brites offer a psychiatric perspective. They propose a relationship that draws from the person-centred conditions of empathy, unconditional positive regard, and congruence, to help clients work through their experience of diagnosis. This enables a co-creation of meaning and understanding of clients' subjective experience that goes beyond giving labels and 'treatment'. The authors state that it is paramount that psychiatric professionals have training in working with assessment according to the needs of each client. They propose a paradigm shift, from a position of focusing on diagnosis, labelling, and treatment to the co-development of a therapeutic relationship as a facilitator of change and the reduction of suffering.

Pallab Majumder, a consultant child and adolescent psychiatrist, emphasizes the need to become more empathic, flexible, non-prejudiced, and open-minded when listening to young people, and to consider cultural attributes. Trust can be developed by establishing relationships, sharing activities, and demonstrating flexibility. Given that the role of the child psychiatrist and his or her relationship with the young person is shaped by society, the law, and the medical profession, he stresses the danger of losing sight of the importance of therapeutic relationship. Attention needs to be given to the relational aspect of practice by psychiatric professionals.

In her work with dissociative identity disorder, previously known as multiple personality disorder, Jo Ringrose stresses the importance of providing a nurturing and secure safe base in therapy. The therapist needs to demonstrate acceptance of the thoughts, feelings, and behaviours the client was previously unable to express for fear of rejection. The therapist's love and acceptance of all aspects of the client's self can lead to the acceptance of the disassociated parts of themselves. Clients who have dissociative identity disorder need help from their therapist to learn how their parts can work together to grow fully. As well as working with a complex configuration of parts of self, therapy will also involve the client working through traumas that were too toxic for them to process at the time.

Zenobia Nadirshaw critiques current professional practice in relation to working with people with learning difficulties. A person with learning difficulties needs to be seen and treated as a person in their own right. Stereotypical, historical, and biomedical approaches need to be replaced. Professionals need to examine their prejudices and biases towards physical disability and/or intellectual disability and 'race' issues. Black and minority ethnic people with learning disabilities in particular remain invisible to helping professionals. Values are imposed on them. The helping professional must accept responsibility and work within the therapeutic process and in the development of the therapeutic alliance. Much progress is needed in the training of professionals in this area.

Key themes

- The therapeutic relationship is considered important in these areas. Although in practice some professionals will work more in relationship, others will work from a diagnostic perspective.
- Attention needs to be given to the development of the therapeutic relationship by professionals with the dual role of mental health professional and therapeutic practitioner.
- More training, both initial training and continuing professional development, is needed for professionals.

> - For people with mental health problems, diagnosis needs to be contextualized within a supportive therapeutic relationship.

Further dimensions of the therapeutic relationship

In their chapter on transcultural and diversity perspectives, Colin Lago and Val Watson propose that therapy has to take into account continuing patterns of discrimination experienced by those in minority groups, accepting that such micro-aggressions can be repeated within the therapeutic relationship. Therapists in transcultural settings need to understand the nature of their own social identity and how this might impact upon the client from a different cultural or social background. Working across difference and diversity has to take into account the continuing patterns of discrimination experienced by those in minority groups in society. If a successful therapeutic relationship is to develop, the therapist cannot ignore issues of difference and diversity when they arise. Training and continuing professional development are recommended.

Stephen Paul and William West consider spirituality in various forms of therapeutic relationships. They note that an effective therapist requires self-knowledge of themselves in relation to spirituality and religion. This usually has to involve one's own personal development. Practitioners need to undertake background reading and access sources relating to spirituality and religion – remembering that the client is unique. Practitioners need to be ready to listen in an embodied way to their clients. The authors recommend personal development work and awareness of issues relating to religion and spirituality in primary training.

Jeannie Wright explores online therapeutic relationships. She notes they are often driven by client preferences. Some clients prefer the convenience, accessibility, and potential anonymity of the Internet-based relationship; some may access it owing to shift work, geographical remoteness, or disability. The client can take more control in online therapy. A 'disinhibition effect' enables some people to access deeper feelings more quickly. However, there are significant risks associated with online therapy. The therapist needs to provide clear information, with careful contracting, including the appropriateness of this modality. The online relationship itself may be 'disembodied'. Lastly, the technology is liable to breakdown. Backup systems may be necessary.

Our handbook ends with a chapter by Andrea Uphoff on neuroscience. Neuroscience evidences much of what we already believed or knew by empirical observation in our practice. Research affirms the provision of loving or caring relationships as directly related to neurological changes and the development of new neural pathways. The author states, 'If we are willing to engage with the material and remain at the forefront of new discoveries, poised to embrace new knowledge and continuing to ask innovative questions, we may also find new nourishment for our clinical practice' (p. 286). She predicts that neuroscience will probably become a requirement of training, including education on the principles of brain function and neuropsychological strategies for intervention. However, she asserts that although principles can inform practice, neuroscience will never represent the human and the complex processes of psychotherapy.

Key themes

- Training is needed in all of these applied areas.
- New developments in both online therapy and neuroscience are here to stay and, in different ways, will change practice. Professionals need to be updated continuously to remain at the cutting edge of practice.

Summary

In this handbook, a number of key professionals have explored the therapeutic relationship from their own models and professional settings. The views of these contributors complement and stand alongside current research into the psychological relationship in the psychological therapies.

- **The therapeutic relationship is instrumental for change in all areas of practice.** For some practitioners, notably relational therapists, it is at the centre of both theory and practice. For others – psychodynamic, existential, humanistic, and transpersonal therapists – it is the medium in which therapy takes place. In the cognitive behavioural, systemic, and family therapies, it is an important adjunct to the task of therapy. In areas in which therapy is not the principal task of the therapist, such as psychiatry, working with learning difficulties, the helping professions generically, there is emphasis on the need to put the therapeutic relationship at the heart of practice.
- **Issues relating to diversity and power need continued attention.** Be it working transculturally, with children, with people with learning difficulties or with spirituality, there is scope for the continued development of training and practice.
- **An integrated coherent approach to practice is necessary.** The therapeutic relationship needs to be contextualized within a clear and consistent framework. In the practice of therapy, that will be within a coherent core model. In helping relationships, this will be integrated in professional practice.
- **All modalities and settings report a move towards relational ways of working.** From person-centred therapy to cognitive behavioural therapy, from group therapy to family therapy, the importance of a focus on the therapeutic relationship has led to new developments in theory with the relationship at the centre.

References

Andrew Sims Centre (2012) *Nursing 2012: Care and Compassion.* Fourth Annual Mental Health and Learning Disabilities Conference, Leeds, 14 June.

National Health Service (NHS) (2013) *Compassion in Practice: One Year On.* London: NHS.

Warburton, G. and Charura, D. (eds.) (2012) The theory of love, *The Psychotherapist,* 52 (Autumn).

Index

MAKING SUCCESSFUL DECISIONS IN COUNSELLING AND PSYCHOTHERAPY
A Practical Guide

David A. Lane and Sarah Corrie
9780335244348 (Paperback)
2012

eBook also available

This book examines some of the factors that are involved in making good decisions, the range of thinking skills we need in order to make effective choices and some of the factors that can prevent us from making sound decisions in our work with clients.

Drawing on both the existing literature and a range of practical exercises, *Making Successful Decisions in Counselling and Psychotherapy* provides invaluable guidance on how to tackle the task of decision-making in 'real world' counselling and psychotherapeutic settings in order to develop a systematic, effective and creative approach.

Key features:

- Draws on both the existing literature and a range of practical exercises
- Provides invaluable guidance on how to tackle the task of decision-making in 'real world' counselling and psychotherapeutic settings
- Offers advice on developing a systematic, effective and creative approach

www.openup.co.uk

OPEN UNIVERSITY PRESS
McGraw - Hill Education

Printed in Great Britain
by Amazon